SCHOOL OF ADVANCED STUDY UNIVERSITY OF LONDON

Institute of Modern Languages Research

Opposing Patriarchy
Women and the Law in Action in Pre-Unification Italy (1815–1865)

imlr books

Established by the Institute of Modern Languages Research, this series (formerly known as igrs books) aims to bring to the public monographs and collections of essays in the field of modern foreign languages. Proposals for publication are selected by the Institute's editorial board, which is advised by a peer review committee of some fifty senior academics in the field. To make titles as accessible as possible to an English-speaking and multi-lingual readership, volumes are written in English and quotations given in English translation.

For further details on the annual competition, visit:
https://modernlanguages.sas.ac.uk/publications/imlr-books/

imlr books Volume 16

Volume Editor
Dr Anne Simon

Opposing Patriarchy
Women and the Law in Action in Pre-Unification Italy (1815–1865)

Sara Delmedico

SCHOOL OF ADVANCED STUDY UNIVERSITY OF LONDON
Institute of Modern Languages Research
2021

Published by the

Institute of Modern Languages Research
School of Advanced Study, University of London
Senate House, Malet Street, London WC1E 7HU
https://modernlanguages.sas.ac.uk

The Institute of Modern Languages Research is an imprint of
University of London Press

Cover image
Statue of the Goddess of Justice at the old Palace of Justice, Rome
Detail from photograph by Chris Foto
Shutterstock ID 414929143

First published 2021

ISBN 978 0 85457 278 6

ISSN 2632-9573 (Print)

Contents

Acknowledgements vii

Note to the Reader ix

Introduction 1

Part 1 The Italian Peninsula in the Pre-Unification Period

1. Building the Nation State: Italian Society between Old Prerogatives and Modernity 23
2. Ideals of Women in Men's and Women's Writings 49
3. Women and the Law in the Nineteenth-Century Italian Peninsula 85

Part 2 Women and Marriage between Civil, Criminal and Canon Law: The Cases of the Kingdoms of Sardinia and Lombardy-Venetia

4. Women and Men beyond Marriage 127
5. Women, Marriage and the Transmission of Property 155
6. Ending Wedlock 187

Conclusion 215

Table 1. Nineteenth-Century Coinage 219

Glossary 221

Bibliography 223

Index 269

Acknowledgements

It is with real pleasure that I express my deepest gratitude to the Institute of Modern Languages Research for including my study in their book series. I also wish to express my sincere gratitude to the Arts and Humanities Research Council and Cambridge Commonwealth, European and International Trust for generously supporting my PhD studies. The Research Scholarship awarded by the Modern Humanities Research Association enabled me to complete the writing up of this study. My thanks also go to the Italian Department at the University of Cambridge for creating such a supportive and enriching environment in which to work.

For her illuminating, meticulous, enthusiastic and invaluable guidance and feedback, I am deeply indebted to my doctoral supervisor Helena Sanson. I am also extremely grateful to Ann Hallamore Caesar, Victor Crescenzi, Trevor Dean, Abigail Brundin, David Laven, Federica Boldrini and Giovanni Minnucci for sharing their expertise and providing me with helpful comments. Sincere thanks also go to the IMLR's anonymous reviewers, to Jane Lewin and to Anne Simon for helping me throughout the publication process. My warmest thanks go to my family and friends for their love and support.

Note to the Reader

Eighteenth- and nineteenth-century primary sources have been transcribed adopting conservative criteria and following the original as closely as possible. Some changes have been made, however, for ease of reading. They are as follows:

(a) *u* and *v* have been distinguished according to modern usage;
(b) ampersands have been expanded to *et*;
(c) other abbreviations have also been expanded;
(d) accents follow modern usage;
(e) some minor changes have been introduced in terms of punctuation and the use of apostrophes to aid comprehension;
(f) upper case is left as in the original text.

Any apparent incongruities in spelling and morphology which have been preserved are part of the original text. The original spelling of titles in the body of the text and the bibliography has been preserved as far as possible. Translations are the author's own unless otherwise indicated. Throughout this study, names of tribunals have been left in Italian. The Italian words for currencies (e.g., scudi, lire) have been preserved as well. Any comparison with the present-day value of money and goods has deliberately been avoided because the economy, the physical means of production and the perception of the value of an asset in the period under consideration were too different from the present to give a consistent equivalence. A table of nineteenth-century coinage and a glossary are included at the end of this study.

Unfortunately, restricted access to libraries and archives due to Covid-19 regulations meant that not all sources were accessible for checking and occasionally information could not be supplied.

Introduction

Strictly standardised and categorised, the traditional views on women still persisted in the nineteenth century. Model women were submissive and obedient and their roles were to be carried out within the family. Not abiding by these visions meant being frowned upon and met with disapproval. In a society which was static and still revolved around centuries-old hierarchical dynamics, women enjoyed a different legal status to men. Society with its moral values moulded the law and they constituted a mutual and binary extension of each other, thus making the analysis of legal sources a significant testimony to views on women. This book addresses the lives of ordinary women and men in their everyday relations with the law. It crosses the boundary of legal history and goes beyond a cold analysis of the law, of legal proceedings, of the courts and their behaviour, revealing the real life of men and women, with their bias, expectations and ambitions, before the law. Reducing the scale of the analysis to the individual and her/his family within a real-life context allows one to identify some of the patterns of behaviour and thought which shaped and defined the mentality of the Ottocento. In this way the relationship between law and society emerges and gives a better sense of the different facets of such a changing society.

The focus of this book is on the legal status of women in the Kingdoms of Sardinia and Lombardy-Venetia during the period from the Restoration (1815) to the Unification of Italy (1861) and the enactment of the first civil code, known as the Pisanelli Code (1865). This periodisation categorises these decades of the Ottocento into a sort of interregnum between the Old Regime – the past, the old, the backward – and the birth of the Italian nation – the new, a point of arrival, something to which to aspire. If the Council of Trent (1545–63) marked a turning point for the institution of marriage, with regard to other legal matters ancient sources such as Justinian's *Corpus Iuris Civilis* were still considered and used. The French conquests introduced several changes which represented a clash between the past and the present; and between various strata of society which struggled to hold onto their prerogatives and others which welcomed the winds of modernity blowing over the Peninsula. The Restoration let these contradictions emerge: alongside monarchs such as the Kings of Sardinia, who tried firmly to return to the past, others – such as the rulers of Lombardy-Venetia – attempted to introduce innovations (for example, the Austrian Civil Code), thus acknowledging these changes. At the end of this interregnum there is the birth of Italy and shortly afterwards the enactment of the Pisanelli Code, a crucial step in the path towards the building of the nation in which, however, women's contribution was disregarded by the reconfirming of their subordinate status.

Analysing this interregnum implies considering changes and continuities between the present and the past: since ancient times, institutions and legal norms had undergone very few mutations and 'criminal and civil law [...] reflected continuity in a view of woman as essentially a dependant of man'.[1] However, a first-hand examination of the law in action reveals challenges to the centuries-long notion and ideology about women: in real life, some women used the law and knew how it functioned in practice; they questioned authority and negotiated their status, showing an image which was quite different from that promoted in conduct books, among other works.

The geographical limits of this work comprise the Kingdoms of Sardinia and Lombardy-Venetia. The choice of these two states was determined by the fact that they present an interesting array of both similarities and differences which make them particularly suitable for a fruitful comparison. With regard to similarities, in these two states, as in all other states across the Peninsula, the age-old notion of women heavily conditioned every aspect of life. Objects of a culturally determined vision of femininity, women within the family and society were mainly valued as childbearing vessels. In an economic context mostly relying on agriculture, the patriarchal and hierarchical idea of the family deeply affected interpersonal dynamics. The structure of Italian society consisted of several types of family (the bourgeois family or the workers' family, for example), which conflicted and interacted with one other. Although social mobility was almost inconceivable – and, as we shall see, often even forbidden – people from different social classes shared similar behaviour, irrespective

1 Olwen Hufton, *The Prospect before Her: A History of Women in Western Europe 1500–1800* (London: HarperCollins, 1995), p. 505.

of their wealth. Even though to elaborate a consistent model would be questionable, a provisional hypothesis can be attempted: despite being different in their standing, lower and upper classes shared a common sense of honour, respectability and dignity which was to be enforced and transmitted to the following generations. This common feature was also reflected in their behaviour towards the transmission of wealth: no matter whether the patrimony to bequeath was land or a piece of furniture, families were concerned to ensure that their goods were going to the 'right' person. As we shall see, across all social classes, men were considered the 'right' people because they would continue the family's name and were therefore entrusted with the task of controlling and administering the family's patrimony. Women contributed with their dowries and/or with other intangible goods, such as morality, obedience, or their ability to work if they belonged to lower classes.

The static society of both Kingdoms was also characterised by the pervasive presence of the Catholic Church, which was entrenched in many aspects of everyday life, and still influenced societies and people's behaviour throughout the Ottocento and beyond. The Church's sense of morality and religiosity was profoundly interiorised by people and had a profound impact on their mentality. However, its force was not only moral: its jurisdiction over non-patrimonial matters related to marriage and the power of its courts transcended the boundaries of the actual Papal States. Canon law strongly intertwined with Roman law and other local sources, affecting not only judicial outcomes but the very essence of the legal framework itself.

Alongside these common traits there was also a major difference between the Kingdoms of Sardinia and Lombardy-Venetia: in the former, the law allowed men to exclude women from inheritance, thus amassing economic power in men's hands; in the latter, women could inherit in the same way as men. Women's status in the two states also differed to the extent that in the Kingdom of Sardinia any legal act by women had to be authorised by a male relative, while in Lombardy-Venetia they could freely administer their goods. In both states, however, the patriarchal, male-dominated society continued to affect interpersonal rules of behaviour and patterns of thought: indeed, people tried to override the law through private acts, which, in practice, resulted in women enjoying an inferior status to men in Lombardy-Venetia, too.

Despite the different status of men and women being widely accepted, there was still room for discord and disputes. Many lawsuits challenged not only a patrimonial set-up but also ideas and commonplaces and sometimes produced unexpected outcomes. If, in theory, 'the social function of the law is first to lay down rules aimed at the avoidance of disputes [...] and second to set out a normative framework to solve disputes which do arise', in real life the distinction was not so pristine.[2] In the nineteenth century the concomitant presence of several sources of law and the extensive recourse to private acts, such as wills or the renunciation of an inheritance, resulted in a number of diverging interpretations of the two levels of the law, that is, 'law in the books' and legal outcomes. In the Kingdom of Sardinia the presence of the *ius commune* as well as of municipal statutes and other *iura propria*, such as the eighteenth-century *Regie Costituzioni*, made the legal framework not entirely coherent.[3] Moreover, the enactment of Napoleon's Code, and its subsequent repeal, sharply increased legal disputes, especially those concerning inheritance, and saw women exploiting the interstices of the law to improve their economic condition. In the Kingdom of Lombardy-Venetia, by contrast, the Austrian Civil and Criminal Codes were introduced in the first decades of the nineteenth century (in 1811 and 1803 respectively). Although they did not allow the recourse to any other legal source, their provisions, too, were often overridden through private acts such as testaments. As we shall see, in both kingdoms, the law was often distorted to women's detriment.

Recovering Women's Voices

Tracing women's legal status requires consideration of various aspects of life and society, including the demographic, economic, political, cultural and social dimensions. The analysis of this wider context is complemented by the examination of contemporary treatises in which the ideal models of women are described. These texts were written by both women and men: they aimed to help women correctly to assess their status and also allowed men to understand

2 David Ibbetson, 'Comparative Legal History: A Methodology', in *Making Legal History: Approaches and Methodologies*, ed. by Anthony Musson and Chantal Stebbings (Cambridge: Cambridge University Press, 2012), pp. 131–45 (p. 135).

3 The *ius commune*, or *utrumque ius*, is the bulk of laws formed by Roman and canon law, shared and used across the Italian Peninsula. An overview on the body of legal rules issued by the Catholic Church can be found in Jean Gaudemet, *Le Droit canonique* (Paris: Fides, 1989). See also Jean Gaudemet, *La Formation du droit canonique médiéval* (London: Variorum, 1980); Jean Gaudemet, *Storia del diritto canonico: ecclesia et civitas* (Cinisello Balsamo: San Paolo, 1998). *Iura propria* refers to the law enacted by states and used in their territories only.

how to handle family life and the roles of men and women. They depicted women as weak-headed, poorly educated, dependent on a male adult and fulfilling their role within the household. Women in the house, within the family, in the private sphere, were deemed to be in the place for which nature had destined them and where they belonged. However, if the private sphere was not women's exclusive domain, men, with their supposed greater firmness of mind, were entitled to monopolise civil life and spaces outside the home. In the words of Ruth Kelso, the public sphere implied 'mingling freely with a multitude of persons in a public place, as is necessary in public relations' and was unsuitable to women's decorum and chastity.[4] The construction of the identities of both women and men was framed by the dichotomy between the private and the public sphere and by the opposition between obedience, a woman's virtue and command, a prerogative of men.[5]

As Joan Kelly-Gadol highlights, the concepts of private and public have changed over time and continue to change, depending on the culture considered;[6] accordingly, the line which divides the two spheres shifts as well. In the case of nineteenth-century Italian society, women began to go beyond the boundary of their private, secluded worlds, that is, their households; their presence in the public sphere became much more intense than ever and, during the upheavals of the Risorgimento, they contributed powerfully to the cause in contexts such as the barricades or the

4 Ruth Kelso, *Doctrine for the Lady of the Renaissance* (Urbana, IL: University of Illinois Press, 1956), p. 14.

5 On this point see Katherine Mitchell and Helena Sanson, 'Introduction', in *Women and Gender in Post-Unification Italy: Between Private and Public Spheres*, ed. by Katherine Mitchell and Helena Sanson (Oxford: Peter Lang, 2013), pp. 1–9 (esp. pp. 2–3). See also Perry Willson, 'Introduction: Gender and the Private Sphere in Liberal and Fascist Italy', in *Gender, Family and Sexuality: The Private Sphere in Italy, 1860–1945*, ed. by Perry Willson (Basingstoke: Palgrave Macmillan, 2004), pp. 1–19 (esp. pp. 1–4). On the dichotomy between the private and public spheres, see also Susan M. Okin, *Women in Western Political Thought* (Princeton, NJ: Princeton University Press, 1992); Lawrence E. Klein, 'Gender and the Public/Private Distinction in the Eighteenth Century: Some Questions about Evidence and Analytic Procedure', *Eighteenth-Century Studies*, 29 (1995): *The Public and the Nation*, 97–109; Jürgen Habermas, *The Structural Transformation of the Public Sphere: An Inquiry into a Category of Bourgeois Society*, trans. by Thomas Burger and Frederick Lawrence (Cambridge, MA: MIT Press, 1996); Jane Rendall, 'Women and the Public Sphere', *Gender and History*, 11 (1999), 475–88.

6 Joan Kelly, *Women, History and Theory: The Essays of Joan Kelly* (Chicago, IL; London: University of Chicago Press, 1984), pp. 10–11.

salons. The private sphere and the public sphere often interacted and overlapped, blurring the boundary between the private and the public. Changes in the political set-up of the Italian Peninsula also entailed mutations in the legal frameworks affecting people, women in particular, and questioned the centuries-long notion of femininity. However, as we shall see, the great majority of people were not yet ready to accept an inclusive redefinition of women's status in law, or to comply with any challenges to the patriarchal and hierarchical Italian society, to the extent that, in the period in question, women even experienced a 'fairly regular pattern of relative loss of status'.[7]

In nineteenth-century Italy women were still 'divided into three acceptable states of being': unmarried, married and widowed women.[8] For centuries this subdivision was reflected in conduct literature for and about women. It is only in the second half of the nineteenth century that conduct literature began considering women outside these states, such as spinsters and separated women, new 'categories' which were frowned upon and often viewed with suspicion, but reflected changes taking place in society at the time.[9] The conduct of these women, too, needed to be normalised and codified, even more so because of their potential disruptiveness. Conduct literature became 'a more diversified phenomenon [...] more reflective of social reality, and covering a wider range of "roles" for women'.[10] Nevertheless, the ideal woman remained the one who played her role within the boundaries of marriage, 'the institution at the heart of the social system',[11] and whose life had significance mainly with regard to the three related phases of existence: the time before, during and after marriage. Marriage, in the words of Trevor Dean and Kate Lowe, 'was understood to be a different act for

7 Joan Kelly-Gadol, 'The Social Relation of the Sexes: Methodological Implications of Women's History', *Signs*, 1 (1976), 809–23 (p. 810). The term 'status' is used in the meaning defined by Kelly-Gadol, i.e., the power to act and the position held within family and society.

8 Lucy Hosker, '"Donne sole" in Post-Unification Italy: The Works of Tommasina Guidi and Emilia Nevers' (unpublished doctoral thesis, University of Cambridge, 2015), pp. 15–18.

9 Hosker, '"Donne sole" in Post-Unification Italy', pp. 15–18.

10 Helena Sanson, 'Introduction: Women and Conduct in the Italian Tradition, 1470–1900: An Overview', in *Conduct Literature for and about Women in Italy, 1470–1900: Prescribing and Describing Life*, ed. by Helena Sanson and Francesco Lucioli (Paris: Classiques Garnier, 2016), pp. 9–40 (p. 33).

11 Hufton, *The Prospect before Her*, p. 59.

women and men'.[12] However, it had a considerable importance for both, being the path to which to aspire, even if this implied giving up individual ambitions and expectations.

A close investigation into everyday reality, beyond the conceptualisation and idealisation of the female sex, questions this longstanding, stereotypical notion of women and uncovers a different scenario. If moralists and educationalists insisted on female obedience and submissiveness, this was perhaps also because in everyday life women showed resistance. Some women did not passively accept their status and even disregarded the existing order and defined rules of society: the ideals promoted by the Enlightenment and the French Revolution had planted their seeds. However, even if some decades ago historians of women's lives such as Gerda Lerner already made clear that 'it is no longer sufficient to view women mainly as members of families',[13] before the law men and women were still perceived predominantly as part of a family and structured their subjectivities within its boundaries. The understanding of the changes taking place during the Ottocento should primarily focus, on the one hand, on the legal importance of the family, a moral body and a sort of 'microstate' within the state, one with its own customs, interiorised and accepted by its members; and, on the other hand, on the impact of the transition towards a society in which the individual became the new centre. It is against this background that this study analyses the relations between men and women, between subjects and authorities; and the ways the law and the judicial system deployed their forces in this context.

Over the centuries, the law underwent several transformations in response to emerging needs, but the broader framework remained substantially unchanged, with ancient sources still having force of law and affecting everyday lives. As we see in the following chapters, the age-old notion of women would continue to have an impact on commonplaces and attitudes for long after the Unification of Italy. The contents of the Pisanelli Code thus reflect a male-dominated elaboration of the law in an equally male-dominated society. Through the analysis of the law in action, this study assesses the extent to

12 Trevor Dean and Katherine J. P. Lowe, 'Introduction: Issues in the History of Marriage', in *Marriage in Italy, 1300–1650*, ed. by Trevor Dean and Katherine J. P. Lowe (Cambridge: Cambridge University Press, 1998), pp. 1–21 (p. 2).

13 Gerda Lerner, 'Placing Women in History: A 1975 Perspective', in *Liberating Women's History: Theoretical and Critical Essays*, ed. by Berenice A. Carroll (Urbana, IL: University of Illinois Press, 1976), pp. 358–67 (p. 360).

which judicial outcomes adhered to the written law, that is, the law preserved and transmitted 'in the books'. In other words, it examines how, in this period of crucial changes, the reality of being a woman interacted with the ideals that had been elaborated over the centuries; and how the theorised notions of womanhood influenced everyday life in concrete and practical ways. The case studies examined in this work concern ordinary people and investigate the experiences of women belonging to different social classes, from both rural and urban contexts: through their actions, these women challenged prejudices, stereotypes and the set-up of the world to which they belonged.

State of the Art

Because of its position at the intersection between social, legal and gender history, this study has a new and interdisciplinary identity. To structure this identity, the works of Paolo Ungari and Manlio Bellomo provide a first general, conceptual and contextual grounding on family law and women's legal status. In particular, in his *La condizione giuridica della donna in Italia* (1970) Bellomo addresses women's legal status from ancient to modern times, describing its evolution through time and making clear the crucial link between family, wealth and society.[14] Bellomo's analysis of the widespread commonplace which pictures women as 'l'immagine riflessa dell'uomo' [man's reflected image] helps to explain the issues concerning the transmission of wealth at that time.[15] In this context, the law itself appeared as a means of ensuring the continuity of the family name and the wealth which was key to its status. Alongside the focus on law and legal changes, Bellomo's work does not neglect to analyse the shifts towards a new understanding of the family and women's role in it which began from the eighteenth century onwards. This helps to identify the many peculiarities of the legal system, the roots of which dated back to a very ancient past and relied on a number of different, and often overlapping, provisions of the *ius commune* and *iura propria*. Paolo Ungari's study of family law, *Storia del diritto di famiglia in Italia (1796–1942)* (1974), examines the law in force, the writings of the jurists of the time, as well as the social and political changes which

14 Manlio Bellomo, *La condizione giuridica della donna in Italia. Vicende antiche e moderne* (Rome: Il Cigno, 1996 [1970]).

15 Bellomo, *La condizione giuridica*, p. 25.

took place.[16] It provides a clear, reliable description of the intricate development of the legal framework concerning family in the last two centuries. The stress on the importance of the family as formative of law and legal customs helps us to understand the extent to which changes such as those promoted by the Enlightenment affected its structure.

The works by Bellomo and Ungari were both written in the 1970s – at a time when Italy was going through critical changes which also involved women – and were the first attempts to provide a systematic study of women's status and the legal framework. In particular, Bellomo's work examines women's status from the Middle Ages to the present, while Ungari's study covers the period from 1976 to the Second World War. They shed light on the way families were structured and perceived, paying attention to the shift from the idea of family as a group sharing identity and power to a more intimate idea of a moral body in which emotions were its prominent component. This process has also been the subject of a themed volume, *Famiglia e mutamento sociale* (1977), edited by Marzio Barbagli,[17] who in his subsequent monograph *Sotto lo stesso tetto* (1984) clearly detects and studies this new attitude within society by adopting a socio-demographic approach.[18] His studies reveal more 'informal' behaviour between family members, which had a deep effect on a centuries-old hierarchical structure and questioned authority within the family. Luciano Guerci examines women's perspective and assesses these new attitudes against the works published at that time, in particular treatises on female conduct, education and morality.[19] He identifies a 'crisi dell'obbedienza' which pushed people to redefine their own roles and sense of self and at the same time to challenge obedience, which was no longer perceived as unquestionable.[20] Therefore, paternal

16 Paolo Ungari, *Storia del diritto di famiglia in Italia (1796–1942)* (Bologna: Il Mulino, 1974).

17 *Famiglia e mutamento sociale*, ed. by Marzio Barbagli (Bologna: Il Mulino, 1977).

18 Marzio Barbagli, *Sotto lo stesso tetto. Mutamenti della famiglia in Italia dal XV al XX secolo* (Bologna: Il Mulino, 1984).

19 Luciano Guerci, *La discussione sulla donna nell'Italia del Settecento: aspetti e problemi* (Turin: Tirrenia Stampatori, 1987); Luciano Guerci, *La sposa obbediente: donna e matrimonio nella discussione dell'Italia del Settecento* (Turin: Tirrenia Stampatori, 1988).

20 Guerci, *La sposa obbediente*, p. 11.

authority, examined in *La paura dei padri nella società antica e medievale* (1983)[21] and sometimes described as a sort of 'metus reverentialis' [reverential fear], informed power relations within kinship groups for centuries, but, as observed by Marco Cavina, started to become more fluid from the eighteenth century onwards.[22]

In the last thirty years, historiography on law and wealth has become more substantial. In his *Famiglia, successioni e patrimonio familiare nell'Italia medievale e moderna* (1994), Andrea Romano focuses on the importance of inheritance laws in preserving family, wealth and therefore status in society.[23] The gender dimension, which is not widely investigated by Romano, is, instead, the core of Giulia Calvi's and Isabella Chabot's edited volume *Le ricchezze delle donne* (1998).[24] This work moves in a new direction by explaining the key role of women in the social and familial context: they were excluded from obtaining a large part of their family's wealth, but, at the same time, women were bearers of their family's honour and also seen as a means by which the power of their families of origin was deployed in society.

The legal dimension on which these works drew is further examined in the studies by scholars such as Trevor Dean and Kate Lowe, Daniela Lombardi and Thomas Kuehn, who emphasise the role played by the law in action and base their analysis on a solid archival investigation into primary sources. Society's key institution – marriage – is the focus of Trevor Dean's and Kate Lowe's edited work on *Marriage in Italy* (1998). Since 'marriage is important because it heralded change', it is also identified as a starting point from which an investigation into views on gender and on female and male roles could be carried out.[25] The authors clearly stress the variety of reasons for which marriages were contracted: it emerges that, even though strategy was extremely important, individuals' needs were not always disregarded. Alongside economic and social reasons, love was also allowed some room in the marriage market. This point,

21 *La paura dei padri nella società antica e medievale,* ed. by Ezio Pellizer, Nevio Zorzetti and Alberto Maffi (Rome: Laterza, 1983).

22 Marco Cavina, *Il padre spodestato. L'autorità paterna dall'antichità a oggi* (Rome: Laterza, 2007).

23 Andrea Romano, *Famiglia, successioni e patrimonio familiare nell'Italia medievale e moderna* (Turin: Giappichelli, 1994).

24 *Le ricchezze delle donne. Diritti patrimoniali e poteri familiari in Italia,* ed. by Giulia Calvi and Isabelle Chabot (Turin: Rosenberg and Sellier, 1998).

25 Dean and Lowe, 'Introduction', p. 1.

often deemed controversial, is discussed in *Storia del matrimonio dal Medioevo a oggi* (2008) by Daniela Lombardi, who also provides an in-depth analysis of rituals and customs of marriage according to social class.[26] By looking at both court records and the law, Lombardi sheds light on how marriage has evolved over time.

The perspective of the law in action is examined by Thomas Kuehn's studies on Renaissance Italy by means of an analysis of legal archival sources through the lens of gender.[27] Kuehn draws attention to the 'familial context, where gender stereotypes were lived and disregarded at times, where women were deeply engaged in roles seen as theirs and not, supposedly, threatening existing order, but rather embodying it'.[28] The author sees family law not as static, but rather as formative of domestic life. Nonetheless, it generated conflicts in which women took part and were able to circumvent and exploit legal limitation to their advantage.

The pivotal role played by marriage means that the analysis of women's legal status should inevitably start by considering the three stages of a woman's life: before, during and after marriage. Several studies have undertaken a close analysis of the extent to which moral and religious limitations influenced behaviour. The works of James Brundage and Jean Delumeau clearly define the notion of sin which became entangled with sexuality and pervaded Western societies from the Middle Ages onwards – or, indeed, earlier, since both Saint Paul and Saint Jerome inveighed against the sinfulness of (especially women's) sexuality.[29] In this regard, Delumeau identifies the concept of sin – and its related fear of punishment – not only as a means to dominate ordinary people but also as deeply afflicting the ecclesiastical elites as well. By focusing on the Italian Peninsula, Gabriella Bonacchi, Oscar Di Simplicio, Margherita Pelaja and Lucetta Scaraffia also provide an interesting picture of the Church, its code of morality and the view of the ecclesiastical authorities'

26 Daniela Lombardi, *Storia del matrimonio dal Medioevo a oggi* (Bologna: Il Mulino, 2008). See also Daniela Lombardi, *Matrimoni di antico regime* (Bologna: Il Mulino, 2001).

27 Thomas Kuehn, *Law, Family and Women: Toward a Legal Anthropology of Renaissance Italy* (Chicago, IL: University of Chicago Press, 1991); Thomas Kuehn, *Family and Gender in Renaissance Italy, 1300–1600* (Cambridge: Cambridge University Press, 2017).

28 Kuehn, *Family and Gender*, p. 20.

29 See, e.g., Neil Adkin, *Jerome on Virginity: A Commentary on the Libellus de virginitate servanda (Letter* 22) (Cambridge: Francis Cairns, 2003); St Paul, 1 Timothy; 1 Corinthians 5 and 6.

behaviour as a sort of anxiety to ensure 'moral order'.[30] However, the Church not only exerted a moral influence on people and society: it had jurisdiction over non-patrimonial matters concerning marriage. As Jean Gaudemet explains, canon law informed many aspects of life and this meant that secular authorities had to establish a close relationship with the Church itself.[31]

In such a context, people's behaviour was subjected to rigorous assessment and was to converge in what was understood to be the correct way of living. To a woman in particular, the time before marriage was key to her future and she had to behave in an honourable way in order to avoid any stain challenging a possible future marriage. Nevertheless, transgressions were part of life and could led to pregnancy or even infanticide:[32] as Giovanni Cazzetta has shown in his *Praesumitur seducta* (1999), seduction and the birth of illegitimate offspring were major concerns for society and this led, from the Enlightenment onwards, to a new understanding of women, who went from being considered victims of their seducers because of their weakheadedness to being stigmatised as accomplices able to manipulate law in their favour by claiming to be victims of seduction when they were, instead, consciously having sexual intercourse in order to claim to be married.[33] However, if 'many found their sexuality beyond the boundaries of accepted behavior', as Guido Ruggiero suggests in *The Boundaries of Eros* (1989),[34] Maurice Daumas, in *Adulteri e cornuti* (2008), demonstrates that adultery was the objective evidence of the double standard by which women and men were judged.[35] Again, this was a powerful

30 Oscar Di Simplicio, *Peccato penitenza perdono. Siena 1575–1800. La formazione della coscienza nell'Italia moderna* (Milan: Franco Angeli, 1994); Gabriella Bonacchi, *Legge e peccato. Anime, corpi, giustizia alla corte dei papi* (Rome: Laterza, 1995); Margherita Pelaja and Lucetta Scaraffia, *Due in una carne. Chiesa e sessualità nella storia* (Rome: Laterza, 2008).

31 Jean Gaudemet, *Le Mariage en Occident. Les mœurs et le droit* (Paris: Cerf, 1987); Gaudemet, *Storia del diritto canonico*.

32 Adriano Prosperi, *Dare l'anima. Storia di un infanticidio* (Turin: Einaudi, 2005); Adriano Prosperi, *Infanticide, Secular Justice, and Religious Debate in Early Modern Europe* (Turnhout: Brepols, 2016).

33 Giovanni Cazzetta, *Praesumitur seducta. Onestà e consenso femminile nella cultura giuridica moderna* (Milan: Giuffrè, 1999).

34 Guido Ruggiero, *The Boundaries of Eros: Sex Crime and Sexuality in Renaissance Venice* (Oxford: Oxford University Press, 1989), p. 15.

35 Maurice Daumas, *Adulteri e cornuti. Storia della sessualità maschile tra Medioevo e modernità* (Bari: Dedalo, 2008), p. 70.

reminder that women's behaviour had to be different from that of men; and their sense of self was to be deployed within the safe walls of their households. Being part of a family in order to avoid being marginalised was therefore key: the worries and concerns single women carried with them are clearly explained by Maura Palazzi;[36] and this was also the reason why families did their best to make widows marry again, as Giulia Calvi and Isabelle Chabot show in their articles on second marriages.[37]

Alongside the socially accepted behaviour, individuals had their own sense of self which often clashed against that of others: in their edited series *I processi matrimoniali degli archivi ecclesiastici italiani*,[38] Silvana Seidel Menchi and Diego Quaglioni explain the many reasons for initiating a dispute, thus showing that both women and men were far from abiding by societal rules. All these works use a number of legal sources – law, jurisprudence and judicial sources – and address marriages, their rituals and the possible subsequent conflicts. Although the studies mentioned above mainly focus on the period before the Napoleonic conquests, their contribution is pivotal to understanding the various dynamics which led to the nineteenth-century context and then to the elaboration of the new legal framework of Italy. Nonetheless, given that the crucial period between the Restoration and the Unification of Italy has not received the scholarly attention it deserves and has often been overlooked, this work is a first attempt to fill this gap.

36 Maura Palazzi, *Donne sole. Storie dell'altra faccia dell'Italia tra antico regime e società contemporanea* (Milan: Mondadori, 1997).

37 Giulia Calvi, 'Reconstructing the Family: Widowhood and Remarriage in Tuscany in the Early Modern Period', in *Marriage in Italy*, ed. by Dean and Lowe, pp. 275–96; Isabelle Chabot, 'Seconde nozze e identità materna nella Firenze del tardo medioevo', in *Tempi e spazi di vita femminile tra medioevo ed età moderna*, ed. by Silvana Seidel Menchi, Anne Jacobson Schutte and Thomas Kuehn (Bologna: Il Mulino, 1999), pp. 493–523.

38 *Coniugi nemici. La separazione in Italia dal XII al XVIII secolo*, ed. by Silvana Seidel Menchi and Diego Quaglioni (Bologna: Il Mulino, 2000); *Matrimoni in dubbio. Unioni controverse e nozze clandestine in Italia dal XIV al XVIII secolo*, ed. by Silvana Seidel Menchi and Diego Quaglioni (Bologna: Il Mulino, 2001); *Trasgressioni. Seduzione, concubinato, adulterio, bigamia (XIV–XVIII Secolo)*, ed. by Silvana Seidel Menchi and Diego Quaglioni (Bologna: Il Mulino, 2004); *I tribunali del matrimonio (secoli XV–XVIII)*, ed. by Silvana Seidel Menchi and Diego Quaglioni (Bologna: Il Mulino, 2006).

Sources and Methodology

The core of this study relies on first-hand investigation of archival documents and primary sources. First, the analysis takes into account the legal framework in order to understand the pluralistic nature of the law in force in the Kingdoms of Sardinia and Lombardy-Venetia and the way it affected women. These sources include municipal statutes, the *ius commune* and other acts, such as the *Costituzioni* enacted in the eighteenth century, and nineteenth-century legal codes. Second, the analysis of the legal framework is complemented by the examination of a corpus of archival material held in state archives in Turin, Milan, Verona and Venice as well as in Church archives, such as the Archbishop's Curia of Turin and Milan; and the Bishop's Curia of Verona. These four cities were chosen for their importance, especially because they were the seat of higher courts such as the Senato of Turin or the Supremo Tribunale of Verona. Crucially, these archives also preserve documents from smaller, surrounding urban centres and rural villages; hence they provide an important body of material to compare and assess the social, economic and legal dynamics in play in the rural and urban contexts of the two Kingdoms.

As Silvana Seidel Menchi points out, sources such as judicial proceedings are very useful as they can offer different keys to interpreting society and people.[39] Besides showing how courts carried out their judgements, these sources also allow us to infer how the law was manipulated by the people involved in a lawsuit and how their words were recorded.[40] Indeed, Charles Donahue argues that '[t]he way in which the witness tells his or her story is more likely to be a product of the witness or of the clerk who recorded the testimony', something which causes considerable distortions in the process of redacting legal records.[41] Nonetheless, detecting the way in which the law was leveraged to comply with people's will is extremely useful as it testifies to their lives, experiences, expectations and ambitions, offering much more than a cold description of legal acts. However, in order to limit the extent of these distortions, a significant bulk of archival material has been examined to identify recurrent features

39 Silvana Seidel Menchi, 'I processi matrimoniali come fonte storica', in *Coniugi nemici*, ed. by Seidel Menchi and Quaglioni, pp. 15–94 (pp. 49–57).

40 Seidel Menchi, 'I processi matrimoniali', pp. 49–57.

41 Charles Donahue, *Law, Marriage, and Society in the Later Middle Ages: Arguments about Marriage in Five Courts* (Cambridge: Cambridge University Press, 2007), p. 7.

which would allow us to consider a case as a representative case study.[42] This approach to sifting through the many disputes examined in archival documents and legal journals enables an in-depth analysis of those cases accounted the most significant for nineteenth-century legal dynamics.

The initial research involved the analysis of a large number of notarial documents such as wills and dowry instruments: from the inventories held in each archive it was possible to locate notaries who were active in the historical period which is the object of the present analysis and whose acts were significant for this study. Each notary rogated for about twenty years, their papers being preserved in folders containing roughly two hundred acts each. Among these acts there were dowry instruments and wills, as well as deeds of sale. Acts such as wills were made by both men and women in equal numbers. The chosen notaries are the following:

1) in Turin, Giovanni Aiassa, Giovanni Pietro Ellena and Giovanni Antonio Partiti, who were active in Turin and in the areas of Pinerolo and Villafranca between 1768 and 1849;
2) in Milan, Giuseppe Alberti and Giulio Caimi, active in Milan and surrounding areas in the mid-nineteenth century;
3) in Verona, Lorenzo Maggi and Giuseppe Merci, respectively from Verona and Cero in the early decades of the nineteenth century;
4) in Venice, Antonio Santibusca and Luigi Sperotti, active in the years from 1801 to 1868.

From this initial corpus of documents, approximately three hundred wills and dowry instruments were identified and selected. The examination of them aimed to assess how these documents were drawn up, by whom and why. Particular attention was given to women's role in this process; and to the interactions between the different family members, especially among male figures who intervened in signing the wills and dowry instruments of their relatives.

In the above-mentioned archives court transcripts were also considered: they came from courts of first instance, courts of appeal, supreme courts and ecclesiastical tribunals. Among others, records have been analysed from the Tribunale di Pinerolo, the Corte di

42 For case studies as a research method, see Robert K. Yin, *Case Study Research: Design and Methods* (Thousand Oaks, CA: Sage, 1994). See also Lisa Webley, 'Stumbling Blocks in Empirical Legal Research: Case Study Research', *Law and Method* (October 2016), 1–21.

Appello di Casale, the Corte di Cassazione di Torino, the Tribunale Civile di Prima Istanza di Venezia, the Tribunale di Appello Generale (Venice) and the Supremo Tribunale di Verona. The analysis of court transcripts shows how people approached the law, their main motives in beginning a lawsuit and whom they involved. Despite being initiated by members of the same family, lawsuits did not always imply a profound fracture within the kinship group. As Renata Ago argues, resorting to a court could often be interpreted as a way to remedy a defective situation and not necessarily as a sign of strong discord.[43] It thus highlights the way people perceived their world and their everyday relations. The court transcripts in question concern roughly three hundred lawsuits. The choice to include in this study only a selection of the documents collected is driven not only by practical reasons, but also by the desire to focus on the peculiarity of the cases, on their protagonists and on how they managed to manipulate the law to their own ends. In particular, the aim is to offer a picture of ordinary nineteenth-century people, from different socio-economic backgrounds, in front of the law.

A third type of primary source to be examined are legal journals. The nineteenth century offers the first examples of journals of jurisprudence published across the Italian Peninsula. This is an extremely significant source, which has not yet attracted the scholarly attention it deserves, especially considering that these legal journals are a rich source of information since they were meant to guide judges, lawyers and jurists in approaching and understanding the *ratio* behind the decisions made by courts; and to help them to handle similar cases. They dealt with civil, criminal and commercial law; and the selection of lawsuits and debates included in their pages mirrors the questions to which authorities paid special attention and which they considered worthy of an in-depth discussion. With an intended readership of legal experts, these journals were edited by renowned jurists such as the lawyers Giovanni Francesco Zini, who edited *Giurisprudenza pratica secondo la legislazione austriaca*, a legal journal for the Kingdom of Lombardy-Venetia published from 1817 to 1845; and Cristoforo Mantelli, editor of *Giurisprudenza del codice civile e delle altre leggi dei regii stati*, one of the two journals for the Kingdom of Sardinia, which was published from 1839 to 1847. The other was *Annali di giurisprudenza*: it was published in Turin from 1838 to 1845

43 Renata Ago, *Economia barocca. Mercato e istituzioni nella Roma del Seicento* (Rome: Donzelli, 1998), pp. xi–xii.

and compiled by a group of prominent legal experts, amongst them Urbano Rattazzi. These journals were usually published annually, even though the *Giornale di giurisprudenza pratica* (1846–62), for example, was fortnightly (but its issues are now collected in yearly volumes).

Cases concerning seduction, extramarital relations, adultery and separation are few: for instance, in the twelve volumes of *Giurisprudenza degli Stati Sardi* (previously called *Giurisprudenza del codice civile e delle altre leggi dei regj stati*) published between 1848 and 1859 there are only twenty cases of separation, one case of adultery, two cases of seduction and one case dealing with extramarital relations. Similar data can be inferred with regard to *Giurisprudenza teorico pratica secondo la legislazione austriaca*. Instead, lawsuits dealing with dowry and other inheritance issues are more numerous: the same volumes of *Giurisprudenza degli Stati Sardi* reported 156 disputes concerning dowries and ninety-two cases regarding wills. Again, the data are similar for Lombardy-Venetia legal journals. Legal journals also enable us to infer how uncertainties and incongruities in the law were confronted and elaborated by courts to produce consistent outcomes. The way cases are described in these journals is very significant, too. With regard to cases concerning adultery, for example, particular attention is paid to the protection of the protagonists' honour by not mentioning their names and by limiting the information given in order to prevent the exposure of their identity.

The case studies examined concern litigations that underwent several stages and give a clear insight into the law in action. These are valuable because they reconstruct the social, moral and cultural issues behind the claims, convey the authorities' position regarding the matters analysed and show how commonplaces and stereotypes influenced judicial outcomes. Legal acts and judicial proceedings alone, however, do not allow us fully to understand a society; therefore, the works of scientists, moralists, theorists and jurists who contributed to shaping ideas about women have also been considered. These works address both men and women; and often assert that their goal was to make women correctly assess their position in society and the role to which they had to adhere. The study of this kind of writing helps us better to comprehend the way the law in action moved, altered the outcomes of judicial proceedings and entered people's minds. The multiple sources of investigation used in this study help us to deduce the very essence of the law in action with all its inherent 'perceptions of processes and how they influence behaviour [so] to understand how laws are understood, and how and why they are applied and misapplied, subverted, complied with or rejected'.[44]

Structure

By studying this material and taking into account all these issues, this work, which is not intended to be an exhaustive study, proposes a revised interpretation of the nineteenth-century images of womanhood. The picture which emerges shows women questioning obedience and challenging authority: they did not hesitate to go before a court to ask for their rights to be enforced and they initiated lawsuits for several reasons. For example, they asked for an addition to their dowries, or wanted the dissolution of their marriage because they claimed that their husbands had passed a disease onto them. Although they were formally in a subordinate position, some women envisioned themselves as worthy members of society, fully entitled to ask for justice.

This work is divided into two parts, each composed of three chapters. The first part describes the Ottocento context, the ideology about women as expressed in public discourse and the legal framework of the Italian Peninsula. In the second part attention turns to relevant case studies from the Kingdoms of Sardinia and Lombardy-Venetia. In Chapter 1 the social, political and economic context of the nineteenth-century Italian Peninsula is examined. This approach allows a stronger focus on Italian society, on the meaning of the family in this context and, within this framework, women's role and contribution to both the family and society. The nineteenth century was a crucial period: alongside political and economic changes, new ideas imbued society and had a strong impact on the sense of self in both women and men. The presence of women beyond the private sphere began to be more intense. Women and men questioned the family's centuries-old hierarchical structure, thus challenging not only their own world but the very heart of society. Chapter 2 provides a picture of ideas about women. The examination explores contemporary views about women amongst scientists, theorists, moralists and jurists. By attempting to rely on a presumed scientific basis, many theories focused on the link between women's weaker bodies and their consequently weaker minds. These views, reinforcing ideals of female domesticity and shared also by many women, gave a solid foundation to women's inferior legal

44 Webley, 'Stumbling Blocks', pp. 2–3.

status. Chapter 3 is devoted to the law in force in pre-Unification states with regard to women. Close attention is paid to the dowry and to how it changed over time. This institution was particularly important because, in the great majority of pre-Unification states, the dowry was the lawful share in an inheritance which a woman was entitled to obtain through her family's patrimony. As it was usually a scant portion of the family's patrimony, the dowry is, therefore, clear evidence of the different status enjoyed by the women and men of the time.

The second part of this volume turns to the individual. It presents and discusses a selection of case studies which cast light on the relations between men and women before and outside wedlock, during marriage and at the time of its dissolution. In particular, Chapter 4 deals with a selection of case studies concerning marriage promises, seduction and extramarital relations. As we shall see, both ecclesiastical and civil authorities aimed at circumscribing relations, especially sexual intercourse, within the boundaries of wedlock, thus ensuring their desired social 'order' as a way of conveying their powers and prerogatives throughout every stratum of society, including the lowest. If people's intimate lives were a major concern to the authorities, the transmission of wealth was an equally important matter: Chapter 5 examines cases about dowries and wills, two crucial instruments which put the continuity of a family's patrimony at stake. Several lawsuits were initiated by women; and the analysis of them shows, in practice, the efforts families made to preserve their patrimony. Finally, Chapter 6 analyses widowhood and separation, two possible moments in a woman's existence which had important implications for both their intimate sphere and the transmission of wealth. In particular, the chapter traces widows' actual access to inheritance and women's requests for separation, focusing on the reasons which drove them before a court to relate issues pertaining to their very intimate lives. Courts aimed both to ensure social order and to meet people's needs; however, the outcomes of these cases were sometimes unexpected and frustrating. Through the analysis of the law in action and of women's use of the law itself, this study offers a contribution to the recovery of the forgotten voices and experiences of those ordinary women who, in their everyday life, reacted against the constraints imposed upon them by society and decided not to accept their status passively. Theirs were small, but nonetheless powerful, acts of resistance against and disruption of the *status quo*.

Part 1
The Italian Peninsula in the Pre-Unification Period

1. Building the Nation State: Italian Society between Old Prerogatives and Modernity

In the late nineteenth century the Italian Peninsula was fragmented into a number of different states. Regardless of their size, these were all economically backwards and mainly agrarian territories, with industrialisation in only a few areas, mostly in the north of the Peninsula. The male-dominated structure of family and society reflected this backwardness and would inform social dynamics for a long time to come. In this context, women had strictly defined roles within the household, even if, as we shall see, their involvement in the Risorgimento process brought them outside their homes. Although this led to a redefinition of women's sense of self, their active participation did not challenge their place in society and their subordinate status with respect to men. This chapter analyses the political, economic and social context of the Italian Peninsula within which women's legal status will be assessed. The new settlement established by the Congress of Vienna (1814–15) left several issues unresolved and eventually gave way to the upheavals which led to the Unification of Italy. After analysing the context of the Ottocento, attention is focused on the family unit and on society, pointing out the efforts of monarchs and families to keep society unchanged, for example, by endorsing same-class marriages. The last section also discusses women's contribution to the Risorgimento, both as a means to participate in the fight against the oppressors and as a way to carve out a corner which enabled them to claim a voice in society.

The Political and Economic Context

After Napoleon's defeat and his exile to Saint Helena (1815), monarchs and diplomats gathered at the Congress of Vienna to develop a new political configuration aimed at ensuring long-lasting peace through the balance of power and the criterion of legitimacy. However, the latter was neglected in favour of the former, as in the case of the Republics of Genoa and Venice, which had been incorporated into the Kingdoms of Sardinia and Lombardy-Venetia respectively.[1] The Austrian Empire became the hegemonic power in the Italian Peninsula at large: it ruled over Lombardy-Venetia, which was formally a single kingdom in personal union with the Empire and exerted its influence over other states through kinship links.[2] While the Duchy of Parma and Piacenza and the Duchy of Lucca were given to Maria Luigia of Habsburg-Lorraine and to Maria Luisa of Bourbon respectively, the overthrown kings were reinstated in all other territories formerly occupied by Napoleon. The Duchy of Modena and Reggio was returned to Francesco IV of Habsburg-Este, who inherited the Duchy of Massa and Carrara after the death of his mother, Maria Beatrice of Este; the Grand Duchy of Tuscany was given back to Ferdinand III of Habsburg-Lorraine; and the Papal States to Pope Pius VII. With regard to the south, the two Kingdoms of Naples and Sicily were unified under the name of the Kingdom of the Two Sicilies, ruled by Ferdinand I of Bourbon.[3] On the one hand, the new order of the Italian Peninsula left intense feelings of dissatisfaction among its people, since, apart from the subjects of the Kingdom of Sardinia, they either felt they were under foreign rules or were dissatisfied with their monarch. On the other hand, it helped to build a shared sense of identity and, consequently, to identify a common enemy against whom to turn during the Risorgimento. The assumption that Italy did in fact exist as a political entity was leveraged by an internalised and longstanding tradition, which, as suggested by Francesco Bruni, converged into the 'coscienza di un orizzonte unico, che ha molte vite virtuali e nessuna istituzionale [...] la cui esistenza è garantita

1 Alberto Mario Banti, *Il Risorgimento italiano* (Rome: Laterza, 2004), pp. 38–41. On the pre-revolutionary set-up, see Marco Soresina, *L'età della Restaurazione, 1815–1860. Gli Stati italiani dal Congresso di Vienna al crollo* (Milan: Mimesis, 2015), pp. 11–13.

2 On the Habsburgs in the Lombardy-Ventia, see Marco Meriggi, *Amministrazione e classi sociali nel Lombardo-Veneto (1814–1848)* (Bologna: Il Mulino, 1983); David Laven, *Venice and Venetia under the Habsburgs, 1815–1835* (Oxford: Oxford University Press, 2002).

3 For a detailed analysis of borders and states after the Congress of Vienna, see Soresina, *L'età della Restaurazione*, pp. 15–19.

dal fatto stesso che tutti la danno per scontata' [awareness of a unique horizon, which has many virtual lives and no institutional [life], [...] the existence of which is guaranteed by the very fact that everyone takes it for granted].[4] The construction of the conceptual Italian community found its meaning in the rhetoric of oppression in which the proud Italian character fought against the oppressors, identified with the Austrian Empire, the Pope or other monarchs, who hindered Italy from becoming a nation, united and under the rule of the Piedmontese king.[5]

In the age of the Restoration, the Italian Peninsula – like much of Southern Europe – was still a largely agrarian territory.[6] For a long time the main character of any demographic and socio-economic evolution remained that of a fast-growing population in the countryside.[7] In his study from 1854 the economist and politician Stefano Jacini, author of several works analysing the economic fabric of the Peninsula, estimated that investment in agriculture was six times higher than in

4 Francesco Bruni, *Italia. Vita e avventure di un'idea* (Bologna: Il Mulino, 2010), pp. 490–91, also pp. 69–103.

5 On the construction of Italian identity, see also Roberto Martucci, *L'invenzione dell'Italia unita: 1855–1864* (Milan: Sansoni, 1999); Alberto M. Banti, *La nazione del risorgimento. Parentela, santità e onore alle origini dell'Italia unita* (Turin: Einaudi, 2000); *Immagini della nazione nell'Italia del Risorgimento*, ed. by Alberto M. Banti and Roberto Bizzocchi (Rome: Carocci, 2002); Banti, *Il Risorgimento italiano*, esp. pp. 53–73; Silvana Patriarca, *Italianità. La costruzione del carattere nazionale* (Rome: Laterza, 2010); Silvana Patriarca, 'Italiani/Italiane', in *Atlante culturale del Risorgimento. Lessico del linguaggio politico dal Settecento all'Unità*, ed. by A. M. Banti and others (Rome: Laterza, 2011), pp. 199–213 (esp. pp. 200–01); Duccio Balestracci, *Medioevo e Risorgimento. L'invenzione dell'identità italiana nell'Ottocento* (Bologna: Il Mulino, 2015), esp. pp. 7–10. On the sense of nation and imagined community, see Benedict Anderson, *Imagined Communities: Reflections on the Origin and Spread of Nationalism* (London: Verso, 1983).

6 Several nineteenth-century surveys highlighted this point. See, e.g., Giuseppe Devincenzi, 'Relazione sull'agricoltura dell'Alto e del Basso Milanese', *Annali universali di statistica*, 81 (1844), 329–38; Stefano Jacini, *La proprietà fondiaria e le popolazioni agricole in Lombardia: Studj economici* (Milan: Borroni and Scotti, 1854), pp. 52–71. On Lombardy see Kent R. Greenfield, *Economia e liberalismo nel Risorgimento. Il movimento nazionale in Lombardia dal 1814 al 1848* (Bari: Laterza, 1964), pp. 11–12. With regard to the Po Valley, see also Alberto Mario Banti, *Terra e denaro. Una borghesia padana dell'Ottocento* (Venice: Marsilio, 1989), pp. 21–34.

7 During the nineteenth century the population growth was affected by several factors, such as bad harvests and epidemics, hence recording a lower increase than the European average. See Athos Bellettini, 'La popolazione italiana

commerce and industry combined.[8] From the Restoration onwards, in almost the entire Peninsula, landowners, politicians, economists and agronomists aimed at, and firmly believed in, modernising agriculture and enhancing it as an economic driver. In the nineteenth century sericulture acquired importance and, amid the debates on how to improve it, there was great demand for more advanced techniques in every agricultural sector.[9] The education of farmers and a prompt response to the demands of the market were the key themes with which various investigations and professional journals were concerned. From the 1840s onwards prices of agricultural products began to rise on international markets, leading to the idea that, even though commerce and industry (both metallurgical and textile) should be taken into account, the economy of the northern areas of Italy could also grow without focusing on industrialisation.[10] In the Italian Peninsula industrialisation began to develop in the 1830s and was characterised by strong regional asymmetry between the North and the South, with infrastructure having a very low impact on the territory.[11]

---

dall'inizio dell'era volgare ai giorni nostri. Valutazioni e tendenze', in *Storia d'Italia*, ed. by Ruggiero Romano and Corrado Vivanti, 6 vols (Turin: Einaudi, 1973), v, *I documenti*, 489–532 (p. 517); Guido Pescosolido, 'L'economia e la vita materiale', in *Storia d'Italia*, ed. by Giovanni Sabbatucci and Vittorio Vidotto, 6 vols (Rome and Bari: Laterza, 1994), i, *Le premesse dell'unità*, 3–118; Soresina, *L'età della Restaurazione*, pp. 168–70. See also Gérard Delille, *Agricoltura e demografia nel Regno di Napoli nei secoli XVIII e XIX* (Naples: Guida, 1977), esp. pp. 12–38; Lorenzo Del Panta, *Evoluzione demografica e popolamento nell'Italia dell'Ottocento: 1796–1914* (Bologna: CLUEB, 1984).

8 Jacini, *La proprietà fondiaria*, p. 139; Greenfield, *Economia e liberalismo*, p. 79. On agriculture in the Italian Peninsula, see also Carlo Cattaneo, *D'alcune instituzioni agrarie dell'alta Italia applicabili a sollievo dell'Irlanda* (Milan: di Giovanni, 1847).

9 Greenfield, *Economia e liberalismo*, pp. 64–70. See also Luigi Serristori, 'Dell'attuale condizione dell'industria in Italia', *Annali universali di statistica*, 85 (1845), 9–19 (pp. 11–16).

10 Pescosolido, 'L'economia e la vita materiale', pp. 64–65. See also Greenfield, *Economia e liberalismo*, pp. 79–190; Gino Luzzatto, *Per una storia economica d'Italia. Progressi e lacune* (Bari: Laterza, 1957), pp. 83–84; Marta Petrusewicz, 'Agronomia: innovatori agrari nelle periferie europee dell'Ottocento', in *Storia dell'agricoltura italiana in età contemporanea*, ed. by Piero Bevilacqua, 3 vols (Venice: Marsilio, 1992), iii, *Mercati* e *istituzioni*, 295–344.

11 Vera Zamagni, *Industrializzazione e squilibri regionali in Italia. Bilancio dell'età giolittiana* (Bologna: Il Mulino, 1978), pp. 197, 200. See also Luciano Cafagna, *The Industrial Revolution in Italy, 1830–1914*, trans. by Muriel Grindrod (London: Collins, 1971), pp. 1–54 (pp. 48–49).

Family and Society

The severe economic backwardness of the Italian Peninsula was reflected in social and cultural dynamics,[12] but its fabric, poised between the past and the future, began to testify to a slow change which affected family structures. Since the end of the eighteenth century, the image of large patriarchal families gathered around a householder had begun to fade and give way to different 'kinds' of families, such as the bourgeois family, the workers' family and the various peasants' families.[13] Several factors contributed to these changes, resulting in a reduction in family size: this could be explained by the transition towards modern *companionate* marriages, which were 'small parental families characterized by love between spouses, as well as between parents and children'.[14] Edward Shorter believes that this transition was also due to a new sense of personal autonomy for women, who actively contributed to the decision to reduce the numerical size of their families.[15] In particular, statistics on Milanese and Florentine upper classes show a change in attitude towards celibacy and spinsterhood. In Dante Zanetti's demographic survey on the Milanese aristocracy,

12 Several studies of the time focused on this point. See, e.g., Enrico Pani Rossi, *La Basilicata libri tre. Studi politici, amministrativi e di economia pubblica* (Verona: Civelli, 1868); Gaspare Finali, *Le Marche: ricordanze* (Ancona: Morelli, 1896); Alfredo Niceforo, *L'Italia barbara contemporanea: Studi e appunti* (Milan: Sandron, 1898).

13 See Peter Laslett, 'Family and Household as Work Group and Kin Group: Areas of Traditional Europe Compared', in *Family Forms in Historic Europe*, ed. by Richard Wall, Jean Robin and Peter Laslett (Cambridge: Cambridge University Press, 1983), pp. 513–64; *La famiglia italiana dall'Ottocento a oggi*, ed. by Piero Melograni and Lucetta Scaraffia (Rome and Bari: Laterza, 1988); *Storia della famiglia italiana, 1750–1950*, ed. by Marzio Barbagli and David I. Kertzer (Bologna: Il Mulino, 1992); Giorgio Vecchio, *Profilo storico della famiglia. La famiglia italiana tra Ottocento e Novecento* (Cinisello Balsamo: San Paolo, 1999), pp. 5–8.

14 Jack Goody, 'Dowry and the Rights of Women to Property', in *Property Relations: Renewing the Anthropological Tradition*, ed. by C. M. Hann (Cambridge: Cambridge University Press, 1998), pp. 201–13 (p. 209). See also Élisabeth Badinter, *L'Amour en plus: histoire de l'amour maternel (XVIIe–XXe siècle)* (Paris: Flammarion, 1981).

15 On companionate marriages, see Edward Shorter, 'Emancipazione femminile, controllo delle nascite e fecondità nella storia europea', in *Famiglia e mutamento sociale*, ed. by Barbagli, pp. 317–59 (pp. 344–46); Kate Fisher, 'Marriage and Companionate Ideals since 1750', in *The Routledge History of Sex and the Body: 1500 to the Present*, ed. by Sarah Toulalan and Kate Fisher (London

for example, the percentage of unmarried men and women in the period between 1600 and 1647 was 49% and 75% respectively, while between 1850 and 1899 the percentage went down to 11.5% and 25%.[16] The increase in the number of marriages did not, however, lead to an analogous increase in the number of births, thus testifying to the voluntary control of births.[17] Although statistics and data samples are not sufficiently large and reliable, demographers explain that the decline of fertility was due to a combination of factors, including a reduction in the size of land plots, which led to a sort of 'proletarianisation' of the rural areas. This meant that the number of farm workers increased and, consequently, the size of their families became smaller.[18]

In the Italian Peninsula many large towns already existed before the onset of industrialisation: urbanisation did not imply a process of 'deruralisation'.[19] Nevertheless, the industrialisation process played an important role in altering the social fabric of the Italian Peninsula, leading simultaneously to the rise of the bourgeoisie as a new class of entrepreneurs and the decline of the nobility.[20] This combination of factors delivered the *coup de grace* to a world which had been exposed to erosion for several decades, a blow which the

---

and New York: Routledge, 2013), pp. 328–48 (p. 329). Breastfeeding also had an impact on the reduction of family size. On this point see Massimo Livi-Bacci, *A History of Italian Fertility during the Last Two Centuries* (Princeton, NJ: Princeton University Press, 1977), pp. 35–48, 285–86.

16 Dante Zanetti, *La demografia del patriziato milanese nei secoli XVII, XVIII, XIX* (Pavia: Università di Pavia, 1972), p. 84.

17 Zanetti, *La demografia del patriziato milanese*, pp. 144–45. A similar decline was recorded among Florentine patricians. See Robert B. Litchfield, 'Caratteristiche demografiche delle famiglie patrizie fiorentine dal sedicesimo al diciannovesimo secolo', in *Saggi di demografia storica*, ed. by Carlo Alberto Corsini and others (Florence: Università di Firenze, 1969), pp. 17–34 (p. 25).

18 See Barbagli, *Sotto lo stesso tetto*, pp. 45–138.

19 Alberto De Bernardi, 'Città e campagna nella storia contemporanea', in *Storia dell'economia italiana*, ed. by Ruggiero Romano, 3 vols (Turin: Einaudi, 1990–91), III (1991), *L'età contemporanea: un paese nuovo*, 252–78 (p. 253).

20 See Alberto Mario Banti, 'Ricchezza e potere. Le dinamiche patrimoniali nella società lucchese del XIX secolo', *Quaderni Storici*, 50 (1982), 629–61 (pp. 646–49); Giuliana Biagioli, 'Patrimoni e congiuntura: crescita, crisi e ripresa di una famiglia nobile toscana fra Sette e Ottocento', in *Ricerche di storia moderna*, ed. by Elsa Luttazzi Gregori and others, 4 vols (Pisa: Pacini, 1976–95), II (1979), *Aziende e patrimoni di grandi famiglie (sec. XV–XIX)*, 297–377 (pp. 332–35). See also James C. Davis, *The Decline of the Venetian Nobility as a Ruling Class* (Baltimore, MD: Johns Hopkins University Press, 1962).

large patriarchal family struggled to resist. As the Milanese jurist Giovanni Carcano observed:

> un notevole cambiamento parmi verificato nel corso di non molti anni nelle abitudini della nostra famiglia [...]. A memoria d'uomini ancor freschi fu tempo in cui era comune tipo fra noi la famiglia patriarcale [...] nella quale i figli maritavano presso i padri, menando loro donne nella casa dei padri [...]. Ora lo sperperarsi e il dividersi [...] è il costume dell'epoca nostra.[21]
>
> [a noteworthy change seems to have occurred in the habits of our family in recent years. [...] Men who are still young remember that there was a time when the patriarchal family was common among us, [...] and in this kind of family, married sons settled with their women in their fathers' homes. [...] Now squandering and dividing [...] are the custom of our current times.]

The same concerns regarding the disintegration of the large patriarchal family were expressed in an interesting portrait of nineteenth-century Lombard society drawn up by the Milanese writer Carlo Ravizza (1811–1848).[22] His novel *Un curato di campagna: schizzi morali* features a country priest trying to persuade families to remain together:

> Le grandi famiglie tendevano più che mai a scomporsi [...] o per l'insubordinazione di un figliuolo, o per l'inerzia di un altro, o per l'invidia gelosa di qualche donna [...] e allora non so dire quanto il buon parroco si sforzasse d'impedire queste scomposizioni [...], "figliuoli miei, abitate una sola casa, fate bollire un sol pentolo, lavorate tutti ed insieme, chè riunendo le vostre forze, riuscirete a quello che disuniti non farete mai".[23]
>
> [Large families tended more than ever to break up [...] either through the insubordination of one son, or by the inertia of another, or through the jealous envy of some woman [...] and so I cannot say how much the good parish priest endeavored to prevent these break ups [...], "my children, live in one house, boil a single pot, work all together, because by gathering your forces you will succeed in what, disunited, you would never achieve".]

21 Giovanni Carcano, *Il codice civile austriaco ed i suoi caratteri* (Milan: Manini, 1860), p. 27.

22 The journal *Guida dell'educatore*, edited by Raffaello Lambruschini, reported that Carlo Ravizza's best known book, *Un curato di campagna: schizzi morali*, was a valuable moral essay and was to 'riuscir grata ad ogn'Italiano, che desideri veder diffusa ne' più umili tugurj una sana morale' [make every Italian who wishes to see good morals spread in the humblest hovels grateful] (*Guida dell'educatore*, 7 (1842), 116–22 (p. 122)).

23 Carlo Ravizza, *Un curato di campagna: schizzi morali* (Milan: Pirola, 1841), p. 30

The *curato di campagna* considered staying united to be both a sign and a source of strength for families, a value to pursue in the face of the pressures of modernity. The patriarchal family, a symbol of a fading world, had its own rules and customs, which were questioned by new ideals introduced since the Enlightenment. (This point will be discussed in the following chapters.) In this context, the 'insubordinazione di un figliuolo' was a major concern for the family, and for society, which rested on a rigid hierarchical structure.

Although Carlo Ravizza refers to large patriarchal peasants' families which owned or rented small plots of land for cultivation, social dynamics among their members presented traits similar to those characterising other kinds of families, such as those belonging to the upper classes. The key in this regard was the possession of goods; and the most sensitive issue for a family was the transmission of this wealth, be it a *latifundium* or a small plot of land, a large sum of money, or just a piece of furniture. In broader terms, a family could be described as a moral body, led by men and composed of several members who recognised themselves as sharing a common name and identity and resided in a family's property.[24] As argued by Cesarina Casanova, belonging to a family also meant being part of a group and:

> i confini della solidarietà o dell'indifferenza si possono cogliere solo chiedendosi in quali occasioni per un individuo potere o non potere attivare una rete di sostegno fosse determinante per il suo successo e quali rapporti in queste occasioni risultassero preferenziali.[25]
>
> [the boundaries of solidarity or indifference can be grasped only by asking on which occasions an individual was or was not able to activate a support network which was decisive for their success and which relationships were preferential on these occasions.]

24 On the notion of family, see also Giulio Vismara, *L'unità della famiglia nella storia del diritto in Italia* (Rome: Apollinaris, 1956); James C. Davis, *A Venetian Family and Its Fortune, 1500–1900: The Donà and the Conservation of Their Wealth* (Philadelphia, PA: American Philosophical Society, 1975), pp. 1–4; Thomas J. Kuehn, 'Household and Family in Ius Commune and Ius Proprium', in *The Household in Late Medieval Cities: Italy and Northwestern Europe Compared*, ed. by Myriam Carlier and Tim Soens (Leuven: Garant, 2001), pp. 37–50; Victor Crescenzi, 'Per una semantica della famiglia (ovvero: di cosa si parla, quando si parla di famiglia?)', in *Il giurista e il diritto. Studi per Federico Spantigati*, ed. by Andrea Bixio and Giuliano Crifò (Milan: FrancoAngeli, 2010), pp. 3–31; Kuehn, *Family and Gender*, pp. 33–52.

25 Cesarina Casanova, *La famiglia italiana in età moderna. Ricerche e modelli* (Rome: Carocci, 2000), p. 63.

Hence, the idea of family, and the mutual support it implied, had blurred boundaries, which were also defined by the sense of shared identity and behaviour and, in time, loosened to allow new members to enter through marriages and births. Over the centuries this large moral body became a smaller and more intimate group; and its hierarchical structure faced a progressive evolution towards a sort of 'verticalisation', with the power usually held in one male hand.[26]

The social, economic and political strength of the family coincided with the strength of its assets, to the extent that the possession of goods made the difference between having, or not having, significance before the law. If the medieval jurist Albericus of Rosciate (1290–1360) maintained that 'familia id est substantia' [the family is its wealth][27] and Bartolus of Saxoferrato (1313–1357) confirmed that 'familia accipitur in iure pro substantia' [the family is taken in law for its wealth],[28] in nineteenth-century society the family was still considered in a similar way. This also implied that its members were only those who were entitled to benefit from its *substancia* and, in the words of Thomas Kuehn, 'property was an ingredient in identity'.[29] In this *familia*, ideas about name, honour and prestige were a legacy of ancient times and were transmitted through the male line only. From the Middle Ages up to the Ottocento this ideal of *familia* continued to be characterised by the behaviour and customs shared by other *familiae* of similar wealth. Their customs had legal value and formed the bulk of customary laws that were enforceable and existent beyond the written law (this point is analysed in Chapter 3).

26 On family structure in the Middle Ages, see Richard A. Goldthwaite, *Private Wealth in Renaissance Florence: A Study of Four Families* (Princeton, NJ: Princeton University Press, 1968); David Herlihy, 'Family Solidarity in Medieval Italian History', *Exploration in Economic History*, 7 (1969), 173–84; Francis William Kent, *Household and Lineage in Renaissance Florence: The Family Life of the Capponi, Ginori, and Rucellai* (Princeton, NJ: Princeton University Press, 1977), pp. 21–62; Romano, *Famiglia, successioni e patrimonio*, pp. 60–85; *La famiglia tardoantica. Società, diritto, religione*, ed. by Valerio Neri and Beatrice Girotti (Milan: LED, 2016).

27 Albericus of Rosciate, 'Familia', in *Dictionarium iuri tam civilis quam canonici* (Venice: [n. pub.], 1581), n. pag.

28 Bartolus of Saxoferrato, *Commentaria in primam infortiati* (Lyon: [n. pub.], 1552), p. 112; Kuehn, *Family and Gender*, pp. 48–51.

29 Kuehn, *Family and Gender*, p. 49.

Women and the Family

In a family, the most prominent figure was represented by the *paterfamilias*, whose personal supremacy enabled him also to be the *dominus* of the *patrimonium* of the *familia*. He was a male adult, head of the family and holder of an almost endless *potestas* over his children and grandchildren.[30] The ambiguous limits of the *potestas* were also extended to wives, who went from being under the authority of their fathers or grandfathers to being under that of their husband after marriage. Since classical times women had been perceived as not being fully part of the family. For example, only grandchildren *ex filio* – and not those *ex filia* – were subject to the *potestas* of the *paterfamilias*. A woman could not have any person subject to her *potestas*[31] and was considered as if she were the only component of her family. A woman was 'familiae suae et caput et finis est' [the beginning and the end of her family], as the Roman jurist Ulpian wrote in the third century.[32] Even though Ulpian described the family of his time, Carla Fayer notes that the characteristics of the Roman household were similar to those of the extended patriarchal peasant families existing

30 The jurist Ulpian described the *familia* as 'plures personae, quae sunt sub unius potestate aut naturae aut iure subiectae' [several people, who are subject to the authority of one [person] either by nature or by law] (*Digest*, 50.16.195.2, 'Ulpianus libro 46 ad edictum'). The *potestas* [authority] is a major characteristic of the *familia* and is defined as the power to command and dispose of people and goods. This authority over family members implied economic dependence on the *paterfamilias*, which meant 'head of a family'. The *paterfamilias* was not subject to any *potestas* and was *sui juris* [of his own right, autonomous, independent]. For the *paterfamilias* in Roman law, see Carla Fayer, *La familia romana: aspetti giuridici ed antiquari*, 3 vols (Rome: "L'Erma" di Bretschneider, 1994), I, 18–19; Jane F. Gardner, *Family and Familia in Roman Law and Life* (Oxford: Clarendon Press, 1998), pp. 6–10; Romano, *Famiglia, successioni e patrimonio*. On paternal authority, see Philippe Ariès, *Padri e figli nell'Europa medievale e moderna*, trans. by Maria Garin (Bari: Laterza, 1968) (orig.: *L'enfant et la vie familiale sous l'ancien régime* (Paris: Plon, 1960)); Giovanni Lobrano, *Pater et filius eadem persona. Per lo studio della 'patria potestas'* (Milan: Giuffrè, 1984), esp. pp. 25–27; Cavina, *Il padre spodestato*. On the role of the *paterfamilias*, see also *La paura dei padri*, ed. by Pellizer, Zorzetti and Maffi.

31 Fayer, *La familia romana*, I, 19.

32 Digest, 50.16.195.5, 'Ulpianus 46 ad edictum'. Among the major works of Gnaeus Domitius Annius Ulpianus (*c*. 170–228?) were the two commentaries *Ad edictum* and *Ad Sabinum*, which supplied about a third of the contents of Justinian's *Digest*. The *Law of Citations* (*Lex citationum*), issued by the Emperor Valentinian III in 426 and later absorbed into the *Codex Theodosianus* (438), states

in several areas of the nineteenth-century Italian Peninsula.[33] One might suggest that the parallels between Roman and peasant families could also be found in other extended patriarchal families, such as those of the nobility, the points in common being the possession of some wealth, the concern for its transmission and the *potestas* that a *paterfamilias* exercised over people and goods. Nonetheless, in the Ottocento the Turinese lawyer Francesco Concone, drawing on Ulpian's words, explained that:

> dovendo le femmine onde lasciar discendenti da sé, passare a marito, che appartiene ad altra famiglia, e con ciò assumere nome diverso, si avevano a considerare, come se cessassero di far parte della famiglia del padre, o almeno ne fossero l'ultimo anello.[34]
>
> [given that women had to produce offspring, they have to marry a man who belongs to another family and assume a different name, as a result, they were to be considered as if they had ceased to be part of the father's family, or, at least, as if they were the last link.]

Women were destined to marry and give birth to children who would perpetuate their husband's lineage.[35] By becoming part of another *familia*, women were excluded from substantial parts of the wealth of their family of origin, because this was to be assigned to the men who would bear the family's name. As argued by the jurist Giovanni Maria Negri:

> [c]essa [...] nei padri medesimi il fomite di accumular sostanze, allorché sanno, che queste devono già pervenire col mezzo delle femmine ad altre ignote famiglie. [Infatti] si veggono [...] sussistere de' secoli, col mezzo de' maschj, li più illustri casati, che ritennero colle loro sostanze lo splendor del loro cognome ad ornamento di queste contrade. I maschj sono quelli che conservano le proprie famiglie, e colle loro cure lo stato e la dovizia di esse.[36]

---

that judges were able to use only the doctrines of the five outstanding jurists Ulpian, Papinianus, Gaius, Modestinus and Paulus to interpret law and reach a decision. See also Albericus of Rosciate, 'Familia'; he maintains that 'mulier non habet familiam' [a woman does not have a family].

33 On this point see Fayer, *La familia romana*, I, 17–21.

34 Francesco Concone, *Giurisprudenza femminile* (Turin: Fumero Maggiore, 1839), p. 144.

35 Kuehn, *Law, Family and Women*, p. 199.

36 Giovanni Maria Negri, *Dei difetti del Codice Civile Italico, che porta il titolo di Codice Napoleone e dei pregj del Codice Civile Austriaco* (Vicenza: Parise, 1815), p. 77.

> [[t]he impetus to accumulate wealth ceases [...] with the fathers themselves as soon as they know that, through the women, it may fall into the hands of unknown families. [In fact] one sees [...] that, for centuries, the most illustrious families have continued to exist through their men, who with their substance kept the splendour of their name to adorn these districts. It is men who preserve their families and, with their care, the status and wealth of those families.]

The sole reason that would drive the *paterfamilias* to acquire wealth was the pursuit of honour and prestige for the *familia* which would bear his name. Amassing wealth for women, who would then give birth to children bearing someone else's name, was pointless. In a world characterised by power relationships, hierarchy, authority and obedience, property was key and determined status, real or vaunted.

In this context, when Napoleon extended the French Civil Code to the conquered regions, its rules governing family law and inheritance were a major challenge to the very foundation of Italian society. Along with the opportunity given to all children to succeed regardless of their sex,[37] Napoleon's *Code Civil des Français*[38] – or, in its Italian version, the *Codice Civile di Napoleone il Grande pel Regno d'Italia*[39] – excluded the rule *paterna paternis, materna maternis* (goods coming from the father's property go to the father's relatives and those from the mother's property to the mother's relatives) to identify the origin of assets to regulate inheritance.[40] These two principles were real novelties for the pre-Unification legal systems, in which

37 Art. 745, in *Codice Civile del Regno d'Italia*, in *Collezione Completa dei Moderni Codici Civili* (Turin: Minerva Subalpina, 1845), pp. 1–139 (p. 43).

38 The Code, which was the work of a committee of jurists appointed by Napoleon and led by Jean-Étienne-Marie Portalis, consisted of 2,281 articles, had the tripartite division of Roman law (*personae, res, actiones*) and was strongly influenced by the Roman law in force in the south of the country. Its Italian translation was applied to the Italian territories by decree on 30 March 1806 and came into force the following day. The code unified the legal régime of the entire Peninsula, with the exception of Sicily, Sardinia and some territories of the Venetia.

39 Despite jurists and politicians demanding the inclusion of changes which would be more suitable to the juridical tradition of the Italian Peninsula, Napoleon's will prevailed and prevented the introduction of codes other than a direct translation of the *Code Civil des Français* (Carlo Ghisalberti, *Unità nazionale e unificazione giuridica in Italia* (Rome: Laterza, 1988), p. 135).

40 Art. 732, in *Codice Civile del Regno d'Italia* (1845), p. 42. Before Napoleon, the goods of a man went to his family of origin at the time of his death, thereby leaving his widow without the possibility of inheriting anything. With Napoleon, the new couple were the key unit and their families of origin no longer had the legal

the predominance of sons and the separation of property between spouses were broadly accepted. The strong resistance to Napoleon's family law, which also challenged parental authority,[41] was not just a fight against the law implemented by the conqueror: it reflected the concerns of the *paterfamilias*, who strove to keep his small 'monarchy' unchanged.[42] Indeed, allowing all children – sons and daughters – to receive the same portion of inheritance meant that properties would be divided into small shares, causing families a loss of status and prestige. This was a situation to be avoided for a society which perpetuated itself and its prerogatives by locking up its assets.

---

significance they had enjoyed previously. As we see in Chapter 3, for example, during the time before and after Napoleon's Code the dowry, which was usually given by fathers, returned to a woman's line if she died without children.

41 Art. 488, in *Codice Civile del Regno d'Italia* (1845), p. 29. In the Napoleonic Code paternal authority ended with the coming of age and the individual becoming emancipated. This entailed his or her being able to undertake juridical acts. Up to the enactment of the French Code and, after the Congress of Vienna, with the recall into force of the law of the Ancien Régime, the coming of age did not lead automatically to emancipation, as on the basis of Roman law a person could be emancipated only by a formal act or after the death of his or her father. However, in many areas of the Italian Peninsula a son was considered emancipated when he attained the age of majority, was married and lived in a different household from that of his father.

42 The parallelism between family and monarchy could be drawn from the words of Cesare Beccaria. He argues that 'vi siano cento mila uomini, o sia venti mila famiglie, ciascuna delle quali è composta da cinque persone, compresovi il capo che la rappresenta; se l'associazione è fatta per le famiglie, vi saranno venti mila uomini, e ottanta mila schiavi; se l'associazione è di uomini, vi saranno cento mila cittadini, e nessuno schiavo. Nel primo caso vi sarà una repubblica, e venti mila piccole monarchie, che la compongono; nel secondo, lo spirito repubblicano non solo spirerà nelle piazze e nelle adunanze della nazione, ma anche nelle domestiche mura, dove sta gran parte della felicità o della miseria degli uomini' [say there are one hundred thousand people, divided into twenty thousand families, each comprising five people, including the head of the family who represents it; then if the association is regarded as consisting of families, there will be twenty thousand persons and eighty thousand slaves; if it is regarded as consisting of individuals, there will be one hundred thousand citizens and no slaves. In the former case, there will be one republic and twenty thousand little monarchies which make it up; in the latter, the republican spirit will be breathed not only in the squares and in public meetings, but also within the home, where much of man's happiness or misery is to be found]. Therefore, considering society as a gathering of families instead of people meant that some individuals were deemed to be subordinate to others (Cesare Beccaria, *Dei Delitti e delle pene* (Paris: Cazin, 1786), p. 144; trans. in *Beccaria: On Crimes and Punishments, and Other Writings*, ed. by Richard Bellamy, trans. by Richard Davies (Cambridge: Cambridge University Press, 1995), p. 60).

The *Code Napoléon*, which was influenced by natural law and inspired by individuals' equality, regardless of social class, attacked this equilibrium, this immobility and this inequality.

From this perspective it is easy to understand the advice given by Ravizza's country priest, who tries to persuade small landowners' families not to send their children to study Latin. The priest 'li consigliava a mandar piuttosto i figli in qualche collegio dove fossero instituite le scuole di commercio, e più volentieri li avrebbe indirizzati a quello che avesse anche una scuola d'agricoltura e delle industrie affini' [suggested to them that they should rather send their children to a school at which they could learn about trade and, even more willingly, to those schools in which they could also learn about agriculture and related industries].[43] In the static Ottocento, staying within the boundaries of one's own social class was praised and also strongly recommended. Attempts to improve the family trade were welcomed, but this was not supposed to lead to transition from one social class to another. New relationships and kinship links were usually created through marriages among people of similar wealth and status. Unlike the Napoleonic Code, which did not recognise class privileges, Italian society firmly discouraged and even punished any attempt at breaking down class barriers and any aspiration to climb the social ladder. Thus, the *Codice Estense* of 1771,[44] which, except for the short Napoleonic period, remained in force in the Duchy of Modena until the advent of the *Codice Estense* in 1851, condemned the marriage of 'disparaggio', that is, a marriage between a man and a woman of different social status.[45] In this act Duke Francesco III declared that it was for the 'importante oggetto del decoro delle famiglie, e del pubblico, e privato interesse' [important goal of families' decorum and for public and private interest][46] that:

> qualunque nobile si accaserà con persona, il cui matrimonio per la di lei vile, e bassa condizione apporti disonore, e vitupero a sé, ed

43 Ravizza, *Un curato di campagna*, p. 45.

44 The *Codice Estense*, also known as *Codice di leggi e costituzioni pel Ducato di Modena*, was promulgated by Francesco III, Duke of Modena, in 1771. All statutes and municipal laws in force before its approval were abolished, but for topics not covered by this *Codice* the use of Roman law was permitted.

45 The Civil Code of Modena was promulgated by Francesco V in 1851. The Code was enacted to reform and attune the law in force in the Duchy. This code, too, recognised the possibility of using other sources of law, such as Roman law, to decide on topics not covered.

46 Art. VII Tit. XIII, in *Codice Estense*, in *Collezione completa*, pp. 787–870 (p. 810).

> alla sua famiglia, non solamente tale nobile incontrerà la Nostra disapprovazione, ma inoltre ci riserviamo a dare contro di lui quei provvedimenti, che secondo le circostanze de' casi crederemo opportuni, e convenienti.[47]
>
> [a noble person whose marriage to a person of a lower status would bring dishonour and disgrace to himself or herself, and to the family, will not only meet with Our disapproval, but we also reserve the right to sanction this person with those measures which we deem appropriate and proper according to the circumstances of the case.]

A marriage of 'disparaggio' was considered to be such a dishonour that the monarch would intervene in person and assess the issue, deciding which provision was appropriate in the specific circumstance. The Duke, who was deeply concerned with keeping the social structure of his Duchy unchanged, also imposed sanctions against parents of humble condition who had contributed, 'col consiglio, od anche con la semplice connivenza' [with advice, or even with simple connivance], to encouraging the marriage between their children and those of higher rank.[48] The importance of social class and the desire for society to remain static were not just a vague wish, but were pursued by the law itself, which contributed to perpetuating class stratification.

However, under some circumstances exceptions were permitted: for example, in the case of the potential impoverishment of some 'illustri casati' [illustrious houses] 'hypergamous' marriages between nobles with scant patrimonies and very wealthy non-noble people were accepted.[49] An interesting example comes from the Papal States, where Tomaso Stramigioli, a wealthy man from Pesaro, married Augusta Antaldi in 1854. She had a dowry of 1,500 scudi,[50] quite meagre for a woman of her status: Augusta belonged to a family

47 Art. VII Tit. XIII, in *Codice Estense*, p. 810.

48 Art. IX Tit. XIII, in *Codice Estense*, p. 810.

49 Hypergamy is defined as marrying a person of higher social status. An overview of the pattern of the evolving definition of hypergamy, which was first used in Indian sociology to define marriage with people of higher castes, can be found in Rhonda R. Buckley, 'Hypergamy', in *The Wiley Blackwell Encyclopedia of Family Studies*, ed. by Constance L. Shehan, 4 vols (Chichester: Wiley Blackwell, 2016), II, 1085–86. For marriage between people belonging to different social classes, see also Marco Meriggi, 'Società, istituzioni e ceti dirigenti', in *Storia d'Italia*, ed. by Sabbatucci and Vidotto, I, *Le premesse dell'unità*, 177–90.

50 State Archive of Pesaro (SAP), Notaio Luigi Perotti, 1854.

of some distinction and antiquity, still well regarded despite her patrimony being hugely impoverished. To Tomaso, this marriage meant entering elite society. Augusta died a few months later and Tomaso married again shortly after. This time he married a woman from a wealthy but non-noble family. Her dowry consisted of three thousand scudi and a trousseau.[51] Since Tomaso's wealth had not doubled within a few months, the difference in the amount of the two dowries tells us much about the customs of the time: Augusta, in addition to cash, brought to her marriage nobility and social status which compensated for her limited dowry. Emilia, the second wife, came from a wealthy family, but could not boast a noble and ancient lineage. To be attractive in the marriage market, her dowry had to be higher than that of a noble, but less wealthy, woman.

Other than creating alliances and acquiring a higher status, marriage was also a way to restore a patrimony by means of the dowry brought by the bride to the new family.[52] For example, Anna Bonaccorsi Dolcini Tredozio was a very wealthy woman from the Romagna region (then part of the Papal States); accordingly, she had an opulent dowry. In 1831 she married Baron Bettino Ricasoli (1809–1880), the future Italian Prime Minister (1861–62 and 1866–67).[53] The marriage allowed Ricasoli to repay his family's debts and to improve and modernise his farms. These cases suggest that monarchs and society's upper strata of the time used a specific strategy: on the

51 SAP, Notaio Luigi Perotti, 1855.

52 On marriage strategies in the Early Modern period and the Enlightenment, see also Raul Merzario, *Il paese stretto. Strategie matrimoniali nella diocesi di Como, secoli XVI–XVIII* (Turin: Einaudi, 1981); Anthony Molho, *Marriage Alliance in Late Medieval Florence* (Cambridge, MA: Harvard University Press, 1994), pp. 236–38; Gérard Delille, 'Strategie di alleanza e demografia del matrimonio', in *Storia del matrimonio*, ed. by Michela De Giorgio and Christiane Klapisch-Zuber (Rome: Laterza, 1996), pp. 283–306; Michela De Giorgio, 'Raccontare un matrimonio moderno', in *Storia del matrimonio*, ed. by De Giorgio and Klapisch-Zuber, pp. 307–90.

53 For further details on Ricasoli's marriage and his wife's dowry, see Daniele Bronzuoli, *Matrimoni e patrimoni. La dote di Anna Bonaccorsi e la strategia imprenditoriale di Bettino Ricasoli* (Florence: Polistampa, 2013). See also Andrea Moroni, 'Antica gente e subiti guadagni. Patrimoni aristocratici fiorentini nell'800', *Biblioteca di storia toscana moderna e contemporanea*, 44 (1997), 1–364 (p. 143); Biagioli, 'Patrimoni e congiuntura', p. 343. See also the marriages of Princes Errico Antonio and Massimo Montalto di Lequile from the Kingdom of the Two Sicilies. The dowries of their wives were explicitly mentioned as paying off several mortgages they had on their properties (Paolo Macry, *Ottocento. Famiglia, élites e patrimoni a Napoli* (Turin: Einaudi, 1988), p. 52). See also the marriage

one hand, monarchs aimed to maintain a powerful class of allies by praising these kinds of marriage; on the other, nobles ensured their survival as an influential body against the challenges brought by the rise of the new bourgeois class.

Moreover, these cases show that the choice of the bride and groom was rarely driven by love: marriage was 'un fatto più che mai "razionale", concertato a tavolino dai genitori o dai membri più influenti della famiglia' [more than ever a 'rational' act, arranged by parents or by the most influential family members].[54] In this context, as Lucetta Scaraffia observes, 'la categoria dell'utile dominava i parametri estetici' [profit dominated over aesthetic parameters].[55] Among property owners marriage complied with families' aspirations to preserve their importance in society by becoming connected to families of similar status and wealth, or to improve their status; among lower classes, marriage was contracted for similar, functional reasons. The ability to work, together with having a small dowry, which for lower classes could consist of some pieces of furniture such as a bed or a wardrobe, made a woman desirable on the marriage market.

Scaraffia suggests that social dynamics in the countryside adhered to a model which always required the presence of a male and a female in the household. This also meant that 'la donna che entra nella famiglia come moglie e che si prepara a sostituire la madre serve a compensare la sorella che se ne esce' [the woman who enters the family as a wife replaces the mother and serves to counterbalance the sister who leaves]:[56] when one member of the couple was missing, he or she was replaced by another person, that is to say, for example, that the daughter-in-law replaced the sister who relocated to another house after her marriage.[57] One might argue that similar behaviour could be inferred not only in contexts where the labour force was crucial: men and women had fundamental and complementary roles in the upper

strategies of the Barraco family (Marta Petrusewicz, *Latifondo. Economia morale e vita materiale in una periferia dell'Ottocento* (Venice: Marsilio, 1990), pp. 13–16).

54 Gaetano Cozzi, *La società veneta e il suo diritto. Saggi su questioni matrimoniali, giustizia penale, politica del diritto, sopravvivenza del diritto veneto nell'Ottocento* (Venice: Marsilio, 2000), p. 41).

55 Lucetta Scaraffia, 'Essere uomo, essere donna', in *La famiglia italiana*, ed. by Melograni and Scaraffia, pp. 193–258 (p. 205).

56 Scaraffia, 'Essere uomo, essere donna', p. 195.

57 Scaraffia, 'Essere uomo, essere donna', pp. 203–07. Similar behaviour is also described in Elena De Marchi, *Dai campi alle filande. Famiglia, matrimonio e lavoro nella "pianura dell'Olona" 1750–1850* (Milan: FrancoAngeli, 2009), pp. 178–82.

strata of society as well, a point borne out by the incidence of remarriage.[58] Indeed, the high mortality rate often resulted in an early end to marriages and, subsequently, remarriages. As Trevor Dean and Kate Lowe explain, 'the question of what the other spouse should do with regard to remarrying was [an] especially severe [dilemma] for women, who were supposed not to be able to function effectively without being married'.[59] On the male side, instead, 'il existe un véritable tabou dans le domaine des travaux domestiques [...] les veufs ne peuvent pas rester sans femme, pas plus que les vieux célibataires qui gardent avec eux une vieille soeur destinée à leur entretien' [there is a real taboo in the field of domestic work, [...] widowers cannot remain without a woman and, for this reason, bachelors keep with them an old sister intended for their support].[60] As family was key for the society of the time, both men's and women's lives were imagined mainly as part of and having a role in it.

Women and Political Participation: The Risorgimento

Leveraged by the ideals of the Enlightenment and the French Revolution, from the beginning of the Ottocento the family began to be loaded with expectations. It was considered the place in which

58 Although the lack of sufficiently comprehensive, reliable data does not allow the proposition of a consistent model, some studies analyse the demographics of remarriage for limited areas. See, e.g., Athos Bellettini, 'Les Remariages dans la ville et dans la campagne de Bologne au dix-neuvième siècle', in *Marriage and Remarriage in Populations of the Past*, ed. by Jacques Dupâquier and others (London: Academic Press, 1981), pp. 259–72; Massimo Livi-Bacci, 'On the Frequency of Remarriage in Nineteenth Century Italy: Methods and Results', in *Marriage and Remarriage in Populations of the Past*, ed. by Dupâquier and others, pp. 347–61; Andrea Schiaffino, 'Quelques données sur le remariage dans un milieu urbain: Bologne aux dix-neuvième et vingtième siècles', in *Marriage and Remarriage in Populations of the Past*, ed. by Dupâquier and others, pp. 397–409; Marco Breschi, *La popolazione della Toscana dal 1640 al 1940. Un'ipotesi di ricostruzione* (Florence: Dipartimento Statistico, 1990); Marco Breschi and others, 'Family Composition and Remarriage in Pre-Transitional Italy: A Comparative Study', *European Journal of Population*, 25 (2009), 277–96.

59 Dean and Lowe, 'Issues in the History of Marriage', p. 21.

60 Martine Segalen, 'Mentalité populaire et remariage en Europe occidentale', in *Marriage and Remarriage*, ed. by Dupâquier and others, pp. 67–76 (p. 67). See also Carlo Alberto Corsini, 'Why is Remarriage a Male Affair? Some Evidence from Tuscan Villages during the Eighteenth Century', in *Marriage and Remarriage*, ed. by Dupâquier and others, pp. 385–95.

citizens were to be educated in a sense of the motherland and civic values were to be instilled.[61] Other than acquiring dignity and self-fulfilment through marriage, women were also asked to transmit patriotic values to their children, even though they themselves were not included in the notion of citizenship. This notion was explained and developed by the German philosopher Immanuel Kant (1724 1804), who argued that only active participation in the political community provided an individual with the status of citizen and guaranteed the power to vote. Those who did not have such power could be treated according to natural law, but they could not be considered active members of the State. The major characteristic needed to be a citizen and to participate in the legislative process was 'sibisufficientia' [independence].[62] The concept of independence was further explored by the French theorist and politician Emmanuel Joseph Sieyès (1748–1836). He argued that 'il est constant qu'un vagabond, un mendiant ne peuvent être chargés de la confiance politique des Peuples' [it is a fact that a vagrant and a beggar cannot be responsible for the political trust of the Peoples];[63] and he raised some doubts that a servant, a person employed by a master, or a foreigner could be accepted as representatives of a state. Accordingly, a woman could not be counted among those having the independence needed to be citizens because, as we see in the following chapters, she enjoyed fewer rights than men and depended on them.[64] The works of Kant and Sieyès,

61 Ilaria Porciani, 'Famiglia e nazione nel lungo Ottocento', in *Famiglia e nazione nel lungo Ottocento italiano. Modelli, strategie, reti di relazioni*, ed. by Ilaria Porciani (Rome: Viella, 2006), pp. 15–54 (p. 50); Roberto Bizzocchi, 'Una nuova morale per la donna e la famiglia', in *Storia d'Italia. Annali 22. Il Risorgimento*, ed. by Alberto M. Banti and Paul Ginsborg (Turin: Einaudi, 2007), pp. 69–96; Ilaria Porciani, 'Disciplinamento nazionale e modelli domestici nel lungo Ottocento: Germania e Italia a confronto', in *Storia d'Italia. Annali 22. Il Risorgimento*, ed. by Banti and Ginsborg, pp. 97–125. On the idea of family and nation, see Alberto Mario Banti, *Sublime madre nostra. La nazione italiana dal Risorgimento al fascismo* (Rome: Laterza, 2011).

62 Immanuel Kant, *On the Old Saw: That May Be Right in Theory but It Won't Work in Practice*, trans. by E. B. Ashton, intro. by George Miller (Philadelphia, PA: University of Pennsylvania Press, 1974 [1793]), pp. 62–65. See also Pietro Costa, *Cittadinanza* (Rome and Bari: Laterza, 2005), p. 48; Jacob Weinrib, 'Kant on Citizenship and Universal Independence', *Australian Journal of Legal Philosophy*, 33 (2008), 1–25 (pp. 2–4).

63 Emmanuel J. Sieyès, *Qu'est-ce que le Tiers-État?* (Paris: [n. pub.], 1789), p. 38.

64 Sieyès, *Qu'est-ce que le Tiers-État?*, pp. 37–38. See also Emmanuel J. Sieyès, *Observations sur le rapport du Comité de constitution concernant la nouvelle organisation de la France* (Versailles: Baudouin, 1789).

analysed and translated into Italian from the early decades of the nineteenth century, contributed to forging the idea of the 'domestic' woman.[65] Lacking the independence and firmness of mind required actively to participate in public life, she was to remain secluded in the private sphere, the place nature had chosen for her.

At the time of the French Revolution, however, the patriotic impulse spread among women as well and the goal of a female *citoyenneté* slowly emerged.[66] The Revolution led to the *Déclaration des droits de l'homme et du citoyen* (1789), which considered only men as citizens: the *Déclaration des droits de la femme et de la citoyenne* (1791) by Olympe de Gouges, as well as Condorcet's work *Sur l'admission des femmes au droit de cité* (1790), firmly challenged women's exclusion from civil rights.[67] In the Italian Peninsula journalists such as Elisabetta Caminer Turra (1751–1796) and Eleonora Fonseca Pimentel (1752–1799) had, since the late eighteenth century, attempted to carve out a space which would allow them to contribute to public discourse. Elisabetta Caminer Turra began working as a journalist for her father's journal *Europa letteraria* in 1768. She addressed several topics without neglecting women's issues, such as the need for education or forced monachisation.[68] Eleonora Fonseca Pimentel, whom Verina Jones defines as 'the journalist and opinion-maker of the Repubblica Partenopea', was in charge of *Il monitore napoletano* from its very foundation on 2 February 1799. She was executed with the reestablishment of the Bourbon monarchy a few months later.[69]

65 E.g., the Pisan jurist Giovanni Carmignani studied Kant's works and described him as having 'immenso ingegno' (Giovanni Carmignani, *Teoria delle leggi della sicurezza sociale*, 3 vols (Pisa: Nistri, 1831), I, 142).

66 Gisela Bock, *Le donne nella storia europea. Dal Medioevo ai giorni nostri* (Rome: Laterza, 2001), p. 59.

67 Olympe de Gouges, *Déclaration des droits de la femme et de la citoyenne*, ed. by Emanuèle Gaulier (Paris: Mille et une nuits, 2003), p. 17; Nicolas Condorcet, *Sur l'Admission des femmes au droit de cité* (Paris: Firmin Didot Frères, 1847), pp. 5–6. On Olympe de Gouges, see Sophie Mousset, *Olympe de Gouges et les droits de la femme* (Paris: Félin, 2003); Sophie Mousset, *Women's Rights and the French Revolution: A Biography of Olympe de Gouges* (New Brunswick, NJ; London: Transaction, 2007). On women and the French Revolution, see also Elisabeth G. Sledziewski, 'Rivoluzione e rapporti fra i sessi. La svolta francese', in *Storia delle donne. L'Ottocento*, ed. by Georges Duby and Michelle Perrot (Rome and Bari: Laterza, 1991), pp. 34–50.

68 Verina R. Jones, 'Journalism, 1750–1860', in *A History of Women's Writing in Italy*, ed. by Letizia Panizza and Sharon Wood (Cambridge: Cambridge University Press, 2000), pp. 120–34 (pp. 122–24).

69 Jones, 'Journalism', pp. 128–30. See also Bruna Bertolo, *Donne del Risorgimento. Le eroine invisibili dell'Unità d'Italia* (Rome: Ananke, 2011), pp. 351–54.

The attempts of these few women to make their voices heard did not mean that women asked for the *droit de cité*:[70] for example, in *Pensieri della libera cittadina I. P. M. alle sue concittadine*, a pamphlet printed in 1797, the anonymous writer argues that:

> se il mezzo più eloquente alla modificazione negl'uomini è la susta del cuore, sarà incontrastabile la grande influenza del nostro sesso, per ridestare dal sonno de' buoni Cittadini, che poi l'amore della libertà, la forza dell'opinione, l'abitudini, l'esempio renderanno ben presto perfetti. Una buona Cittadina non dovrebbe stimar il suo attinente, il suo amico, che in proporzione alla di lui attività per meritare dalla patria.[71]
>
> [if the most eloquent means of change in men is the heart's springs, the great influence of our sex will be indisputable; to reawaken good Citizens from sleep and make them perfect thanks to love of freedom, power of opinion, habits [and] example. A good female citizen should consider her relative, her friend, only in relation to his activity which makes him worthy of the homeland.]

Although the writer defines herself as a female citizen, she confines herself to merely describing the influence women could have on

70 An analysis of women's participation in the eighteenth-century events of the Italian Peninsula can be found in Richard J. Evans, *The Feminists: Women's Emancipation Movements in Europe, America and Australasia, 1840–1920* (London: Routledge, 2013), pp. 136–37; Annarita Buttafuoco, 'Straniere in patria. Temi e momenti dell'emancipazione femminile italiana dalle Repubbliche giacobine al fascismo', in *Esperienza storica femminile nell'età moderna e contemporanea: Atti del seminario*, ed. by Anna Maria Crispino, 2 vols (Rome: Unione donne italiane circolo "La Goccia", 1988), II, 91–124 (pp. 95–97); Annarita Buttafuoco, 'La causa delle donne. Cittadinanza e genere nel triennio "giacobino" italiano', in *Modi di essere. Studi, riflessioni, interventi sulla cultura e la politica delle donne in onore di Elvira Badaracco*, ed. by Annarita Buttafuoco (Bologna: EM, 1991), pp. 79–106; Gabriella Bonacchi and Angela Groppi, *Il dilemma della cittadinanza: diritti e doveri delle donne* (Rome: Laterza, 1993); Maria Teresa Guerra Medici, *La cittadinanza difficile* (Camerino: Università di Camerino, 2000); Nadia M. Filippini, 'Donne sulla scena politica: dalle Municipalità del 1797 al Risorgimento', in *Donne sulla scena pubblica. Società e politica in Veneto tra Sette e Ottocento*, ed. by Nadia M. Filippini and others (Milan: FrancoAngeli, 2006), pp. 81–137 (esp. pp. 85–123); Gian Luca Fruci, 'Cittadine senza cittadinanza. La mobilitazione femminile nei plebisciti del Risorgimento (1848–1870)', *Genesis*, 5 (2006), 21–55. See also Pietro Costa, 'Diritti/Doveri', in *Atlante culturale del Risorgimento*, ed. by Banti and others, pp. 270–84; and Antonio Chiavistelli, 'Rappresentanza', in *Atlante culturale del Risorgimento*, ed. by Banti and others, pp. 343–58.

71 Anon., *Pensieri della libera cittadina I. P. M. alle sue concittadine* (Venice: Zatta, 1797), p. 5.

male citizens. Similarly, in her *Breve difesa dei diritti delle donne* (1794), Rosa Califronia, a self-styled Roman countess, set out to defend women's rights, which she describes as 'l'autorità legittima di fare, e di avere, o di ricuperare ciò che è proprio' [the rightful authority to do, and to have, or to recover what a person owns].[72] With this aim she attempted to refute the 'accusations' against women as being 'prive di ragione', 'pazze', 'piene di vizi [e] causa d'ogni male' ['without reason', 'crazy', 'full of vices and the cause of all evil'].[73] Califronia, too, did not go further than responding to the commonly held view of women and did not make any explicit claim to rights. In her *Schiavitù delle donne* (1797) Carolina Arienti Lattanzi (1771–1818) goes slightly further and addresses women's inferior status. She also points out that the 'istituzione delle doti ci divenne pregiudicievole da che fossimo escluse dall'avere un'eguale diritto coi maschi alla distribuzione della paterna eredità' [institution of the dowry became prejudicial to us because it hindered us from having the same right as males to paternal inheritance].[74] Her arguments, however, were not taken up by others and did not have any consequences.

With the Restoration, the overthrown monarchs made a strong effort to return to the past by reinforcing the legal framework of the Ancien Régime, even if several articles from Napoleon's Code (e.g., those on mortgages and contracts) were left unchanged. However, the ideals of the Enlightenment and the French Revolution had a significant impact on the Italian Peninsula and, from the very first years of the French conquests, testified to the 'dilatazione degli spazi del dibattito politico' [expansion of spaces for public debate].[75] This led to the active participation of several strata of the population, not only in public debate but also in the Risorgimento process as a whole.[76] Alongside the political redefinition of states' boundaries, the Risorgimento was a movement which saw people from different

72 Rosa Califronia, *Breve difesa dei diritti delle donne scritta da Rosa Califronia contessa romana* (Assisi: Taglioretti, 1794), p. VII.

73 Califronia, *Breve difesa*, pp. XII–XXXIV.

74 Carolina Lattanzi, *Schiavitù delle donne*, ed. by Gilberto Zacchè (Mantua: Edizioni Lombarde, 1976), p. 41; Jones, 'Journalism', pp. 126–27. Carolina Lattanzi also worked as an editor for the *Corriere delle dame* from 1804 until her death in 1818.

75 Banti, *Il Risorgimento italiano*, pp. 6–11.

76 Bibliography on the Italian Risorgimento is vast. Recent studies which touch upon participation in the process across social classes include, e.g., John A. Davis

social classes experiencing a sense of unity and sharing the common aim of fighting against their oppressors. Women, too, participated in this process.[77] They served the cause in different ways and their participation was not only limited to what society considered respectable for a woman, such as the organisation of hospitals and charities, as in the case of Cristina Belgiojoso.[78] An important contribution to the process of the Risorgimento also came from various literary salons where people gathered, discussed and shared their ideals of patriotism. Among the most famous salons were those of Clara Carrara Spinelli Maffei in Milan and Bianca Rebizzo in Genoa.[79] Other women, such as Countess Teresa Casati Confalonieri,

---

and Paul Ginsborg, *Society and Politics in the Age of the Risorgimento: Essays in Honour of Denis Mack Smith* (Cambridge: Cambridge University Press, 2002); Banti, *Il Risorgimento italiano*; *Storia d'Italia*, ed. by Banti and Ginsborg; *Fare l'Italia: unità e disunità nel Risorgimento*, ed. by Mario Isnenghi and Eva Cecchinato (Turin: UTET, 2008); Lucy Riall, *Risorgimento: The History of Italy from Napoleon to Nation State* (New York, NY: Palgrave Macmillan, 2009).

77 On women's participation see Renata Pescanti Botti, *Donne nel Risorgimento italiano* (Milan: Ceschina, 1966); Fruci, 'Cittadine senza cittadinanza'; Elena Sodini, *Le carte di Felicita Bevilacqua. Famiglia, nazione e patriottismo al femminile in un archivio privato (1822–1899)* (Verona: Cierre, 2010). A number of works were published on the occasion of the 150th anniversary of Unification. See, e.g., Bertolo, *Donne del Risorgimento*; *Donne del Risorgimento*, ed. by Elena Doni and others (Bologna: Il Mulino, 2011); Laura Guidi, Angela Russo and Marcella Varriale, *Il Risorgimento invisibile. Patriote del Mezzogiorno d'Italia* (Naples: Comune di Napoli Edizioni, 2011); Marcella Varriale, '"Perché anche noi siamo cive[s]": reti amicali e familiari nel Carteggio Ranieri', *Chronica Mundi*, 12 (2017), 73–98.

78 Cristina Trivulzio di Belgiojoso has been the object of a number of studies, e.g., more recently, *Cristina di Belgiojoso: politica e cultura nell'Europa dell'Ottocento*, ed. by Ginevra Conti Odorisio, Cristina Giorcelli and Giuseppe Monsagrati (Casoria: Loffredo, 2010); *"La prima donna d'Italia". Cristina Trivulzio di Belgiojoso tra politica e giornalismo*, ed. by Mariachiara Fugazza and Karoline Rörig (Milan: FrancoAngeli, 2010); Gianna Proia, *Cristina di Belgiojoso. Dal salotto alla politica* (Rome: Aracne, 2010); Maria Grosso and Loredana Rotondo, '"Sempre tornerò a prendere cura del mio paese e a rivedere te". Cristina Trivulzio di Belgiojoso', in *Donne del Risorgimento*, ed. by Doni and others, pp. 65–94; Sharon Wood, 'Murder in the Harem: Cristina di Belgiojoso', in *Women and Gender in Post-Unification Italy*, ed. by Mitchell and Sanson, pp. 135–52.

79 Maria Teresa Mori, *Salotti. La sociabilità delle élite nell'Italia dell'Ottocento* (Rome: Carocci, 2000); Cristina Gastel Chiarelli, *Niente zucchero nel calamajo: lettere di Giuseppe Verdi a Clara Maffei* (Milan: Archinto, 2005); Bertolo, *Donne del Risorgimento*, pp. 41–45, 62–64; Mirella Serri, 'La piccola grande tessitrice. Clara Maffei', in *Donne del Risorgimento*, ed. by Doni and others, pp. 111–22.

Metilde Viscontini Dembowski, Maria Gambarana Frecavalli, Bianca Milesi, Camilla Besana Fé and Teresa Sopranzi Agazzini, played a meaningful role in secret revolutionary societies, among which was the Società delle Giardiniere, the female branch of the Carbonari movement.[80] In particular, in 1822 the frequent trips to Turin by Teresa Sopranzi Agazzini raised suspicions among Milanese authorities. She was brought before the special committee which dealt with political crimes and questioned about her relationship with the patriot Federico Confalonieri.[81] The strength of her relationship emerges from the short transcript of her interrogation:

> Commissione: Ha mai ricevuto pieghi da consegnare a Confalonieri?
> Teresa: No.
> Commissione: Un piego che doveva essere trasmesso al principe di Carignano?
> Teresa: No.
> Commissione: Sicura?
> Teresa: Non ho ricevuto alcun piego diretto al principe di Carignano né il mio onore permette che io esponga ciò che non è.[82]
>
> [Committee: Have you ever received any bundles of papers to be delivered to Confalonieri?
> Teresa: No.
> Committee: A bundle of papers that was to be given to the Prince of Carignano?
> Teresa: No.
> Committee: Are you sure?
> Teresa: I have not received any bundle of papers for the Prince of Carignano and my honour does not allow me to say what is not.]

Teresa Sopranzi Agazzini not only had a close relationship with Confalonieri, but was also entrusted with handling messages to the Prince of Carignano, the King of Sardinia. It is worth noting the way she brought her social status into play by suggesting that things were as she reported them and that questioning her words would besmirch her honour.

Some women became protagonists in other crucial subversive activities and crimes in the name of Italy.[83] For example, in the Papal

80 See *Donne del Risorgimento*, ed. by Doni and others.

81 State Archive of Milan, Processi Politici, 43, 1112 and 1127.

82 State Archive of Milan, Processi Politici, 43, 1127.

83 See also *Stato degli inquisiti dalla S. Consulta per la rivoluzione del 1849* (Rome: Vittoriano, 1937), p. 8.

States there were, by 1851, many political offences pending before the courts. These related to the period from 1848 to 1849 and were differentiated between crimes considered 'simply political' and 'political accompanied by a common crime'. Many women who were to be prosecuted were aged between seventeen and fifty-three and belonged to different social classes. In addition to some 'subversive' episodes, the participation of some women was more decisive. A case in point is that of Caterina Baracchini, a woman from Rome, who distributed clandestine prints, hid several people who were sought by the Papal police and in general played a crucial role among the conspirators at the time of the 1849 Roman Republic. The sentence, which condemned her to fifteen years in prison, describes her as a 'fiera mazziniana, era socia e con essa non si faceva alcun mistero delle cose della Società. Aveva un ruolo rilevante nella direzione della Società' [a proud Mazzinian, she was an associate and there were no secrets from her regarding the affairs of the Society. She had an important role in the direction of the Society].[84] Many women also served the cause through the fervent dissemination of ideas (e.g., Sara Nathan or Jessie White Mario),[85] while others fought, and were killed, on the barricades.[86] Finally, some women also became involved in illicit activities in connection with the gangs of brigands which became a phenomenon in Southern Italy.[87]

84 *Stato degli inquisiti dalla S. Consulta,* p. 103.

85 On Sara Levi Nathan, see Stefania Pallunto, *Sara Levi Nathan* (Pesaro: Comune di Pesaro, 1993); Anna Maria Isastia, *Storia di una famiglia del Risorgimento. Sarina, Giuseppe, Ernesto Nathan* (Turin: Università Popolare di Torino, 2010). On Jessie White Mario, see David Lewis, *Jessie White Mario: An English Heroine in the Liberation of Italy* (Oxford: Eureka, 2006); Bertolo, *Donne del Risorgimento,* pp. 132–51.

86 Bertolo, *Donne del Risorgimento,* pp. 271–305; Elena Doni, 'Rose bianche per un soldato. Colomba Antonietti', in *Donne del Risorgimento,* ed. by Doni and others, pp. 25–33.

87 For an overview of brigandage, see Andrea Carteny, 'Il brigantaggio in Italia tra Risorgimento e questione meridionale: un'introduzione al tema', *Chronica Mundi,* 11 (2016), 249–71; John Dickie, 'A World at War: The Italian Army and the Brigandage 1860–1870', *History Workshop Journal,* 33 (1992), 1–24; Natascia Tieri, *Il brigantaggio post unitario. Un'analisi di sociologia storica* (Rome: Aracne, 2013); Gaetana Mazza, *Tra storia e storie. Banditismo, brigantaggio e milizie civili nel meridione d'Italia dal XVI al XIX secolo* (Rome: Aracne, 2015); Franco Gaetano Scoca, *Il brigantaggio postunitario nel dibattito parlamentare (1861–1865)* (Naples: Editoriale Scientifica, 2016); and, with specific reference to women, Marjan Schwegman, 'Horrific Heroines: Female Brigandage, Honour and Violence in Post-Unification Italy, 1860–1870', in *Women and Gender in post-Unification Italy,* ed. by Mitchell and Sanson, pp. 111–31.

In summation, women's presence in the Risorgimento was significant: they conspired and fought side by side with men, carried tricolour cockades and showed their support for the cause.[88] Rather than seeking emancipation, however, they primarily aimed to contribute to the liberation from foreign oppressors and to national unification. Despite being a sign of women's desire actively to participate in society and have roles beyond the household, their participation did not lead to a clear redefinition of ideas on women.[89] Once peace was reached, most women returned to their traditional role of angel of the hearth. As we see in the next chapter, their subordinate status was indisputable: notions about women were rooted in ancient beliefs and also often shared by the women themselves.

88 The 'Registro delle persone di Fano e suo distretto pregiudicate in opinione politica' (30-12-1834), held in the Archivio of the Biblioteca Federiciana of Fano, reports the names of various women: e.g., Maddalena Tranquilli, 'libera col vestire una foggia di tre colori e con il parlare il linguaggio [...] del più deciso, ed accanito liberalismo' [free by dressing in a three-coloured style and speaking the language [...] of the most decisive and fierce liberalism]; or the wife of the head of the hospital who wore tricolour cockades. See also *Registro di Pesaro e suo distretto pregiudicate in opinione politica (12-6-1835)*, published in *Studia Oliveriana*, 10 (1990).

89 See also Derek Beales and Eugenio F. Biagini, *The Risorgimento and the Unification of Italy* (London: Longman, 2002), pp. 136–41.

2. Ideals of Women in Men's and Women's Writings

In the eighteenth and nineteenth centuries the image of women was strictly standardised and categorised. The legacy of traditional views which had prevailed since the time of Tertullian (*c.* 155–*c.* 220 AD) or even earlier and depicted women as either pious, virginal and obedient or temptresses and *ianua diaboli* [the Devil's doors] still persisted and influenced attitudes. Even if it was no longer to the same extreme degree, theorists and moralists, as well as physicians and jurists, still considered women to be different to men. Starting from the scientific assumption that weaker female bodies resulted in women being less able to develop rational, consistent ideas, they justified women's different role and position within society and developed many works of conduct literature aimed at helping them to deal with everyday life. A number of tracts also addressed men and were written to inform and explain female and male perspectives, as well as outlining how to assess their different status correctly. This chapter analyses the different theories and points of view which were elaborated to assert women's subjugation by men. As we shall see, these ideas were also shared by some women educationalists, who endorsed the commonly held idea of the domestic woman, ideally a wife and mother,[1] whose life was to be spent within her home, where womanly virtues were more useful. However, the events of the Risorgimento brought women outside their homes and led them to redefine their sense of themselves and also to question the boundaries between the private and public spheres.

1 On this point see Badinter, *L'Amour en plus*, pp. 13–15.

The Ideology on Women

The analysis of the differences between the sexes serves to assert women's incapacity and, as explained by Ian Maclean, this was considered 'a feature of higher animals, [...] postulated in plants and even metals by alchemists, and essential to mystical understandings of the universe'.[2] For centuries, women's alleged incapacity and their *infirmitas, imbecillitas* and *levitas* were explained by considering their different body temperature and humours. Hippocratic physicians considered women to be hotter than men but, as it was imagined that they absorbed liquids like a sponge, their need to excrete these excess fluids resulted in them being more unstable.[3] Aristotle and Galen instead claimed that men were hotter and drier than women and thus more perfect, as hotness and dryness were considered by them to be characteristics of perfection. The female principle was cold, wet, passive, deprived, 'the result of a generative event not carried through to its final conclusion', requiring the male principle to complete itself.[4] According to Galen, women and men had similar organs, but as those of women were internal, this implied they were imperfect and even mutilated.[5] The Greco-Roman theories of bodily humours and female imperfection persisted for centuries and as late as the thirteenth century Thomas Aquinas claimed that a woman was a *mas occasionatus*, a defective male for whom nature's intentions

2 Ian Maclean, *The Renaissance Notion of Woman: A Study in the Fortunes of Scholasticism and Medical Science in European Intellectual Life* (Cambridge: Cambridge University Press, 1980), p. 30.

3 On women and physiology, see Gail Kern Paster, 'Unbearable Coldness of Female Being: Women's Imperfection and the Humoral Economy', *English Literary Renaissance*, 28 (1998), 416–40; Helen King, *Hippocrates' Woman: Reading the Female Body in Ancient Greece* (London: Routledge, 1998), pp. 31–33. See also Ippocrate, *Natura della donna*, ed. by Valeria Andò (Milan: Rizzoli, 2000).

4 Maclean, *The Renaissance Notion of Woman*, p. 30.

5 For an overview of these theories, see Maclean, *The Renaissance Notion of Woman*, pp. 28–46; Thomas Laqueur, *Making Sex: Body and Gender from the Greeks to Freud* (Cambridge, MA; London: Harvard University Press, 1992), pp. 194–207; Guerci, *La discussione*, pp. 143–60 (esp. pp. 144–46); Londa Schiebinger, *The Mind Has No Sex? Women in the Origins of Modern Science* (Cambridge, MA; London: Harvard University Press, 1991 [1989]), pp. 163–64; Hufton, *The Prospect before Her*, pp. 23–58; Margaret L. King and Albert Rabil Jr., 'The Other Voice in Early Modern Europe: Introduction to the Series', in *The Contest for Knowledge: Debates over Women's Learning in Eighteenth-Century Italy*, ed. by Rebecca Messbarger and Paula Findlen (Chicago, IL: University of Chicago Press, 2005), pp. xi-xxxi (pp. xii–xiv).

had not been fully accomplished.[6] In the sixteenth century, although physicians' *observationes* contributed to a better understanding of the human body – see, for example, the *Observationes anatomicae* (1561) by Gabriele Falloppio (1523?–1562) – women were still considered to be inferior to men because their weaker body was deemed to have an impact on their mind.

The comparison between male and female bodies and the impact on their respective minds would affect the elaboration of theories for a long time beyond the sixteenth century. At the end of the eighteenth century the Swiss physiognomist Johann Kaspar Lavater (1741–1801), who was inspired by the Neapolitan scholar Giovan Battista Della Porta (1535–1615) and by the British philosopher Thomas Browne (1605–1682), explained that the physical characteristics of women, 'tender, yielding, easily wounded, sensible, and receptible',[7] were also manifested in their minds. In particular, the tenderness of female organs meant that women were 'formed to maternal mildness and affection',[8] a weakness which strongly contrasted with men's mental and physical strength. A woman, who in the words of Thomas Browne in *Religio Medici* (1643) was 'the Rib and crooked Piece of Man',[9] had the function of comforting man 'like angels, and to lighten his cares'.[10] Women were the:

> counterpart of man, taken out of man, to be subject to man, [the] light texture of their fibres and organs, [the] volatility of feeling, render them so easy to conduct and to tempt; so ready of submission to the enterprise and power of the man.[11]

Despite the softness and tenderness of their bodies, Della Porta had already warned in his *De humana physiognomonia* (1586) that women

6 Thomas Aquinas, *La somma teologica. Testo latino e italiano* (Bologna: Edizioni Studio Domenicano, 1985 [1265–73; first published in 1485]), p. 193. See also Arturo Bernal Palacios, 'La condiciòn de la mujer en sancto Tomàs de Aquino', *Escritos del Vedat*, 4 (1974), 285–355.

7 Johann Kaspar Lavater, *Physiognomy: Or the Corresponding Analogy between the Conformation of the Features, and the Ruling Passions of the Mind* (London: Tegg, 1866 [1775–78]), pp. 181–82. The German original work by Lavater was translated into Italian from the French version with the title of *L'arte di conoscere gli uomini dalla loro fisionomia* (Milan: Agnelli, 1808).

8 Lavater, *Physiognomy*, pp. 181–82.

9 Thomas Browne, *Religio Medici: Or, the Christian Religion, as Professed by a Physician; Freed from Priest-Craft and the Jargon of Schools*, 2 vols (London: Curll, 1736), II, 92.

10 Lavater, *Physiognomy*, pp. 181–82.

11 Lavater, *Physiognomy*, pp. 181–82.

were 'ladr[e] e pien[e] d'inganni' [thieves and full of deception].[12] Based on his study of physiognomy, he pointed out how close observation of people's physical features could explain their personality traits. For example, Della Porta asserted that women have features similar to those of leopards and consequently were just as treacherous.[13] Lavater's works on physiognomy, as well as those of Della Porta and Browne, were later taken into account by Cesare Lombroso (1835–1909), who, towards the end of the nineteenth century, expounded his theories on the correspondence between physiognomic characteristics and the inclination to commit a crime.[14]

Based on these ideas, men of letters and educationalists believed that women were inferior to men and therefore needed to be treated differently. Alongside more traditionally misogynistic views, women were usually described as having a vivid imagination and bodies that strongly affected their minds. As the Genoese philosopher Paolo Mattia D'Oria explained in his *Ragionamenti* (1716), imagination prevails over the power of the intellect, preventing women from being able to restrain themselves and reach real virtue.[15] Despite having some similarities to men, and perhaps even the ability to build empires and states, women were 'incapaci del grande officio di legislatore' [incapable of the great office of legislator] because this required a level of wisdom which they simply did not, and could not, have.[16]

With the Enlightenment new ideas and values began to take shape: 'Education was at the hearth of the Enlightenment project'.[17] As Ann Hallamore Caesar explains, it radiated out 'not only in ground-breaking works that specifically addressed the subject, but also indirectly by infiltrating and informing the growing volume

12 Giovan Battista Della Porta, *De humana physiognomonia libri sex*, ed. by Alfonso Paolella (Naples: Edizioni scientifiche italiane, 2013), p. 88.

13 Della Porta, *De humana physiognomonia*, pp. 87–90.

14 See, e.g., Cesare Lombroso, *L'uomo delinquente* (Milan: Hoepli, 1876); Cesare Lombroso and Guglielmo Ferrero, *La donna delinquente: La prostituta e la donna normale* (Turin: Bocca, 1903 [1893]).

15 Paolo-Mattia D'Oria, *Ragionamenti di Paolo-Mattia D'Oria indirizzati alla signora donna Aurelia d'Este duchessa di Limatola ne' quali si dimostra la donna, in quasi che tutte le virtù più grandi, non essere all'uomo inferiore* (Frankfurt: [n. pub.], 1716), p. 313.

16 D'Oria, *Ragionamenti*, pp. 343–44.

17 Ann Hallamore Caesar, 'Gender, Genre and Education. Writing about Conduct in Eighteenth-Century Venice', in *Conduct Literature for and about Women in Italy*, ed. by Sanson and Lucioli, pp. 119–34 (p. 119). On Enlightenment theories on women's nature see also Paul Hoffman, *La Femme dans la pensée des*

of printed matter directed at an emergent literate middle class with secular and worldly ambitions'.[18] This also led to new attitudes towards women and motherhood; and to lively debates on women's education and their potential contribution as a 'madre educatrice' to the well-being of families and society. Even though female identity was 'il riflesso di un immaginario maschile [...] nella cultura scritta, [...] di una serie di modelli comportamentali, espressione anche di una determinata rappresentazione dell'ordine sociale' [the reflection of male imagination [...] in written culture, [the reflection] of a series of behavioral models, which are an expression of a certain representation of the social order],[19] the importance of women's role in the development and upbringing of children was particularly highlighted.[20] Women's education became an issue which was broadly discussed and deeply analysed in tracts and conduct books. The point was that women who began to study were 'una realtà che andava assumendo un'inusitata e inquietante ampiezza di dimensioni' [a situation which was taking on an unusual and disturbing breadth of dimensions].[21] They also attained some success to the extent that in 1723 the famous Accademia dei Ricovrati of Padua held a disputation

Lumières (Paris: Ophrys, 1977); Badinter, *L'Amour en plus*, pp. 154–55; Susan Dalton, *Engendering the Republic of Letters: Reconnecting Public and Private Spheres in Eighteenth-Century Europe* (Montreal & Kingston: McGill-Queen's University Press, 2003).

18 Hallamore Caesar, 'Gender, Genre and Education', p. 119.

19 Carmela Covato, 'Educata a non istruirsi: un'introduzione al problema', in *E l'uomo educò la donna*, ed. by Carmela Covato and Maria Cristina Leuzzi (Rome: Editori riuniti, 1989), pp. 25–45 (p. 27).

20 Helena Sanson, '"La madre educatrice" in the Family and Society in Post-Unification Italy: The Question of Language', in *Women and Gender in Post-Unification Italy*, ed. by Mitchell and Sanson, pp. 39–63 (pp. 44–50). See also Helena Sanson, *Women, Language and Grammar in Italy, 1500–1900* (Oxford: Oxford University Press, 2011), pp. 251–52. On women's education see also *L'educazione delle donne. Scuole e modelli di vita femminile nell'Italia dell'Ottocento*, ed. by Simonetta Soldani (Milan: FrancoAngeli, 1989); Simonetta Ulivieri, *Educare al femminile* (Pisa: ETS, 1995); Simonetta Ulivieri, *Le bambine della storia dell'educazione* (Rome and Bari: Laterza, 2003); Anna Ascenzi, *Il Plutarco delle donne. Repertorio della pubblicistica educativa e scolastica e della letteratura amena destinata al mondo femminile nell'Italia dell'Ottocento* (Macerata: EUM, 2009), pp. 17–28; Morena Corradi, '"Un esercito femminile": educazione e nation-building nell'Italia del secondo Ottocento', *Chronica Mundi*, 14 (2019/ 2020), forthcoming.

21 Guerci, *La sposa obbediente*, p. 12.

intended to address the question of whether or not women were to be admitted to the study of sciences and of the noble arts,[22] with Giovanni Antonio Volpi insisting that women should not study in order to avoid the risk of endangering the good order of family and society.[23]

Nevertheless, if not a 'mutamento *di* ruolo, non mancarono le istanze a favore di un mutamento *nel* ruolo' [change *of* role, there was no lack of requests in favour of a change *in* the role]:[24] the rise of the idea of the 'madre educatrice' [mother educator] implied that 'women themselves required a better education, to ensure that they, in turn, would be able to better educate their own children'.[25] As we shall see, the future success of children came to be viewed as conditional on their mothers, since, as the Neapolitan jurist and philosopher Gaetano Filangieri (1753–1788) argued, 'esse gli nudriscono e gli educano ne' primi anni della vita; esse spargono i primi semi del vizio o della virtù ne' loro teneri cuori' [they nourish and educate them in the early years of life; they scatter the first seeds of vice or virtue into their tender hearts].[26] Therefore, women's role within the household was increasingly regarded as a matter of great importance and, alongside the function of nourishing their children, they were also entrusted with the task of educating them. In particular, they were charged with educating children about the moral values which upheld civil society.[27] The rise of the idea of the 'madre educatrice' meant that emphasis was placed on women's function as educators of their children but, at the same time, the role of the father, who took decisions regarding education, was still upheld. Mothers therefore provided their children with their very first education, which was

22 On this point see Fiamma Lussana, 'Misoginia e adulazione: ambiguità dell'immagine femminile nel secolo dei Lumi', *Studi Storici*, 2 (1984), 547–58; Luisa Ricaldone, 'Eighteenth-century Literature', in *A History of Women's Writing in Italy*, ed. by Panizza and Wood, pp. 95–106; Rebecca Messbarger, *The Century of Women: Representations of Women in Eighteenth-Century Italian Public Discourse* (Toronto: University of Toronto Press, 2002), pp. 21–48.

23 Giovanni Antonio Volpi, *Che non debbono ammettersi le donne allo studio delle scienze, e delle belle arti* ([n.p.]: [n. pub.], 1723), pp. 8–10. See also Guerci, *La discussione*, pp. 171–72; and Messbarger, *The Century of Women*, pp. 36–40.

24 Guerci, *La sposa obbediente*, pp. 13–14.

25 Sanson, '"La madre educatrice"', pp. 44–50 (p. 45).

26 Gaetano Filangieri, *La scienza della legislazione*, 8 vols (Genoa: Gravier, 1798 [1780]), VII, 215.

27 Badinter, *L'Amour en plus*, pp. 252–53.

normally first approved and endorsed by the father.[28] The premise that quality of mind was contingent on the strength of one's body remained unquestioned and consequently it was men, not women, who debated the degree to which women should and could study in order to fulfil this new role.

In the Italian Peninsula various works published during the Enlightenment in France, such as Jean-Jacques Rousseau's *Émile, ou De l'éducation* (1762), were known and influenced this debate.[29] In this work Rousseau explains that women were created for men and, therefore, 'toutes les réflexions des femmes en ce qui ne tient pas immédiatement à leurs devoirs, doivent tendre à l'étude des hommes ou aux connaissances agréables qui n'ont que le goût pour objet' [all the reflections by women on what is not immediately related to their duties must tend to the study of men or to pleasant knowledge that has only taste as its object].[30] He concedes that women and men depend on one another, but argues that their dependence was not equal,[31] as women were made 'pour plaire et pour être subjuguée' [to please and to be subjugated].[32] Rousseau believed that women's minds were not strong enough to bear prolonged reflection and high concepts, as 'la femme a plus d'esprit, et l'homme plus de génie' [the woman has more spirit and the man more genius].[33] The search for abstract and speculative truths, principles and axioms of science was not suitable for them, as they did not have the ability to concentrate and their minds were mainly practically oriented. This is why their education also had to relate to

28 Carlo Pancera, 'Figlie del Settecento', in *Le bambine nella storia dell'educazione*, ed. by Simonetta Ulivieri (Rome: Laterza, 2006), pp. 189–213 (p. 195).

29 On l'*Émile* see also Badinter, *L'Amour en plus*, pp. 237–94; Carmela Covato, *Sapere e pregiudizio: l'educazione delle donne fra '700 e '800* (Rome: Archivio Guido Izzi, 1998), pp. 41–45; Carmela Covato, 'Educare bambine dell'Ottocento', in *Le bambine nella storia dell'educazione*, ed. by Ulivieri, pp. 215–46 (esp. pp. 220–23); Alberto Mario Banti, *L'onore della Nazione. Identità sessuali e violenza nel nazionalismo europeo dal XVIII secolo alla Grande Guerra* (Turin: Einaudi, 2005), pp. 56–58; Anna Rossi-Doria, *Dare forma al silenzio. Scritti di storia politica delle donne* (Rome: Viella, 2007), pp. 114–15, 118. For an overview of the debate on women in France, see Élisabeth Badinter, 'Préface', in *Qu'Est-ce qu'une femme? Antoine Léé*, ed. by Élisabeth (Paris: P.O.L., 1989), pp. 9–47.

30 Jean Jacques Rousseau, *Émile ou de l'éducation*, ed. by François and Pierre Richard (Paris: Garnier, 1951 [1762]), p. 488.

31 Rousseau, *Émile*, p. 455.

32 Rousseau, *Émile*, p. 446.

33 Rousseau, *Émile*, p. 489.

practicalities.[34] Rousseau asserts that women's minds would never develop and be able to reach the same high level of concentration as men.[35]

For this reason it was useless to force women's nature, since the impact of their bodies on their minds could not be avoided and, as the Bolognese physician Petronio Ignazio Zecchini (1739–1793) maintained in his *Dì geniali della dialettica delle donne ridotto al suo vero principio* (1771),[36] they were not able to overcome physical constraints in the same way men were.[37] Because of their 'perpetuo irritamento dell'utero' [perpetual irritation of the uterus], women were destined to remain 'prigioniere del loro "materiale macchinamento" e non abbandonare mai la femminil debolezza per acquistare la viril costanza e risolutezza' [prisoners of their 'material mechanics' and never to abandon their feminine weakness and acquire virile constancy and determination].[38] Various writers criticised these theories:[39] in his *Lana caprina. Epistola di un licantropo* (1772), for example, Giacomo Casanova (1725–1798), deriving his ideas from René Descartes's 'mind-body dualism',[40] maintained that women were able to think and reason like men and that their education, and not their uterus, was the cause of their apparent inferiority.[41]

34 Rousseau, *Émile*, pp. 488–89.

35 Rousseau, *Émile*, p. 472.

36 On Zecchini, see also Guerci, *La discussione*, pp. 157–59; Messbarger, *The Century of Women*, pp. 66–68; Dalton, *Engendering*, pp. 13–16.

37 Petronio Ignazio Zecchini, *Dì geniali della dialettica delle donne ridotta al suo vero principio* (Bologna: S. Tommaso D'Aquino, 1771), p. 45.

38 Zecchini, *Dì geniali della dialettica*, pp. 45, 10.

39 On the controversy raised after the publication of Zecchini's *Dì geniali della dialettica delle donne*, see also Marta Cavazza, 'Women's Dialectics, or the Thinking Uterus: An Eighteenth-Century Controversy on Gender and Education', in *The Faces of Nature in Enlightenment Europe*, ed. by Lorraine Daston and Gianna Pomata (Berlin: BWV, 2003), pp. 237–57.

40 On this point see Anna Rossi-Doria, *Il primo femminismo: 1791–1834* (Milan: UNICOPLI, 1993), pp. 128–29; Gonzalo Rodriguez-Pereyra, 'Descartes's Substance Dualism and his Independence Conception of Substance', *Journal of the History of Philosophy*, 46 (2008), 69–89. On Descartes, see also Schiebinger, *The Mind has no Sex?*, pp 170–75.

41 Giacomo Casanova, *Lana Caprina: Lettre d'un lycanthrope* (Paris: Librairie de la société casanovienne, 1926 [1772]), pp. 29–32.

Women, their World and their Education

Even if most scholars were convinced that women lacked a firm stance and were not able to grasp lofty mental concepts, some also argued that this condition should not be stigmatising. In his major study *Système physique et moral de la femme* (1775), which was widely known at the end of the eighteenth century and later translated into Italian in Naples in 1829, the French physician Pierre Roussel (1742–1802) stated that, on account of their own weaknesses, women were more inclined to empathise with unfortunate people.[42] This natural piety could form the foundation of social virtues. Therefore, Roussel argued that women's qualities, even if they were not as brilliant as the talents of men, were more useful in society.[43]

The precise nature of these female traits thus continued to be the subject of sustained attention from those who were interested in proving the scientific rationale for women's subordinate status. The French physiologist Pierre Jean George Cabanis (1757–1808), for example, endorsed the idea of the domestic woman. In his works, which were translated into Italian from 1802 onwards, he argued that the softness of women's brain matter allowed their physical movements to be prompter.[44] This 'promptitude' had an impact on their general sensitivity and made them feel insecure and powerless; and, consequently, women pursued the attention of others in order to fortify their existence by means of those (i.e., the men) whom they considered able to protect them.[45] This repeated behaviour exacerbated women's already weak nature and caused them to become even weaker and more insecure than they originally were. Cabanis, too, proposed a model in which women performed their roles within the household and men governed the public sphere: this was because women paid great attention to things pertaining to everyday life, that is, small things, while men's minds were destined for the great challenges the public sphere entailed.[46] Cabanis argued, however, that women's motivation in attending to

42 Pierre Roussel, *Sistema fisico e morale della donna seguito dal Sistema fisico e morale dell'uomo e da un frammento sulla sensibilità*, 2 vols (Naples: Manzi, 1829 [1775]), II, 65.

43 Roussel, *Sistema fisico e morale*, II, 66–67.

44 Pierre-Jean George Cabanis, *Rapports du Physique et du moral de l'homme*, 2 vols (Paris: Fortin, Masson, 1843 [1802]), I, 201.

45 Cabanis, *Rapports du Physique*, I, 197.

46 Cabanis, *Rapports du Physique*, I, 197.

small domestic matters was their desire to make a positive impression on men because their world developed entirely in relation to men, on whom they completely depended, even in relation to their own happiness.[47]

Similar ideas had already been expressed by the Ligurian moralist Gaspare Morardo (1738–1817), who, in his *L'arte di conservare e accrescere la bellezza delle donne* (1800–01), argued that women always had the 'irrequieto desio di piacere agli uomini di attirarsi la loro stima e i loro cuori' [restless desire to please men to attract their esteem and their hearts]. This intense desire to be appreciated by men had always been 'l'energica molla di tutte le donnesche operazioni [...] l'oggetto di tutti i pensieri e di tutte le cure delle donne' [the energetic spring of all women's actions, the object of all women's thoughts and care]; and even their imagination, which was ready, vibrant and vivid, led them 'in ogni tempo alle virtù più ardue e alle più strepitose azioni' [at all times to [undertake] the most arduous virtues and the most sensational actions].[48] These actions were carried out solely to please and gain the admiration of men, 'questa essendo l'invincibile lor passione' [this being their invincible passion].[49] For this reason men considered marriage to be a major achievement for women: through it, they were redeemed, given value and the privilege of being guided throughout life by their husband.[50]

As Luciano Guerci argued, 'giustificare la subordinazione e l'obbedienza della moglie non costituì un particolare problema: la naturale debolezza – di corpo e di spirito – della donna provava che la condizione della moglie non poteva che essere una condizione di inferiorità' [justifying the subordination and obedience of the wife was not a particular problem: the natural weakness – of a woman's body and spirit – proved that the condition of the wife could only be a condition of inferiority].[51] On this point, for example, in his *La religione, dimostrata e difesa* (1805) Abbot Alessandro Maria Tassoni maintains that nature gave men a manifest superiority over women: '[O] si risguardi la robustezza, forza e coraggio, che ordinariamente ha più l'uomo, o si consideri anche la penetrazione, intendimento e giudizio, di cui più generalmente è dotato' [[E]ither look at vigour,

47 Cabanis, *Rapports du Physique*, I, 215.

48 Gaspare Morardo, *L'arte di conservare ed accrescere la bellezza delle donne* (Turin: Morano, 1800–01), pp. 85–86.

49 Morardo, *L'arte di conservare*, pp. 85–86.

50 Morardo, *L'arte di conservare*, pp. 85–86.

51 Guerci, *La sposa obbediente*, p. 121.

strength and courage, of which man normally has much more [than a woman], or consider also the discernment, understanding and judgement with which he is more generally endowed].[52] This meant that a husband and wife had equal rights in marriage, but 'il marito è superiore, ma la superiorità è di preminenza, di ordine, di governo, non un potere tirannico ed assoluto' [the husband is superior, but this is a superiority of pre-eminence, of order, of government, not a tyrannical and absolute power].[53]

A similar line of thought was also developed in a pamphlet published in Milan in 1819 and signed by an 'avvocato Leopold', who defined himself as 'the husbands' mentor'. The author claimed that marriage gives 'il marito di tutta la matrimoniale autorità, della paterna potenza, e di tutto il reggimento della famiglia: alla moglie conferisce il nome, il domicilio e tutto il patrocinio del marito' [the husband all the matrimonial authority, all the paternal power and all the government of the family; to the wife it confers a name, a home and all the patronage of her husband].[54] Since nature was deemed to provide men with much more discernment and intelligence than women, it followed that women were to be subject to them. He nevertheless conceded that women were to be considered their husbands' other halves.[55]

These works dealing with marriage and the way women had to behave towards their husbands began to flourish from the eighteenth century onwards. They focused on obedience and responded to the 'preoccupazioni legate a fenomeni sociali in cui si scorgeva una crisi dell'obbedienza che minacciava la stabilità delle gerarchie esistenti' [concerns related to social phenomena in which a crisis of obedience was perceived as a threat to the stability of existing hierarchies].[56] Women, Luciano Guerci observed, 'tendevano a sfuggire [...] al controllo del marito [e] non obbedivano più con la stessa docilità e prontezza con cui avevano obbedito in passato' [tended to escape from the control of their husband and no longer obeyed with the same docility and promptness with which they had obeyed in the past].[57] Therefore, these writings were also a means of steering disobedient

52 Alessandro Maria Tassoni, *La religione, dimostrata e difesa* (Naples: Società Editrice, 1854 [1805]), pp. 550–51.

53 Tassoni, *La religione,* p. 551.

54 Leopold, *Il mentore dei mariti e delle mogli o sia sposizione dei mezzi di essere felici nel matrimonio in tutte le classi diverse della società* (Milan: Giegler, 1819), p. 15.

55 Leopold, *Il mentore,* pp. 56, 64–65.

56 Guerci, *La sposa obbediente,* p. 11.

57 Guerci, *La sposa obbediente,* p. 12.

women back on course and helping them to understand correctly the role for which nature had destined them.

Although women were considered subject to men and it was imagined that their whole world revolved around the impression they wanted to make on men, their sweet feelings, their aptitude for empathy and their natural piety were attributes which would allow them to fit into the role of the first educators of their offspring. The continued emphasis on seclusion and small things played an important role in the understanding of women as educators, since young children required the concentrated attention within the home that only women could give. However, even if most of these features were natural, women needed to work on themselves to become good mothers and educators. In particular, as the Venetian abbot Giovanni Bellomo, in his *Saggio sopra il più conveniente sistema di femminile educazione* (1832), maintains, women 'moralmente forman gli uomini' [morally form men] and were crucial to obtain domestic happiness.[58] This meant that if they focused carefully on their deeds, 'ne viene di conseguenza che a un tempo stesso si migliori il pubblico costume' [public habits improved at the same time as a result].[59]

A few years later this view was also endorsed by the educationalist and linguist Raffaello Lambruschini (1788–1873), who believed that motherhood and the ability to take care of children was a skill women possessed naturally, but that some training was needed. As 'fanciulli accorti e ardimentosi […] scuotendo un giogo sì lieve signoreggiano le loro timide educatrici' [prudent and daring children, […] shaking such a light yoke, dominate their shy educators], women should acquire a 'ragionata educazione dell'infanzia' [reasoned education of childhood].[60] Later, the education of young boys was to be entrusted to male educators.[61] Lambruschini also focused on the distinction between 'educazione', which was 'educazione del cuore, educazione della mano' [education of the heart, education of the hand] and, therefore, embedded with moral values, and 'istruzione',

58 Giovanni Bellomo, *Saggio sopra il più conveniente sistema di femminile educazione* (Venice: Tasso, 1832), p. 30.

59 Bellomo, *Saggio sopra il più conveniente sistema*, p. 30.

60 Raffaello Lambruschini, *Sull'utilità della cooperazione delle donne bennate al buon andamento delle scuole infantili per il popolo* (Milan: Stella, 1834), p. 8.

61 Lambruschini, *Sull'utilità della cooperazione*, p. 8.

which had an intellectual connotation.[62] In his *Guida dell'Educatore*, Lambruschini criticises women who 'o sono poco istruite [...] o pretendono d'essere letterate' [are poorly educated or pretend to be literates];[63] and in reply to one of his readers, a woman who pointed out that Lambruschini wanted almost to remove 'il titolo e le facoltà di madre a una donna che si occupi dello studio delle lettere' [the title and capability of motherhood from a woman who deals with the study of letters], he explains that he blamed only those women who claimed to be cultured and neglected their duties to dedicate themselves to the study of literature.[64] Lambruschini, like the great majority of nineteenth-century moralists and theorists, believed that a woman's primary duties were being a mother and a good wife; therefore studying and gaining some culture were to be considered only a secondary goal. A woman within the family was in the place where God wanted her to be and from there she could do her best for society, because she could do the best for her family, both as a wife and mother. Mothers should be the first educators of children and their behaviour was crucial as it was considered 'educazione indiretta' [indirect education].[65] If men had 'robustezza ed ardimento' [robustness and boldness], women easily outmatched them in virtues naturally carried in their hearts, such as love and patience.[66] Instead, men, who had the strength to bear 'i patimenti e le fatiche' [sufferings and labours], were not able to stand the boredom of looking after babies, as 'solo l'inesauribile capacità di abnegare sé stessa, di cui è dotata la figlia del dolore, resiste a prove sì lunghe e sì difficili' [only the inexhaustible ability to deny oneself, with which the daughter of sorrows is endowed, can withstand such long and difficult trials].[67]

Lambruschini argued that 'l'incremento della civiltà europea, la piega che han presa i nostri costumi' [the improvement of European civilisation, the turn that our customs have taken] allowed women to go beyond the role of mere guardians of household order and

62 Lambruschini, *Sull'utilità della cooperazione*, p. 13. On the distinction between 'educazione' and 'istruzione' see also Sanson, '"La madre educatrice"', p. 52; Covato, 'Educata a non instruirsi'.

63 Lambruschini, *Guida dell'educatore*, 1 (1836), 38.

64 Lambruschini, *Guida dell'educatore*, 2 (1836), 63–65.

65 Lambruschini, *Guida dell'educatore*, 3 (1836), 84–85.

66 Lambruschini, *Sull'utilità della cooperazione*, p. 6.

67 Lambruschini, *Sull'utilità della cooperazione*, p. 7.

welfare and to acquire an indirect social power. This power was to be valued and directed to enable women to 'conspire' 'con bell'armonia all'ordine e al lustro della città' [with beautiful harmony to the order and lustre of the city].[68] Conversely, if 'la dimenticheremo, l'abbandoneremo a sé medesima [...] ella sarà una forza perturbatrice, un principio di collisione, di scompiglio, di morte' [we will forget her, abandon her to herself, [...] she will be a disturbing force, a principle of collision, disarray, death].[69] The root of this power was to be found in a sort of inspiration and influence which women could put in place to improve society and its values.

Women and Motherhood

Alongside treatises the journalism of the time also promoted the ideal virtues of the good woman, mother and wife.[70] Women's education and behaviour were to be taken into account even before the birth of their children. In a journal addressing women, *Studii per le donne italiane*, published in Milan from 1837 to 1838, great attention was paid to values such as morality, sacrifice and modesty. For example, in one of its articles the Milanese writer and journalist Giovan Battista De Cristoforis prescribed that mothers' thoughts and deeds were to be calm and sober, as 'pensieri ed opere non concordanti col dovere [...] sono infausti preludi alla sanità del nascituro' [thoughts and works not consonant with duty [...] are inauspicious preludes to the health of the unborn child].[71] Later, as children became older, the education of males and females was necessarily to be diversified. As highlighted by the French theorist Jeanne Louise Henriette, known as Madame Campan, in her treatise *De l'Education*, translated into Italian in 1827 as *Dell'educazione*, a boy should be educated by his mother only until the age of seven. Since women, due to their temperament, were not able to stand challenging situations, after that age 'l'austerità degli studj, la violenza dei giuochi, quella degli esercizj, tutto quello insomma che far si deve per l'educazione degli uomini, per dare una forte tempra al loro animo, troppo urterebbe la sensibilità squisita d'una madre' [the austerity of studies, the violence of games, that of exercises, all that is to be done for the education of men, to give a

68 Lambruschini, *Sull'utilità della cooperazione*, p. 7.

69 Lambruschini, *Sull'utilità della cooperazione*, p. 12.

70 See Ascenzi, *Il Plutarco delle donne*, pp. 11–50.

71 Giovan Battista De Cristoforis, 'Filosofia pratica', *Studii per le donne italiane*, 1 (1837), 35–43 (p. 36).

strong temper to their soul, would have too great an impact on the exquisite sensitivity of a mother].[72]

The different role and status enjoyed by men and women in society meant that the destinies of males and females changed at the point when their education needed to be differentiated. Girls were to be well-educated for their pre-established duties as good wives and mothers: although a woman was part of a new family after her marriage, her conscientious acquittal of her duties was a source of pride for her original family as well.[73] Girls' education had to be carried out within the household and was primarily entrusted to mothers, who were required to watch over them attentively.[74] Mothers were encouraged to consider every aspect of life and not to disregard the importance of entertainment and making friends. In the essay *La buona madre*, translated into Italian in 1846, the French Jesuit Firmin Pouget relates the story of three 'wise' mothers who wanted to 'preservare le loro figlie dal contagio del secolo e dalle cattive compagnie, senza condannarle alla solitudine ed all'isolamento' [preserve their daughters from the contamination of our time and from bad company, without condemning them to solitude and isolation].[75] These mothers, together with their young daughters, often met at one of their houses, but only 'dopo i divini ufficii [e] dopo aver compiti i domestici lor doveri' [after the divine offices [and] after having performed their domestic duties].[76] Pouget stresses the importance of the mothers' presence, which never made the daughters feel under close surveillance but, instead, comforted them. He regards these girls as an example of total obedience and abnegation, to be praised and emulated by every woman who wanted to fit smoothly into the place which nature and society had assigned her.[77]

If educationalists and men of letters agreed that an educated woman would be a better mother, particularly to her daughter,[78] they also shared the idea that her education was to be limited, because, as Anna Ascenzi observes, 'la donna colta era destinata a rimanere

72 Madame Campan [Jeanne Louise Henriette], *Dell'educazione*, 2 vols (Milan: Rezzi, 1827), I, 86.

73 Pancera, 'Figlie del Settecento', p. 195.

74 Guerci, *La sposa obbediente*, pp. 69–74.

75 Firmin Pouget, *La buona madre, o sia vita di Teresa di Lamourous fondatrice e prima superiora della casa di misericordia di Bordeaux* (Milan: Boniardi-Pogliani, 1846), p. 11.

76 Pouget, *La buona madre*, p. 11.

77 Pouget, *La buona madre*, pp. 11–13.

78 Badinter, *L'Amour en plus*, pp. 252–53.

una figura potenzialmente eversiva, destabilizzante, e comunque scomoda' [the educated woman was destined to remain a potentially subversive, destabilising and in any case uncomfortable figure].[79] The Piedmontese man of letters and politician Cesare Balbo (1789–1853) believed that, since women carried out their roles in the domestic realm because 'il regno delle donne è in casa' [the women's realm is the house],[80] they would benefit from an education focused on a secluded life, on loneliness, quiet and activities related to managing a house.[81] This kind of education would reflect their future lives. Men, on the other hand, would benefit from a multitude of companions and a certain degree of roughness, which would be the image of the world in which they would live.[82]

Balbo, strongly influenced by Rousseau and Cabanis, argued that women's main role was to comfort men. Along with activities related to their domestic realm, he conceded that women could be further educated, they could 'abbellire l'ingegno, che è la parte più amabile di esse' [beautify ingenuity, which is the most lovable part of them], but they should never demonstrate that they were very well educated; and everything they said had to appear spontaneous, as a different, but always simple, expression of their affections.[83] Women's education should be aimed, above all, at enabling them to provide good company for men, because a woman's charm 'sta nella sua dipendenza; la sua forza, nella sua debolezza; la sua potenza, nel suo diritto di aver protezione' [is in her dependence; her strength in her weakness; her power, in her right to protection].[84] He suggested not stimulating women too much intellectually, because many activities, even 'se non nocciono al dovere, nocciono alla grazia femminile, che sta sopra ogni cosa nella moderazione, nella dolcezza, nella tranquillità' [if they do not harm duty, they harm feminine grace, which is above all in moderation, sweetness, tranquility].[85] Balbo deplored the 'vice'

79 Ascenzi, *Il Plutarco delle donne*, p. 48.

80 Cesare Balbo, *Pensieri ed esempi: opera postuma; con l'aggiunta dei Dialoghi di un maestro di scuola pure inediti* (Florence: Le Monnier, 1856), p. 156.

81 On this point see also Anna Maria Rao, 'Il sapere velato. L'educazione delle donne nel dibattito italiano di fine Settecento', in *Misoginia: la donna vista e malvista nella cultura occidentale*, ed. by Andrea Milano (Rome: Dehoniane, 1992), pp. 243–310.

82 Balbo, *Pensieri ed esempi*, pp. 156–58.

83 Balbo, *Pensieri ed esempi*, pp. 159–60.

84 Balbo, *Pensieri ed esempi*, p. 316.

85 Balbo, *Pensieri ed esempi*, p. 316.

of exaggerating women's education and industriousness; and claimed that 'quelle professore di matematica, di lingua greca, di legale, e peggio di chirurgia, che furono già all'Università di Bologna, mi paiono più mostri che miracoli' [those Professors of Mathematics, of Greek, of Law and, worse, of Surgery who graduated at the University of Bologna seem more monsters than miracles].[86]

The man of letters and educationalist Niccolò Tommaseo (1802–1874) had a similar vision of women's roles in society and stressed that their lives were sanctified by two major functions, obedience and love.[87] Their education did not need to go further than giving them the possibility to say 'con proprietà e con chiarezza parte di quel che sentono in cuore' [with command and clarity part of what they feel in their hearts]; and, if they would like to improve themselves a little more, they could learn 'a fare interi i concetti proprii, non a rubacchiare gli altrui, o a ripeterli infiacchiti e rimpiccoliti' [to be able to have their own ideas, not to steal them from others, or to repeat them weakened and shrunken].[88] Tommaseo, like many other theorists of his time, was convinced that women were not born to be learned[89] and pointed out that 'real education' started when the educators' role finished: for men this was at the time of their graduation or when they began to work, while for women it was at the time of their marriage.[90] Culture acquired by women was understood as a corruption of their spirit, to the extent, he added, that in a learned woman it was even difficult to find true love and generosity. Conversely, a woman, who would read 'libri semplici di religione, di morale di storia [...] educherà il proprio ingegno a fin d'educare i figli proprii, o, se di proprii non n'ha, quelli de' congiunti e de' poveri' [simple books on religion, on morals from history [...] will educate her mind in order to educate her own children, or, if she does not have her own, those of her relatives and of the poor] and, by so doing, she would fulfill herself.[91] To this kind of woman, studies would not be a 'balocco o pericolo, ma dovere e salvezza' [pastime or danger, but duty and salvation].[92] Moreover,

86 Balbo, *Pensieri ed esempi*, p. 159.

87 Niccolò Tommaseo, *La donna. Scritti varii* (Milan: Agnelli, 1872 [1868]), p. 256.

88 Tommaseo, *La donna*, p. 257.

89 Tommaseo, *La donna*, p. 259.

90 Niccolò Tommaseo, *Delle nuove speranze d'Italia, presentimenti da un'opera di Niccolò Tommaseo* (Florence: Le Monnier, 1848), p. 95.

91 Tommaseo, *La donna*, p. 259.

92 Tommaseo, *La donna*, p. 260.

when literature, gallantry, politics or disbelief extinguished in the female soul the flame which created candid words and sudden feelings, a woman, 'per dotta e arguta che sia' [no matter how learned and witty she is], would become something 'di schifoso da mettere ribrezzo e pietà: peggio che cadavere, mostro' [disgusting to have aversion to and pity for: worse than a corpse, a monster].[93]

Learned women had 'misunderstood' their role in society. Acquiring a high degree of education was pointless for them and they were not considered able to reach the same level as men in terms of culture and knowledge. Along with entering an unnatural condition, if they diverted from the role assigned to them by society and nature, women would even run the risk of harming their health. Marriage and especially motherhood were their 'natural' condition; and being married was the only status thought to permit them to enjoy good health and to reach old age. The French doctor Alexis Delacoux (1792–1860), in his *Hygiène des femmes, ou Préceptes de santé à leur usage dans la vie privée* (1829), translated into Italian in the following year with the title *Igiene delle donne, ossia Precetti di salute all'uso loro nella vita privata,* argued that no institution was more edifying to women than marriage. Therefore, '[dalla] duplice condizione di sposa e di madre deriva una sequela d'obbligazioni' [a number of duties emerge from her dual status of wife and mother] which are enough to fill every moment of a woman's life.[94] Every job that could be done outside a woman's domestic realm, that is, the home, was a 'ver[a] depravazion[e] moral[e]; imperocché la donna non è chiamata a condurre l'aratro, ed a tenere lo scettro delle nazioni, più che l'uomo non sia fatto per tener l'ago ed il fuso' [real moral depravity; because a woman is not called to lead the plow and to hold the sceptre of nations, just as a man is not made to hold the needle and the spindle].[95] As women were 'dotate di mente fina e dilicata' [endowed with a fine and delicate mind] and could learn easily, they could better profit from observing and following examples than from hard studies.[96] He maintained that evidence demonstrated that the study of geography, history and languages was more harmful than

93 Niccolò Tommaseo, *Dell'educazione. Osservazioni e saggi pratici* (Venice: Andruzzi, 1842), p. 19; Tommaseo, *La donna,* p. 257.

94 Alexis Delacoux, *Igiene delle donne, ossia Precetti di salute all'uso loro nella vita privata traduzione dal francese di N. P.* (Milan: Pirotta, 1830), p. 125.

95 Delacoux, *Igiene delle donne,* p. 125.

96 Delacoux, *Igiene delle donne,* p. 128.

beneficial; and that society would then suffer a number of premature losses: 'Quante giovinette, quante donne giovani succumbono, sia a malattie di petto, a affezioni cerebrali qui pressoché endemiche' [How many young girls, how many young women succumb, both to chest and brain diseases, which [are] almost endemic here].[97]

Education for women was thus to be limited to simply enabling them to be aware of their duties. In the eyes of these theorists, women whose education had gone too far would not accomplish any long-lasting achievement.[98] In *Un curato di campagna* (mentioned above) Carlo Ravizza gives some practical examples of the various risks which women who devoted too much time to their education might incur. The country priest relates the cases of Gaetana Agnesi (1718–1799), the renowned Milanese mathematician and philosopher, and Maria Pellegrina Amoretti (1756–1787), from Oneglia near Genoa, the first woman to earn a degree in 'ragion civile' [law], in Pavia in 1777:[99] they both studied hard but this deeply affected their lives and brought them suffering or premature death. In the case of Gaetana Agnesi, 'dopo poch'anni di festeggiamento e di gloria, fu vista tutt'a un tratto comparire a Milano trista e dimessamente vestita' [after a few years of celebration and glory, she was suddenly seen in Milan sadly and simply dressed],[100] while the fate of Maria Pellegrina Amoretti was even worse. He describes in detail the story of Amoretti as a prodigy who went to Pavia to take two very difficult exams at the Faculty of Law: ten professors, 'increduli della sua scienza e disdegnosi d'un femminile addottoramento, le proposero le più sottili questioni, finché, maravigliati, unanimamente la dichiararono degnissima d'approvazione' [incredulous of her knowledge and disdainful of a woman obtaining a degree, asked her the most subtle questions, until, marvelling, they unanimously declared her most worthy of approval].[101] Amoretti's performance was certainly deemed to be 'unnatural' for a woman and all these efforts of mind compromised

97 Delacoux, *Igiene delle donne*, pp. 116–17.

98 Guerci, *La discussione*, pp. 170–72.

99 On the life of Agnesi see Giovanna Tilche, *Maria Gaetana Agnesi* (Milan: Rizzoli, 1984); Massimo Mazzotti, *The World of Maria Gaetana Agnesi, Mathematician of God* (Baltimore, MD: Johns Hopkins University Press, 2007). On Amoretti, see Giovanni Zaffignani, *L'università e la ragazza. La verità sulla prima laurea in legge ottenuta in Europa da una donna Maria Pellegrina Amoretti, Pavia, 1777* (Acirerale: Bonanno, 2010).

100 Ravizza, *Un curato di campagna*, p. 226.

101 Ravizza, *Un curato di campagna*, p. 227.

her weak health.[102] Moreover, these triumphs 'le pesavano sul cuore quasi un rimorso' [weighed on her heart almost like regret] and after a few years she died. Ravizza's priest explains that the task of women was to educate and to do charitable acts; and whoever turned their talents to other tasks denied humankind many occasions for happiness and improvement.[103] Ravizza's country priest claims that women should not look to improve their dignity with great achievements and education, because Christianity already redeemed and ennobled them through the indissolubility of marriage and monogamy.[104]

As Luciano Guerci explains, 'gli scrittori devoti [dicevano che] Dio medesimo aveva assegnato alla donna un ruolo subalterno' [devout writers [said that] God himself had assigned a subordinate role to woman][105] and entrusted men with a sort of 'délégation des pouvoirs de Dieu' [delegation of powers from God].[106] For example, Giacomo Polatti, a priest from Vicenza, wrote *Della protezione accordata alla donna dal cristianesimo* (1844), a pamphlet composed for the marriage of one of his parishioners, the noble Ottaviano Mocenigo from Venice. In this he argues that in places where 'è impedita o distolta la salutare influenza del Cristianesimo' [the healthy influence of Christianity is prevented or diverted], women fatally fell under the yoke of slavery and soon entered the dirty world of licentiousness.[107] Marriage, particularly a Christian marriage, was a considerable benefit for women and they should be content with this achievement.

The link between women and Christianity was particularly emphasised in the nineteenth century. In particular, the Catholic Church acknowledged the importance of 'rinvigorire il sentimento religioso femminile e di far maturare nella donna cattolica una più

102 Ravizza, *Un curato di campagna*, p. 229.

103 Ravizza, *Un curato di campagna*, p. 230.

104 Ravizza, *Un curato di campagna*, pp. 230–31. For the role of women as described by Christian doctrine, see Maclean, *The Renaissance Notion of Woman*, pp. 6–27 (esp. pp. 23–24); King and Rabil, 'The Other Voice in Early Modern Europe', pp. xv–xvi.

105 Guerci, *La sposa obbediente*, p. 131.

106 Badinter, *L'Amour en plus*, pp. 24, 17–19, 21–27. See also Élisabeth Badinter, *L'Un est l'autre: des relations entre hommes et femmes* (Paris: Jacob, 1992 [1986]), pp. 191–240.

107 Giacomo Polatti, *Della protezione accordata alla donna dal cristianesimo* (Vicenza: Paroni, 1844), p. 26.

salda consapevolezza del proprio ruolo e dei propri compiti familiari' [reinvigorate[ing] the religious sentiment of women and of developing in the Catholic woman a firmer awareness of her own role and family duties].[108] To this end, 'il tipo di formazione degli educandati di antico regime non era più sufficiente e adatta alla condizione mutata dei tempi' [the type of training [given by] the old regime of boarding schools was no longer sufficient and suited to the changed requirement[s] of the times].[109] Alongside a drive to improve the quality of education given by those schools run by nuns, a number of new 'educandati' were founded to provide education to girls from the middle and upper classes.[110] These 'educandati' also came to be led by laywomen and were intended to prepare girls for their future domestic duties and to help them to become good wives and mothers, educated to understand their role within the family and society more broadly, through 'l'interiorizzazione dei valori proposti come esemplari' [the internalisation of the values [which are] offered as examples].[111]

Moralists repeatedly stressed the importance of domesticity. Women's values were primarily to be put into practice in the private sphere, where they had the crucial task of running their household. The treatise by the French abbot Frédéric-Edouard Chassay, *I doveri delle donne nella famiglia* (1852), was translated by the Florentine poet Isabella Rossi Gabardi Brocchi, who considered this work 'piena di luminose verità, di profonda conoscenza del mondo e del cuore femmineo' [full of luminous truth, of profound knowledge of the world and of the female heart].[112] Chassay warns women that 'una

108 Ascenzi, *Il Plutarco delle donne*, p. 31.

109 Ascenzi, *Il Plutarco delle donne*, p. 32.

110 Bibliography on women's education in the Ottocento is vast. See, e.g., *E l'uomo educò la donna*, ed. by Covato and Leuzzi; Silvia Franchini, *Élites ed educazione femminile nell'Italia dell'Ottocento. L'Istituto della SS. Annunziata di Firenze* (Florence: Olschki, 1993); Simonetta Ulivieri, *Educare al femminile* (Pisa: ETS, 1995); Simonetta Soldani, 'La fortunosa conquista di un'istruzione secondaria da parte delle giovani italiane', in *La donna in Italia: 1848–1914: unite per unire*, ed. by Emanuela Bruni, Patrizia Foglia and Marina Messina (Cinisello Balsamo: Silvana, 2011), pp. 15–26 (pp. 15–16). See also the case of the schools of 'mutuo insegnamento', created to teach literacy to lower classes (Soresina, *L'età della Restaurazione*, pp. 98–99).

111 Franchini, *Élites ed educazione femminile*, pp. 2–3, 58. See also Philippe Ariès, *L'Enfant et la vie familiale sous l'Ancien Régime* (Paris: Plon, 1960), p. 435; Ulivieri, *Educare al femminile*, p. 125.

112 Frédéric Edouard Chassay, *I doveri delle donne nella famiglia* (Milan: Volpato, 1856), p. ii.

casa mal diretta allontana tutti coloro che dovrebbero compiacersene' [a badly managed house drives away all those who should be pleased with it], including their husbands, who would certainly look for 'costose distrazioni' [expensive distractions] elsewhere.[113] Women needed help in assessing the importance of their duties correctly, because they were not intelligent enough to do so by themselves. Indeed, women's nature was 'più viva che attiva, più agitata che intraprendente, e credono d'aver mosso delle montagne quando hanno mutato di luogo qualche frammento di paglia' [more alive than active, more agitated than enterprising; and [women] believe they have moved mountains when they have just changed the position of a few fragments of straw].[114]

Many female moralists themselves complied with this commonly accepted prejudice about female inferiority and also wrote essays and books to explain how to tackle their condition. The Bolognese Anna Pepoli Sampieri (1783–1844), for example, was 'intimamente persuasa che le donne non siano destinate a partecipare dei pubblici affari' [thoroughly persuaded that women are not destined to participate in public affairs] and therefore believed that their education had to focus on, and be limited to, the role and duties for which nature had created them.[115] Obedient angels of the hearth, they were defined by their domestic duties and depended on their husbands, who, in turn, were required to treat 'dolcemente le mogli, e loro comandino con buon modo' [their wives sweetly and command them in a good manner].[116] This hierarchy within the family was the natural order, given that men were 'in intelligenza e in altezza di senno [...] di lungo spazio superiori' [greatly superior [...] in intelligence and in depth of mind] to women.[117] For this reason, sons and daughters were to be educated in different ways and women could provide a crucial contribution in this regard. Pepoli Sampieri endorsed the ideas already proposed by male theorists and educationalists, who thought that women's nature was not adequate to educating sons for their adult roles in society.

113 Chassay, *I doveri delle donne*, p. 82.

114 Chassay, *I doveri delle donne*, p. 128.

115 Anna Pepoli Sampieri, *La donna saggia ed amabile. Libri tre* (Capolago: Elvetica, 1838), p. 117.

116 Pepoli Sampieri, *La donna saggia*, p. 61.

117 Pepoli Sampieri, *La donna saggia*, p. 61.

They could be in charge of the education of sons in their early years, but not beyond.[118] This was because:

> lo spirito loro è bene acconcio ad acquistare molte nozioni di cose speciali; [...] esse mirabilmente riescono nello stile epistolare, se sono nel raccontare avvenimenti o novelle, nel descrivere usi e costumi, di leggiadra vivacità spirano tutte le osservazioni loro sugli oggetti particolari, ma che piuttosto si fermano agli effetti che alla ricerca delle cause. Dal che nasce che nelle scienze e nelle arti di rado sono prime, essendo cosa manifestamente provata che, quante volte trattisi di considerazione di sottili ragionamenti di grandi combinazioni, dove sia necessità di stabilire principii o leggi, le donne sono sempre state trovate inferiori agli uomini.[119]

> [their spirit is well suited to acquiring the basics on many special things; [...] they succeed admirably in the epistolary style, if they are recounting events or short stories, describing habits and customs, all their observations on particular objects express graceful vivacity, but [these observations] stop at the effects rather than at the search for the causes. From this, it arises that they are rarely at the forefront in sciences and arts, it being something clearly proven that, so often [when] considering matters of subtle reasoning, regarding complex issues where it is necessary to establish principles or laws, women have always been found to be inferior to men.]

On the contrary, as far as daughters were concerned, mothers could and should be in charge of their education until they were married, avoiding, first of all, anything that would 'ispirare alla sua figliola amore per le cose frivole e dispendiose' [inspire her daughter's love for frivolous and expensive things].[120]

The typical female virtues such as sweetness and meekness were widely transposed and re-proposed by women[121] and shaped the idea of model women and wives, who were above all submissive and obedient. As explained by the Turinese writer Giulia Molino Colombini (1812–1879) in her *Sulla educazione della donna*, women's lives had to lean on men's sturdiness 'come viti al pioppo' [like vines on a poplar], because they were 'collocate sulla terra per essere guidate, anziché per reggere altrui' [placed on earth to be guided,

118 Pepoli Sampieri, *La donna saggia*, p. 113.

119 Pepoli Sampieri, *La donna saggia*, p. 114.

120 Pepoli Sampieri, *La donna saggia*, pp. 113–14.

121 Ascenzi, *Il Plutarco delle donne*, p. 27.

rather than to support others].[122] Despite arguing that women were created to depend on men, Molino Colombini valued the importance of education, mainly as a means to 'recare rimedio alla leggerezza femminile' [remedy female fickleness].[123] In addition, if studying the sciences was to help women's minds to acquire 'nerbo e dirittura' [strength and honesty], 'l'educazione del cuore e della mente' [the education of the heart and mind] was pivotal.[124] Moreover, when providing girls with an education, mothers had to lead by example.

The role of mothers was also emphasised by Caterina Franceschi Ferrucci (1803–1887), who, in her *Degli studii delle donne* (1853), stressed that a mother worthy of that name 'non ommetterà cosa alcuna per conservare l'ordine stabilito dalla natura, e la misura prescritta dalla religione e dalla morale, nella mente e nel cuore delle sue figlie' [will not omit anything to preserve the order established by nature, and the measure prescribed by religion and morals, in the minds and hearts of her daughters].[125] Despite emphasising the importance of education, complying with the role established by nature was the main aspect on which to focus when preparing a girl for adulthood. In a letter to Raffaello Lambruschini dated 1871 and included in her *Epistolario* (published posthumously in Turin in 1910), Franceschi Ferrucci reasserts this idea by arguing:

> Stoltissima [è] l'opinione di quelli, i quali vorrebbero che le donne avessero in comune cogli uomini gli uffici, e gli onori: sicché in luogo di attendere ai casalinghi lavori, e ad allevare i loro figlioli perdessero in gare ambiziose la pace dell'animo, la verecondia, e la dignità della vita.[126]
>
> [It is a very foolish opinion of those [people] who would like women to have offices and honours in common with men, so that instead of doing their housework and raising their children they would lose the peace in [their] souls, modesty and dignity of life.]

122 Giulia Molino Colombini, *Sulla educazione della donna: pensieri* (Turin: Fory and Dalmazzo, 1851), p. 10.

123 Molino Colombini, *Sulla educazione della donna*, p. 110.

124 Molino Colombini, *Sulla educazione della donna*, pp. 91, 110.

125 Caterina Franceschi Ferrucci, *Degli studii delle donne* (Turin: Pomba, 1853), p. 13.

126 Caterina Franceschi Ferrucci, *Epistolario di Caterina Franceschi Ferrucci: edito ora la prima volta, con lettere di scrittori illustri a lei* (Reggio Emilia: Guidetti, 1910), p. 358.

Women had to be content with carrying out housework and going beyond this natural order would also have meant their lives lost dignity. Women, as Carmela Covato observes, 'sono state educate a non istruirsi, ma ad apprendere rigide regole di comportamento finalizzate ad interiorizzare un destino quasi sempre esclusivamente domestico' [have been educated not to educate themselves, but to learn strict rules of behaviour aimed at internalising an almost exclusively domestic destiny].[127] This is why Franceschi Ferrucci explains that a woman, when looking at her son's cradle, 'già vede e onora l'uomo' [already sees and honours the man].[128] Their different destiny and the hierarchical set-up of nineteenth-century society are clear from her son's very first days: in this context, mothers could do their best to care for their sons and to teach them honour and respect, a role to be fulfilled within the household, in the domestic realm, in which they could also appropriately express their individuality enhanced by a good education.

This view of the 'domestic woman' whose world revolved entirely around her husband and her family was also shared by the Milanese educationalist Luisa Amalia Paladini (1810–1872). In her *Manuale per le giovinette italiane* (1851) she explains how to become a good wife and mother and, therefore, a good and fulfilled woman. Despite considering women as companions to men, Paladini stresses that their main task was to ensure that:

> lo stanco padre di famiglia trovi in casa sua tutto ordinato, tutto piacevole all'occhio, tutto ridente [e] che la casa sia per esso un tempio di sicuro riposo e di affetti dolcissimi che lo ristorino delle sue tante cure e fatiche.[129]
>
> [the tired father of the family finds everything tidy in his house, all pleasing to the eye, everyone laughing; and that the house is a temple of safe rest and sweet affections for him which will restore him from his many cares and efforts.]

A woman was allowed to acquire some culture, as 'anziché distoglierla dall'adempimento di un tal dovere glielo rende più facile ed aggradevole' [instead of diverting her from the fulfillment of such

127 Carmela Covato, 'Istruzione femminile e metamorfosi dell'identità in Italia fra Ottocento e Novecento', in *Conduct Literature for and about Women in Italy*, ed. by Sanson and Lucioli, pp. 283–99 (p. 283).

128 Franceschi Ferrucci, *Degli studii delle donne*, p. 10.

129 Luisa Amalia Paladini, *Manuale per le giovinette italiane* (Florence: Le Monnier, 1866 [1851]), p. 93.

a duty, [it] makes it easier and more pleasant] and would enable her to be considered a reliable companion by her husband, who could then even ask her opinion 'ne' casi dubbi e difficili' [in doubtful and difficult cases].[130] Women could also acquire some rough knowledge of the law, as this would help them better to educate their children to comply with it.[131] By contrast, studying sciences was neither necessary nor useful to women. She allows that studying some botany or natural history could help, but the deep study of one science was to be avoided, as it would hinder them from carrying out their duties.[132] In Paladini's view, too, women were first of all mothers and wives: their education had to facilitate the superior tasks of men in the world beyond the family.

Jurists on Women's Status

Following the path of physicians and moralists, jurists, too, endorsed the idea that women were inferior to men. The views of jurists in pre-Unification Italy (and beyond) continued to reflect the same misogynistic views and prejudices that were expounded in the discourses of moralists and men of letters. Alongside their general *infirmitas* and *levitas animi,* women would be prevented from correctly assessing the value of objects because of their *imbecillitas.* For this reason they were deemed to lack the ability to understand and conclude a legal transaction and were to be prevented from undertaking any contracts. In particular, because of these characteristics – assumed to be peculiar to women – it was imagined that they wasted all their money on superfluous things. As we see in the next chapter, in almost the entire Italian Peninsula women could not administer their goods, a state of affairs which was considered a form of protection for both women and society.

In this regard, the Pisan criminalist Giovanni Carmignani, in his *Teoria delle leggi della sicurezza sociale* (1831), observes that 'la tutela perpetua, alla quale in altre età fu sottoposta la donna può essere considerata come una guarentigia pubblica contro le offese, di cui la debolezza del sesso cedendo alle malvage altrui suggestioni può essere ragione' [the perpetual protection to which a woman was subjected in other times can be considered a public guarantee

130 Paladini, *Manuale,* p. 94.

131 Paladini, *Manuale,* p. 94.

132 Paladini, *Manuale,* p. 118.

against the offences which can be caused by the weakness of their sex, [making them] yield to the wicked suggestions of others].[133] Women needed to be protected against confidence tricks because their softer, weaker spinal brain, the *cerebralis medulla*,[134] hindered them from developing ideas and left them some steps behind men in achieving full maturity.[135] Women also lacked the firm mind needed to understand civil law and to undertake obligations.[136] Contracts by women were valid only with the approval of a male relative and a judge. It was a form of 'guarentigia pubblica' [public protection] because, according to the Neapolitan jurist Domenicantonio Galdi, 'ordinariamente gli uomini sono più capaci delle donne di ben governare gli affari particolari' [ordinarily men are more capable than women of governing detailed affairs].[137]

These ideas were taken into account by the laws of many states in the Italian Peninsula, where, as we see in Chapter 3, several legal norms limited women's administration of their assets. In areas such as the Kingdom of Lombardy-Venetia, women did not need any authorisation, in particular marital authorisation, and this led several voices to criticise what was considered to be a real threat to a family's assets and public order. Scholars and jurists broadly discussed whether women's minds were able properly to administer their patrimony and compared their legal status as a result of this code with others in force in the Italian Peninsula. The key point in the debate was again the possibility that women might spend their whole patrimony on frivolities. The jurist Giovanni Carcano, for example, in his commentary on the Austrian Code in force in Lombardy-Venetia, describes its results with these words: 'padre senza maestà, madre senza onore, donne senza freno' [father without majesty, mother without honour, women without restraint], because enforcing 'una comune misura, l'individuo, la persona, tutti li eguaglia, e quindi tutti li sposta e li abbassa' [a common measure makes the individual, the

133 Carmignani, *Teoria delle leggi della sicurezza sociale*, III, 311–12.

134 Giovanni Carmignani, *Juris criminalis elementa* (Pisa: Nistri, 1833 [1808]), p. 44.

135 Carmignani, *Teoria delle leggi della sicurezza sociale*, II, 172.

136 Carmignani, *Juris criminalis elementa*, p. 44.

137 Domenicantonio Galdi, *Enciclopedia legale, ovvero Repertorio alfabetico di legislazione, giurisprudenza e dottrina in materia di dritto civile, commerciale, criminale, amministrativo, canonico, pubblico, naturale e delle genti*, 5 vols (Naples: Marghieri, 1864–68), II, 757.

person, all equals, and therefore displaces and lowers everyone].[138] Thanks to this code, a woman:

> commercia, compera, vende, giuoca alla borsa, s'impegna nel cambio, dona agli amanti, riceve il prezzo dell'adulterio, fomenta gli scialaqui e le insubordinazioni dei figli, disperde il proprio patrimonio, e ciò tutto senza che sappia, senza che abbia diritto di divieto il marito.[139]
>
> [trades, buys, sells, plays on the stock market, engages in money-changing, gives gifts to lovers, receives the benefits of adultery, fosters the waste and insubordination of her children, loses her wealth – and all this without her husband knowing, without him having the right to stop her.]

Carcano, as well as other jurists, did not consider the possibility that women could use their money appropriately, but rather focused on the fact that the lack of marital authorisation would unavoidably lead to misuse.

Other than being convinced that women's objective was to spend their patrimony on whims, jurists also insisted on the need to take their morality into consideration. In his posthumous work *Trattati inediti di giurisprudenza* (1854), the Tuscan jurist Francesco Forti believed that 'la frivolezza ed il puttanesimo del sesso' [the frivolity and harlotry of [the female] sex] were such that, in the Italian Peninsula, no wise legislator would ever establish a system in which goods were held in common by spouses.[140] Forti endorsed the 'Quintus Mucius presumption', according to which it had to be assumed that all assets belonging to women had been purchased with their husbands's money, in order to 'escludere il sospetto che se li sieno guadagnati facendo commercio del proprio corpo' [rule out the suspicion that they were earned by trading their bodies].[141] This presumption was deemed to guarantee women's reputations and to avoid any inquiry over the origin of money.

138 Carcano, *Il codice civile austriaco*, p. 29.

139 Carcano, *Il codice civile austriaco*, p. 28.

140 Francesco Forti, *Trattati inediti di giurisprudenza* (Florence: Viessieux, 1854), pp. 456–57.

141 Forti, *Trattati inediti*, pp. 456–57. The Quintus Mucius presumption was named after the Roman jurist Quintus Mucius Scaevola (*c*. 140–*c*. 82 BC), who introduced it into the legal framework. See *Digest* 24.1.51. It was meant to avoid the suspicion that women could have bought the goods through illegal trade. See also Philippe-Antoine Merlin, *Dizionario universale ossia repertorio ragionato di giurisprudenza e quistioni di diritto*, trans. by Filippo Carillo, 14 vols (Venice: Antonelli, 1834–42), IV, 1035–36.

A very small number of jurists held that women could be favoured by the allegedly unstable nature of their minds. Women's nature and their difficulties in understanding the law were to be taken into consideration when indicting them for a crime. In this regard, Carmignani, as mentioned earlier, assumed that it was almost impossible to imagine that the heart of a woman could harbour the hateful force necessary to commit a crime.[142] However, if this happened, women's minds and their inconstant feelings were to be considered and those who committed crimes were to be judged more mildly than men. This was especially aimed at not exacerbating any contradiction to civil laws.[143] The same thought was expressed by Luigi Stella, a Roman lawyer who, in an article published in the journal *Archivio Giuridico* in 1869, explained that two 'anomalies' persisted in women: a perpetual childhood and a permanent infirmity.[144] He argued that women's *imbecillitas* made them change easily and go from being enthusiastic to disheartened; these feelings, combined with menstruation, pregnancy and childbirth, were transformations which disrupted the normal state of life. Therefore, their childish spirits and the great vitality and instability of their feelings did not allow criminal law to be retained in women's memories. In particular, Stella claimed that they obeyed the law without understanding its essence and that this was to be taken into account.[145]

Carmignani and Stella were rare exceptions in a context in which the great majority thought that women should be debarred from undertaking any act of civil life, but that there was no general reason which could justify or excuse a woman who committed a crime. For example, Pellegrino Rossi, a jurist and diplomat who served as Prime Minister of the Papal States in 1848, wrote in his *Trattato di diritto penale* (1832) that there were crimes, or infringements of the law, which were more excusable if committed by women. Examples of such infractions were political crimes, the importance and immorality of which could be unknown to a woman. However, he explained that it was impossible to establish general rules in this respect and women were to be treated the same as men with regard to crimes.[146] Lawmakers also shared this point of view. For example,

142 Carmignani, *Teoria delle leggi della sicurezza sociale*, II, 175.

143 Carmignani, *Teoria delle leggi della sicurezza sociale*, II, 175–76.

144 Luigi Stella, 'Alcune considerazioni sulla minore responsabilità penale della donna', *Archivio Giuridico*, 4 (1869), 76–83.

145 Stella, 'Alcune considerazioni sulla minore responsabilità', p. 79.

146 Pellegrino Rossi, *Trattato di diritto penale* (Milan: Borroni and Scotti, 1832), p. 244.

the *Regolamento sui delitti e sulle pene* (1832), the criminal code of the Papal States, explicitly reported that 'non dispensa dalla pena né la condizione né il sesso' [neither status nor sex exempts [anyone] from punishment].[147] Nineteenth-century women were not deemed able to understand the law, but they were subject to it just as men were.

The debate on women's legal status which took place in the Ottocento could be attributed to the rapid changes which took place in the Italian legal framework. As we shall see, some norms, especially those included in the Napoleonic Code stating that men and women had equal inheritance rights, were a major challenge to eighteenth- and nineteenth-century society and its legal system. The many works regarding women's legal status could be interpreted as a way to make public people's concerns and to resist changes which the legal system did and would undergo. Some theorists maintained that women were to be given greater importance in society, although still under the guidance of men. Gian Domenico Romagnosi (1761–1835), a jurist and philosopher from the Duchy of Parma, stressed that even if 'le leggi vogliano favorire l'equo trattamento delle donne, esso non deve giungere al punto d'intieramente abbandonarle a loro stesse' [laws want to promote fair treatment for women, this must not go so far as to abandon them entirely to themselves].[148] He reported the experience of 'viaggiatori filosofi, che hanno attentamente esaminata la parte morale delle popolazioni del globo' [travelling philosophers, who have carefully examined the moral side of the peoples of the world][149] and drew on the general opinion that the heart was the organ which prevailed in women, whereas in men it was the mind that prevailed. In his *Istituzioni di civile filosofia ossia di Giurisprudenza Teorica* (1825), he points out that, both for their own best interests and for the preservation of order within families, women should only be given 'libertà protetta e specialmente sostenuta dall'autorità sociale' [protected freedom and especially supported by social authority].[150] He compares women to a 'fanciullo ignaro dei pericoli o imprudente' [child unaware of the dangers or impulsive], for whom economic freedom would be a 'barbarie palliata' [concealed barbarism].[151]

147 Art. 2, in *Regolamento sui delitti e sulle pene* ([n.p.]: [n. pub.], 1832), p. 3.

148 Gian Domenico Romagnosi, *Opere. Istituzioni di civile filosofia ossia di giurisprudenza teorica*, 4 vols (Florence: Piatti, 1839), IV, 436.

149 Romagnosi, *Opere*, III, 1460.

150 Romagnosi, *Opere*, IV, 436.

151 Romagnosi, *Opere*, IV, 437.

Indeed, 'la natura ha disposto che il consiglio sia unito alla forza, e l'affetto alla debolezza' [nature has ordered that reason be united with strength, and affection with weakness].[152] This would explain the hierarchical structure of marriage which, as the Roman jurist Filippo Maria Renazzi (1747–1808) claimed, was 'divina legem sancitum' [sanctioned by divine law].[153]

If theorists and jurists stressed that women were important, they also highlighted and insisted on a vague concept of their importance in society without any further specification. This point can also be inferred from the words of Carcano, who argued that 'grandi parole furono fatte per emancipare la donna' [great words were said to emancipate woman] and suggested doing even better: 'eleviamola, coordinandola' [elevate them by coordinating them].[154] Alongside this vague argument there was no suggestion of how to implement this 'elevation'. Backing the usual view that attributed reason to men and liveliness of imagination and exquisiteness of feeling to women, he claimed that all these faculties had an important value, but reason was the one that governed things. Women should be 'socially' valued but, above all, guided through life by men; for this reason, women should in turn honour men 'con fiducia ed affetto, poiché [loro] guardia e tutela' [with trust and affection, since they are their guard and protection].[155]

Acknowledging Women's Participation

These views on women remained unchallenged even during the Risorgimento, when women's participation in the Italian cause was strong and noted by many people. The Turinese man of letters and philosopher Vincenzo Gioberti, in his *Delle condizioni presenti e future d'Italia* (1848), described women's participation in the cause as a phenomenon that needed to be 'specialmente avvertito; perché esso è al parer mio uno dei sintomi più atti a dimostrare che siam giunti a maturità civile, e a pieno essere di coscienza come nazione' [especially noticed, because in my opinion this is one of the symptoms which most effectively shows that we have reached civil maturity and are

152 Romagnosi, *Opere*, IV, 437.

153 Filippo Maria Renazzi, *Elementa juris criminalis. Liber primus. De delictis generatim* (Bologna: Francisci Cardinali & Caroli Frulli, 1826 [1773–75]), pp. 198–99.

154 Carcano, *Il codice civile austriaco*, p. 29.

155 Carcano, *Il codice civile austriaco*, p. 29.

fully conscious as a nation].[156] This idea, however, did not result in a challenge to women's status. The description of women's features provided an insight into his views:

> [I]l carattere essenziale della virilità consiste nell'autonomia, per cui l'uomo [...] non dipende che da sé stesso; onde a sé solo si appoggia, in sé solo confida, sostiene senza essere sostenuto, protegge senza esser protetto, e ha una piena coscienza delle proprie forze, come quelle che sono svolte e maturate compitamente; giacché la coscienza non è altro che l'intelligenza adulta, esplicata, messa in atto e avente il possesso di sé medesima. L'indole opposta, cioé la femminilità, risiede per contro in una coscienza incoata e confusa, che non erompe in riflessione, e non si estrinseca che sotto la forma istintiva del sentimento; onde la donna si sente debole, bisognosa di appoggio e di aiuto: il suo amore è un abbandono, che ella fa di sé medesima a un essere più forte che la protegge.[157]

> [[T]he essential character of virility consists in autonomy, for which man [...] depends only on himself; hence he relies only on himself, in himself alone he trusts, he sustains without being sustained, he protects without being protected, and has a full awareness of his own strengths, such as those which are carried out and matured fully; since consciousness is nothing more than adult intelligence, explicit, implemented and in possession of itself. On the other hand, the opposite disposition, that is, femininity, resides in a blind and confused consciousness, which does not burst forth in reflection and does not express itself except in the instinctive form of feeling; hence the woman feels weak, in need of support and help: her love is an abandonment which she makes of herself to a stronger being who protects her.]

Women's presumed 'coscienza incoata e confusa' [unconscious and confused consciousness] was still the main excuse for preventing women from engaging in activities imagined to require excessive intellectual effort for the weak female mind, such as the study of abstract sciences or politics.[158]

156 Vincenzo Gioberti, *Delle condizioni presenti e future d'Italia* (London: [n. pub.], 1848), p. 10. Similar comments were expressed by Cesare Balbo, who maintained that 'quel precipitarsi delle donne nella carità, quel rimpiazzar la famiglia propria coll'universale [è] il maggior forse de' progressi morali dell'età nostra' [that rush of women into charity, that replacing of one's own family with the universal, is perhaps the greatest of the moral achievements of our age] (Balbo, *Pensieri ed esempi*, p. 316).

157 Vincenzo Gioberti, *Il Gesuita moderno*, 5 vols (Naples: Batelli, 1849), IV, 255.

158 Women's supposedly inchoate, confused reason was also taken into consideration by Roussel, who pointed out that women's fickle imagination and

Participation in the public sphere was an exclusive prerogative of men, because women were 'l'angelo della famiglia' [the angel of the family] and had a 'diversità di tendenze, di vocazioni speciali' [variety of tendencies, of special vocations],[159] as the patriot Giuseppe Mazzini wrote in *Doveri dell'Uomo* (1860). He was convinced that even if men were not superior to women, the two sexes had 'funzioni distinte nell'Umanità' [different functions in Humanity].[160] Mazzini claims that their qualities were very 'useful' in society: women could help with charity work, volunteering at hospitals and orphanages; and could collect and distribute alms and also funds for the Italian cause. These 'different functions' did not seem to include political participation. In the Italian Peninsula, where most men did not have the right to vote either, women were not even taken into consideration in this regard. Mazzini explains that:

> oggi, la metà della famiglia umana, la metà dalla quale noi cerchiamo ispirazioni e conforti, la metà che ha in cura la prima educazione dei nostri figli, è per singolare contraddizione, dichiarata civilmente, politicamente, socialmente ineguale, esclusa da quell'Unità. A voi che cercate, in nome d'una verità religiosa, la vostra emancipazione, spetta di protestare in ogni modo, in ogni occasione, contro quella negazione dell'Unità. L'*emancipazione della donna* dovrebbe essere continuamente accoppiata per voi coll'*emancipazione dell'operaio*, e darà al vostro lavoro la consacrazione d'una verità universale.[161]

> [today, half of the human family, the half from which we seek inspiration and comfort, the half who take care of the early education of our children, are by singular contradiction declared civilly, politically socially unequal, excluded from that Unity. It is up to you who seek your emancipation, in the name of a religious truth, to protest in every way, on every occasion, against that denial of Unity. The *emancipation of women* should continuously go together with the *emancipation of the worker* and will give your work the consecration of a universal truth.]

---

the structure of their minds debarred them from being able to hold the broader views of politics and those great moral principleswhich men could easily hold (Roussel, *Sistema fisico e morale della donna*, II, 66–67). Cabanis added that women were able to assess their inferior condition and voluntarily dismissed any great effort of mind because they understood that they were not able to bear the mental effort this activity required (Cabanis, *Rapports du Physique*, I, 195).

159 Giuseppe Mazzini, *Dei doveri dell'uomo* (Milan: RCS, 2010 [1860]), p. 81.

160 Mazzini, *Dei doveri dell'uomo*, p. 81.

161 Mazzini, *Dei doveri dell'uomo*, p. 148.

Alongside a clear acknowledgement of the different status of women and men, Mazzini's use of the term 'emancipation' could be interpreted as a need for a more inclusive society which would neglect neither workers nor women. As Paolo Passaniti argued, the 'discorso sulla famiglia e sulla donna come titolare di diritti negati dalla storia che i proletari dovranno riscrivere secondo giustizia' [discourse on the family and on women as holders of rights denied by history which proletarians will have to rewrite according to justice] would be the ideological foundation of the first demands for women's rights.[162] Mazzini also stressed the need for a better education for women, intended both for the acquisition of moral values and for studying. Weak-headedness, which was identified as a normal characteristic of women and used to assert their inferiority, was considered by Mazzini to be illusory and the result of the poor, unequal education provided to them.[163] In a letter to the Member of the Italian Parliament Salvatore Morelli dated August 1867, he claims that women's emancipation:

> sancirebbe una grande verità religiosa, base a tutte le altre, la unità del genere umano; e associerebbe, nella ricerca del vero e del progresso umano comune, una somma di facoltà e di forze, isterilite in oggi da quella inferiorità che dimezza l'anima.[164]
>
> [would sanction a great religious truth, the foundation of all the others, the unity of humankind; and would associate, in the search for truth and common human progress, a sum of faculties and forces made barren today by that inferiority which halves the soul.]

Mazzini's views reflected the new sensitivity which had begun to spread among theorists and politicians and resulted in more inclusive proposals and ideas.

As mentioned earlier, physical characteristics were thought to be reflected in women's minds and therefore used to assert women's subjugation. However, with the Enlightenment, the French Revolution with its novelties and expectations and the Risorgimento with the changes which took place in the economic structure as well as in the political order, women's nature and role in society started

162 Paolo Passaniti, *Diritto di famiglia e ordine sociale. Il percorso storico della società coniugale in Italia* (Milan: Giuffrè, 2011), pp. 208–09.

163 Passaniti, *Diritto di famiglia*, pp. 80–81.

164 Salvatore Morelli, *La donna e la scienza, o, La soluzione del problema sociale* (Naples: Società Tipografico-editrice, 1869), p. LXXXIX; see also Giuseppe Mazzini, *Scritti editi e inediti*, 25 vols (Milan: Daelli, 1886), xv, 2–3.

to be progressively questioned. As a result, some timid hints about women's status were made: as we see in the next chapter, from a strictly legal standpoint the two acts promulgated in the Kingdom of Sardinia and in the Duchy of Modena, in 1837 and 1851 respectively, could be considered a first, important achievement. These new laws allowed women to succeed to their parents' inheritance, although not to the same extent as their brothers. Nonetheless, for women the path to obtaining the same legal status as men was still very long. Ancient stereotypes still persisted and there were no substantial changes in attitude which could lead to a more inclusive approach to their status, especially during the development of new legal norms.

3. Women and the Law in the Nineteenth-Century Italian Peninsula

Marriage and death were the two principal points in life at which the hierarchical structure and external standing of families could be challenged. Both implied changes in a family's structure and opportunities for renegotiating positions, altering power structures and redistributing authority within the household.[1] Consequently, governments and law-makers paid special attention to these events, crucial as they were to 'maintain[ing] the hierarchical system on which the economy, and indeed the whole society rested'.[2] As we saw in Chapter 1, the family 'accipitur in iure pro substantia'; and inheritance laws were key for those who had a *substancia* to transmit. Marriage and death involved the transfer of property, which was to be devolved in the correct way and to a nominated person, normally a man carrying forward the family name. In this context, the existence of any related women and the number of goods to which they were entitled was to be carefully assessed.

Since assets bestowed status and power, families were concerned about the possible fragmentation of their property and goods: this would lead to a loss of prestige for the family. Hence, the possibility of woman inheriting a large portion of the family assets was not to be considered, because this would hinder the continued material prosperity of her natal family and enrich other families instead. For this reason, families adopted strategies to minimise the risk of property being broken up. 'The chief feature of the traditional European family was its instability', as André Burguière and François

1 David R. Green and Alastair Owens (eds), *Family Welfare: Gender, Property, and Inheritance since the Seventeenth Century* (London: Praeger, 2004), p. 8.

2 Goody, 'Dowry and the Rights of Women to Property', p. 203.

Lebrun point out;[3] and thus families controlled the transmission of their wealth by limiting the number of their children, by managing celibacy and spinsterhood and by making full use of *fideicommissa*, majorats, *inter vivos* donations and testaments. This strategy would ensure that property was transferred to the right person. Wills in particular were used across all social classes: even people belonging to lower classes bequeathed their few possessions or money by this means,[4] in addition to using wills to specify arrangements for their funerals, give testimonies of their faith in God and the Celestial Court and bequeathing various donations to the Church.[5] The law reinforced families' efforts to preserve their patrimony in its entirety by excluding women from inheritance. The compensation for this exclusion was the dowry, a woman's rightful share of her family's patrimony.

The Dowry from Ancient Times to the Nineteenth Century

The dowry is a very old institution. In the pre-Justinian era its provision was a moral and social obligation; and not providing a daughter with a dowry brought dishonour on the family and was a

3 André Burguière and François Lebrun, 'The One Hundred and One Families of Europe', in *A History of the Family*, ed. by André Burguière and others, 2 vols (Cambridge: Polity Press, 1996), II, 11–94 (p. 15).

4 See Michel Vovelle, 'La morte nella mentalità e nella pratica religiosa', in *Società, Chiesa e vita religiosa nell'Ancien régime*, ed. by Carla Russo (Naples: Guida, 1976), pp. 231–82 (esp. pp. 231–41); Maria Antonietta Visceglia, 'Corpo e sepoltura nei testamenti della nobiltà napoletana', *Quaderni Storici*, 50 (1982), 583–614; Maura Piccialuti, *L'immortalità dei beni. Fedecommessi e primogeniture a Roma nei secoli XVII e XVIII* (Rome: Viella, 1999), pp. 139–63. The French historian Philippe Ariès argues that up to the eighteenth century the will was used to express faith and decisions regarding the salvation of one's body and soul. In the second half of the eighteenth century he reports a sort of secularisation of wills. Ariès attributes this behaviour not to a de-Christianisation of society, as suggested by Michel Vovelle, but to a distinction made by the testator between the transmission of goods and the expression of personal feelings, which reduced the will to a mere document (Philippe Ariès, *Western Attitudes toward Death: From the Middle Ages to the Present*, trans. by Patricia M. Ranum (London: Marion Boyars, 1994 [1976]), pp. 63–65). See also Michel Vovelle, *Piété baroque et déchristianisation en Provence au XVIIIe siècle. Les attitudes devant la mort d'après les clauses des testaments* (Paris: Plon, 1973), pp. 608–14. With regard to the Italian Peninsula, this did not hold completely true, yet in the mid-nineteenth century a large part of most wills was dedicated to decisions concerning religious services and expressions of faith.

5 See also Macry, *Ottocento: famiglia, élites e patrimoni a Napoli*, pp. 69–77.

sign of extreme poverty.[6] Around the time of the Byzantine Emperor Justinian in the sixth century[7] the giving of a dowry assumed the character of a legal obligation.[8] This meant that a father had to provide a dowry even if his daughter had her own *peculio*, as the wealth of a *filiusfamilia* was called. During the Early Middle Ages the custom of establishing a dowry lost its importance due to the presence of other institutions such as the *faderfio*, a marriage gift of negligible value given to the groom by the bride's family, particularly in use in areas conquered by the Lombards.[9] Over time, the value of the *faderfio* increased considerably and evolved to become a sort of compensation for women's exclusion from inheriting.[10] In the twelfth century, when its value became very high and the rediscovery of the *Corpus Iuris Civilis* of Justinian led to a revival of the Roman dowry, the two terms were often used interchangeably.[11] The use of the dowry became predominant and the *faderfio* was completely abandoned. The preference for the Roman dowry might have been because it was associated with the right to register a mortgage guaranteeing the goods which were part of it, something which was not possible with the *faderfio*.

From the Middle Ages onwards the dowry, as a custom, began to replace a daughter's rightful share of the paternal inheritance and

6 Fayer, *La familia romana*, II, 673.

7 The Byzantine Emperor Justinian issued the collection of laws known as *Corpus Iuris Civilis* between 529 and 534. The *Corpus* is composed of *Code* (*Codex*), *Digest* or *Pandects* (*Digesta* and *Pandectae*), *Institutes* (*Institutiones*) and *Novels* (*Novellae Constitutiones*).

8 Fayer, *La familia romana*, II, 717–37.

9 On the *faderfio*, see Federico Criscuolo, *La donna nella storia del diritto privato italiano* (Palermo: Caronna & Macoclin, 1885), pp. 49–50; Manlio Bellomo, *Ricerche sui rapporti patrimoniali tra coniugi* (Milan: Giuffrè, 1960), pp. 61–63. Enrico Galluppi claims that the *faderfio* was 'solo un corredo di vestimenti per la propria persona' (Enrico Galluppi, *La successione dei conjugi nella storia interna del diritto italiano* (Rome: Civelli, 1873), p. 58). At the time of the Lombards a husband also acquired a right of guardianship over his wife known as the *mundium*. Alongside the guardianship, a husband acquired sole rights over her properties. The *mundium* also implied that a husband was obliged to protect his wife and was responsible for her. See Emma Southon, *Marriage, Sex and Death: The Family and the Fall of the Roman West* (Amsterdam: Amsterdam University Press, 2017), pp. 34–37. On the *mundium*, see also Francesco Brandileone, *Saggi sulla storia della celebrazione del matrimonio in Italia* (Milan: Hoepli, 1906), pp. 4–9; Ennio Cortese, 'Per la storia del mundio in Italia', *Rivista italiana per le scienze giuridiche*, 3 (1955/1956), 323–474.

10 Manlio Bellomo, 'Dote (diritto intermedio)', *Enciclopedia del diritto*, 16 vols (Milan: Giuffrè, 1958–65), IV, 8–32 (p. 9).

11 Bellomo, 'Dote', p. 9.

was a means to 'dissociare le donne dall'asse maschile del lignaggio, in concomitanza con l'affermazione della concezione agnatizia della famiglia' [dissociate women from the male axis of the lineage, in conjunction with the affirmation of the conception of the family being perpetuated solely through the male line].[12] Later on, when the custom of excluding women from inheritance was transcribed into municipal Statutes, the *exclusio propter dotem* gained the force of law and became part of the *iura propria* of the *communes*.[13] In the first statutes of the eleventh century there are only traces of this provision, but after the thirteenth century every statute across the Peninsula excluded women from succession.[14] Women were excluded from inheriting, but at the same time they became entitled to the indisputable right to a dowry and its amount began to be determined by law. Dowries were often equal to the Falcidian Quarter or to the *legitima portio*,[15] but this equality was not always a stringent requirement: some statutes only provided that it was to be 'congrua', that is, 'appropriate', a case in point being the Statute of Parma,[16] or that of Vigevano (then in Piedmont, nowadays in Lombardy), which did not make any reference to its amount.[17] Upon receiving a dowry, women were often asked to sign a document in which they renounced any further right to their paternal inheritance, even though their dowry was the only wealth to which they were entitled by law. These acts were usually drawn up before a notary, also signed by the groom or his *paterfamilias*[18] and aimed to exclude any possible interpretation of the

12 Casanova, *La famiglia italiana*, p. 92.

13 Bellomo, *Ricerche sui rapporti patrimoniali*, pp. 163–84.

14 Francesco Ercole, 'L'istituto dotale nella pratica e nella legislazione statutaria dell'Italia superiore', *Rivista italiana di scienze giuridiche*, 45 (1909), 191–302 (pp. 212–13). To my knowledge, no provision allowing women to inherit has been found in any statute of the Italian Peninsula to date.

15 The Falcidian Quarter was named after the Lex Falcidia (40 BC), which stated that a maximum of three-quarters of the net estate could be disposed of in wills.

16 *Decisioni del Supremo tribunale di Revisione con note ed opuscoli relativi del cavaliere Francesco Melegari: Dal 27 aprile al 28 dicembre 1829* (Parma: Carmignani, 1832), pp. 121–23.

17 *Giurisprudenza Italiana*, 2 (1849), 671–97 (p. 694).

18 This kind of act was called 'cautela' [precaution] and was often referred to as 'cautela del De Luca', named after the jurist Giovanni Battista De Luca (1613?–1683). See Giovanni Battista De Luca, *Il dottor volgare, ovvero Il compendio di tutta la legge civile, canonica, feudale e municipale, nelle cose più ricevute in pratica, moralizzato in lingua italiana*, 6 vols ([n.p.]: [n. pub.], 1673), VI, 36–39; Ungari, *Storia del diritto di famiglia*, p. 66. In Sicily and the Mezzogiorno this 'cautela' was

law that would lead to a request for further money or goods. Paolo Ungari observes that in practice women were asked to renounce almost every protection granted by Roman law or any municipal or state law.[19] Along with the dowry, women were given the *corredo,* also called the *scherpa* or *fardello,* a trousseau formed of goods such as clothes, furniture, textiles and jewels. These were usually mentioned in the dowry instruments, while other goods which were not part of a dowry were called *paraphernalia.*[20]

In return for the dowry and the *faderfio,* the bride was also entitled to receive a marriage gift. Gifts *propter nuptias* provided by the groom were called the *tertia, morgengabe* or *quarta* and *meffio* or *meta*: these gifts were usually a third or quarter of the groom's patrimony, or were equal to half the amount of the bride's dowry.[21] The *tertia, quarta* and *meta* were not usually delivered to the bride herself but remained in the husband's possession; hence the wife was considered a creditor in this regard and was able to obtain her marriage gift only upon her husband's death.[22] Thus, at first both spouses were asked to contribute 'ad sustinenda onera matrimonii' [to bear the burden of marriage].

---

also called 'cautela di Maranta', named after the jurist Roberto Maranta (1476–1530?). See Roberto Maranta, *Speculum aureum et lumen aduocatorum praxis ciuilis* (London: Symphorianum Beraud, 1573), pp. 877–95. In addition, 'per meglio fortificare le rinunzie medesime, lo sposo ovvero il marito, [...] promettea rendere indenni a proprie spese coloro, a cui pro si rinunziava, laddove la rinunzia si rescindesse dal magistrato' [in order the better to strengthen the renunciations themselves, the groom or the husband, [...] promises to indemnify at his own expense those in whose favour renunciations were made, if these were rescinded by the magistrate] (Vincenzo Lomonaco, *Storia de principii della legislazione* (Naples: Azzolino, 1844), p. 210).

19 Ungari, *Storia del diritto di famiglia,* p. 54.

20 Julius Kirshner argues that during the Middle Ages non-dotal goods were classified as *parapherna* or *paraphernalia* and *bona non dotalia.* The former were movable goods brought by the wife to the husband's household for her own use, or for her and her husband to use in common, while the *bona non dotalia* were the assets belonging to the wife which she did not bring into her husband's household. He adds that fourteenth- and fifteenth-century Florentine statutes refer only to the single category of *bona non dotalia* (Julius Kirshner, 'Materials for a Gilded Cage: Non-Dotal Assets in Florence, 1300–1500', in *The Family in Italy: From Antiquity to the Present,* ed. by David I. Kertzer and Richard P. Saller (New Haven, CT; London: Yale University Press, 1991), pp. 184–207). Nineteenth-century law and jurisprudence did not make any distinction and the terms *paraphernalia* and *bona non dotalia* seem to coincide.

21 Bellomo, *Ricerche sui rapporti patrimoniali,* pp. 2–5.

22 For considerable detail, see Bellomo, *Ricerche sui rapporti patrimoniali,* pp. 35–37.

Nevertheless, families were reluctant to give these groom's gifts and, from the twelfth century onwards, the *odium quartae* [hatred towards the *quarta*] began to emerge.[23] This aversion towards all nuptial gifts by the groom – not only towards the *quarta* – resulted at first in the promulgation of laws which reduced their overall amount and, eventually, in their suppression altogether.[24] In the *commune* of Genoa, for instance, the *tertia* had already been abolished in 1143.[25] From this time onwards the financial burden of the marriage began to shift completely to the bride's side.

This was because the dowry was given to the new family not only for the wife's needs but also to support the common household. Based upon Roman law, the person holding the dowry, usually the husband or the father-in-law, had a duty to support its owner, which meant that 'sustentationem sufferre et alimenta praestare et medicinae eius succurrere' [maintenance, food and medicines were to be given].[26] The term *sustentatio* also included clothes and jewellery for everyday display. A woman, instead, was only entitled to obtain the *antifactum* or *controdote*, usually a third of the dowry's value. Like other marriage gifts, the *antifactum* was not delivered to the bride or to her family, but remained in the possession of the husband until his death: upon widowhood, a woman went from having the right to a third or a quarter of her husband's patrimony to only being given a sum based on the amount of her dowry.

As mentioned earlier, it was at this time that the *Corpus Iuris Civilis* of Justinian was rediscovered and studied by various jurists. According to Mario Ascheri these 'jurists [...] persuaded the public powers that Roman-canon *ius commune* elaborated by them amounted to a kind of concentrated wisdom'.[27] Through the jurists' writings and analysis this corpus of laws began to be known and used for cases not covered by statutes and customs.[28] Moreover, jurists contributed

23 Francesco Brandileone, 'Studi preliminari sullo svolgimento dei rapporti patrimoniali fra coniugi in Italia', *Archivio giuridico*, 67 (1901), 201–81 (p. 206).

24 Bellomo, *Ricerche sui rapporti patrimoniali*, pp. 5–18.

25 David Herlihy, 'The Medieval Marriage Market', *Medieval and Renaissance Studies*, 6 (1976), 3–27 (p. 8).

26 *Digest*, 24, 3, 22, 8, Ulpianus libro 33 Ad Edictum.

27 Mario Ascheri, *The Laws of Late Medieval Italy (1000–1500): Foundations for a European Legal System* (Leiden: Brill, 2013), p. 269.

28 On the study of the *Corpus Iuris Civilis* and the glossators, see *Studies in the Glossators of the Roman Law: Newly Discovered Writings of the Twelfth Century*, ed. by Hermann Kantorowicz and William Warwick Buckland

to the formation of the law through their *consilia*, namely, learned opinions concerning cases already before judges.[29]

With regard to Justinian's *Corpus Iuris Civilis*, the parts in which women were considered inferior to men were broadly highlighted and discussed; conversely, provisions for equal inheritance rights were ignored. The Codex expressly states that 'all [...] descendants through the male line, whether males or females, shall be equally and alike called to the right of statutory succession in case of intestacy'; and the Novels iterated that no difference should exist between males and females eligible for an inheritance.[30] The exclusion of women came from their supposed inferiority (see Chapter 2) and from the belief that the *familia* continued through the male line. However, Cesarina Casanova argues that:

> la disparità o l'eguaglianza come criteri di successione non erano valori in se stessi: il valore era la stabilità della proprietà e le modalità di trasmissione dei beni vi si adattarono a seconda delle possibilità offerte dal contesto produttivo e della sua elasticità.[31]
>
> [disparity or equality were not, in themselves, attributes to be used as criteria for inheritance: the aim was to maintain the integrity of the property; and methods of passing on the assets had been made to comply with the possibilities offered by the production context and its flexibility.]

This means that the exclusion of those members considered by society to be weaker and less able to contribute to the standing of a family, e.g., women, was simply practised in order to preserve the wealth and the prestige of families and not as a goal to pursue in its own right.

(Cambridge: Cambridge University Press, 1938); Francesco Calasso, *Medio Evo del diritto* (Milan: Giuffrè, 1954), pp. 503–606. See also Ennio Cortese, *Le grandi linee della storia giuridica medievale* (Rome: Il cigno Galileo Galilei, 2001); and Ennio Cortese, *Il Rinascimento giuridico medievale* (Rome: Bulzoni, 1992).

29 On this point see Trevor Dean, *Crime and Justice in Late Medieval Italy* (Cambridge: Cambridge University Press, 2007), pp. 95–109. On *consilia* about disputes concerning dowries, see, e.g., Chiara Valsecchi, 'L'istituto della dote nella vita del diritto del tardo Cinquecento: i *Consilia* di Jacopo Menochio', *Rivista di storia del diritto italiano*, 52 (1994), 205–85.

30 'Nullam vero esse volumus differentiam in quacumque successione aut hereditate inter eos qui ad hereditatem vocantur masculos ac feminas' (Justinin, *Corpus iuris civilis*, Novel 118, 4; see also Codex 6, 58, 14, 1 and Novel 127, 1–2).

31 Casanova, *La famiglia italiana*, pp. 109–10.

In the Italian Peninsula during Middle Ages, the absence of any sons meant the estate of the deceased was inherited by relatives belonging to the male line, such as brothers. Male relatives from a woman's family of origin were of great importance, even after her marriage. As Paolo Macry observes, the uncle (the father's brother) was a prominent figure to whom a woman could report in the event of her father's death.[32] Among wealthy families *fideicommissa* or majorats were often established;[33] or men managed their patrimony together in a joint proprietorship known as *fraterna*, a kind of consortium usually led by the first-born son. Its members lived in the same house and sat at the same table in a 'communio ad eundem panem et vinum' [fellowship sharing the same bread and wine].[34] This was not only a custom but could be included among the 'socio-political necessities' which Andrea Romano suggests were used to 'garantire la conservazione dell'unità familiare intorno al patrimonio' [ensure family unity over the patrimony].[35] Thus family members not only shared 'bread and wine', but also the common goal of preserving the patrimony in its entirety, that is, avoiding the fragmentation of the *substancia* which gave value *in iure* to a family. A woman's dowry could include real estate, but was mainly and preferably given in cash. By giving cash, families avoided relinquishing properties which could serve as a symbol of the family's strength and, at the same time, money could more easily be invested by the husband.[36]

During the Middle Ages the ownership of properties was also of crucial concern to law-makers: numerous statutes provided norms to avoid properties being given to people from other *communes*. These norms tried to limit marriages between women and men of different *communes* by imposing several restrictions. To discourage these marriages, the statutes of Pesaro and Senigallia, for example,

32 On this point see Macry, *Ottocento: famiglia, élites e patrimoni a Napoli*, pp. 38–41.

33 The institution of the *fideicommissum* was not used before the fifteenth century. See Romualdo Trifone, *Il fedecommesso: storia dell'istituto in Italia* (Naples: Pierro, 1914); Maria Carla Zorzoli, 'Della famiglia e del suo patrimonio: riflessioni sull'uso del fedecommesso in Lombardia tra Cinque e Seicento', *Archivio storico lombardo*, 115 (1989), 91–148; Piccialuti, *L'immortalità dei beni*.

34 Camillo Fumagalli, *Il diritto di fraterna nella giurisprudenza da Accursio alla codificazione* (Turin: Bocca, 1912), p. 44.

35 Romano, *Famiglia, successioni e patrimonio*, p. 11.

36 A dowry could also include rights to goods, the release of debts, or movables (Julius Kirshner, 'Pursuing Honor While Avoiding Sin: The "Monte Delle Doti" of Florence', *Quaderni di studi senesi*, 41 (1978), 1–82 (p. 2)).

stipulated that wealthy women who wanted to marry outside the *commune* had to pay a huge tax; whereas men could not have any right over their wives' dowry if they did not relocate to their wives' *commune* of origin.[37] The 1255 Statute of Parma prohibited the creation of dowries using any properties that were within the territory of the *commune*, especially with 'case e castella' [houses and castles].[38] Along with preventing any loss of status for the family, the aim was to avoid these properties being owned by people from a different *commune* who might be rivals or even enemies. Even if a family could not provide a daughter with a dowry other than real estate, the statutes did not permit the sale of property in the *commune* (within the city walls). Property in the countryside, however, could be freely sold; hence in towns such as Camerino women from the *contado* who married people from inside the *commune* were allowed to bring dowries twice as large as those which women from the *commune* who married husbands from the countryside were permitted take with them.[39] In this case the main aim of the rule could have been to allow capital to pour into the *commune* in order to promote trade.

During the twelfth century the value of a dowry was still affordable for a family. An example often cited is Canto XV of the Paradiso, in which Dante wrote that at the time of his ancestor Cacciaguida the birth of a daughter did not cause fear to her father because the dowry did not exceed the proper measure.[40] In the Renaissance, as society changed, dowries increased considerably in value and even became ostentatious. The value of a dowry was an indicator of social prestige and 'poteva portare in più occasioni la famiglia della donna a compromettere il suo equilibrio economico impegnandosi a versare somme troppo elevate per le sue possibilità' [on several occasions

37 Antonio Pertile, *Storia del diritto italiano: dalla caduta dell'Impero Romano alla codificazione*, 8 vols (Turin: Unione tipografico-editrice, 1892), III, 323.

38 Pertile, *Storia del diritto italiano*, III, 323.

39 E.g., the Statute of Camerino (1578), cited in Pertile, *Storia del diritto italiano*, III, 324. See also Federico Criscuolo, *La donna nella storia del diritto privato italiano* (Palermo: Carini, Caronna and Macoclin, 1885), pp. 63–64; Maria Teresa Guerra Medici, 'Diritto statutario e condizione della donna nella città medievale dei secc. XII–XIV', *Rivista di storia del diritto italiano*, 65 (1992), 319–36 (pp. 321–22); Ungari, *Storia del diritto di famiglia*, pp. 68–69.

40 'Non faceva, nascendo, ancor paura/la figlia al padre, ché 'l tempo e la dote/ non fuggien quinci e quindi la misura', in Dante Alighieri, *La Divina Commedia*, ed. by Giorgio Petrocchi (Turin: Einaudi, 1975), p. 339.

could lead the woman's family to compromise their economic stability by committing to pay sums too high for their means].[41] Conversely, having only sons meant that the family 'fortune was safe from devastating daughters whose need for dowries might compel withdrawal from capital', as argued by Frederic Lane when describing the Venetian Barbarigo family.[42]

Some towns responded to this increase in the value of dowries by establishing strict limits by law. For example, in Venice (in 1420) women could have at most a dowry of sixteen hundred *ducati*;[43] in Rome (in 1400) a dowry of eight hundred *fiorini* plus a trousseau worth six hundred *fiorini* was allowed; in Foligno (in 1589) twelve hundred scudi were the maximum permitted dowry in the town itself and two hundred in the countryside.[44] The amount of a dowry was also framed by local custom. In the Kingdom of Naples, for example, dowries could be created on the basis of the 'uso di Proceri e Magnati'. This custom was only in force among the 'Proceri' and 'Magnati', namely the ancient nobility who exercised jurisdictional powers within their fiefs.[45] Alongside this custom there was the 'Patto di Capuana e Nido',[46] a pact which could be signed at the time of the

41 Casanova, *La famiglia italiana*, p. 90.

42 Frederic C. Lane, *Andrea Barbarigo: Merchant of Venice, 1418–1449* (Baltimore, MD: Johns Hopkins University Press, 1944), p. 39. On dowries in Venice, see Stanley Chojnacki, 'Dowries and Kinsmen in Early Renaissance Venice', *The Journal of Interdisciplinary History*, 5 (1975), 571–600 (pp. 571–72). On dowries in Florence, see Lauro Martines, *The Social World of the Florentine Humanists, 1390–1460* (London: Routledge and Kegan Paul, 1963), pp. 37–38, 200; Virginia Cox, 'The Single Self: Feminist Thought and the Marriage Market in Early-Modern Venice', *Renaissance Quarterly*, 48 (1995), 513–81; Alberto Tenenti, *L'Italia del Quattrocento. Economia e società* (Rome: Laterza, 1996), pp. 123–24.

43 Stanley Chojnacki, *Women and Men in Renaissance Venice* (Baltimore, MD: Johns Hopkins University Press, 2000), pp. 56–57.

44 Pertile, *Storia del diritto italiano*, p. 322. For a study of the size of dowries among the Neapolitan nobles, see Maria Antonietta Visceglia, 'Linee per uno studio unitario dei testamenti e dei contratti matrimoniali dell'aristocrazia feudale napoletana tra fine Quattrocento e Settecento', *Mélanges de l'Ecole française de Rome. Moyen-Âge, Temps modernes*, 95 (1983), 393–470 (esp. pp. 447–59).

45 Visceglia, 'Linee per uno studio unitario', p. 459.

46 The origin of the Pact of Capuana and Nido is unknown. At the beginning of the fourteenth century King Charles II of Naples (1248–1309) ordered the collection of customs from Naples and confirmed the use of the principle *paterna paternis, materna maternis* to settle an inheritance. King Ferdinand the Catholic (1452–1516) then formally allowed for the possibility of entering into the 'patto di

marriage agreement and which was also available to non-nobles and to those not belonging to the 'sedili' of Capuana or Nido.[47]

After this period in which the value of dowries increased, their amount became more restrained and once again became equal to, or even lower than, the legitime. However, as establishing a dowry implied a great financial commitment, during the fifteenth century various Monti delle Doti or Monti di Maritaggi were created, either among families or at the municipal level. These Monti were a sort of *tontina* aimed at providing dowries for subscribers' female relatives, thus allowing for a delay in a family's economic effort.[48] Moreover, some families consigned female members to convent life as a way to avoid spending a large part of the family's patrimony on a dowry. Even though nunneries also required a dowry (also called 'elemosina'), it was much smaller than that required for a marriage.[49]

Capuana e Nido' (Anon., *Del patto di Capuana e Nido, e de' suoi effetti. Dissertazione* (Naples: Trani, 1823), pp. 42–50).

47 The Sedili, or Seggi or Piazze, were administrative institutions of the Kingdom of Naples, formed by families of high standing. They were named after the area to which they pertained and had different prerogatives. See Camillo Tutini, *Dell'origine e fundazione de' seggi di Napoli, del tempo in che furono istituiti* (Naples: Gessari, 1754); Alfonso Di Letizia, *Degli usi de' proceri, e magnati e di Capuana, e Nido* (Naples: Perger, 1786); Cesare Marini, *Lezioni di dritto civile novissimo,* 4 vols (Naples: Osservatore medico, 1830–32), I (1830), 390–91; Nicola Del Forno, *La storia civile del Regno di Napoli in compendio* (Naples: De Dominicis, 1841), p. 85; Visceglia, 'Linee per uno studio unitario', esp. pp. 459–70.

48 *Tontines* are investment plans by which several subscribers pay an agreed sum into a fund and receive an annuity which increases as members die. See Flavia Luise, 'Famiglia e società a Solofra tra il 1640 e il 1676 nei capitoli matrimoniali e nei testamenti', *Mélanges de l'Ecole française de Rome. Moyen-Age–Temps modernes,* 95 (1983), 299–338 (pp. 316–20); Gérard Delille, 'Un esempio di assistenza privata: i monti di maritaggio del Regno di Napoli (secoli XVI–XVIII)', in *Timore e carità. I poveri nell'Italia moderna,* ed. by Giorgio Politi, Maria Rosa and Franco Della Peruta (Cremona: Libreria del Convegno, 1982), pp. 227–81; Anthony Molho, *Marriage Alliance in Late Medieval Florence* (Cambridge, MA: Harvard University Press, 1994), pp. 27–179; Isabelle Chabot and Massimo Fornasari, *L'economia della carità. Le doti del Monte di pietà di Bologna (secoli XVI–XX)* (Bologna: Il Mulino, 1997).

49 On this point see Vismara, *L'unità della famiglia nella storia del diritto in Italia,* pp. 259–61; Ungari, *Storia del diritto di famiglia,* p. 57. De Luca explains also that 'la regola, la quale così dispone, in maniera che se la figlia d'un Principe, ovvero di un signore grande, alla quale, volendosi maritare convenisse una dote di cento, e più mila scudi, elegga di farsi monaca, in tal caso a sua dote congrua, e di paraggio, sarà quella ch'è solita darsi al Monastero, ancorché fosse di scudi mille, e meno' [the rule dictates that if the daughter of a Prince, or of a great gentleman, who would be given a dowry of a hundred, even a thousand scudi, if wanting to

Nevertheless, in the eighteenth century sending women to a nunnery without a true vocation was regarded with some criticism; the man of letters Ludovico Antonio Muratori comments on this point that:

> molte Nobili ma povere Zittelle, le quali o non v'è maniera di maritarle, o altro ripiego non v'ha per isgravarne la Casa, [sono confinate] in un Monistero, dove son fortunate, se con vera vocazione rinunziano al Mondo: infelici, se il contrario.[50]

> [many noble but poor spinsters who either have no way of getting married, or have no other way of relieving the financial burden on their homes [are confined] to a Nunnery, where they are lucky if they renounce the world with a true vocation, but unhappy if the opposite is true.]

The expression 'isgravarne la Casa' used by Muratori clearly underlines the problem with dowering a daughter: a dowry was a significant financial commitment; and a family, if not wealthy enough, had to look for solutions to maintain its economic strength without threatening its honour. However, if the case of Arcangela Tarabotti provides us with a clear depiction of a forced monachisation,[51] it

---

marry, should decide to become a nun, her appropriate and similar dowry will be the one that is usually given to the Nunnery, which could be a thousand scudi or less] (De Luca, *Il dottor volgare*, III, 111).

50 Ludovico Antonio Muratori, *Della pubblica felicità, oggetto de' buoni principi* (Lucca: [n. pub.], 1749), p. 279. On nunneries, see also Gabriella Zarri, 'Monasteri femminili e città (secoli XV–XVIII)', in *Storia d'Italia. Annali 9. La Chiesa e il potere politico dal Medioevo all'età contemporanea*, ed. by Giorgio Chittolini and Giovanni Miccoli (Turin: Einaudi, 1986), pp. 357–429 (esp. pp. 420–29); Gabriella Zarri, *Recinti. Donne, clausura e matrimonio nella prima età moderna* (Bologna: Il Mulino, 2000), pp. 203–49. See also Katherine J. P. Lowe, *Nuns' Chronicles and Convent Culture in Renaissance and Counter-Reformation Italy* (Cambridge: Cambridge University Press, 2003). On forced monachisation see also Giuliano Marchetto, 'Il volto terribile del padre. "Metus reverentialis" e matrimonio nell'opera di Tomás Sánchez', in *I tribunali del matrimonio*, ed. by Seidel Menchi and Quaglioni, pp. 269–88; Anne Jacobson Schutte, *By Force and Fear: Taking and Breaking Monastic Vows in Early Modern Europe* (Ithaca, NY: Cornell University Press, 2011); Anne Jacobson Schutte, 'Genitori, figli e monacazione forzata: norme ecclesiastiche versus patria potestà (secc. XVII–XVIII)', in *Famiglia e religione in Europa nell'età moderna. Studi in onore di Silvana Seidel Menchi*, ed. by Giovanni Ciappelli, Serena Luzzi and Massimo Rospocher (Rome: Edizioni di Storia e Letteratura, 2011), pp. 147–59.

51 See Arcangela Tarabotti, *L'Inferno monacale di Arcangela Tarabotti*, ed. by Francesca Medioli (Turin: Rosenberg and Sellier, 1990); Jutta Gisela Sperling, *Convents and the Body Politic in Late Renaissance Venice* (Chicago, IL: University of Chicago Press, 1999), pp. 31–36.

should be pointed out that nuns did not always view their convents as prisons. Gabriella Zarri, in particular, observes that nunneries were often 'una estensione della famiglia patriarcale, un contenitore per l'eccedenza demografica, ma anche un solido centro di potere e di possibilità di autorealizzazione per le donne, [un] luogo privilegiato per affermare e accrescere l'onore della famiglia' [an extension of the patriarchal family, a place to store the demographic surplus, but also a solid centre of power and of potential self-fulfillment for women, a privileged place in which to affirm and increase the honour of the family].[52] From a formal point of view, the institution of the dowry did not undergo any substantial changes for centuries. The new role of educator assigned to women in the eighteenth century did not by any means lead to a corresponding improvement in their legal status.

In force since the Middle Ages, the *ius commune*, together with customary law and municipal statutes, remained basically unchanged until the Enlightenment, when some states of the Italian Peninsula issued their *Costituzioni*.[53] The establishment of these acts was part of a broader process driven by the need to create a coherent legal and jurisprudential framework: from the sixteenth century onwards several collections of the *communes opiniones doctorum* (the opinions of leading jurists),[54] court decisions and legal acts were published.[55] With regard to the law, the enactment of the *Leggi e costituzioni di S. M. il Re di Sardegna* in 1723 was a first attempt to organise the legal framework systematically. Another, similar act was produced in the Duchy of Modena, namely the *Codice Estense* of 1771.[56] Despite aiming progressively to repeal all the existing sources of law, it was still possible to use the *ius commune*.[57] These were mainly collections

52 Gabriella Zarri, 'Presentazione', in Arcangela Tarabotti, *Lettere familiari e di complimento*, ed. by Meredith Kennedy Ray and Lynn Lara Westwater (Turin: Rosenberg and Sellier, 2005), pp. 7–17 (pp. 9–11).

53 See also Ungari, *Storia del diritto di famiglia*, pp. 39–40.

54 On the *communis opinio doctorum*, see Antonio Padoa-Schioppa, *A History of Law in Europe: From the Early Middle Ages to the Twentieth Century* (Cambridge: Cambridge University Press, 2017), pp. 297–99.

55 On this point see Adriano Cavanna, *Storia del diritto moderno in Europa*, 2 vols (Milan: Giuffrè, 1979), I, 258–69.

56 An overview can be found in Cavanna, *Storia del diritto moderno in Europa*, I, 278–92.

57 Cavanna, *Storia del diritto moderno in Europa*, I, 278–82, 287–93.

of acts already in force to which very few additions were made and did not introduce any improvement to women's circumstances.[58]

The French Revolution: The Jacobin Constitutions and the Napoleonic Code

The eighteenth-century French conquests led to the founding of the Sister Republics.[59] At first, the decrees issued by the French revolutionaries were enforced in these territories. Then each republic began to elaborate its own *Costituzione*. During the period from 1789 to 1795 the legislation which emerged from the French Revolution was driven by a bourgeois, secular conception of the family and the state. This resulted in canon law, for example, being replaced by a secular law on marriage.[60] Other than abolishing *fideicommissa* and the feudal hierarchy of persons, these laws considered women

58 The sole source of law which granted equal rights to every individual was the Statute of San Leucio, promulgated by the Bourbon King Ferdinand IV in 1789 and limited to the silk weavers' colony of San Leucio, a village 30 km from Naples. The Statute given by the King provided equal inheritance rights for males and females, the dowry was abolished and the making of wills was forbidden (Victor Marcadé, *Spiegazione teorico-pratica del Codice Napoleone contenente l'analisi critica degli autori e della giurisprudenza*, 5 vols (Naples: Marghieri, Giachetti, 1874), v, 94; Carlo Nardi, 'Una legislazione egualitaria d'un re assolutista: il codice della colonia di S. Leucio', *L'Eloquenza*, 49 (1959), 96–111; Giulio Vismara, *Il diritto di famiglia in Italia dalle riforme ai codici. Appunti* (Milan: Giuffrè, 1978), p. 8; Ungari, *Storia del diritto di famiglia*, pp. 61–62; *L'utopia di Carolina. Il Codice delle leggi leuciane*, ed. by Nadia Verdile (Naples: La stamperia digitale, 2007); Nadia Verdile, 'Tra leggi illuminate e lettere private: il 1789 di Maria Carolina d'Asburgo', *Archivio per la Storia delle Donne*, 5 (2008), 71–106).

59 The Sister of Jacobins Republics were founded as a result of French conquests in various areas of Europe. In the Italian Peninsula several republics were also founded. The largest ones were the Cisalpine, the Cispadane, the Roman and the Parthenopean Republics. See Melchiorre Roberti, *Milano capitale napoleonica: la formazione di uno stato moderno, 1796–1814* (Milan: Fondazione Treccani, 1946); Carlo Ghisalberti, *Le costituzioni giacobine (1796–1799)* (Milan: Giuffrè, 1973); Carlo Ghisalberti, *Dall'antico regime al 1848. Le origini costituzionali dell'Italia moderna* (Rome: Laterza, 1974), pp. 61–85; Stuart J. Woolf, *Napoleon's Integration of Europe* (London: Routledge, 1991); Carlo Ghisalberti, *Istituzioni e società civile nell'età del Risorgimento* (Rome and Bari: Laterza, 2005), pp. 16–41; Mauro Lenci, 'The Battle over "Democracy" in Italian Political Thought during the Revolutionary *Triennio*, 1796–1799', in *The Political Culture of the Sister Republics, 1794–1806*, ed. by Joris Oddens, Erik Jacobs and Mart Rutjes (Amsterdam: Amsterdam University Press, 2015), pp. 97–106.

60 Vismara, *Il diritto di famiglia*, p. 25.

and later-born sons as individuals with equal rights to inherit from their parents. With the Thermidorian Reaction, and later with the enactment of the Napoleonic Code, many principles which had inspired the Revolution were put aside.[61] The French Code, applied in the Italian Peninsula under the name of *Codice Civile di Napoleone il Grande pel Regno d'Italia*, reintroduced some peculiarities of the Ancien Régime's legal framework, such as the punishment of adultery or the requirement to obtain parental consent for a marriage.[62]

Although scholars consider the family-law provisions of the Napoleonic Code reactionary in comparison to the Constitutions of the Sister Republics of Italy and to what the Revolutionaries had envisioned, to the Italian Peninsula this code 'appariva l'immagine stessa della rivoluzione [e] uno *standard* giuridico che ancora per molti decenni si presenterà come una meta' [appeared to be the very image of the Revolution and a legal standard which would for many decades continue to present itself as a goal [to which to aspire]].[63] The chance given to all children to inherit from their parents, regardless of their sex,[64] was a disruptive novelty for the

61 The law promulgated in the areas conquered by the French was called *droit intermédiaire*, which refers to those laws enacted between 1789 and 1804, namely from the time the Assemblée Nationale proclaimed itself the Assemblée Nationale Constituante (9 July 1789) up to the promulgation of the Napoleonic Code (21 March 1804). It is called *intermédiaire* to evoke the idea of a transition period between the Ancien Régime and the Napoleonic Code. The French legal historian Eric de Mari argues that the term *intermédiaire* did not reflect the disruptive context in which the *droit* was promulgated. He instead suggests that *révolutionnaire* would be more appropriate (Eric de Mari, 'Le Droit intermédiaire. Posture juridique, imposture politique et vacuité d'une convention', *La Révolution française, Rupture(s) en Révolution*, 5 (2011) <http://lrf.revues.org/340> [accessed 22 September 2020]). However, it should be noted that, on 12 June 1795, Decree 21 prairial year III abolished the word *révolutionnaire* (John Hardman, *The French Revolution: The Fall of the Ancien Régime to the Thermidorian Reaction, 1785–1795* (London: Arnold, 1981), pp. 220–21). On the reactionary shift of the French Revolution see also Noah C. Shusterman, *The French Revolution: Faith, Desire, and Politics* (London: Routledge, 2014); Ian Davidson, *The French Revolution: From Enlightenment to Tyranny* (London: Profile Books, 2016).

62 Vismara, *Il diritto di famiglia*, pp. 32–39. See also Ghisalberti, *Istituzioni e società civile*, pp. 42–59.

63 Ungari, *Storia del diritto di famiglia*, pp. 104, 93–124; Ghisalberti, *Istituzioni e società civile*, pp. 25–51. For a discussion on the reactionary nature of the Napoleonic Code see Jean-Louis Halpérin, *L'Impossible Code Civil* (Paris: Presses universitaires de France, 1992), pp. 276–77. See also James Gordley, 'Myths of the French Civil Code', *The American Journal of Comparative Law*, 42 (1994), 459–505.

64 Art. 745, in *Codice Civile del Regno d'Italia* (1845), p. 43.

nineteenth-century legal system.[65] Marriage became a pact between individuals and susceptible, therefore, to divorce. Even though it reconfirmed the primacy of men over women and enforced marital authorisation as a legal requirement for any act of a wife's public life, the Napoleonic code was not welcomed in the Italian Peninsula. In fact, the French Emperor challenged a centuries-long equilibrium founded on the consolidation of a family's fortune in its entirety through *fideicommissa* and majorats, on strong land immobilisation and on a rigidly patriarchal and authoritarian family structure, one implemented through the management of marriage, celibacy and spinsterhood.[66] By proclaiming that all heirs were to be treated equally,[67] the Napoleonic Code threatened the *familia* of the Ancien Régime, a body which 'accipitur in iure pro substantia' and *accipitur* in society for the role and the prestige it possessed and represented.[68]

Along with the Code's disruptive and unpopular regulations, the most significant legacy of the Napoleonic conquests was codification. During the Ancien Régime, jurists, judges and other scholars helped to shape the law with their *interpretatio,* in addition to the several sources which collaborated in the formation of the legal framework.[69] With codification, on the contrary, the legislative power assumed

65 Vismara, *Il diritto di famiglia,* pp. 47–52; Ungari, *Storia del diritto di famiglia,* pp. 93–124.

66 Alberto M. Banti, 'I proprietari terrieri nell'Italia centro-settentrionale', in *Storia dell'agricoltura italiana,* ed. by Bevilacqua, III, 45–103.

67 As Halpérin points out, despite being considered egalitarian, 'il y a dans le Code civil des personnes *plus égales* que d'autres: les maris par rapport aux femmes' [in the Civil Code there are some people who are *more equal* than others: husbands versus wives] (Halpérin, *L'Impossible Code Civil,* p. 276).

68 See also Vismara, *Il diritto di famiglia,* p. 46.

69 The assumption that laws did not cover every aspect of life meant they had to be interpreted. From ancient Roman jurisconsults to medieval glossators to modern jurists, laws have been interpreted, clarified and explained. For further discussion, see Emilio Betti, *Teoria generale della interpretazione,* 2 vols (Milan: Giuffrè, 1955), II, 789–866; Victor Crescenzi, 'Problemi dell'interpretatio nel diritto comune classico', in *El Dret Comù i Catalunya: Actes del II Simposi Internacional, Barcelona, 31 maig 1 juny del 1991,* ed. by Aquilino Iglesia Ferreiròs (Barcelona: [n. pub.], 1992), pp. 167–206; Michael Stolleis, 'Judicial Interpretation in Transition from the *Ancien Régime* to Constitutionalism', in *Interpretation of Law in the Age of Enlightenment: From the Rule of the King to the Rule of Law,* ed. by Yasutomo Morigiwa, Michael Stolleis and Jean Louis Halpérin (Dordrecht: Springer, 2011), pp. 3–17.

the exclusive right to make laws[70] and henceforth the state became the only existing authority; the legal privileges of particular groups were no longer recognised;[71] and the feudal legacy of 'soggezione di persona a persona' [subjugation of one person by another] was abolished.[72] Mario Enrico Viora argues that laws before the enactment of the Napoleonic Code were qualified as 'consolidazioni' rather than codes, namely compilations and collections of various decrees and acts already in force.[73] A code, by contrast, is an autonomous source of law.[74] Applied to almost the entire Italian Peninsula (albeit formally under different governments), Napoleon's Code – which is considered the first code of law in the modern era – was therefore the sole law and excluded any resort to other sources. It was complete, exhaustive and served as a regulatory framework for the development of codes in the nineteenth century.

Women and the Law during the Restoration

With Napoleon's defeat and the Congress of Vienna, the deposed monarchs were restored to power in their own states. The *Codice Civile pel Regno d'Italia* was repealed and the previous legal system was reinstated with the exception of some norms which simplified matters relating to private contracts or mortgages.[75] As Paolo Ungari writes with regard to family law, the Restoration resulted in a 'vera e propria

70 Paolo Grossi, 'Assolutismo giuridico e diritto privato nel secolo XIX', *Rivista di storia del diritto italiano,* 64 (1991), 5–17 (pp. 6–7); *The Rule of Law: History, Theory and Criticism,* ed. by Pietro Costa and Danilo Zolo (Dordrecht: Springer, 2007), p. 325.

71 Banti, 'I proprietari terrieri nell'Italia centro-settentrionale', p. 47.

72 *Raccolta degli atti del governo di S. M. il Re di Sardegna dall'anno 1814 a tutto il 1832,* 22 vols (Turin: Pignetti and Carena, 1842), VI, 389.

73 For a further discussion of the term 'consolidations', see Mario E. Viora, *Consolidazioni e codificazioni. Contributo alla storia della codificazione* (Turin: Giappichelli, 1967); Natalino Irti and Francesco Santoro-Passarelli, 'Consolidazioni e codificazioni delle leggi civili', *Atti dei Convegni Lincei,* 106 (1994), 245–52 (pp. 245–47). A different point of view is expressed by Ugo Petronio, 'Una categoria storiografica da rivedere', *Quaderni fiorentini per la storia del pensiero giuridico moderno,* 13 (1984), 705–17.

74 On this point see Giuseppe Galasso, 'Il contesto storico: l'età del *Codice*', *Atti dei Convegni Lincei,* 221 (2006), 9–18; Paolo Grossi, '*Code Civil*: una fonte nuovissima per la nuova civiltà giuridica', *Atti dei Convegni Lincei,* 221 (2006), 19–42.

75 An overview of this point is found in Soresina, *L'età della Restaurazione,* pp. 25–51.

reazione politico-morale inflessibile' [genuine and appropriate, unyielding moral and political reaction].[76] Reverting to the previous legal system meant that a subsidiary recourse to Roman law, customary law and municipal statutes for topics not covered in the acts issued by monarchs was again possible and canon law was still complementary to the *iura propria* of the pre-Unification Italian states.[77] The Restoration reconfirmed the Catholic Church's jurisdiction on non-patrimonial matters related to marriage, such as its dissolution. Marriage was, in fact, regulated by the formalities prescribed by the Catholic Church; ecclesiastical jurisdiction and canonical impediments were brought back into force and often rules from canon law were integrated by stricter prescriptions by the state.[78] With regard to marriage, for example, parental consent was not needed according to canon law. In the Duchy of Modena, however, it was formally required by the *Codice Estense* and people marrying without this approval were put under sanctions. This had the following implications:

> per porre qualche ritegno ai disordini, agl'inconvenienti, e alle dissensioni, che producono nelle famiglie i matrimonii, che si contraggono da' figli senza saputa, o consenso de' loro padri [gli alimenti che gli ascendenti dovranno prestare saranno] i frutti della metà della legittima da calcolarsi di tempo in tempo su le forze del loro patrimonio, nella quale metà sola della legittima sarà in arbitrio degli stessi ascendenti d'istituirlo, privandoli di tutto il resto della loro successione.[79]
>
> [to put some restraint on the disorders, inconveniences and dissensions which arise in families due to marriages contracted by

76 Ungari, *Storia del diritto di famiglia,* p. 125.

77 For a discussion of the Napoleonic Code and law in pre-Unification Italian states, see Guido Astuti, 'Il Code Napoléon in Italia e la sua influenza sui codici degli stati italiani successori', *Accademia nazionale dei Lincei,* 179 (1973), 176–237; Stefano Solimano, 'L'edificazione del diritto privato italiano: dalla Restaurazione all'Unità', *forum historiae iuris* <http://www.forhistiur.de/2005-05-solimano/> [accessed 6 December 2020]. On the use of canon law see also Paolo Grossi, *A History of European Law* (Chichester: Wiley-Blackwell, 2010), pp. 31–32.

78 Marriage was to be celebrated according to the formalities enshrined by the Catholic Church. This provision was included in the *Codice per gli Stati di Parma, Piacenza e Guastalla* (Art. 34), the *Codice Estensi* (Art. 74), the Civil Code of the Kingdom of Sardinia (Art. 108) and the *Codice per lo Regno delle Due Sicilie* (Art. 67). For further discussion on this point see Passaniti, *Diritto di famiglia,* pp. 163–203. On marriage and canon law see Jean Gaudemet, *Sociétés et marriage* (Strasbourg: Cerdic, 1980); Gaudemet, *Le Mariage en Occident.*

79 Art. I Tit. XIII, in *Codice Estense,* p. 809.

> children without their families knowing, or without the consent of their parents, [the allowance that the parents will have to provide] [to the couple] will be the proceeds from half of the lawful inheritance to be calculated from time to time on the strengths of their assets; it will be at the discretion of the parents to award this half of the lawful inheritance to their child, depriving them of the rest of their inheritance.]

This behaviour could be interpreted as a way of complementing paternal authority: as Marco Cavina points out, while 'i sommovimenti sociali e bellici scompaginavano l'ordine domestico[,] il Duca [si faceva] carico dei compiti paterni mal praticati, indossando le vesti di padre supplente' [social and wartime upheavals disrupted the domestic order, the Duke [took] charge of paternal duties which were not properly carried out, taking on the role of a substitute father].[80] The wives and any resulting children from marriages contracted without parental consent were not entitled to any alimony or assets from inheritance.[81] These rules were made with the intention of limiting marriages between people belonging to different social classes. Nevertheless, as we see in Chapter 4, a marriage – being a lifelong bond sanctified by God – was considered indissoluble and valid even if contracted without the parents' consent.

Whereas jurisdiction on personal matters related to marriage was handled by the Church, acts undertaken by the restored monarchs and related to family law had the main purpose of maintaining the 'pietrificazione della società italiana e [l']irrigidimento programmatico delle sue frontiere di classe' [petrification of Italian society and the systematic tightening of its class boundaries].[82] Secular laws were driven by an agnatic conception of the family, which gave preference to the descendants of the male line. Soon after the Congress of Vienna an edict issued in the Kingdom of Sardinia on 18 November 1817 enabled the introduction of *fideicommissa* and majorats, which had been abolished with the *Regio Editto* on 29 July 1797.[83] These two institutions were considered particularly important for the wealth of both the state and of the families themselves. As stated in the *Codice Estense*, for example, their objective was 'la conservazione, e il sostegno delle principali famiglie degli Stati' [the conservation and

80 Cavina, *Il padre spodestato*, pp. 153–54.

81 Art. II Tit. XIII, in *Codice Estense*, p. 809.

82 Ungari, *Storia del diritto di famiglia*, p. 125.

83 *Raccolta degli atti del governo di S. M. il Re di Sardegna dall'anno 1814 a tutto il 1832*, 22 vols (Turin: Pignetti and Carena, 1842), VI, 388–91.

support of the most prominent families of the States].[84] The Pope's *Regolamento Legislativo e Giudiziario per gli affari civili* also allowed majorats.[85] Despite rulers being eager to reintroduce these institutions, probably driven by the desire to meet the elite's expectations, jurists and theorists had not been favourably inclined towards them well before the winds of revolution started blowing. In particular, in 1742 Ludovico Antonio Muratori claimed that: 'chiamo io superbia quella di una creatura [...] che voglia far da padrone [...] non solamente allorché spira l'ultimo fiato, ma per moltissimi anni anche dopo la morte sua' [I call it pride when a creature [...] wants to be the master [...] not only up to his last breath, but also for many years after his death].[86] The critique against institutions such as *fideicommissa* could be explained by the fact that, other than favouring only one member of a family and neglecting all others, they also limited any possibility of dividing goods and using them freely and more efficiently.

In addition to these acts, immediately after the Restoration the monarchs of the Italian Peninsula started developing new legal codes. The ideals of the Enlightenment and the French Revolution, along with nearly twenty years of rule, had introduced institutional and juridical innovations which were settled into people's minds and could no longer be anachronistically deleted; however, they could possibly be adapted to the new order.[87] As previously mentioned, while many legal institutions, such as those of commercial law, were maintained as they were in the Napoleonic Code, in terms of family law it was, *tout court*, a return to the past. The repeal of the Napoleonic Code and the return to the previous legal system implied the reintroduction of the separation of property between spouses.

84 Art. I Tit. XXXIII, in *Codice Estense*, p. 828. The Code of the Duchy of Modena from 1851 also allowed majorats. See Art. 864–881, in *Codice Civile per gli Stati Estensi* (Modena: Eredi Tipografi Reali, 1851), pp. 184–88.

85 Art. 38, in *Regolamento Legislativo e Giudiziario per gli affari civili*, in *Collezione completa*, pp. 871–94 (p. 877).

86 Ludovico Antonio Muratori, *Dei difetti della giurisprudenza* (Venice: Pasquali, 1742), p. 146; see also the opinion of Giovanni Battista De Luca (Piccialuti, *L'immortalità dei beni*, pp. 90–107).

87 See, e.g., Cosimo Semeraro, *Restaurazione. Chiesa e società. La 'seconda ricupera' e la rinascita degli ordini religiosi nello Stato pontificio (Marche e Legazioni 1815–1823)* (Rome: LAS, 1982), p. 49; Alberto Aquarone, 'La restaurazione nello Stato Pontificio e i suoi indirizzi legislativi', *Archivio della Società romana di storia patria*, 78 (1955), 119–88 (pp. 152–60); Gabriella Santoncini, *Sovranità e giustizia nella Restaurazione pontificia. La riforma della organizzazione della giustizia criminale nei lavori preparatori del Motu Proprio del 1816* (Turin: Giappichelli, 1996), pp. 5–20.

There were a few exceptions to this rule, as for example on the island of Sardinia, where a marriage custom to celebrate weddings known as *a sa sardisca* existed. In contrast with other parts of the Italian Peninsula, according to this custom goods acquired by spouses were part of a property in common between them.[88]

The return to the law in force during the Ancien Régime also meant that, in most states of the Italian Peninsula, daughters were again excluded *propter dotem* [because of the dowry] from inheriting and sometimes did not even have the right to obtain an amount equal to the *portio legitima*. In varying manners and degrees, families from all social classes established dowries for their daughters, even during the Napoleonic period. Their provision was considered to be essential for their 'collocamento', literally their 'placement'. Given that women were able to inherit from their parents, the dowry was just meant to be an advance on their inheritance, but, as we see in more detail in Chapter 5, in practice this norm was overridden by acts that the women signed to renounce further rights.

Marriage was a matter of public and private interest. Having a dowry enabled a woman to join society as a subject worthy of respect. Not having a dowry was considered a dreadful situation across all social classes, to the extent that charities provided dowries for poor but deserving girls.[89] In nineteenth-century jurisprudence,

88 The custom of celebrating the *a sa sardisca* weddings was preserved until 1865. It was mainly carried out by the lower classes and included the common property of all the goods of the spouses, or just the common property acquired after marriage. For a broader discussion on *a sa sardisca* weddings, see Melchiorre Roberti, 'Per la storia dei rapporti patrimoniali fra coniugi', *Archivio Storico Sardo*, 1 (1908/1909), 273–92; Ennio Cortese, *Appunti di storia giuridica sarda* (Milan: Giuffrè, 1964); Giulio Vismara, 'Momenti di storia della famiglia sarda', *Studi sassaresi* (1971), 181–203; Antonio Marongiu, *Saggi di storia giuridica e politica sarda* (Padua: CEDAM, 1975); Antonio Marongiu, 'Il matrimonio "alla sardesca"', *Archivio Storico Sardo di Sassari*, 7 (1981), 85–93; Maria Margherita Satta, 'Struttura familiare e modelli di trasmissione dell'eredità', in Anna Maria Cecaro and others, *Donne e società in Sardegna: eredità e mutamento. Materiali e strumenti di ricerca* (Sassari: Iniziative culturali, 1989), pp. 59–78 (pp. 67–72); Loredana Garlati, 'La famiglia tra passato e presente', in *Diritto della famiglia*, ed. by Salvatore Patti and Maria Giovanna Cubeddu (Milan: Giuffrè, 2011), pp. 1–48 (p. 10). The regime of common property of goods was also used in other areas of the Italian Peninsula, such as Sicily. On this island, this custom was called *more Latinorum* (Ungari, *Storia del diritto di famiglia*, pp. 70–71).

89 See, e.g., Art. XVIII, in *Costituzioni di Modena*, in which these institutions aimed at giving a dowry to poor girls are mentioned (in *Collezione completa*, 787–870 (p. 798)); and the Archivio della Biblioteca Federiciana (Fano), 1846,

the term 'collocamento' occurred frequently. The 'collocamento' of a woman was fundamental to her family and a safeguard for society. Reaching a 'collocamento onesto e decente' [an honest and decent placement] was an undertaking which would bring prestige to the family, as well as being a real economic deal. As explained in a judicial proceeding from 1855, 'onestà' [honesty] in a juridical sense meant honour, dignity and comfort: a 'collocamento onesto' was one which had these characteristics.[90] The 'collocamento' was important among all social classes and often women who worked saved their money to establish a dowry for themselves. The establishment of a dowry made a woman attractive on the marriage market and, at the same time, allowed her to keep safe the goods that were part of the dowry, given that a dowry could not be freely

---

Documenti vari, where documents show that many dowries were drawn to celebrate the election to the papacy of Pope Pius IX in that year. See also David I. Kertzer and Wendy Sigle, 'The Marriage of Female Foundlings in Nineteenth-Century Italy', *Continuity and Change,* 13 (1998), 201–20. In some cases, state lotteries were aimed at providing dowries (Maria Chiara Marcucci, 'Le "zitelle" e il gioco del lotto a Fano (1857–1860)', *Nuovi Studi Fanesi,* 10 (1995), 169–94. Dowries were sometimes established from the legacies of noblewomen. See *Ragnatele di rapporti. Patronage e reti di relazione nella storia delle donne,* ed. by Lucia Ferrante, Maura Palazzi and Gianna Pomata (Turin: Rosenberg and Sellier, 1988), in particular the chapters by Lucia Ferrante, 'Patronesse e patroni in un'istituzione assistenziale femminile (Bologna sec. XVII)' (pp. 59–79); Angela Groppi, 'Una gestione collettiva di equilibri emozionali e materiali. La reclusione delle donne nella Roma dell'Ottocento' (pp. 130–47, esp. pp. 134–38); Laura Guidi, 'La "passione governata dalla virtù": benefattrici nella Napoli ottocentesca' (pp. 148–65); Marina D'Amelia, 'La conquista di una dote. Regole del gioco e scambi femminili alla Confraternita dell'Annunziata (secc. XVII–XVIII)' (pp. 305–43); and Ida Fazio, 'La Signora dell'Oro. Carità femminile, potere e controllo sociale in una comunità siciliana tra Sette e Ottocento' (pp. 80–98). Despite its importance, a dowry was not a precondition for a woman to contract a valid marriage. In this regard, the Decretum of Gratian (1075/80–1145/47) states: '[N]ullum sine dote fiat coniugium' [Let there be no marriage without a dowry]. However, since the Middle Ages jurists and glossators have pointed out that the consent of the two spouses was the only condition required for a valid marriage. On marriage without dowry, see also Bellomo, *Ricerche sui rapporti patrimoniali,* p. 67; Bellomo, 'Dote', p. 10; Sara McDougall, 'Women and Gender in Canon Law', in *The Oxford Handbook of Women and Gender in Medieval Europe,* ed. by Judith M. Bennett and Ruth Mazo Karras (Oxford; New York: OUP, 2013), pp. 163–80 (esp. pp. 166–67).

90 See *Giornale del Foro ossia Raccolta di regiudicate romane e straniere,* 1 (1855), p. 89. See also Béat Philippe Vicat, *Vocabularium juris utriusque,* 3 vols ([n.p.]: Ex officina Bousquetiana, 1759), II, 94. Here the term *honestum* stands for 'decorum, conveniens honorique congruum est'.

spent – either by their husbands or by the women themselves – without the authorisation of a judge.[91]

The return to the previous legal system and the new acts issued after the Restoration returned the Italian Peninsula to the fragmented legal scenario of the past. In the Papal States for example, with the return of Pope Pius VII to his throne women were again excluded from inheritance because of the dowry. The Pope issued his first *motu proprio* on 16 July 1816: he explicitly affirmed that a dowry was to be equal to the legitime.[92] The following *motu proprio*, that of 1824, states that a dowry was simply to be 'congrua' [appropriate] and 'la misura della congruità si determina avuto riguardo alla condizione della famiglia, alle forze del di lei patrimonio, all'uso vigente nella medesima, ed alla consuetudine osservata nel luogo dalle altre famiglie di eguale condizione' [the appropriate amount is determined by taking into account the status of the family, the strengths of its patrimony, the customs in force in the same family and the customs in force among other families of equal condition in the same place].[93] Hence, the dowry went from being equal to the legitime to just having a legal requirement to be appropriate, something which was difficult to define precisely as the term 'appropriate' included a broad range of qualities. The *motu proprio* issued in 1827 and the *Regolamento legislativo e giudiziario* of 1834 iterated this principle.[94]

The measure of 'appropriateness' can be inferred from a case from 1852 in which a woman called Umbellina Livi entered into a legal dispute against her brothers.[95] In 1831 their father Francesco Livi

91 On this point, see Ida Fazio, 'Valori economici e valori simbolici. Il declino della dote nell'Italia dell'Ottocento', *Quaderni storici*, 78 (1992), 291–317.

92 The law enacted in the nineteenth century did not describe how the legitime was calculated. As we have seen, Roman law was used for topics not covered by these codifications. According to Novel 18, 1 of the *Novellae Constitutiones*, enacted by Justinian from 534 until his death in 565, the *legitima portio*, or portion of estate which could not be bequeathed by will, was a third of the deceased's estate if there were four or fewer children and half if there were more than four children.

93 Art. 117, in *Moto proprio della Santità di Nostro Signore Papa Leone XII in data dei 5 ottobre 1824 sulla riforma dell'amministrazione pubblica della procedura civile e delle tasse dei giudizi* (Rome: Poggioli, 1824), pp. 22–23.

94 Art. 20, in *Regolamento legislativo e giudiziario per gli affari civili*, p. 876.

95 *Giornale del Foro ossia Raccolta di regiudicate romane e straniere*, 2 (1853), 166–70 (p. 169). This case is described in more detail in Sara Delmedico, 'The Dowry in Mid-Nineteenth-Century Papal States: The Case of Umbellina Livi', in

died; nine years later she asked for her dowry.[96] Although the family lived in Rome, where the children (two sons and four daughters) of the deceased had been educated, they were originally from Albano, a small town near the capital city of the Papal States. This town was also where the family had its assets. As her brothers wanted to give her a dowry of one thousand scudi, as was customary in Albano, Umbellina appealed to the Sacra Rota, which ultimately decided that a dowry of two thousand scudi was more appropriate.[97] The court explained that in order to establish the amount of a dowry the criterion to be used was the town where a family lived permanently and:

> in tali giudizj, [...] la congruità della dote deve desumersi non da una certa misura dalla legge assegnata, per es. dalla legittima, ma dalle ricerche di fatto sul consueto di famiglie simili, sul decoro e sulla convenienza delle nozze contratte, e da altri elementi opportuni a determinare il ragionevole arbitrio dei giudici.[98]
>
> [in such judgments, [...] the appropriate size of the dowry must be inferred not from a specific measure ruled by the law, for example, by the legitime, but by factual research on the custom of similar families, on the decorum and suitability of the contracted wedding, and on other appropriate elements to determine a sound ruling from the judges.]

As the estate of their father amounted to 34,307 scudi, the *legitima portio* – calculated on the basis of Roman law – should have been roughly three thousand scudi for each daughter. This means that the dowry established for Umbellina Livi was just two-thirds of the legitime.

Another case in point is that of Serafina Bonizi Poggi, a woman from Rome who claimed that her dowry was not 'congrua'.[99] The daughter of a wealthy Roman merchant, Serafina had married an older man and had gone to live with him in Tolfa, a town in the countryside near Civitavecchia. She maintained that her dowry of eight thousand scudi was not sufficient and that as a consequence

Gender and Generations: Spaces, Times, Identity, ed. by Ekaterina Lung, Gabriella Valera and Christopher Heath (= *Chronica Mundi*, 13 (2018)), pp. 92–106.

96 At the age of twenty-five a woman was entitled to ask for her dowry (Art. 28, in *Regolamento legislativo e giudiziario per gli affari civili*, p. 876).

97 On the prerogatives of the tribunal of the Sacra Rota or Ruota, see Domenico Bernini, *Il tribunale della S. Rota Romana* (Rome: Bernabò, 1717); Kirsi Salonen, *Papal Justice in the Late Middle Ages: The Sacra Romana Rota* (London: Routledge, 2016).

98 Salonen, *Papal Justice*, p. 167.

99 *Giornale del Foro ossia Raccolta di regiudicate romane e straniere*, 1 (1854), 136–43 (p. 136).

her social status had deteriorated. According to the court, 'la parità della condizione [doveva] desumersi dall'opinione del paese e non dalla materiale forza dei rispettivi patrimoni' [the difference in status had to be deduced from local attitudes and not from the material strength of the respective assets].[100] The Sacra Rota rejected her claim and argued that the daughter of a shopkeeper, although wealthy, who had married a landlord or a country merchant, had entered into a family of higher status than her own. She had also moved from Rome to the province and this was not to be considered an unfavourable circumstance, as often even young Roman women preferred the province to a large city, because there they were 'contente di vivere nella affezione dei mariti, [di] occuparsi nella educazione della prole, riverite e salutate da tutti, mentre in Roma, in tanta abbondanza di signorìa nostra e straniera sarebbero appena conosciute' [happy to be basking in the affection of their husbands, to take care of the education of their offspring, revered and greeted by all, while in Rome, in such abundance of both local and foreign nobility, they would hardly have been known].[101] Hence, a scant dowry could be compensated for by a woman being known and greeted, intangible goods which, in the opinion of the court, would make her content and fulfilled. A man, on the other hand, needed the 'physical' assets of the family's patrimony such as money, lands and houses to be properly rewarded. Another criterion used to define the appropriateness of a dowry was the education families gave to their children and their 'exterior display', or how they dressed and the nature of their lifestyle. In Serafina's case, the bride's father – even though wealthy – was 'alieno dal lusso [e] conduceva la famiglia con una esibizione molto modesta' [averse to luxury and led the family with a very modest display]; consequently, the dowry did not need to be very opulent and she was to be content with the dowry she had received.[102]

In the Duchy of Modena, the *Codice Estense* of 1771, repealed at the time of Napoleon and again in force after his defeat, prescribed that daughters be excluded from the inheritance of their parents' estate if they had brothers.[103] As in the Papal States, they were entitled to an appropriate dowry and the concept of appropriateness was

100 *Giornale del Foro ossia Raccolta di regiudicate romane e straniere*, 1 (1854), p. 136.

101 *Giornale del Foro ossia Raccolta di regiudicate romane e straniere*, 1 (1854), p. 139.

102 *Giornale del Foro ossia Raccolta di regiudicate romane e straniere*, 1 (1854), p. 141.

103 Art. I Tit. XXXIV, in *Codice Estense*, p. 832.

described as 'corrispondente alla qualità della dotanda, e dello sposo, alle forze del patrimonio degli obbligati a dotare, e all'uso, e alla pratica della famiglia, e del luogo' [corresponding to the quality of the woman receiving the dowry and of the groom, to the strengths of the assets of those obliged to provide the dowry and to the customs and habits of the family and of the place].[104] Women's legal status slightly improved with the Code of 1851, which stated that children could inherit their father's and mother's property without gender distinction. Nonetheless, the Code pointed out that 'se all'eredità concorrono maschi e femmine, la porzione di ciascun maschio deve superare della metà quella che tocca a ciascuna femmina; cosicchè la porzione del maschio stia a quella della femmina come tre a due' [if males and females compete for an inheritance, the portion given to each male must exceed that which is owed to each female by half; so that the portion of the male corresponds to that of the female by three to two].[105]

The situation in the Grand Duchy of Tuscany was similar to that in the other pre-Unification states where women were only entitled to receive a dowry. In Article 6 of his *Legge sulle successioni intestate,* issued on 18 August 1814, Grand Duke Ferdinand III ruled that daughters and other female offspring were excluded from inheriting from their male relatives.[106] The following article specified that women were also excluded from inheriting from their mother.[107] Although the portion inherited by a woman was to be equal to the *legitima portio* of the inheritance of both parents, Article 36 allowed dowries lower than the *legitima portio.* However, in this case other goods given to women to reach the amount of the legitime had to be considered *bona extra dotalia.*[108] The distinction was that the dowry was to be secured against the husband's properties and could be used only after a judge's authorisation, whereas the *bona extra dotalia* could be freely spent. In particular circumstances, a dowry could be higher than the legitime without affecting the rights of other heirs. In a judgement delivered by the Regia Ruota Fiorentina in May 1817, for example, it was noted that a dowry of three thousand scudi was

104 Art. I Tit. XIV, in *Codice Estense,* p. 810.

105 Art. 911, in *Codice Civile per gli Stati Estensi* (1851), p. 194.

106 Art. 6, in *Legge sulle successioni intestate,* in *Collezione completa,* 895–936 (p. 897).

107 Art. 7, in *Legge sulle successioni intestate,* p. 897.

108 Artt. 32–47, *Legge sulle successioni intestate,* p. 897.

not over-large if the father's assets were worth 25,000 scudi.[109] In this case, the deceased had had three sons and two daughters; and one of the daughters had already been dowered thirty-seven years earlier. The court ruled that the dowry was not too high if 'l'età della dotanda è avanzata, quando il patrimonio è capace di sopportarla, e quando concorrono altre circostanze, che la dimostrano giusta' [the age of the woman receiving a dowry is advanced, when the family assets are able to bear it and when other circumstances concur which show it to be appropriate].[110] Given that the bride was no longer young, granting her a higher-than-usual dowry would have made her more attractive on the marriage market, allowing her to marry, which, as we have seen, was considered the natural condition and primary goal of a woman.

In the Duchy of Lucca, the Napoleonic Code remained in force even after the defeat of the French emperor. Nonetheless, some parts of the code, such as those pertaining to family law and conflicting with local customs, were modified by decrees. The *Decreto relativo alle successioni intestate*, promulgated by the Duchess Maria Luisa of Bourbon on 22 November 1818, repealed some articles of the Napoleonic Code concerning inheritance; and Articles 55 to 71 of Chapter IX, *Della dote, e degli altri compensi dovuti alle Femine*, stated that daughters were excluded from the *ab intestato* inheritance of their fathers, but could succeed to their mothers who died intestate.[111] They were entitled only to a dowry equal to the legitime, calculated according to parameters set out in Roman law. If daughters had already been provided with a dowry higher than the legitime, it should not be reduced unless it affected the interests of other offspring; if it was lower, daughters could ask for an addition.

In the Kingdom of Sardinia, King Carlo Emanuele III promulgated the *Regie Costituzioni* in 1770 and confirmed the dowry as the only right women enjoyed over any parental inheritance.[112] After the Congress of Vienna, the *Regie Costituzioni* were reinforced, as had happened

109 *Decisioni del Foro Toscano inedite dall'anno 1815, all'anno 1819*, ed. by Lorenzo Cantini and Domenico Nenci, 5 vols (Florence: Stamperia del Giglio, 1824), III, 303–13.

110 *Decisioni del Foro Toscano*, III, 311.

111 Artt. 12–22 and Artt. 55–71, in *Decreto relativo alle successioni*, in *Collezione completa*, 937–948 (pp. 942, 944–45).

112 The *Leggi e Costituzioni di Sua Maestà il Re di Sardegna* were promulgated by Vittorio Amedeo II of Savoy in 1723 and 1729. King Carlo Emanuele III reworked these laws and promulgated a new version of these *Regie Costituzioni* in 1770.

with the law of other states in the Italian Peninsula. Then, in 1827 King Carlo Felice promulgated the *Leggi civili del Regno di Sardegna*. This code, however, was only in force on the isle of Sardinia.[113] In 1837 King Carlo Alberto promulgated the Civil Code of the Kingdom of Sardinia, which permitted all legitimate children or their descendants to inherit from their father, mother and any other relative,[114] even if the establishment of a dowry was still contemplated.[115] Article 943 declared that:

> trattandosi di successione al padre od altro ascendente paterno maschio la porzione di successione che spetterebbe alla femmina o suoi discendenti, eredi e non della medesima, sarà devoluta a titolo di subingresso [...]. Tale subingresso non avrà però luogo che in favore di que' fratelli e discendenti da essi, che saranno in grado di conservare la famiglia, e per la circostanza del proprio stato propagarla.[116]

> [in the case of succeeding a father or other male paternal ancestor, the portion of the inheritance which would belong to the female or her

113 To be enforced on Sardinia, edicts of Piedmontese monarchs needed to undergo a separate enactment. The eighteenth-century *Regie Costituzioni* were also enforced with the edict of 15 January 1770 (Alessandro Lattes, 'Le leggi civili e criminali di Carlo Felice pel Regno di Sardegna', in *La Sardegna di Carlo Felice e il problema della terra*, ed. by Carlino Sole (Cagliari: Editrice sarda Fossataro, 1967), pp. 403–509 (p. 409); Paolo Grossi, 'Per la storia della legislazione sabauda in Sardegna: il Censore dell'agricoltura', *Annali della Facoltà Giuridica dell'Università di Macerata*, 26 (1963), 197–240 (pp. 201–03); Francesco Aimerito, *La codificazione della procedura civile nel Regno di Sardegna* (Milan: Giuffrè, 2008), pp. 151–53). For an overview on law on the island of Sardinia, see Guido Astuti, 'Gli ordinamenti giuridici degli Stati Sabaudi', in *Storia del Piemonte*, ed. by Dino Gribaudi (Turin: Casanova, 1960), pp. 487–562; Antonello Mattone, 'Assolutismo e tradizione statutaria. Il governo sabaudo e il diritto consuetudinario del Regno di Sardegna (1720–1827)', *Rivista storica italiana*, 116 (2004), 926–1007.

114 Art. 931, in *Codice civile per gli Stati di S. M. il Re di Sardegna*, in *Collezione completa*, 587–785 (p. 651). The King of Sardinia Carlo Alberto (1798–1849) started working on codification just a month after his accession to the throne (r. 1831–49). The Civil Code of the Kingdom of Sardinia was promulgated in 1837 and incorporated many aspects of the Napoleonic Code (Gian Savino Pene Vidari, 'L'attesa dei codici nello Stato Sabaudo della Restaurazione', *Rivista di storia del diritto italiano*, 68 (1995), 107–52 (p. 127)). This code was extended to the island of Sardinia with a decree on 20 November 1847 (Soresina, *L'età della Restaurazione*, p. 26).

115 Art. 1517, in *Codice civile per gli Stati di S. M. il Re di Sardegna*, p. 665.

116 Art. 943, in *Codice civile per gli Stati di S. M. il Re di Sardegna*, p. 673. The terms 'in ragione del proprio stato' [by reason of their state] meant that if they were priests or interdicted, they were not allowed to take over the *subingresso*.

descendants, whether or not they are her heirs, will be transferred as a *subingresso* [...]. This *subingresso*, however, will only be used to favour those brothers and their descendants who will be able to preserve the family and, due to their circumstances, be able to propagate it.]

It is worth noting the use of the terms 'conservare' and 'propagare', that is, to 'preserve' and 'propagate', which are substantially the same words as used in the eighteenth-century *Costituzioni* of the Kingdom of Sardinia, underlying, once again, that family was crucial to Italian society, as was its conservation.[117] The discussion will return to the Kingdom of Sardinia in the following chapters. Throughout the entire Peninsula only three codes allowed all children to succeed to their parents equally, regardless of gender. These were the *Codice per lo Regno delle Due Sicilie*, promulgated by Ferdinand, King of the Two Sicilies, on 26 March 1819;[118] the *Codice per gli Stati di Parma, Piacenza e Guastalla*,[119] promulgated by Duchess Maria Luigia in 1820; and the *Codice civile universale austriaco pel Regno Lombardo-Veneto*, the Italian version of the 1811 *Allgemeines Bürgerliches Gesetzbuch* (*ABGB*),[120] introduced into Lombardy-Venetia on 1 January 1816. These three Codes still allowed for the establishment of a dowry, which, however, was just to be considered an advance on their paternal inheritance.[121]

117 The *subingresso* was the right to take over the hereditary portion from a woman, who was compensated with a portion of inheritance equal to the legitime (Art. 945, in *Codice civile per gli Stati di S. M. il Re di Sardegna*, p. 673).

118 Art. 667, in *Codice per lo Regno delle Due Sicilie*, in *Collezione completa*, 231–369 (p. 274).

119 Art. 837, in *Codice civile per gli stati parmensi*, in *Collezione completa*, 371–514 (p. 422).

120 Artt. 730–734, in *Codice civile universale austriaco pel Regno Lombardo-Veneto*, in *Collezione completa*, 141–230 (p. 187). For an overall discussion on the *Allgemeines Bürgerliches Gesetzbuch*, see Grossi, *A History of European Law*, pp. 90–93. On the influence of the *ABGB* on the elaboration of other nineteenth-century laws of the Italian Peninsula, see *L'ABGB e la codificazione asburgica in Italia e in Europa: atti del Convegno internazionale, Pavia, 11–12 ottobre 2002*, ed. by Ettore Dezza and Pio Caroni (Padua: CEDAM, 2006); Ettore Dezza, *Lezioni di storia della codificazione civile: il Code civil (1804) e l'Allgemeines Bürgerliches Gesetzbuch (ABGB, 1812)* (Turin: Giappichelli, 1998). For a discussion on the *ABGB* regarding women's legal status, see Maria Rosa Di Simone, 'La donna nella storia del diritto austriaco: tradizione e innovazione tra medioevo e Settecento', in *Donne tra storia e politica*, ed. by Agata Cecilia Amato Mangiameli (Turin: Giappichelli, 2012), pp. 24–43; Maria Rosa Di Simone, 'La condizione giuridica della donna nell'ABGB', *Historia et ius*, 9 (2016), paper 3, 1–29.

121 Art. 1353, in *Codice per lo Regno delle Due Sicilie*, p. 314; Art. 1329, in *Codice per gli Stati di Parma, Piacenza e Guastalla*, in *Collezione completa*, 371–514 (p. 449); Art. 1218, in *Codice civile universale austriaco pel Regno Lombardo-Veneto*, p. 214.

With the exception of Lombardy-Venetia, the law also debarred women from making contracts and managing their assets, making them subject to men in every aspect of their lives. As we saw in Chapter 2, ideas of women's weak-headedness contributed to shaping the commonly held opinion that they were unable to deal with money and contracts. These preconceived ideas were deeply rooted in the entire Italian Peninsula (even in areas where women could administer their own wealth) and explained why women needed to obtain authorisation if they wanted to make any kind of contract. Depending on the state where it was required, this authorisation was to be given by their husband, or by their father, or by a male relative and/or by the judge. During the Middle Ages, this authorisation was included in municipal statutes, though with varying degrees of harshness.[122] With the introduction of the Napoleonic Code into the conquered Italian territories, authorisation to make contracts became merely marital and therefore only affected married women. As such it generally improved unmarried women's agency for a few years[123] but, at the same time, once again highlighted the importance of the family.

By the time of the Restoration – and the consequent return to previous laws – women again needed to obtain authorisation, and not just from their husbands. Article 52 of the Pope's *Regolamento Legislativo e Giudiziario per gli affari civili*, for example, associated women with 'pupilli, minori, interdetti' [pupils, minors and interdicted people] and stated that their contracts were valid only after the approval of a judge.[124] The *ratio* of this provision was effectively described in a judgement made by the tribunal of the Sacra Rota in 1859. This case was about a woman, a subject of the Pope, who had signed a bill of exchange while she was in France. As she did not want to pay the sum back, she was sued by her creditor. The Roman judges ruled against the creditor and maintained that if female subjects of the Papal States were allowed to go abroad and make contracts without the due formalities:

> le patrie leggi, che loro vietano di contrattare, potrebbero essere assai facilmente fraudate [e per una donna che] voglia spendere in

122 See Victor Crescenzi, 'L'autorizzazione maritale e il problema storico della capacità della donna coniugata di disporre dei propri beni', in *Mujeres y derecho. Una perspectiva histórico-jurídica. Encuentro de historiadores del derecho. Actas*, ed. by Francisco L. Pacheco Caballero (Barcellona: Associació Catalana d'História del Dret, 2015), pp. 127–85. For a nineteenth-century overview on this authorisation, see *Giurisprudenza del codice civile*, 2 (1839), 89–110.

123 Artt. 215–223, in *Codice Civile del Regno d'Italia* (1845), p. 13.

124 Art. 52, in *Regolamento Legislativo e Giudiziario per gli affari civili*, p. 878.

vanità ed in capricci tutto il suo patrimonio basterebbe andare per poco tempo all'estero, ed ivi contrarre tutte quelle obbligazioni che vuole, e delle quali dovrebbero i giudici del nostro Stato ordinare la esecuzione.[125]

[the laws of the homeland which forbid [women] from undertaking contracts could very easily be circumvented; and [for a woman who] wants to spend all her assets on vanity and whims it would be [easy] enough to go abroad for a short time and, when there, to commit to all the obligations she wishes and the judges of our state would then be expected to order the enforcement of them.]

Ideas about women's weak-headedness could also be inferred in a similar case brought before the court of Genoa in 1856[126] in which a woman named Clelia Massone renounced her paternal inheritance.[127] The case revolved around the argument that the formalities required for such an act had not been correctly observed. The tribunal ordered that Clelia should ask for the required authorisation because 'i diritti, di cui la medesima pretese lo esperimento, possono essere stati da una donna facilmente scambiati con quelli che le erano riservati dalla legge' [the rights that this woman presumed to challenge could easily have been exchanged by her for those which were legally reserved for her].[128] The situation was similar in the entire Peninsula, with the exception of Lombardy-Venetia, where there were no such rules and women could freely administer their own assets.[129] As we shall see later,

125 *Giornale del Foro, raccolta di regiudicate romane e straniere*, 1 (1859), 248–50.

126 Art. 1211, in *Codice civile per gli Stati di S. M. il Re di Sardegna* (Turin: Stamperia reale, 1837), p. 328. This code explicitly rules that married women needed authorisation. However, given that in the Kingdom of Sardinia children were under the *potestas* of their father or grandfather until a formal act of emancipation was made, it follows that women were not freely able to undertake any legal act, even though of age (Artt. 210–211, in *Codice civile per gli Stati di S. M. il Re di Sardegna*, p. 60).

127 *Giurisprudenza degli Stati Sardi*, 6 (1856), 543–45.

128 *Giurisprudenza degli Stati Sardi*, 6, p. 544.

129 For nineteenth-century legal discussions over marital authorisation after Unification, see Aniello Vescia, 'Se l'autorizzazione maritale sia necessaria alla moglie il cui marito è inabilitato', *Archivio giuridico*, 38 (1887), 33–43; Antonio Scevola, *L'autorizzazione maritale ed il mandato conferto dalla moglie al marito* (Turin: Unione Tipografico-Editrice, 1888); Emilio Bianchi, 'La inabilitazione e l'assenza del marito in materia di autorizzazione maritale, osservazioni sull'art. 135 N.° 1 del Codice civile italiano', *Archivio giuridico*, 40 (1888), 552–66. For a study on marital authorisation and the path towards its abolition, see Monica

when the Pisanelli Code was enacted in 1865 marital authorisation became compulsory in Lombardy-Venetia as well, thus considerably worsening the legal status of women in this area.[130]

Women's juridical status as subordinate to men was broadly accepted in most pre-Unification states. However, Italian society was slowly changing. The French Revolution and the nineteenth-century upheavals of the Risorgimento involved the participation of several strata of society and provoked demands for more democratic and inclusive institutions. Moreover, women also became involved and their participation did not go unnoticed. The need for new legal norms may have emerged, and been fully heeded, during the short life of the Roman Republic of 1849, when the Commissione Provvisoria di Governo dello Stato Romano prohibited the establishment of the dowry, repealed the exclusion of women from *ab intestato* inheritance and enabled women who were of age to make contracts without any formalities. However, the Commissione Provvisoria also confirmed that married women could not enter into obligations without their husbands' permission.[131] These few improvements did not last long. When the Pope returned to power he repealed these norms and the Papal States returned to their previous legal system, which remained unchanged until the Unification of Italy.

Women and Civil Rights before Unification

The codes and statutes of pre-Unification Italy rarely took women into account outside the sphere of family law. Often women were not even mentioned during discussions of who might be entitled to vote.[132] Among the various statutes issued in the 1840s, the Tuscany

Fioravanzo, 'Sull'autorizzazione maritale. Ricerche attorno alla condizione giuridica della donna nell'Italia unita', *Clio*, 30 (1994), 641–725; Giulia Galeotti, 'L'autorizzazione maritale nel primo codice civile unitario: un istituto "estraneo" alla tradizione italiana?', *Dimensioni e problemi della ricerca storica*, 2 (2005), 155–82.

130 The only known protest made by women against the requirement for marital authorisation was the petition of *female citizens* to extend the rights enjoyed by women of Lombardy-Venetia to all the women of the new Kingdom of Italy (Mariachiara Fugazza, 'Il lungo cammino dei diritti', in *La donna in Italia: 1848–1914*, ed. by Bruni, Foglia and Messina, pp. 67–78 (p. 67)).

131 Artt. 11, 12, 16, 58, in *Raccolta delle leggi, decreti, ordinanze e regolamenti del governo dello stato romano* (Bologna: Tiocchi, 1849), pp. 67, 70.

132 In the eighteenth and nineteenth centuries, providing women with civil rights was not the subject of many debates. The common opinion was that a

Election Law of 3 March 1848 was the only one explicitly to exclude women.[133] Conversely, Article 24 of the Albertine Statute stated that 'tutti i regnicoli [...] godono ugualmente i diritti civili e politici e sono ammissibili alle cariche civili e militari, salvo le eccezioni determinate dalla legge' [all subjects [...] enjoy civil and political rights equally and are eligible for civil and military positions, except for cases specifically determined by law].[134] The *Statuto fondamentale pel governo temporale degli Stati della Chiesa*, granted by Pope Pius IX, allowed subjects some minor representation and indicated the amount of wealth or the professions which rendered people eligible to vote, but it did not state the sex of potential voters. Similarly, the *Costituzione della Repubblica Romana*, approved on 3 July 1849, introduced universal suffrage, specifying requirements to be eligible as voters and citizens.[135] In particular, Article 17 stated that 'ogni cittadino che gode i diritti civili e politici a 21 anni è elettore, a 25 è eleggibile' [every citizen who enjoys civil and political rights at the age of 21 can vote, [and] at 25 is eligible [to stand for election]].[136] Although these three statutes made generic references to subjects and citizens, there was no claim or doubt that they meant to address only men: women, as we saw in Chapter 1, were not included in notions of citizenship and their exclusion was indisputable.[137]

woman who voted 'non solo mostrerebbe una completa imperizia, ma il suo stesso decoro sarebbe in continuo contrasto con le passioni che l'agiterebbero maggiormente' [would not only display complete inexperience, but her own decorum would be in continual conflict with the passions that would greatly agitate her] (Stella, 'Alcune considerazioni sulla minore responsabilità', p. 81).

133 Art. 8, in *Raccolta delle leggi del 3 marzo e 26 aprile 1848 e successive 15 e 16 luglio 1859 per la formazione delle liste elettorali* (Florence: Stamp. Governativa, 1859), p. 19.

134 Art. 24, in *Statuto del Regno di Sardegna, 4 marzo 1848* (Padua: Salmin, 1866), p. 10.

135 Artt. 16–20, in Carlo Rusconi, *La Repubblica romana del 1849*, 2 vols (Turin: Cassone, 1850), II, 126.

136 Costituzione della Repubblica Romana, Tit. III Art. 17, in *Raccolta delle leggi, decreti, ordinanze e regolamenti del governo dello Stato Romano*, 3 vols (Bologna: Tiocchi, 1849), I, 47.

137 On this point see also Raffaele Romanelli, 'Electoral Systems and Social Structures. A Comparative Perspective', in *How Did They Become Voters? The History of Franchise in Modern European Representation*, ed. by Raffaele Romanelli (The Hague and London: Kluwer Law International, 1998), pp. 1–36 (pp. 21–22).

At the municipal level, Article 12 of the *Decreto sull'ordinamento de' municipj*, issued during the Roman Republic on 31 January 1849, specified that charities were allowed to vote. As these bodies had an interest in the civic life of a town, they were deemed to be worthy of expressing their ideas. The same article, however, explicitly excluded charities led by women.[138] Furthermore, Article 14 of the *Regolamento comunale* – issued in the Grand Duchy of Tuscany on 20 November 1849 – ordered that women, like minors and interdicted people, exercised their right to vote through those who represented them, either by law or by mandate.[139] It is difficult to understand whether they effectively exercised this right, but this article might indicate that the male adult, namely the *paterfamilias*, who represented women, minors and interdicted people was theoretically supposed to exercise the vote on behalf of his entire family.

In Lombardy-Venetia women who had sufficient wealth were able to nominate representatives in municipalities and could also be elected through a representative.[140] Article 68 of the *Patente sovrana 12 aprile 1816 N. 45* ruled that:

> le donne, i pupilli, i minori, gl'interdetti, come ancora i luoghi pii, collegi università ed in generale qualunque stabilimento pubblico intestato nelle tavole del censo [...] può essere eletto deputato, ed il procuratore od amministratore che lo rappresenta non debbe avere alcuna delle eccezioni personali indicate nello stesso capitolo primo.[141]
>
> [women, pupils, minors, interdicted people, as well as religious institutions, colleges, universities and in general any public establishment registered in the census tables [...] can be elected as a representative; and the procurator or administrator who represents them should not have any of the personal exceptions that are mentioned in Chapter One.]

It should be noted, however, that this provision was enforced in small municipalities only. With regard to larger towns, Article 37

138 Art. 12, *Decreto sull'ordinamento de' municipj*, 31 gennaio 1849, Tit. III, Della formazione della rappresentanza comunale, in *Raccolta delle leggi, decreti, ordinanze e regolamenti del governo dello Stato Romano*, I, 48.

139 Emanuele Repetti, *Compendio storico della città Firenze, sua comunità, diocesi e compartimento fino all'anno 1849* (Florence: Tofani, 1849), p. 402.

140 Nidia Danelon Vasoli, *Il plebiscito in Toscana nel 1860* (Florence: Olschki, 1968), pp. 109–10; Marco Meriggi, *Milano borghese. Circoli ed élites nell'Ottocento* (Venice: Marsilio, 1992), p. 199; Giulia Galeotti, *Storia del voto alle donne in Italia. Alle radici del difficile rapporto tra donne e politica* (Rome: Biblink, 2006), p. 25.

141 *Atti del governo di Lombardia. Parte prima dal 1° gennajo al 30 giugno 1816* (Milan: Imperiale Regia Stamperia, 1816), p. 252.

of the same *Patente* clearly pointed out that 'non sono proponibili ai consigli comunali [...] i pupilli, i minori, le donne, gl'interdetti' [pupils, minors, women and interdicted people [...] cannot be proposed to city councils].[142] Women could exercise these rights when pupils, minors and interdicted people were also allowed to do so, thus confirming that this was not an acknowledgement of women's equality but a pre-eminence given to wealth, the *substancia* which after five centuries still informed the legal system. In the Italian Peninsula some demands for civil rights were first made at the time of the plebiscite for annexation to Piedmont. Women expressed their involvement in the Italian cause, as well as their desire to participate effectively, through messages addressed to the King of Sardinia; by setting up separate ballot boxes in private homes; or by casting their votes at meetings of men, sometimes even in the same polls.[143]

The Unification of Italy

The Unification of Italy under the rule of King Vittorio Emanuele II meant that the law in force in the Kingdom of Sardinia was extended to the entire Peninsula. On 25 April 1859, shortly before Unification, the Piedmontese parliament gave the government full legislative

142 *Atti del governo di Lombardia. Parte prima dal 1° gennajo al 30 giugno 1816*, pp. 244–45.

143 Alessandro Alessandrini, *I fatti politici delle Marche dal 1 gennaio 1859 all'epoca del plebiscito* (Macerata: Libreria editrice Marchigiana, 1910), p. 398. See also Fruci, 'Cittadine senza cittadinanza'; Gian Luca Fruci, 'Il sacramento dell'unità nazionale: linguaggi, iconografia e pratiche dei plebisciti risorgimentali (1848–70)', in *Storia d'Italia*, ed. by Banti and Ginsborg, pp. 567–605. Two cases of women being allowed to vote on account of their own merits are known. They were the eighteen-year-old poetess of Recanati, Maria Alinda Bonacci, who was allowed to vote because of her artistic merits; and Marianna De Crescenzo, called La Sangiovannara, a tavern-keeper of Monte Calvario a Napoli who actively participated in the upheavals of 1848 (Gian Luca Fruci, 'Alle origini del momento plebiscitario risorgimentale (1797–1870)', in *Verso l'unità. Conferenze e laboratori didattici organizzati con la collaborazione della Domus Mazziniana: Pisa, ottobre – novembre 2010*, ed. by Alessandra Peretti (Ospedaletto: Pacini, 2011), pp. 43–56 (pp. 46–47)). In his work on Garibaldi Marc Monnier reports that La Sangiovannara 'a tout un quartier sous ses ordres' and, having fought as a soldier, '[elle] a obtenu de voter comme un citoyen' (Marc Monnier, *Garibaldi: histoire de la conquête des Deux-Siciles* (Paris: Lévy frères, 1861), p. 371). See also Marcella Varriale, 'Marianna De Crescenzo', in *Dizionario biografico degli italiani*, 100 vols (Rome: Istituto della Enciclopedia Italiana, 1960–2020), xc (2017) <https://www.treccani.it/enciclopedia/sangiovannara_%28Dizionario-Biografico%29/> [accessed 1 June 2021].

and executive powers which paved the way for a new phase of legal codification, ending with the approval and publication of three new codes on 20 November 1859: the Criminal Code, the Criminal Procedure Code and the Civil Procedure Code.[144] On the same day, Law 3788 was approved; it stated that the government would submit a bill to parliament in order to unify the law in both the new and old provinces of the Kingdom.[145] Immediately after Unification a committee chaired by Vincenzo Miglietti began to work on a new code in consultation with jurists and judges. The project started with the revision of the Kingdom of Sardinia Civil Code and was presented by Minister of Justice Giovan Battista Cassinis to Parliament in June 1860.[146] A second draft was presented by Miglietti, who became the new Minister of Justice. In the meantime, Law 2248 on municipal and provincial government was approved on 20 March 1865: Article 26 stated that women were explicitly excluded from the electorate.[147] Finally, the new Minister of Justice, Giuseppe Vacca, submitted another draft of the Civil Code to parliament, which, after various amendments by legislative committees, became law on 25 June 1865, with Decree 2358. The Civil Code for the Kingdom of Italy entered into force on 1 January 1866.[148]

The path towards the drafting and promulgation of the Civil Code for the Kingdom of Italy, far from being a smooth process, was preceded 'da un processo di unificazione giuridica in cui il discorso sulla condizione giuridica della donna non è affrontato' [by a process of juridical unification in which the discourse on the juridical condition of women was not addressed] and did not introduce significant innovations.[149] The Pisanelli Code, named after Giuseppe Pisanelli, the Minister of Justice who had a major role in its drafting (even though he was no longer serving in that office

144 These three Codes were promulgated with the *Regi Decreti* 3783, 3784 and 3786.

145 Alberto Aquarone, *L'unificazione legislativa e i codici del 1865* (Milan: Giuffrè, 1960), p. 3; Francesco Santoro-Passarelli, *Libertà e autorità nel diritto civile: altri saggi* (Padua: CEDAM, 1977), pp. 13–26.

146 See Stefano Solimano, *Il letto di Procuste: diritto e politica nella formazione del Codice civile unitario. I progetti Cassinis (1860–1861)* (Milan: Giuffrè, 2003); Passaniti, *Diritto di famiglia*, pp. 210–22.

147 Alessandro De Sterlich, *Annotazioni alla legge sull'amministrazione comunale e provinciale del 20 marzo 1865* (Naples: Trani, 1865), p. 170.

148 On the path to the promulgation of the Pisanelli Code, see Passaniti, *Diritto di famiglia*, pp. 229–67.

149 Passaniti, *Diritto di famiglia*, p. 205.

at the time of its promulgation), was largely based on the content and structure of the Napoleonic Code: while it abolished the right of males to succeed before females in *ab intestato* inheritances[150] and introduced an age limit to parental *potestas* over their children, the Code of 1865 maintained the usual hierarchical order by which women were subject to men. Moreover, marital authorisation was reinforced and also extended to former Lombardy-Venetia, where a similar institution had not existed since the Restoration.[151]

According to the Pisanelli Code both sons and daughters came of age at twenty-one.[152] If they wanted to marry, they were obliged to ask for parental consent up to the age of twenty-five in the case of men and twenty-one in the case of women.[153] One can argue that this distinction was made because rulers still thought of women as entering 'aliene famiglie' [other families] and of men as being invested in the fundamental mission of preserving their *famiglia*: hence for men the decision to enter into a marriage had to be more carefully evaluated than for women.[154] The jurist Domenicantonio Galdi, in his commentary on the *Codice civile del Regno d'Italia*, explained that 'il maggior favore col quale devonsi facilitare i matrimoni delle femmine [...] sul riflesso che per la femmina lo stato matrimoniale è non solo naturale, ma in certa guisa una necessità sociale' [the greater encouragement with which women's marriages must be facilitated [...] is because of the consideration that, for a woman, having marital status is not only natural, but in some ways a social necessity].[155] Like the Napoleonic Code, the Pisanelli Code ruled that if parents did not share the same view about the marriage of their children, the father's will prevailed.[156] Children could appeal to a court if permission to marry was denied.[157] The report by the Minister of Justice which accompanied the publication of the Civil Code explained that it was important to give a daughter the chance to state

150 Art. 736, in *Codice civile del Regno d'Italia: corredato della relazione del Ministro Guardasigilli fatta a S. M. in udienza del 25 giugno 1865* (Turin: Botta, 1865), p. 228.

151 Artt. 134–137, in *Codice civile del Regno d'Italia* (1865), p. 28.

152 Art. 323, in *Codice civile del Regno d'Italia* (1865), p. 63.

153 Art. 63, in *Codice civile del Regno d'Italia* (1865), p. 14.

154 Giovanni Maria Negri, *Dei difetti del Codice Civile Italico, che porta il titolo di Codice Napoleone e dei pregj del Codice Civile Austriaco* (Vicenza: Parise, 1815), p. 77.

155 *Codice civile del Regno d'Italia*, ed. by Domenicantonio Galdi (Naples: Marghieri and Perrotti, 1865), pp. 148–49.

156 *Codice civile del Regno d'Italia*, ed. by Galdi, pp. 148–49.

157 Art. 67, in *Codice civile del Regno d'Italia* (1865), p. 14.

her case before a court if by denying his consent a father could 'per avventura rapire alla figlia una propizia occasione' [by chance steal a propitious opportunity from his daughter], highlighting, once again, the presumed importance of marriage to a woman.[158] Interestingly, the report adds that this opportunity was given to both sons and daughters, because '[r]iconosciuto il diritto del richiamo all'autorità giudiziaria nella figlia[,] fu equo provvedimento il parificare nello esercizio di questo diritto la condizione del figlio maschio, [altrimenti] non si saprebbe intendere il perché della differenza tra i due sessi' [once it is acknowledged that a daughter has the right to refer to the judicial authority, it was a fair provision to make the exercise of this right equal in a son's case, otherwise the difference between the two sexes would not be understandable].[159] As we can infer from these words, the different juridical status of men and women was not perceived as discrimination. The requirement for parental consent to a marriage was considered crucial: in a dissertation on parental *potestas* drawn up by a law student in 1872 this point is made clear:

> Benissimo fece il nostro legislatore a riprodurre la legge Giustinianea discostandosi così dal Diritto Canonico onde evitare il più possibile i matrimoni inconsiderati e perché non si addivenga ad un atto così solenne, spinto solo dal valore di violenta passione.[160]
>
> [Our legislator did very well to comply with Justinian's law, thus deviating from Canon Law in order to avoid unwise marriages as much as possible, so that such a solemn act would not be undertaken solely because of a violent passion.]

In the Napoleonic Code, before contracting a marriage children of age were also required to ask for advice from their parents through a respectful and formal act known as 'atti rispettosi' [respectful acts].[161] These 'atti rispettosi' were no longer required by the Pisanelli Code. In both the Napoleonic and the Pisanelli Codes the institution of a

158 The report was written by Giuseppe Pisanelli, who was no longer Justice Minister at the time of the enactment of the Code (*Codice civile del Regno d'Italia* (1865), p. XVIII). On the debate on women's legal status, see Maria Rosa De Simone, 'Le discussioni sui diritti delle donne per il Codice civile unitario', in *Avvocati protagonisti e rinnovatori del primo diritto unitario*, ed. by Stefano Borsacchi and Gian Savino Pene Vidari (Bologna: Il Mulino, 2014), pp. 95–121.

159 *Codice civile del Regno d'Italia* (1865), p. XVIII.

160 Amilcare Galeotti, *La patria potestà: tesi di laurea del dott. Amilcare Galeotti* (Siena: Lazzeri, 1872), p. 56.

161 Art. 151, in *Codice Civile del Regno d'Italia* (1865), p. 10.

dowry was considered, but not mandatory. Given that, according to these codes, daughters were able to inherit in the same way as sons, the dowry no longer replaced women's rightful share of the inheritance. The implication of this was that, even though a dowry was still important, not having one slowly became socially acceptable.[162] Moreover, as Valerio Pocar and Paola Ronfani attest, in the new Civil Code, 'la famiglia come tale non era considerata un soggetto di diritto' [the family as such was not considered a legal entity], thus placing more value on the individual.[163] Nevertheless, the idea that the family had influence as a body was still considered in the Criminal Code of 1889, *Il codice penale per il Regno d'Italia*, when dealing with crimes against 'il buon costume e dell'ordine delle famiglie' [the morals and the order of the family] such as adultery and infanticide.[164]

The Pisanelli Code, while resolving the uncertainties and contradictions of the existing body of law, did not take into account the social unrest which had been in place in Italy since the early decades of the Ottocento. Immediately after the Restoration governments had to deal with a number of forces which co-existed in the Italian Peninsula, but at the end of the century these divisions had become even deeper. New ambitions and old prerogatives were becoming apparent; and new social classes were rising and seeking their place in society. After Italian Unification the state was forced to acknowledge new ideas and expectations and then to face the agricultural crisis and the transition towards industrialisation, with the various social, cultural and psychological issues these changes provoked.[165] Despite women's increased participation in Italian society, especially in the labour market, women's contributions exercised no influence on the drafting of the new Code; and relations within the family were still strongly balanced towards the husbands' authority and, as Paolo Passaniti argues, 'alla fine anche un genitore è di troppo' [in the end one of the parents is too many].[166] With the exception of inheritance rights, women's status remained basically unchanged: the dichotomy of obedience and protection within marriage and women's subaltern

162 See Fazio, 'Valori economici e valori simbolici'.

163 Valerio Pocar and Paola Ronfani, *La famiglia e il diritto* (Rome: Laterza, 1998), p. 14.

164 Artt. 331–363, in *Il codice penale per il Regno d'Italia*, ed. by Giulio Crivellari (Rome: Unione Tipografica, 1889), pp. 123–33.

165 Grossi, 'Assolutismo giuridico', p. 16.

166 Passaniti, *Diritto di famiglia*, p. 213.

position were reaffirmed. The former Kingdom of Sardinia unified the country from a political and juridical perspective and tried to build an identity which went beyond a mere imagined community. However, while creating the Italian nation and aiming at 'fare gli italiani' [forging Italians], once again lawmakers neglected the 'italiane' [Italian women].[167]

167 The well-known expression 'fatta l'Italia bisogna fare gli Italiani' is among the stereotypes of national rhetoric: it indicates the strong desire to build a nation and, at the same time, the difficulties such a process implies (Simonetta Soldani, 'Introduzione', in *Fare gli italiani. Scuola e cultura nell'Italia contemporanea*, ed. by Simonetta Soldani and Gabriele Turi (Bologna: Il Mulino, 1993), pp. 9–34 (pp. 17–25); Alberto M. Banti, *Il Risorgimento italiano* (Rome: Laterza, 2004), pp. 221–22, document 45).

Part 2

Women and Marriage between Civil, Criminal and Canon Law: The Cases of the Kingdoms of Sardinia and Lombardy-Venetia

4. Women and Men beyond Marriage

If it was presupposed that women and men belonged to strictly separate spheres, that is, the public and the private, the law, instead, permeated and intruded into every aspect of people's lives. The extent of its intrusiveness could be inferred from its concern with very intimate matters regarding the personal sphere, such as personal relations between men and women. The law, and the authorities responsible for its enforcement, exerted their influence over people's behaviour and attitudes and even ruled against situations which were beyond the established and desirable social order. The first section of this chapter is devoted to the marriage promise and describes its importance in society for both the betrothed and their families; a broken promise could even be interpreted as an offence to one's honour, a concept which, alongside morality, was shaped and valued by the Church and by society. This meant that sexual intercourse outside the marriage bond was not looked upon kindly, often even forbidden, and was deemed to cause 'disordine', or cast a lifelong moral stigma on those involved. The second and third sections of the chapter are dedicated to seduction and extramarital relations: the former is useful in this analysis as it was viewed as closely related to infanticide; the latter because it was considered a major challenge to the social order. This chapter aims to shed light on the authorities' attitude towards these issues in the Kingdom of Sardinia and in Lombardy-Venetia. As we shall see, ideas and behaviour were similar in both states and strongly influenced people's attitude towards morality and marriage, with canonical impediments intertwining with secular laws.

The Promise to Marry

As we saw in the previous chapter, the Catholic Church had jurisdiction over non-patrimonial matters regarding marriage. Even though the states of the Italian Peninsula had their own laws, formalities for engagement, marriage and its dissolution were prescribed by ecclesiastical authorities. From the early Middle Ages to the nineteenth century and beyond, the Church's jurisdiction and the decisions of its courts had effects beyond the boundaries of secular states. Although, as Diego Quaglioni argues, 'non si possa acconsentire alla schematica opposizione di un matrimonio formale, che nascerebbe solo con Trento e col decreto *Tametsi*, a un matrimonio aformale, che sarebbe il matrimonio medievale' [it is not possible to adhere to the idea [that there is] systematic opposition between a formal marriage, which would be born only with Trent and with the *Tametsi* decree, and an informal marriage, which would be medieval marriage], the Council of Trent undoubtedly represented a turning point in the institution of marriage.[1] On this occasion, among other matters, the Church reorganised and formally settled its rules concerning marriage, thus strongly reaffirming that its rules were *the rules*, to be observed and complied with. From 1563 onwards marriage, which up to that moment had been a pact between two individuals able to give consent, had to abide by the rules prescribed by the Council's Canons. Chapter I of its twenty-fourth Session, the decree known as *Tametsi* adopted on 11 November 1563, declared that a marriage was valid only if concluded in the presence of a priest, *in facie ecclesiae* (before the Church).[2] Conversely:

> [q]ui aliter, quam praesente parocho, vel sacerdote, de ipsius parochi seu ordinarii licentia, et duobus vel tribus testibus, matrimonium contrahere attentabunt, eos sancta synodus, ad sic contrahendum

1 Diego Quaglioni, '"Sacramenti detestabili". La forma del matrimonio prima e dopo Trento', in *Matrimoni in dubbio*, ed. by Seidel Menchi and Quaglioni, pp. 61–79 (p. 74).

2 An overview of marriage and the Council of Trent can be found in James A. Brundage, *Law, Sex and Christian Society in Medieval Europe* (Chicago, IL: University of Chicago Press, 1987), pp. 562–65; Gaudemet, *Le Mariage en Occident*, pp. 286–95. See also Ottavia Niccoli, 'Baci rubati. Gesti e riti nuziali in Italia prima e dopo il Concilio di Trento', in *Il gesto nel rito e nel cerimoniale dal mondo antico ad oggi*, ed. by Sergio Bertelli and Monica Centanni (Florence: Ponte alle Grazie, 1995), pp. 224–47; Daniela Lombardi, 'Fidanzamenti e matrimoni dal Concilio di Trento alle riforme settecentesche', in *Storia del matrimonio*, ed. by De Giorgio and Klapisch-Zuber, pp. 215–50; Daniela Lombardi, 'Intervention by Church and State in Marriage Disputes in Sixteenth- and Seventeenth-Century Florence', in *Crime, Society and the Law in Renaissance Italy*, ed. by Trevor Dean and K. J. P. Lowe (Cambridge: Cambridge University Press, 1994), pp. 142–56; Lombardi, *Matrimoni di antico regime*, pp. 99–118; Jutta Gisela Sperling, 'Marriage at the Time of the Council of Trent (1560–70): Clandestine Marriages, Kinship Prohibitions, and Dowry Exchange in European Comparison', *Journal of Early*

omnino inhabiles reddit, et hujusmodi contractus irritos et nullos esse decernit, prout eos praesenti decreto irritos facit, et annullat.[3]

[[t]hose who shall attempt to contract marriage other than in the presence of the parish priest, or of some other priest by permission of the said parish priest, or of the Ordinary, and in the presence of two or three witnesses: the holy Synod renders such individuals wholly incapable of thus contracting [a marriage] and declares such contracts invalid and null, as by the present decree it invalidates and annuls them.]

A marriage contracted *in facie ecclesiae* was a sacramental, indissoluble bond sanctified by God. It usually followed the *sponsalia* [betrothal], in which the couple promised to marry through words of consent. From the time of the Council of Trent until the nineteenth century, according to canon law consent to marry was personal and freely given through *verba de futuro* or *verba de praesenti* [words of the future; or words of the present].[4] While the former were considered just an engagement and it was, therefore, to some extent possible to have a breach of the promise, the latter were an indissoluble marriage. This point was questioned by one of the most prominent eighteenth-century canonists, Jacob Anton Zallinger zum Thurn (1735–1813), who maintained that *sponsalia* through *verba de futuro* followed by consummation equated to a valid marriage in places where the Canons of the Council of Trent had not been published.[5] Canon

Modern History, 8 (2004), 67–108; Diego Quaglioni, 'Segni, rituali e simboli nuziali nel diritto', in *I tribunali del matrimonio*, ed. by Seidel Menchi and Quaglioni, pp. 43–63. On marriage and canon law, see Gaudemet, *Sociétés et marriage*, pp. 425–47. For a study of marriage before the Council of Trent, see Silvana Seidel Menchi, 'Percorsi variegati, percorsi obbligati: elogio del matrimonio pre-tridentino', in *Matrimoni in dubbio*, ed. by Seidel Menchi and Quaglioni, pp. 17–60; Lombardi, *Matrimoni di antico regime*, pp. 35–68.

3 Council of Trent, *Sess. XXIV*, Chapter I; text translated in 'The Council of Trent. The Twenty-Fourth Session', in *The Canons and Decrees of the Sacred and Oecumenical Council of Trent*, ed. and trans. by James Waterworth (London: Dolman, 1848), pp. 192–232 (p. 197) <https://history.hanover.edu/texts/trent/ct24.html> [accessed on 30 April 2020].

4 On consent and the Council of Trent, see Jean Gaudemet, 'L'Apport de la doctrine canonique aux droits occidentaux en matière de mariage', in *Ius canonicum in Oriente et Occidente*, ed. by Stefan Korta and others (Frankfurt: Peter Lang, 2003), pp. 167–95 (pp. 169–79). On the marriage promise, see also Donahue, *Law, Marriage, and Society*, pp. 16–33; Margherita Pelaja, 'La promessa', in *Storia del matrimonio*, ed. by De Giorgio and Klapisch-Zuber, pp. 391–416; Lombardi, *Storia del matrimonio*, pp. 33–34.

5 The jurist Jakob Anton von Zallinger Zum Thurm (1735–1813) maintains: 'Olim tamen, ante Decretum Concilii Tridentini de matrimoniis

law did not require the parents' consent to contract marriage, but secular lawmakers, aware of the importance of the family and its formation, included this approval as a formal requirement in their *iura propria,* as, for example, in the eighteenth-century *Costituzioni.* As the marriage bond fell under the Church's jurisdiction, these laws only regulated the access enjoyed by the insubordinate sons and daughters to their potential wealth, allowing their parents to provide them with smaller portions of alimony and inheritance than their more obedient offspring.[6] This meant that a marriage concluded without the parents' approval, although strongly discouraged, was a valid bond once contracted.[7]

A marriage promise was an impedient impediment: the betrothed were barred from marrying someone else. However, if a marriage was concluded in spite of the impediment, the bond was not void.[8] A marriage promise could be broken if one of the betrothed could demonstrate that certain formalities had not been taken into consideration, or if he or she had good reason to refuse to marry the other party. A broken promise was a matter pertaining to canon law and complaints had to be filed with the Bishop's Curia, which also had the power to remove impedient and diriment impediments

---

clandestinis, et nunc etiam in locis, ubi illud Decretum non viget, siquis post sponsalia de futuro sposam carnaliter cognorat, praesumebatur consensum de praesenti in matrimonium praestitisse, et quidem praesumptione juris et de jure, contra quam non admittebatur probatio' [Once, before the decree of the Council of Trent on clandestine marriages, and now also in those places in which the decree has no force, if someone, after having contracted a betrothal through words of future, carnally knew his bride, it was presumed that it proved that consent to marriage through words of present was given and indeed a *juris et de jure* presumption, against which no evidence was admitted] (Jakob Anton von Zallinger Zum Thurm, *Institutiones juris ecclesiastici, maxime privati, ordine Decretalium,* 5 vols (Augsburg: Sons of Matthäus Rieger, 1793), IV, 7). See also the case described in Sara Delmedico, *Breve studio sulla condizione giuridica della donna nello Stato Pontificio dell'Ottocento* ([n.p.]: Lulu, 2014), pp. 24–26.

6 See, e.g., Artt. 8–9, in *Leggi, e costituzioni di Sua Maestà* (Turin: Stamperia Reale, 1770), pp. 324–25; Artt. I–II Tit. XIII, in *Codice Estense,* p. 809. See also Lombardi, *Storia del matrimonio,* p. 150.

7 On parental consent to marriage in municipal statutes, see Trevor Dean, 'Fathers and Daughters: Marriage Laws and Marriage Disputes in Bologna and Italy, 1200–1500', in *Crime, Society and the Law,* ed. by Dean and Lowe, pp. 85–106 (pp. 89–90).

8 Impediments to marriage can be impedient or diriment: impedient impediments make a marriage illicit but valid, whereas diriment impediments invalidate it. Impedient impediments can be simple vows, a prior promise of marriage, or a lack of solemnities. On impediments, see also Francesco

(diriment impediments will be analysed later in this chapter). The formalities regarding betrothals were not regulated by law and were, rather, a private agreement.[9] Among the upper classes these took the form of written acts, which were usually formalised before a notary because a breach of promise had to be strictly avoided, considering the financial investment a marriage represented for a family. Among the lower classes, notarised promises were less usual and the betrothed often formalised their commitment through a private, sometimes oral, agreement. If there was no written document, in the event of a breach of the marriage promise appellants had to rely on the evidence they were able to produce before the Curia.

In the following cases brought before the Bishop's Curia of Verona, in Lombardy-Venetia, the varying weight of the plaintiffs' evidence led to quite different outcomes. In 1830, for example, Andrea Buttarini – a boatman from Lonato, near Verona – wrote to the Bishop's Curia to establish an impediment to the marriage of Camilla Bettanini with Giuseppe Papa.[10] Andrea maintained that Camilla had promised to marry him and, to prove his case, brought a witness before the Curia. As was the usual procedure, the Curia summoned Camilla to explain why she had broken her promise. The woman maintained that the promise had been made under the condition that her parents approved the marriage, but they did not. Andrea's claim was rejected, because the Curia ruled that according to canon law a promise was valid if made 'coram testibus, non coram teste' [before witnesses and not before one witness only], as in this case.[11] The sentence also stemmed from the Curia's assumption that Andrea just wanted to exact a 'leggiadra vendetta' [light revenge] on Camilla, rather than really wanting her to keep the promise.[12]

Mercanti, *Compendio di diritto canonico con illustrazioni istorico-dogmatiche*, 4 vols (Prato: Guasti, 1832), I, 448–49; Charles Edward Smith, *Papal Enforcement of Some Medieval Marriage Laws* (Port Washington, NY: Kennikat Press, 1972 [1940]), pp. 5–53; Donahue, *Law, Marriage, and Society*, pp. 18–32.

9 For an overview of betrothals after the Council of Trent, see Lombardi, 'Intervention by Church and State', p. 145; Julius Kirshner, *Marriage, Dowry, and Citizenship in Late Medieval and Renaissance Italy* (Toronto: University of Toronto Press, 2015), p. 52. See also Kuehn, *Family and Gender*, pp. 104–12.

10 Bishop's Curia of Verona, Matrimoniorum, Processi, 1830–1844, doc. 26.

11 Bishop's Curia of Verona, Matrimoniorum, Processi, 1830–1844, doc. 26.

12 Bishop's Curia of Verona, Matrimoniorum, Processi, 1830–1844, doc. 26.

Women were not always the weaker party in the dispute and often strategies and disputes related to marriage were arranged together with their family.[13] Across all classes, a broken marriage promise also had social implications. A case in point is that of Giovanni Battista Civieri, a man from Verona. He was far from just plotting a 'leggiadra vendetta' against the woman to whom he had once been engaged: in fact, his desire to marry her was real and he had standing proofs to impede her marriage to another man. He went before the Bishop's Curia of Verona to ask that the permission given to Luigia Ruzzenenti to marry the other man, Giovanni Battista Pagani, be withdrawn. Luigia's promise to marry him was 'indubitata' [undoubted] and Civieri proved it by showing a number of letters she had written to him.[14] Luigia was a minor under the custody of her paternal uncle Paolo since her parents had died several years earlier; and in 1844 was promised to Civieri in the first instance. However, her uncle Paolo, 'per effetto di manifesta ingiustizia, ed a fine di fare un'onta alla famiglia Civieri, seppe indegnamente indurre, [...] Dio sa con quali mezzi' [as a result of manifest injustice, and in order to insult the Civieri family, he was able shamefully to induce, [...] God knows by what means], his niece Luigia to accept the hand of Pagani, a merchant.[15]

Civieri deplored much more than a broken promise or the unfair behaviour of Luigia's uncle: he particularly highlighted that Paolo deliberately wanted to 'fare un'onta' [bring shame] to his family, thus emphasising the crucial link between promises and honour, as well as the need to defend his family's prestige before society, not to mention his desire to marry Luigia. Civieri pointed out that they promised to marry 'di moto loro proprio non indotti da alcuno' [by their own actions, not induced by anyone] and such a promise could

13 On this point see, e.g., the case described by Elena Papagna in which a girl continued to procrastinate over the date of her marriage with her fiancé because she was trying to secure a wealthier match (Elena Papagna, 'Storie comuni di sposi promessi. I processi della curia arcivescovile di Trani nel tardo Settecento', in *I tribunali del matrimonio*, ed. by Seidel Menchi and Quaglioni, pp. 459–95 (pp. 480–83)).

14 Bishop's Curia of Verona, Matrimoniorium, Processi, 1845–1868, doc. 27.

15 Bishop's Curia of Verona, Matrimoniorium, Processi, 1845–1868, doc. 27. Despite being extremely different from a medieval *vendetta*, this *onta* is somewhat comparable to a sort of insult made to one member in order to offend the whole family, highlighting the idea of honour, which was highly valued across all social classes. See also Trevor Dean, 'Marriage and Mutilation: Vendetta in Late Medieval Italy', *Past and Present*, 157 (1997), 3–36 (esp. pp. 3–5).

not be withdrawn 'a piacere d'uno di loro senza l'adesione espressa ed assentita dell'altro contraente' [at the pleasure of one of them without the express and assented adherance of the other contractor].[16] Furthermore, Beatrice, Luigia's aunt and the wife of Paolo, had even obliged him (Civieri) to buy furniture for their future bedroom. This might have been a strategy on the part of Luigia's family to ascertain that Civieri was a reliable person: asking him to make such a purchase was not a negligible commitment for individuals belonging to the lower classes.

The letters Civieri brought before the Curia to prove the promise had all been put in writing by Luigia between 29 September 1845 and 18 October 1846. Their inspection testified to the existence of genuine feelings between the two and not to a mere arranged engagement. In September 1845, for example, Luigia wrote that she was very happy to know he loved her 'di vero core' [with a true heart]; and a month later, despite signing off the letter with the word 'distintamente' [yours truly], she specified that she would always be 'la tua' [his].[17] On 8 December of the same year something happened between her uncle and the Civieri family, but Luigia assured Civieri that she would be 'sempre fedele fino alla morte' [always loyal until death]; this time, she signed off with 'di vero amore e non ti scordar di me e sono la tua' [of true love and do not forget me and I am yours].[18] A few weeks later, the situation seems to have worsened to the extent that she wrote 'ti prego di non abbandonarmi e porta pazienza che tutto si finisce' [please do not abandon me and have patience knowing that everything ends]; in July 1846, she again confirmed 'non dubitare che altro non amarò che te' [do not doubt that I will love only you].[19]

The evidence to support Civieri's claim was sound. However, in June 1847 Luigia and Pagani – the man her uncle wanted her to marry – put up the banns in the local church of San Zeno Maggiore. Civieri immediately reported to the Curia in order to stop the wedding from taking place. On 2 August 1847 the Curia summoned the girl to clarify her position: Luigia confirmed that she wanted to marry Civieri. Despite having put up the banns for her marriage to another man only a few months earlier, she finally married Civieri on 1 November 1847.[20] There is no written evidence explaining why

16 Bishop's Curia of Verona, Matrimoniorium, Processi, 1845–1868, doc. 27.

17 Bishop's Curia of Verona, Matrimoniorium, Processi, 1845–1868, doc. 27.

18 Bishop's Curia of Verona, Matrimoniorium, Processi, 1845–1868, doc. 27.

19 Bishop's Curia of Verona, Matrimoniorium, Processi, 1845–1868, doc. 27.

20 San Zeno Maggiore, Matrimoni, 1817–1848, doc. 28.

Luigia and her family changed their minds again. One might argue that, since a broken marriage promise was a breach of canon law as well as of the shared rules of society (which were often as strong and influential as the written law), the authoritativeness of the Church, together with the need to avoid stigma, may have led Luigia's family to abide by the original promise made to Civieri. A broken marriage promise was a thorny issue, the regulation of which was far from simple: the Curia usually tried to persuade the parties involved to comply with it, given that, in practice, forcing them to marry against their will could be quite difficult.

Seduction of a 'Zitella onesta'

Along with the broken marriage promise, seduction, which implied sexual intercourse, was an equally significant matter and a source of great concern.[21] In the Settecento the wave of new ideas which, as we saw in Chapter 2, led to the redefinition of women's role in society as the first educators allowed the possibility of considering them capable of understanding the implication of sexual consent. Up to that moment, a woman *semper praesumitur seducta* [was always

21 On seduction by a promise of marriage, see Giorgia Alessi, *Processo per seduzione: piacere e castigo nella Toscana leopoldina* (Catania: [n. pub.], 1988); Alain Boureau, 'L'imene e l'ulivo. La verginità femminile nel discorso della Chiesa nel XIII secolo', *Quaderni storici*, 25 (1990), 791–803; Giorgia Alessi, 'Il gioco degli scambi: seduzione e risarcimento nella casistica cattolica del XVI e XVII secolo', *Quaderni storici*, 25 (1990), 805–31; Lombardi, 'Intervention by Church and State', pp. 154–56; Cazzetta, *Praesumitur seducta*, pp. 136–46; Margherita Pelaja, *Matrimonio e sessualità a Roma nell'Ottocento* (Rome and Bari: Laterza, 1994), pp. 51–59, 154–73; Lombardi, *Matrimoni di antico regime*, pp. 392–412; Luca Faoro, '"Nefandum dogma". Seduzione e promessa di matrimonio in una comparsa trentina del XVII secolo', in *Matrimoni in dubbio*, ed. by Seidel Menchi and Quaglioni, pp. 431–528; Daniela Hacke, 'La promessa disattesa: il caso di Perina Gabrieli (Venezia 1620)', in *Matrimoni in dubbio*, ed. by Seidel Menchi and Quaglioni, pp. 395–413; Georgia Arrivo, *Seduzioni, promesse, matrimoni. Il processo per stupro nella Toscana del Settecento* (Rome: Edizioni di Storia e Letteratura, 2006); Giorgia Alessi, 'Stupro non violento e matrimonio riparatore. Le inquiete peregrinazioni dogmatiche della seduzione', in *I tribunali del matrimonio*, ed. by Seidel Menchi and Quaglioni, pp. 609–40. On the Church's attitude to sex, see Margherita Pelaja, *Scandali. Sessualità e violenza nella Roma dell'Ottocento* (Rome: Biblink, 2001); Pelaja and Scaraffia, *Due in una carne*; Ginevra Diletta Tonini Masella, *Donne sole, modelle, prostitute. Marginalità femminili a Roma fra Sette e Ottocento* (Rome: Edizioni di storia e letteratura, 2012), pp. 71–84. On the marriage promise in the period before the Council of Trent, see Dean, 'Fathers and Daughters'.

presumed to have been seduced]: this entailed the notion that if she gave consent to sexual intercourse (a *stuprum* or *stupro*), this was due to her *fragilitas*, because her will was always assumed to be 'honest'.[22] Until the nineteenth century the term *stuprum* was used to define sexual intercourse with an unmarried woman or with a widow with an honourable position in society.[23] The use of this term, which defined an intercourse contrary to accepted morality, was intended to recall the sense of shame and dishonour caused by sexual relations taking place outside the marriage bond. Although it was deemed an illicit form of intercourse, it did not imply violence.[24] The *stuprum* could be 'semplice' [simple] or 'qualificato' [qualified]; and the distinction was between the absence or presence of a marriage promise.

The ability to give consent instead meant that a woman might be guilty of having had illicit intercourse and being a *socia criminis* [an associate of the crime], not merely a seduced victim. As an accomplice she was fully aware of the implications of her actions and claiming seduction was considered a way to obtain an easy marriage. As highlighted by Giovanni Cazzetta, the rhetoric of the 'abusi delle donne' [abuses by women], that is, women who consciously manipulated the law in their favour in order to be married, led to several proposals to decriminalise the seduction of women who gave their consent.[25] These proposals aimed to avoid 'il risultato "mostruoso" di premiare col diritto donne colpevoli' [the 'monstrous' result of rewarding guilty women with a favourable law].[26] In this regard, for example, in the mid-eighteenth century Ludovico Muratori reported the case of a minister who, aiming to stop the 'esorbitanza negli Stupri' [the exorbitant amount of sexual intercourse with unmarried women], enacted a law through which 'facile riusciva l'accusare e costrignere gli Stupratori a sposare o a dotar le Zittelle' [it was easy to accuse and

22 On this point, see Cazzetta, *Praesumitur seducta*, esp. pp. 15–95.

23 On the term *stuprum*, see *Digest* 48.5.35 (34), *Ad legem Iuliam de adulteriis coercendis*: 'stuprum in vidua vel virgine vel puero committitur' [fornication is committed with a widow, a virgin, or a boy]. For the use of the term *stuprum* from the time of Justinian's *Corpus Iuris Civilis* up to the Middle Ages, see Maria Morello, 'Per una ricostruzione giuridica dello *stupro* e della violenza sulle donne nell'età dello *ius commune*', *Studi Urbinati. Scienze giuridiche, politiche ed economiche*, 64 (2013), 101–29; for the Middle Ages see also Brundage, *Law, Sex and Christian Society*, pp. 28–29.

24 The definition of rape was *stupro violento* [violent *stuprum*].

25 On consent in the law, see Cazzetta, *Praesumitur seducta*, pp. 163–84.

26 Cazzetta, *Praesumitur seducta*, esp. pp. 17, 125–32.

force the seducers to marry or provide dowries to the spinsters].[27] Muratori claimed that the impact of this provision on society had been negative: 'le povere fanciulle si sentivano tratte a fallare per la facilità loro somministrata di veder premiati o ricompensati i lor falli' [poor girls felt encouraged to commit faults because of the ease with which they were given to see their faults financially recognised or rewarded].[28] He also argued that both men and women could become prey to this kind of disorder; and a law that was not sufficiently harsh would consequently worsen society's morality.[29] On this point it is very interesting to note that Muratori considered both sexes prone to committing immoral acts. For men, however, these 'disorders' could be forgiven as they would not bear any visible, long-lasting signs; for women, these *falli* would leave a mark and a blemish which could only be removed through marriage or, eventually, by obtaining a dowry which would re-instate their value on the marriage market and make them respectable wives. Although Muratori refers to them as 'poor girls', according to eighteenth-century discourse on women a woman rapidly evolved from being a person unable to understand the dishonesty of her actions and whose consent was defective to an individual fully aware of her actions: in other words, a person who, with actual malice, wanted to ensnare a man and achieve a marriage, the primary goal of every woman.

This meant that the claim of an honest unmarried woman, a *zitella onesta*, had to be carefully assessed.[30] She could report to the Bishop's Curia to initiate a lawsuit against her seducer and put in place an impediment to bar him from contracting marriage with someone else. For example, in a dispute reported in the journal *Giurisprudenza del codice civile* and brought before an unnamed tribunal of the Kingdom of Sardinia, a man, together with his father, asked the secular judge

27 Ludovico Antonio Muratori, *Della pubblica felicità, oggetto de' buoni principi* (Lucca: [n. pub.], 1749), pp. 102–03.

28 Muratori, *Della pubblica felicità*, pp. 102–03.

29 Muratori, *Della pubblica felicità*, pp. 102–03.

30 The term 'zitella' originated from 'cita' and 'zita', which meant young unmarried girl (Manlio Cortellazzo and Paolo Zolli, 'Zitella', in *Dizionario etimologico della lingua italiana*, 5 vols (Bologna: Zanichelli, 1979–88), v; Salvatore Battaglia, 'Zitella', in *Grande dizionario della lingua italiana*, 21 vols (Turin: UTET, 1961–2002), xxi, 1083). The term *zitella*, 'with the passage of time, morphed into "spinsters"' (Hosker, '"Donne sole" in Post-Unification Italy', p. 85). On the figure of the *zitella* in conduct literature, see Hosker, '"Donne sole" in Post-Unification Italy', pp. 85–113.

to order the Archbishop's Curia of Vercelli to remove the impedient impediment which was hindering his marriage.[31] Despite being rejected by the court due to lack of jurisdiction (as we saw, these matters pertained to the Church's courts), the case is significant in terms of understanding how people tried to circumvent this kind of issue. This man had sexual intercourse with a woman and made her pregnant. He then wanted to marry another woman, possibly of higher status, but the pregnant woman reported him to the Archbishop's Curia of Vercelli and asked for an impediment to be put in place to bar his marriage to someone else. The seducer and his father asked to 'levare [...] l'impedimento impediente nascente dalla deflorazione [...] mediante cauzione di pagare quella indennità che potesse alla medesima essere dovuta' [remove [...] the impedient impediment arising from taking the virginity of the woman [...], by means of a promise to pay the indemnity that could be due to the woman].[32] In their minds, compensation would simply pay off the problem, which was a 'deflorata' [deflowered] and pregnant woman who gave consent to sexual intercourse after being promised marriage. As argued by Giorgia Alessi, since the sixteenth century tribunals such as the Roman Sacra Rota had decreed that a seducer could choose either to provide the seduced woman with a dowry or to marry her, while 'le antiche norme avevano addossato [quest'obbligo] cumulativamente' [ancient rules had imposed [this obligation] cumulatively].[33] This aimed to avoid 'alla famiglie più nobili o facoltose l'onta di un matrimonio coatto con sedotte di bassa condizione' [[bringing upon] the noblest or wealthiest families the shame of a forced marriage with a seduced women of low status].[34]

The seduction of a *zitella onesta* was a major challenge to the common, shared sense of honour and morality and was to be deterred. The Austrian Criminal Code, the *Codice penale dei crimini, dei delitti e delle contravvenzioni* (1852), punished seduction by promise of marriage with a fine and a prison sentence of between three months and a year.[35] The 'disonorata' [dishonoured] was also entitled to

31 *Giurisprudenza del codice civile*, 5 (1842), 149–51.

32 *Giurisprudenza del codice civile*, 5 (1842), p. 149.

33 Alessi, 'Il gioco degli scambi', p. 809. See also Alessi, 'Stupro non violento e matrimonio riparatore'.

34 Alessi, 'Il gioco degli scambi', p. 809.

35 Art. 506, in *Codice penale dei crimini, dei delitti e delle contravvenzioni colle ordinanze sulla competenza dei giudizi penali, e col regolamento sulla stampa del 27 maggio 1852 per l'impero d'Austria* (Vienna: Manz, 1869), p. 177.

compensation.[36] The jurist Luigi Oldrati explains that the Code of 1852 changed the word 'deflorata' [deflowered], which had been used in the previous Code (the *Codice penale dei delitti e delle gravi trasgressioni di polizia* of 1803),[37] into dishonoured.[38] In particular, he notes that 'deflorazione è il vocabolo usato dai criminalisti ad esprimere il delibamento del fior verginale, e la nuova legge avendo sostituito al verbo deflora quello di disonora, pare abbia voluto estendere l'azione anche alla persona già deflorata' [deflowering is the word used by criminalists to mean the deprivation of virginity; and the new law, having replaced the verb deflower with dishonour, seems to have been intended to extend also to the possibility of demanding compensation for a person who has already been deflowered].[39] In other words, this greater protection was also provided to women who had already lost their modesty, which was not uncommon since a marriage promise 'per una zitella è forte stimolo a cedere alle voglie del seduttore' [is a strong incentive for a spinster to succumb to the seducer's desires].[40] Oldrati implied that women, who were not deemed to have the same strength of character as men, could easily fall prey to unscrupulous seducers, putting their honour at risk and irreversibly damaging their reputation.[41]

36 Art. 506, in *Codice penale dei crimini [...] per l'impero d'Austria* (1869), p. 177.

37 On the Austrian Criminal Code of 1803 see *Codice penale universale austriaco (1803)*, ed. by Sergio Vinciguerra (Padua: Cedam, 2001).

38 Luigi Oldrati, *Codice penale austriaco attualmente in vigore nel regno Lombardo-Veneto con osservazioni teorico-pratiche e confronto coll'antecedente abrogato* (Milan: Manini, 1852), p. 432.

39 Oldrati, *Codice penale austriaco*, p. 432. In this passage it is worth noting the unusual use of the term 'persona', considering that nineteenth-century codes and tracts usually report 'femmina' or 'donna'. This might testify to a progressive shift in some jurists' minds from the idea that men and women should be considered individuals with different rights and duties to a more inclusive approach. It could also mean that women were beginning to be considered worthy of enjoying rights based not purely on their biological nature, but because they were 'persone'.

40 Oldrati, *Codice penale austriaco*, p. 432.

41 On honour and reputation, which were important both for married and unmarried women, see Hacke, 'La promessa disattesa', pp. 402–04; Laura Turchi, 'Adulterio, onere della prova e testimonianza. In margine a un processo correggese di età tridentina', in *Trasgressioni*, ed. by Seidel Menchi and Quaglioni, pp. 305–50 (esp. pp. 318–19). On the rhetoric of the danger posed by seducers, see Cazzetta, *Præsumitur seducta*, pp. 330–38.

Poised between the rhetoric of the 'abuses by women' and the need to protect women, law-makers considered seduction a very sensitive question as it often entailed a pregnancy: alongside a possible request to be married, a seduced woman could also ask for alimony to support her children. Key in this context was the question of the attribution of paternity. By impeding the search for paternity, legislators aimed to remove what was considered an obsolete and outdated rule of the Ancien Régime and, above all, to abolish this 'privilege' given to 'donne non oneste' [dishonest women].[42] In the Kingdom of Sardinia, nineteenth-century law did not allow the search for paternity except in two specific cases: if a man explicitly declared himself to be the father of a child (in a written document), or in the case of a proven rape.[43] By contrast, in Lombardy-Venetia paternity could be attributed to a man who, after investigation by the court, was believed to have had sexual intercourse with a woman, provided that her child was born within the appropriate period.[44]

The search for paternity was crucial to win support for children born outside wedlock. Illegitimate children were a cause of great concern: even though the law provided them with the possibility of gaining support from their fathers, claiming to have been seduced and obtaining a favourable ruling as a result was not an easy task for a woman.[45] A good example of this is the lawsuit concerning A. P., a woman seduced by a promise of marriage. She had a long-lasting love affair with D. (both the plaintiff and the defendant were identified by their initials only) and gave birth to two girls in the years after the promulgation of the 1837 Civil Code of the Kingdom of Sardinia.[46] Before the court of Cagliari she claimed that, while the current code required valid betrothals to be made in writing (through a private act or before a notary), D. had promised to marry her when the 1827 *Leggi civili* of King Carlo Felice were in force and this Code did not contain such a rule. A. P. was not able to prove when and whether the marriage promise had effectively been made; and therefore, in the absence of written evidence, she had no way of claiming any

42 Cazzetta, *Præsumitur seducta*, p. 149.

43 Artt. 180 and 185, in *Codice civile per gli Stati di S. M. il Re di Sardegna*, p. 603.

44 Art. 163, in *Codice civile universale austriaco pel Regno Lombardo-Veneto*, p. 156.

45 Art. 166, in *Codice civile universale austriaco pel Regno Lombardo-Veneto*, p. 157. On the right of natural children to receive alimony, see Gian Savino Pene Vidari, *Ricerche sul diritto agli alimenti* (Turin: Giappichelli, 1970). See also Cazzetta, *Præsumitur seducta*, pp. 147–49.

46 *Giurisprudenza degli Stati Sardi*, 7 (1857), 661–62 (p. 661).

legal protection. Given that a natural child could be recognised on the basis of Articles 180 and 185 and that, with the Code of 1837, the search for paternity was not allowed, she was not even able to ask for any support for her daughters.

The court, however, issued a contradictory sentence: A. P. could not make any claim for her daughters but, surprisingly, she was allowed to obtain compensation for having been seduced. Indeed:

> essa ha incontrovertibilmente diritto ad una competente indennità pel danno morale e materiale arrecatole dall'appellante suddetto, coll'averla, secondo quanto venne concludentemente stabilito dalla prova testimoniale, con lusinghiere promesse indotta nei primi anni della sua adolescenza a far paghe le amorose sue voglie; senza che a farle perdere siffatto diritto giovar possano al D... i fatti di non castigata condotta contro di essa articolati; si perché nulla di veramente positivo venne a tale riguardo accertato, e si ancora perché in ogni caso egli stesso ha da tenersi in colpa, se coll'avere esso medesimo fatto primamente deviare dal retto sentiero una giovinetta inesperta, le segnò primo la via della sregolatezza.[47]

> [she has the incontrovertible right to appropriate compensation for the moral and material damage caused by the above-mentioned appellant, by having been induced, according to what has been conclusively established by testimonies, by flattering promises to satisfy his loving desires in the early years of her adolescence; she would not lose such a right in favour of D... [because of] the facts that have been told about her unchaste conduct; both because nothing really certain was ascertained in this regard and also because, in any case, he has to be considered guilty, given that he had made an inexperienced girl deviate from the right path and first led the way in recklessness.]

To support this argument, the court explained that A. P. had asked for fifteen thousand lire in compensation and D. had offered only one thousand lire: the fact that the seducer offered this sum meant he acknowledged the harm caused to A. P. and was, in fact, guilty. With the judgement of 11 August 1857, the court of Cagliari condemned D. to pay one thousand lire. Even more striking than the large difference between the compensation asked for and the amount effectively received by A. P. is that the court mentioned that she had given consent to sexual intercourse after his *flattering promises*, but argued that it was impossible to prove the marriage promise. The court also ruled that D. was the seducer of A. P. and she had the *incontrovertible* right to obtain compensation for the moral and material damage suffered.

47 *Giurisprudenza degli Stati Sardi*, 7, p. 662.

On the other hand, A. P.'s daughters were completely neglected and were not given any support, as they were illegitimate children and their paternity could not be ascertained. The reading of this sentence is once again a powerful reminder of the pivotal importance of the family, a sacred bond established through marriage, which in addition to access to its wealth would also provide children with status and worth.

Along with compromising their reputation and leading an immoral life, women who had illicit sexual intercourse were also considered to be at risk of committing infanticide.[48] As the Milanese lawyer Lino Ferriani points out in his *La infanticida nel codice penale e nella vita sociale* (1886), 'ci furono sempre donne che si macchiarono le mani nel sangue dei loro neonati o per evitare l'onta e lo scandalo, o perché spinte dalla miseria cresciuta nella corruzione, o per lucro infame, o per anima abbruttita sino dall'infanzia' [there have always been women who have stained their hands with the blood of their babies to avoid shame and scandal, or because [they were] driven by misery that grew in corruption, or for ignominious profit, or through a soul corrupted since childhood].[49] However, he admits that women were not completely to blame. Those who truly 'arma[no] la mano dell'infanticida' [arm the infanticide's hand] were the seducers of honest women:[50] they belonged to the upper class, they were wealthy and therefore had more vices than others.[51] As we shall see later in this chapter, this idea contradicts the commonplace one that considered the poor as more vicious and prone to committing sins. Loredana Garlati suggests that this 'new understanding of infanticide emerged with the Enlightenment principles'; and its interpretation became 'attached to an undefended female, victim of society, its values, and of men's deceitful seduction'.[52] Women were considered *sociae criminis* or undefended victims, depending on the circumstances: this contradictory approach may be explained by the

48 On infanticide, see Tommaso Pedìo, *La soppressione del neonato per causa di onore* (Milan: Giuffrè, 1954), pp. 10–22; Prosperi, *Dare l'anima*; Loredana Garlati, 'Honour and Guilt. A Comparative Study on Regulations on Infanticide between the Nineteenth and Twentieth Century', in *Family Law and Society in Europe from the Middle Ages to the Contemporary Era*, ed. by Maria Gigliola Di Renzo Villata (Cham, NY: Springer International Publishing, 2016), pp. 257–81; Prosperi, *Infanticide, Secular Justice, and Religious Debate*.

49 Lino Ferriani, *La infanticida nel codice penale e nella vita sociale: Considerazioni* (Milan: Dumolard, 1886), p. 73.

50 See also Cazzetta, *Præsumitur seducta*, p. 335.

51 Ferriani, *La infanticida*, p. 73.

52 Garlati, 'Honour and Guilt', p. 259.

difficulties in understanding and accepting women's new sense of self, which emerged from the Enlightenment onwards and led to a redefinition of their role, although this change was still to be played out within the family.

Moreover, infanticide did not always carry the same significance. Alongside the distinction between infanticide committed voluntarily or caused by withholding care from the newborn baby, criminalists also distinguished between the killing of a legitimate child and that of an illegitimate one.[53] In the Kingdom of Sardinia, the punishment for infanticide could be reduced by 'uno o di due gradi riguardo alla madre che lo abbia commesso sulla prole illegittima, quando concorrono circostanze attenuanti' [one or two degrees against the mother who committed [infanticide] of illegitimate offspring when mitigating circumstances arise].[54] The criminal code of Lombardy-Venetia made the same distinction: infanticide was punished with 'duro carcere in vita, se il figlio era legittimo; se questi era illegittimo, ha luogo la pena del duro carcere da dieci a venti anni' [hard life imprisonment if the baby was legitimate; if the baby was illegitimate, a hard prison sentence of ten to twenty years].[55] Clearly, legitimate children were deemed to have more value than illegitimate ones because they were born within wedlock and would bear the family name. Conversely, an illegitimate child would be stigmatised even during adulthood and would occupy an ambiguous place in society, to the extent that, in some legal proceedings, people indicted with crimes were mentioned with the term 'spurio' [illegitimate, fake, spurious] added to their names, indicating that their birth was an indelible spot which would affect their lives forever, even though the case had nothing to do with their being illegitimate.[56] Moreover, a man of illegitimate birth who, in adulthood, wanted to receive ordination needed to ask for the *dispensatio natalium*, a dispensation granted by ecclesiastical authorities which cleaned up his uncertain birth and allowed him to enter Christendom as a person worthy of respect.[57] This shared sense of honour attributed value to people on

53 Oldrati, *Codice penale austriaco*, p. 121. See also *Giurisprudenza degli Stati Sardi* (1852), 733–34.

54 Art. 579, in *Codice Penale per gli Stati di S. M. il Regno di Sardegna* (Turin: Minerva Subalpina, 1840), p. 98.

55 Oldrati, *Codice penale austriaco*, p. 121.

56 See, e.g., the case of Domenico *spurio* Belloni, indicted for rape in Macerata at the end of the nineteenth century, in State Archive of Macerata, Processi Penali, 1891, doc. 164.

57 Galdi, *Enciclopedia legale*, II, 709.

the basis of their birth: hence the fact that women were given a lower penalty if the infanticide was committed against an illegitimate child stems from a general comprehension of their need to protect their reputation.

This attitude towards people born outside wedlock did not mean the infanticide of an illegitimate child was not prosecuted. In a case heard before the court of final appeal of Turin, Giuseppa Bouvard, a thirty-year-old peasant, demanded a reduction of her punishment. Previously, she had been convicted for having killed her baby and condemned to forced labour for life by the court of Chambéry in Savoie, which at the time was part of the Kingdom of Sardinia.[58] Before the court of Turin she argued that homicide, including that of a baby, implied premeditation. Her child was, rather, 'di recente nato' [newborn] and consequently she had had no time to plan a possible infanticide. She also asked to be condemned according to Article 579 of the Criminal Code, which dealt specifically with the infanticide of an illegitimate child and gave milder punishments. The court gave this description:

> Le 30 juin 1850, sur les onze heures du matin, la recourante est accouchée d'un enfant du sexe masculin [...]. Cet enfant a été présenté le jour même de sa naissance au recteur de la paroisse de Perjussy, qui l'a baptisé, et inscrit sur les registres des actes de l'état civil; et [...] la recourante lui a donné la mort dans la Commune d'Arenthon, pendant la nuit du 30 juin au 1er juillet. [...] la naissance de cet enfant a été connue, et légalement constatée.[59]
>
> [On 30 June 1850, at eleven o'clock in the morning, the appellant gave birth to a male child [...]. This child was presented to the rector of the parish of Perjussy on the same day of his birth, who baptised him and wrote his name in the register of births; and [...] the appellant killed him in the municipality of Arenthon during the night of 30th June to 1st July. [...] The birth of this child has been known, and legally established.]

On 15 March 1851 the tribunal of Turin rejected the appeal and confirmed the punishment based upon Article 582 (voluntary homicide without mitigating circumstances).[60] It is interesting to

58 *Giurisprudenza degli Stati Sardi* (1851), 56–59.

59 *Giurisprudenza degli Stati Sardi* (1851), p. 58. Part of the case is reported in French as this was the language spoken in the Savoie. Tribunals used both Italian and French. Decisions transcribed in legal journals are also in both languages.

60 Art. 582, in *Codice Penale per gli Stati di S. M. il Re di Sardegna*, p. 98.

note that the newborn baby was first baptised and then killed. Even though the behaviour of Giuseppa was unclear, one could argue that this testifies to her piety. Giuseppa might have been aware that according to Catholic dogma she would deserve Hell but, despite not being able or willing to look after her child and presumably having the intention to commit infanticide, she wanted her baby to become a true Christian and to be received in Heaven as only the baptised could. Baptism was intended as a moment of creation, with the soul entering the body as the result of divine intervention.[61]

In Lombardy-Venetia investigations and proceedings regarding infanticide were similar to those in the Kingdom of Sardinia. A case described in the journal *Giurisprudenza pratica secondo la legislazione austriaca* concerned a twenty-three-year-old woman, Anna K., who was a housekeeper in a manor in an unspecified area of the countryside. Until this occasion she had never been under investigation.[62] Her father had died many years earlier and her mother did the same job in a nearby manor. Anna K., as well as Giuseppa Bouvard, belonged to the 'human type' which committed infanticide as described by Adriano Prosperi in his monograph on the subject: servants or humble labourers, almost always unmarried.[63] Usually they did not have any close relatives, such as a mother or a father, living with them or supporting them.

Court records reported that Anna K. was arrested on the basis of Article 264 of the *Codice penale dei delitti e delle gravi trasgressioni di polizia* (1803) in February 1822.[64] In compliance with the terms of Article 264 she was deemed to have committed infanticide because 'l'ingrossamento del suo corpo l'avea fatto riguardar da tutti come gravida' [the swelling of her body had made everyone see that

61 On baptism, see also Prosperi, *Infanticide, Secular Justice, and Religious Debate*, pp. 161–230.

62 *Giurisprudenza pratica secondo la legislazione austriaca*, 17 (1831), 67–88.

63 Prosperi, *Infanticide, Secular Justice, and Religious Debate*, p. 67.

64 This article explicitly rules that evidence of infanticide might come from the following combined circumstances: 'quando sia seguito un improvviso rimarchevole cambiamento del corpo, senza che appaja la Creatura, che ne doveva essere la causa, e che dalla visita, da queste circostanze occasionata, siasi rilevata la certezza di un parto poc'anzi accaduto' [when a sudden remarkable change of the body shape has happened, without the creature who was the cause of it appearing, and that from the medical examination undertaken for this reason, it had been ascertained that a birth had just happened] (Art. 264, in *Codice de' delitti e delle gravi trasgressioni politiche* (Vienna: Stamperia Reale, 1803), p. 117).

she was pregnant]; then, all of a sudden, she returned to her usual physical appearance, without anyone having heard of her giving birth.[65] Even though there were no traces of the baby, she was subjected to inspection by an obstetrician, who confirmed that Anna had given birth three weeks earlier at the most. This testimony forced Anna to reveal the truth: eight days after Easter, she had been seduced by the son of her master and then 'esserselo ingrossato il ventre, arrestati i suoi benefici, ed essersi quindi creduta gravida' [her belly swelled, her menstruation stopped and she thought she was pregnant].[66] On 20 January 1822, nine months after the seduction had taken place, two other girls who worked as housekeepers in the same house went to dance in a nearby inn, leaving Anna alone. She was already in bed when she felt a strong pain and went to the commode 'dove senza dolori qualche cosa da lei passò nel recipiente' [where something passed painlessly from her into the container].[67] Anna gave a confused description of what had happened to her and insisted that everything 'passò tra la precipitazione e l'irriflessione' [had happened through haste and thoughtlessness].[68] She then returned to bed and, when her co-workers came back from their evening out, did not mention what had happened.

Since Anna shared the bed with the other two girls, one of them inevitably noticed that she seemed suddenly to have lost weight and reported this fact during the trial.[69] The evidence and the testimonies were all against Anna, who had no way of escaping the indictment. She admitted to having understood 'qual nero attentato avesse commesso contro la propria prole, che lo avrebbe pianto per tutta la vita, ma che allora non era corsa col pensiero alle tristi conseguenze, e così dicendo proruppe in dirotto pianto' [what an awful outrage she had committed against her offspring, that she would have mourned all her life long, but at the time she had not understood the sad consequences of her act and, so saying, she burst into tears].[70] Anna secretly carried out her entire pregnancy without being able

65 *Giurisprudenza pratica*, 27 (1831), p. 80.

66 *Giurisprudenza pratica*, 27 (1831), p. 82

67 *Giurisprudenza pratica*, 27 (1831), p. 80.

68 *Giurisprudenza pratica*, 27 (1831), p. 80.

69 Sleeping in the same bed was very common among lower classes and one bed was commonly used by the whole family, leaving no room for intimacy (Lombardi, *Matrimoni di antico regime*, pp. 211–12).

70 *Giurisprudenza pratica*, 17 (1831), p. 83.

'to seek the advice and experience of married women or widows'.[71] During birth, she was alone and without any support, as she also was during the trial. Anna claimed that she did not remember what had happened to her baby and made no mention of cutting the umbilical cord. Instead, she insisted that everything went on very quickly and that she had not understood what was happening. Whether Anna's ignorance of the consequences of her seduction was genuine or just an attempt to escape conviction, she was nonetheless sentenced to two years of imprisonment for infanticide by voluntarily omitting the care a newborn needed.

Beyond the specific case and indictment of this young woman, the analysis of the court records as reported by *Giurisprudenza pratica* has value in that it shows which issues were taken into consideration by the law in action. Although a crucial link between seduction and infanticide was acknowledged, protection of the women involved receded more and more, to the extent that jurists even highlighted 'le solite scuse che le accusate sogliono addurre per ischivare le pene criminali nei casi d'infanticidio' [the usual excuses that the accused usually cite to avoid criminal penalties in infanticide cases].[72] The journal stressed that the first excuse a woman used to avoid indictment was that she had given birth to a stillborn. The second most recurrent claim was that she was not aware of being pregnant. An infanticide also used to say that she was:

> sorpresa e sopraffatta dall'impreveduto parto ed abbia perciò partorito secretamente e senza assistenza; che nell'atto del parto abbia perduto affatto ogni presenza di mente, e che non abbia saputo più che cosa si facesse del feto; finalmente che per ignoranza non abbia prestato all'infante la necessaria cura ed assistenza e per esempio non abbia reciso ed annodato il vincolo umbellicale; dal che i medici asseriscono dover conseguire il dissanguamento e la morte.[73]
>
> [surprised and overwhelmed by the unexpected birth and therefore gave birth secretly and without assistance; that in the act of giving birth she lost all presence of mind and that she no longer knew what was to be done with the foetus; finally, that out of ignorance she did not give the baby the necessary care and assistance and, for example, she did not cut and tie the umbillical cord, from which the doctors assert that bleeding and death would have followed.]

71 Prosperi, *Infanticide, Secular Justice, and Religious Debate*, p. 123.

72 Prosperi, *Infanticide, Secular Justice, and Religious Debate*, p. 85.

73 Prosperi, *Infanticide, Secular Justice, and Religious Debate*, p. 86.

Judges were to pay particular attention to the excuse of 'perdere i sentimenti' [losing her feelings], which was often used to remove the 'imputazione morale' [moral imputation], but, in the opinion of doctors, this situation rarely happened during easy and regular childbirths.[74] What emerges from these nineteenth-century *communes opiniones* is 'una tela intrisa di ambiguità' [a canvas imbued with ambiguity][75] on which women were still considered unable to understand civil law and were to be hindered from undertaking any legal act but, at the same time, were regarded as perfectly able to elaborate excuses in order to evade criminal law and therefore deserving of punishment in the same way as men.

Extramarital Relations

Alongside seduction, which affected 'honest' girls, extramarital relations, that is, sexual intercourse outside marriage, were also not allowed and even punished. Public authorities and society as a whole paid great attention to issues causing disorder and 'scandalo pubblico' [public scandal], events conflicting with the moral, behavioural and cultural structures around which society revolved. As we shall see, authorities tried their best to circumscribe sexual intercourse within the boundaries of wedlock, both by removing possible obstacles to marriage (e.g., canonical impediments) and by punishing situations which could not be solved in other ways, as when the parties involved were already married to other people. Sexual intercourse outside the marriage bond was defined in terms of 'pratiche disoneste' [dishonest practices] or 'commercio illecito' [illicit trade], explicitly conferring a moral stigma and, at the same time, defining sex within marriage as honest and licit.

In the Kingdom of Sardinia the *pratiche disoneste* were handled as a crime and punished according to Article 437 of the *Codice Penale*. The sentence depended upon whether the people involved were married or not and made no formal distinction between men and women: unmarried people could risk up to one year in prison; a married person who had sexual intercourse with an unmarried person could undergo one to two years of prison; if both were married, they would be condemned to imprisonment of two to three years.[76] This article did not mention adultery: the boundaries between adultery

74 See also *Giurisprudenza pratica*, 13 (1830), 176–77.

75 Cazzetta, *Praesumitur seducta*, p. 338.

76 Art. 437, in *Codice Penale per gli Stati di S. M. il Regno di Sardegna*, p. 76.

and extramarital relations were blurred and related to the way they were perceived (adultery is discussed in Chapter 6, when the causes of separation are examined). Extramarital relations, which were often also adulterous, had an impact on society's sense of honour and authorities felt the need for redress. A case for adultery had to be initiated by the betrayed spouse, who could also decide not to initiate it at all. Illicit sexual intercourse was a public matter and a crime against 'il costume pubblico' [public habits], whereas adultery was a crime against 'l'ordine delle famiglie' [the order of families].[77]

This is illustrated in a judgement of 17 August 1855 regarding a man whose family name was Ellena (no other details about his identity are given) and who was given a three-year sentence in prison for having had an affair with a woman, a certain Duverney.[78] They both lived in Chambéry and were both married to other people, yet they persisted in their relations, which provoked a *scandalo pubblico* in the local community. The mayor of Chambéry demanded their arrest and the tribunal, after having questioned the witnesses, enforced their punishment on the basis of Article 437. The case was appealed by Ellena: he argued that his punishment was unjust as none of the people who had borne witness against him should have been allowed to do so. In particular, he claimed that neither the mayor nor the police could testify as this was not an office but an instance case. The difference relied on the possibility of the case being initiated by public authorities (office case) or by a person who had a claim (instance case). Ellena maintained that the lawsuit could have been initiated only by his spouse, who had been betrayed and had motive to seek redress. He also argued that Article 437 punished concubinage and that the nature of his and his lover's relationship did not fall into this category, because they did not live together and the law condemned not 'gli atti di fornicazione, ma l'insulto fatto alla società ed alla religione con legami illegali imitanti il matrimonio, con carattere di comune abitazione, letto, vita e nome' [acts of fornication, but the insult made to society and religion by illegal bonds imitating marriage, such as sharing the same house, bed, life and name].[79] Other than claiming that a public authority was not allowed to bear witness in such a case, Ellena also tried to highlight that 'le relazioni illecite tra persone di sesso diverso sono affare di coscienza' [illicit relationships between people of different sexes are

77 *Codice Penale per gli Stati di S. M. il Regno di Sardegna*, pp. 76, 90.

78 *Giurisprudenza degli Stati Sardi*, 6 (1856), 714–16.

79 *Giurisprudenza degli Stati Sardi*, 6 (1856), p. 715.

a matter of conscience].[80] In contradiction of Ellena's point, this case confirms that nineteenth-century society firmly believed that sex was not solely an intimate matter and that public authorities were allowed to intrude into a person's intimate life. Ellena's argument was essentially wrong: Article 437 did not punish concubinage; rather, that was Article 526. Both the court of first instance and that of appeal pointed out that Article 437 precisely stated that 'toutes les relations illicites qui ont été fréquentes et ont amenés le scandale public' [all illicit relationships which had been frequent and led to public scandal] were to be punished. The sentence was appropriate because it had been ascertained that:

> la femme Duverney avait des relations illicites avec Ellena, qu'elle entrait chez lui de jour et de nuit, que ces relations, dont ce dernier s'était même vanté, avaient le caractère de scandal public, et que les deux prévenus étaient mariés.[81]
>
> [the Duverney woman had illicit relations with Ellena, that she entered his house day and night, that these relations, of which the latter even boasted, had the character of a public scandal and that the two defendants were married [to other people].]

It is worth noting that the court emphasised the characteristics of this relationship which fitted its definition of public scandal: their sexual relations were frequent; and the woman entered the man's house at all hours of the day.

In Lombardy-Venetia, by contrast, sexual intercourse was not punished, arguably because 'lo scandalo dell'inquisizione sarebbe spesso un male maggiore dell'impunità' [the scandal of an inquiry would often cause a greater evil than would impunity].[82] However, the moral authority and rules of the Catholic Church strongly influenced attitudes towards these issues. Session XXIV of the Council of Trent's Canons states that those who carried out *dishonest practices* were warned three times and, if they persisted in behaving in such a way, excommunicated, regardless of their status or social class. Although punishment was deemed to be applied to people of any class and status, closer attention was paid to the poor, who were considered to fall prey to incontinence more easily,[83] which was '[il vizio] il più vile,

80 *Giurisprudenza degli Stati Sardi*, 6 (1856), p. 715.

81 *Giurisprudenza degli Stati Sardi*, 6 (1856), p. 715.

82 Oldrati, *Codice penale austriaco*, p. 104.

83 *Raccolta di alcune notificazioni, editti, ed istruzioni: opera utilissima a tutti gli ecclesiastici*, 5 vols (Venice: Pitteri, 1740), III, 29.

il più schifoso, il più abbominevole' [[the vice] which was the vilest, the most disgusting, the most abominable].[84]

In 1855, for example, the Milanese Curia wrote a letter to the local lieutenancy suggesting they allow a couple to marry as soon as possible. The case concerned a woman from Busto Arsizio (a town forty kilometres from Milan) who wanted to marry the man with whom she had lived in previous years. As her husband, from whom she had been legally separated since 1847, had just died, she did not want to wait the time prescribed by the law before remarrying. The Curia explained the situation with these words: 'La sconsigliata si diede ad altro uomo libero [...] e con esso visse in riprovevole concubinato, con quanto rumore e con qual danno di cattivo esempio, non è a dirsi' [The thoughtless woman gave herself to another free man and lived with him in reprehensible concubinage, with what rumor and damage [caused by their] bad example is unmentionable].[85] The choice of terms used serves as a notable example of the attitudes of the Ottocento. The woman is described as *thoughtless*, possibly meaning she was prey to her feelings, thus reconfirming the stereotype of women as not able correctly to assess what was right and wrong. Along with the disappointment which emerges from this letter, it could also be noted that this couple had lived together for many years and the Church could do nothing but morally condemn them.[86] The situation of this *thoughtless* woman, however, was redeemable: by allowing the couple to marry immediately, 'si verrebbe in tal modo a por fine immediata ad un disordine che generi e genera tanto scandalo' [in this way the disorder that would cause and causes so much scandal would end].[87]

The Church, and secular authorities as well, tended to do their best to favour marriage. As we have seen, ecclesiastical authorities had significant powers over canon law outside the boundaries of the Papal States. Alongside impedient impediments such as the marriage promise discussed earlier in this chapter, the local bishop could also remove the fourteen types of diriment impediments which rendered

84 Michele Piano and Giovanni Labus, 'Meditazione VI, Sul vizio della disonestà. *A spiritu fornicationis libera nos, Domine*', in Michele Piano and Giovanni Labus, *Istruzioni dogmatiche parrocchiali e discorsi evangelici; coll'aggiunta di due ragionamenti* (Milan: Manini, 1839), pp. 691–94.

85 Milan, Archivio Diocesano, Carteggio Ufficiale, April 1855, doc. 472.

86 On this point, see also Pelaja, *Matrimonio e sessualità a Roma nell'Ottocento*, pp. 174–82.

87 Milan, Archivio Diocesano, Carteggio Ufficiale, 1855 Aprile, doc. 472.

a person incapable of validly contracting a marriage.[88] Affinity, for example, was a diriment impediment for which the Bishop's Curia had the power to issue a dispensation. It was defined as 'una specie di parentela originata dalla copula carnale o sia lecita o illecita, purché sia sufficiente alla generazione' [a kind of kinship originating from carnal conjunction, be it licit or illicit, as long as it is sufficient for the generation [of children]];[89] and could exist between a man and a woman's blood relations and vice versa.[90] This was an impediment which individuals very often asked to remove: it frequently happened that a widow or a widower continued to have relations with the family of her or his deceased spouse and even married another member of the in-law family. In these cases, the new couple usually reported to the Curia and explained their motivation for marrying, which was often simple and aimed at surviving everyday life.

A case in point is that of Francesco Gerardo Turri and Amalia Civali, who, in 1863, went before the Bishop's Curia of Verona to ask for the necessary dispensation. Amalia, aged thirty-seven, was the widow of Giovanni Turri, the brother of Francesco Gerardo, aged forty. The two described their actual condition and pleaded to be allowed to marry. They admitted to having had sexual intercourse before the death of Amalia's husband and even believed that the son she had was the child of Francesco Gerardo and not her late husband. Moreover, Amalia was again pregnant and Francesco Gerardo was the father. They made no mention of any feeling or love existing between them; further still, Francesco Gerardo added that he was in extreme need of a woman to carry out housework and assist his aged parents. They also stressed to the Curia that they were both 'miserabilissimi' [very poor] and, taking into consideration the 'mali commessi' [evils that have been committed], would not find other spouses. However, the most important argument in favour of the removal of the impediment might have been that, if they were married, 'sarebbe levato lo scandalo e provveduto alla donna, che altrimenti così abbandonata si darebbe ad una vita cattiva' [the scandal would be removed and the woman would be looked after, otherwise she would abandon herself to a bad life].[91] As Margherita Pelaja argues, the Church saw people as prone to sin, 'sempre sull'orlo dell'orgasmo'

88 Mercanti, *Compendio di diritto canonico*, I, 450.

89 Mercanti, *Compendio di diritto canonico*, I, 459–60.

90 Pelaja and Scaraffia, *Due in una carne*, pp. 105–10.

91 Bishop's Curia of Verona, Matrimoniorum, Dipense, 1863.

[always on the verge of orgasm],[92] and therefore every action to avoid scandal and promote marriage was to be taken.[93] The couple in this case touched the right chord by highlighting the scandal and the risk Amalia faced of falling into a 'vita cattiva' [bad life]: the impediment to marriage was removed and they were allowed to marry.[94]

Confining sexual intercourse within the boundaries of marriage was a primary goal to pursue. James Brundage highlights the fact that authorities were convinced 'fornication was [...] the basic type of illicit sex, a sordid business that fouled the body while it sullied the soul';[95] and these ideas were delivered by both temporal and secular authorities in states such as the Kingdom of Sardinia and Lombardy-Venetia. Sin and grace, however, were 'a concern of all people, from the theologians to the most modest peasants, [and much] more than a means of governing Christian society';[96] and, as Jean Delumeau observes, 'spiritual fear most deeply afflicted the Christian elites themselves'.[97]

In such a context, confession, and possibly repentance, were solutions given to society, which was thought of as being in a constant, crucial tension between sin and salvation;[98] and, at the same time, they were a means of confirming the Catholic Church's power and influence beyond the boundaries of its secular state. Many tracts explained how, in practice, to tackle sensitive and difficult situations in which people's morality was at risk, given that, as argued by Luciano Guerci, 'gli agguati del peccato della carne [sono] onnipresenti' [the traps of the sin of the flesh [are] omnipresent] and the sin 'ci stringe d'assedio e si cela sotto le più

92 Pelaja and Scaraffia, *Due in una carne*, p. 155.

93 On the Church, sin and the law, see also Nicholas Davidson, 'Theology, Nature and the Law: Sexual Sin and Sexual Crime in Italy from the Fourteenth to the Seventeenth Century', in *Crime, Society and the Law*, ed. by Dean and Lowe, pp. 74–98.

94 On female prostitution, see Michela Turno, *Il malo esempio. Donne scostumate e prostituzione nella Firenze dell'Ottocento* (Florence: Giunti, 2003); Ginevra Diletta Tonini Masella, 'Il buon nome delle donne. Matrimonio, professione e reputazione nella Roma dell'Ottocento', *Storia delle donne*, 6/7 (2010/2011), 139–55; Tonini Masella, *Donne sole, modelle, prostitute*, pp. 111–56.

95 Brundage, *Law, Sex and Christian Society*, p. 205.

96 Jean Delumeau, *Sin and Fear: The Emergence of a Western Guilt Culture, XIII–XVIII Centuries* (New York: St. Martin's Press, 1990), p. 248.

97 Delumeau, *Sin and Fear*, p. 321.

98 Guerci, *La discussione*, pp. 41–57.

innocenti apparenze' [besieges us and is hidden underneath the most innocent of appearances].[99] For example, in his *Istruzione pratica per i confessori novelli* (1832) the priest Filippo Maria Salvatori explains that 'in tre ore circa di lavoro seguito mi riesce di fare una confessione generale anche di 50 e 60 anni' [in about three straight hours of work I can make a general confession of even 50 or 60 years].[100] Confession, a prerequisite for absolution, had to be complete and sincere; but receiving a confession was a thorny issue even for an experienced priest, who had to pay particular attention to avoiding any contact with the sinner, especially if this was a woman, as 'il volto della donna è come un vento che brucia la pelle' [a woman's face is like a wind that burns the skin].[101] Despite these efforts and training, once confession and repentance were obtained it was difficult to find a person who would not fall into sin again. Carrying out dishonest practices brought such 'danno spirituale, peggiore di tutti gli altri, sì è la gran difficoltà che incontrano i disonesti ad emendarsi, la gran facilità a morire impenitenti e dannarsi' [spiritual damage, worse than all other types of damage, given the great difficulty dishonest people have in amending themselves and the great ease of dying unrepentant and damned].[102]

By controlling marriage and sexuality, the Catholic Church penetrated the fabric of Italian society and imposed its own sense of morality, which was to be pursued and praised as the 'correct' way of conducting oneself in life and society. This is because 'sexual beliefs and practices exert power, not only over individual conduct, but also over the ways in which institutions themselves grow and develop [having] significant bearings upon property interests, household structure, and notions about morality, among many other things'.[103] Preventing the *disordine* that dishonest practices could cause to society was not just a way to avoid scandal and ensure

99 Guerci, *La discussione*, pp. 42–43.

100 Filippo Maria Salvatori, *Istruzione pratica per i confessori novelli: divisa in due parti* (Turin: Marietti, 1832), p. 271. On confession and the Church, see also Peter Brooks, *Troubling Confessions: Speaking Guilt in Law and Literature* (Chicago, IL: University of Chicago Press, 2000), pp. 90–102; Pelaja and Scaraffia, *Due in una carne*, pp. 101–48.

101 Antonio Pierozzi, *Defecerunt Summula confessionalis utilissima* (Venice: Bindoni and Maffei Pasini, 1538), p. 32. Antonio Pierozzi is also known as Antoninus of Florence (1389–1459).

102 Piano and Labus, *Istruzioni dogmatiche*, p. 694.

103 Brundage, *Law, Sex and Christian Society*, p. 1.

peace: the intrusiveness into the intimate sphere of an individual was a means of control and also a mission entrusted to the authorities.[104] When prison was not enough to discourage illicit intercourse, moral condemnation and the menace of perdition were put into play, as the ultimate goal was an ideal society in which things moved in the correct way, with people subservient to authority, and where the law and hierarchical order did not incur any challenge.

104 See also Delumeau, *Sin and Fear*, pp. 320–22; Di Simplicio, *Peccato penitenza perdono*; Bonacchi, *Legge e peccato*; Christopher F. Black, *Church, Religion and Society in Early Modern Italy* (Basingstoke: Palgrave Macmillan, 2004); Irene Fosi, *La giustizia del papa. Sudditi e tribunali nello Stato Pontificio in età moderna* (Rome and Bari: Laterza, 2007).

5. Women, Marriage and the Transmission of Property

If intrusion into people's intimate personal sphere was a way to exert control over society and enforce the established order, lawmakers and authorities also paid attention to matters regarding the transmission of wealth. Through dowries and inheritance, the ownership of wealth changed, thus challenging the equilibrium on which both families and society depended. While in the Kingdom of Sardinia the dowry was a woman's lawful share of her parents' inheritance, in Lombardy-Venetia women could inherit to the same degree as their male relatives, with the dowry being just an advance on the portion of inheritance to which they were entitled at their parents' death. However, cultural shackles were still very strong; and despite being under the rule of Austrian law, Lombardy-Venetia shared social rules with other areas of the Italian Peninsula. In particular, the prominence given to men can be inferred from many private acts, such as wills, which attempted to override the law and debarred women from accessing the due portion of their family's wealth. Drawing on archival material and legal journals, including the *Annali di Giurisprudenza* or *Giurisprudenza pratica secondo la legislazione austriaca,* this chapter analyses attitudes towards dowries and inheritance by examining a legal disquisition as well as a select number of cases. With regard to the Kingdom of Sardinia, the cases are judicial proceedings concerning dowries; cases regarding Lombardy-Venetia instead pertain to wills and demonstrate the distorting intent with which the latter were sometimes used. These case studies, taken together, help us to understand the expectations, mentality and behavioural patterns of nineteenth-century society.

Women's Exclusion from Inheritance in the Kingdom of Sardinia

As we saw earlier in Chapter 3, the dowry was a crucial institution in most areas of the Italian Peninsula. In the Kingdom of Sardinia, it was the only inheritance portion to which women had a right, except for the short period of the French conquests, when they were entitled to inherit in the same way as men. With the repeal of the Napoleonic Code after the Congress of Vienna, the *Regio Editto* of 21 May 1814 stipulated that the *Regie Costituzioni* of 1770 and other acts promulgated up to 23 June 1800 again had the force of law.[1] This meant that women's access to inheritance was once again limited to an 'appropriate' dowry. The measure of this appropriateness was calculated by considering the family's goods and dowries given 'alle persone di simil grado, secondo la consuetudine del luogo' [to people of similar status, according to the custom of the place].[2] For married women, an appropriate dowry was 'quella dote, colla quale sieno state onestamente ricapitate' [that dowry with which they were honestly placed].[3] As we shall see, this concept had fluid boundaries which were sometimes questioned before courts.

Having a dowry also implied that a woman was excluded from inheriting from her mother[4] and had no right to her relatives' patrimony. Especially during the first half of the nineteenth century, these norms led to several disputes, to the extent that jurists felt the need to clarify some points related to women's exclusion. In 1838 the *Annali di giurisprudenza*, an authoritative journal of jurisprudence for the Kingdom of Sardinia, published a disquisition on the maxim 'tot dotes quot hereditates' [as many dowries as inheritances], that is, whether an amount corresponding to an appropriate dowry was due to a woman on each *ab intestato* inheritance.[5] This was meant to explain that, although a patrimony could substantially increase after receiving several inheritances, a woman who was already dowered was not entitled to any addition. In this disquisition, as well as in the

1 Regio Editto, N. 9, in *Raccolta degli atti del governo di Sua Maestà il Re di Sardegna dall'anno 1814 a tutto il 1832*, 22 vols (Turin: Pignetti and Carena, 1842), I, 15–18.

2 Art. 6, Lib. V, Tit. 7, in *Leggi, e costituzioni di Sua Maestà*, p. 336.

3 Art. 6, Lib. V, Tit. 7, in *Leggi, e costituzioni di Sua Maestà*, p. 336.

4 Art. 3, Lib. V, Tit. 7, in *Leggi, e costituzioni di Sua Maestà*, 2 vols (Turin: Stamperia Reale, 1770), I, 336.

5 *Annali di giurisprudenza raccolta mensile pubblicata da una società di avvocati e causidici*, 1 (1838), 41–51.

cases reported in the following sections, the issue contained many contradictions and inconsistencies: the difficulties in dealing with the enormous bulk of laws, all in force at the same time, and the need to interpret the law without provoking a disruptive effect on society consistently affected the coherence of the legal framework.[6]

The disquisition stated that, even if women were excluded *propter dotem* by law, at the opening of each inheritance they had to be considered as if they were heirs in order correctly to assess their case. The reasoning behind this principle was that, if the assets increased considerably, the dowry, too, might be subject to a re-assessment of its appropriateness. *Annali di giurisprudenza* pointed out that the crucial point to consider was whether a woman was married or not, because 'la differenza che passa tra la maritata e la nubile sta riposta nel modo di determinare la *congruità* della dote, che venne loro lasciata, o costituita' [the difference between the married woman and the maiden is the means of determining the *appropriateness* of the dowry which was bequeathed to them or established for them].[7] Even though the *Regie Costituzioni* did not explicitly make such a distinction, the journal argued that the appropriateness was to be determined at the time of marriage, given that an unmarried woman could also have a dowry which could have been bequeathed in a will or promised before her marriage and then formally established after this event. The journal specified that a woman who was 'recapitata onestamente' [honestly placed] 'è rimossa dalle successioni che a di lei favore si aprono' [is removed from the successions which open up in her favour], because a married woman was always assumed to be appropriately dowered.[8] On this basis there was no reason to grant her further rights. As we shall see, a possible consequence of this principle was that if, for example, a woman had received a dowry appropriate to her status from a relative, she would even be excluded from inheriting from her father.

Annali di giurisprudenza next gave a number of examples of late-eighteenth-century lawsuits which allowed room for questions. In 1781, for example, Rosalia Caccia – already married and dowered – was denied the inheritance of her deceased sister Polissena; but their

6 On the lack of coherence in the nineteenth-century legal system, see Paolo Grossi, 'Tradizione e modelli nella sistemazione post-unitaria della proprietà', *Quaderni Fiorentini per la storia del pensiero giuridico moderno*, 5/6 (1976/1977), 202–338 (pp. 203–06).

7 *Quaderni Fiorentini per la storia del pensiero giuridico moderno*, 5/6, pp. 203–06.

8 *Annali di giurisprudenza*, 1 (1838), 41–56 (p. 51).

sister Felicita was able to inherit because she was still unmarried and had no dowry. In another case, decided in 1795, a court denied Maddalena Gallea Bussolino, who was also already married and enjoyed a dowry provided by an uncle, the ability to inherit from her mother and her sister because she was already *recapitata* and dowered.[9] Conversely, in a judgement passed a few years earlier, in 1740, the court maintained that, as Rosalia Anna had inherited a sum of money from her mother and then established her dowry by herself, she was still able to succeed to her father, 'senza punto far caso della circostanza se [...] fosse maritata, o nubile' [without paying attention to the circumstances of her being married, or unmarried].[10] As mentioned earlier, the formal act of establishing a dowry prevented the free use of the money and goods which were part of it, thus keeping them safe for the time of widowhood. In the case of Rosalia Anna, the decision relied on the assumption that her dowry was not established in such a way as to remove her from the succession because it was not given by 'ascendenti paterni, o materni, o da trasversali' [paternal, maternal or ancillary ancestors].[11] It is clear that this interpretation of the law contradicted what the journal claimed at the beginning of the disquisition, namely that a married woman was always assumed to be appropriately dowered and, therefore, removed from the successions which open in her favour.

Annali di giurisprudenza added that judges often granted more than one dowry to women: 'sembrando loro troppo rigorosa l'esclusione [...] ravvisavano ottimo consiglio il mitigare l'asprezza della legge, allorché l'occasione si presentava di farlo senza sovvertirne il letterale precetto' [as excluding [women] seemed too harsh, they considered it to be a very good idea to mitigate the law when they had the opportunity to do it without subverting the literal precept].[12] The journal argued that there were always solid reasons which permitted an exception and courts had to assess carefully whether money or goods already given to women could be considered appropriate dowries or not. For example, in 1837 a court ordered that a woman, Giacinta Regis, could obtain a dowry from the patrimony of her brother Domenico. The decision highlighted that, even though she had already been given a dowry from her father's estate, Giacinta was not yet married and was allowed to

9 *Annali di giurisprudenza*, 1, p. 51.

10 *Annali di giurisprudenza*, 1, p. 52.

11 *Annali di giurisprudenza*, 1, pp. 52–53.

12 *Annali di giurisprudenza*, 1, p. 49.

reassess the appropriateness of her dowry on the basis of the wealth left by her deceased brother.[13]

With regard to unmarried women, the value of their dowries had to be carefully evaluated and they had the right to examine their appropriateness on the basis of the quality and quantity of their family's assets. If a dowry left by an ancestor or by other relatives was still appropriate, it was not to be increased; rather, if it ceased to be appropriate, especially in comparison to people of similar status according to the customs of that area, addition should be made to that dowry.[14] As this principle emerged from this disquisition alongside the written law, its interpretation was far from pristine and the maxim *tot dotes quot hereditates* needed to be interpreted on a case-by-case basis and not taken literally. With regard to dowries, given their pivotal importance in areas such as the Kingdom of Sardinia various sources of law coexisted and their interpretation led to contradictions, overlaps and inconsistencies which often resulted in unexpected court judgements.

The Roncalli: A Wealthy Family in Piedmont

In the Kingdom of Sardinia, despite being debarred from accessing a large portion of their parents' patrimony women had to be present when the formal act of establishing their dowry was signed. A case regarding litigation that took place in Piedmont, which was part of the Kingdom of Sardinia, is illustrative of this rule. The dispute involved members of a large patriarchal family, the Roncalli, and highlights the considerable difference between the portion of family assets which women and men were entitled to receive. Furthermore, it gives an interesting perspective on how courts dealt with the many co-existing and sometimes conflicting laws. The Roncalli family lived in the Kingdom of Sardinia, in Vigevano, a town fifty kilometres from Milan. They were very close to the Duchy of Milan, which would become part of the Kingdom of Lombardy-Venetia, and had several social and economic relationships in that area. Alongside the custom of using the scudi of Milan as currency, inhabitants often signed legal acts based on the Duchy's local statutes. In such cases judges had not only to tackle the dispute itself, but also to deal with different sources of law.

13 *Annali di giurisprudenza*, 1, p. 47.

14 *Annali di giurisprudenza*, 1, p. 51.

Maria Longhi and Giuseppe Roncalli had one son and six daughters. An image of the family tree will help us to understand the at times intricate developments of the case brought to court. The Roncalli were very wealthy and were able to provide each of their daughters with a dowry worth 3,833 Milanese scudi, as well as a trousseau worth 540 scudi. As Cesarina Casanova observes, a family's choices of continuity corresponded 'all'entità delle risorse, materiali e simboliche, […] e al quadro istituzionale e normativo che condiziona le loro possibilità di disporne' [to the amount of material and symbolic wealth [they had], […] and to the institutional and regulatory framework that shapes their ability to dispose of them].[15] Such were the Roncalli family's choices in the interests of continuity: they gave very good dowries to all their daughters, but it was their son Vincenzo who was the 'chosen' one. Entrusted with the goal of carrying forward the family's name and status, he was entitled to inherit the great majority of their patrimonies and, above all, their physical assets, namely estates and land.

Two daughters, Giacoma and Gioanna, married in 1802 and 1809 respectively. They both went to live in Milan and their dowries were established on the basis of the Statutes of Milan. Giacoma's dowry was established on 9 December 1802 and was given to Serafino Sanchioli, father of her husband Giuseppe. Gioanna married seventeen-year-old Giuseppe Antonio Negroni. In Gioanna's case, the dowry instrument, dated 20 January 1809, reports that it was Clara Sassi – mother of Giuseppe Antonio – who gave consent to her son's marriage and received 'in her hands' her daughter-in-law's dowry.[16] According to the Statutes of Milan, a woman was able to make contracts if she was a widow and had no male relatives and this fact was to be proven by an oath.[17] A widow was also able to give consent to her children's

15 Casanova, *La famiglia italiana*, p. 43.

16 State Archive of Turin (AST), Casale, Corte di Appello, First Quarter of 1849, n. 31. A summary of this case can also be found in *Giurisprudenza Italiana*, 2 (1849), 671–97. Casale is a town in the Monferrato area and is now called Casale Monferrato. However, in judicial proceedings it is just cited as Casale.

17 See Statute 328, in *Statuti di Milano: volgarizzati con note, e spiegazioni* (Milan: Galeazzi, 1773), pp. 177–79. The oath had long been highly significant for the confirmation of a legal transaction if the validity of the latter was doubtful. Various jurists maintained that 'col mezzo del giuramento si riconoscevano efficaci anche obblighi che il diritto civile rifiutava di riconoscere' [through the oath, obligations that civil law refused to recognise were also taken as effective]; and its importance was granted by the legal value it had in Canon law, in which 'valeva a costituire una propria obbligazione ogni qual volta la promessa fosse

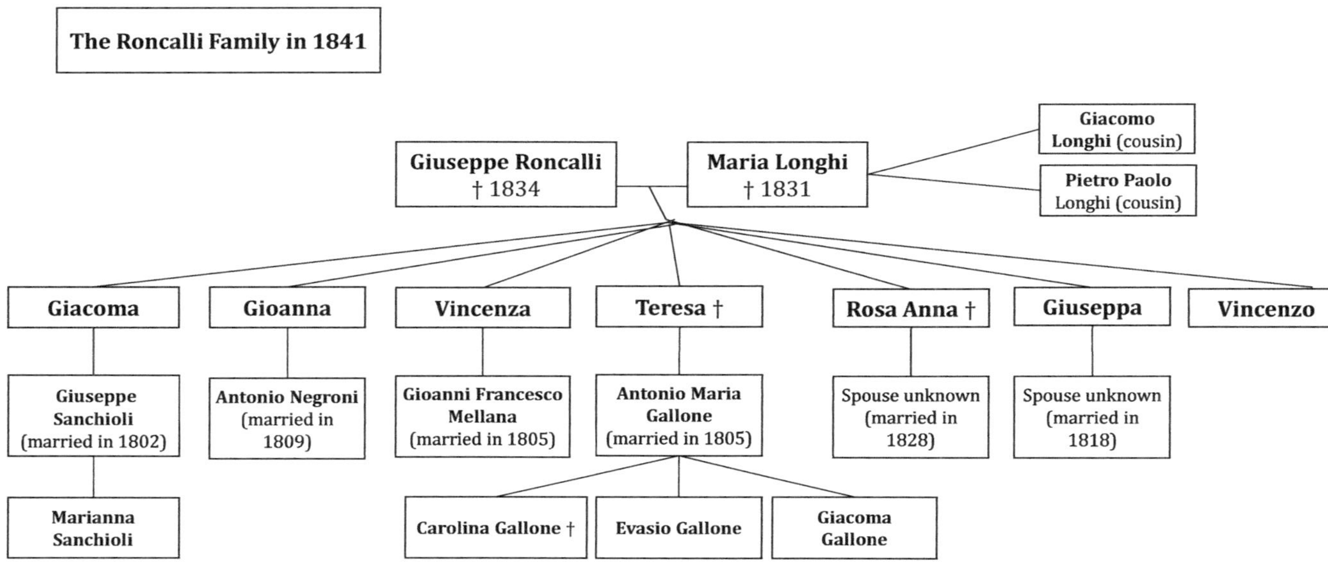
The Roncalli Family in 1841
Giuseppe Roncalli † 1834
Maria Longhi † 1831
Giacomo Longhi (cousin)
Pietro Paolo Longhi (cousin)
Giacoma
Gioanna
Vincenza
Teresa †
Rosa Anna †
Giuseppa
Vincenzo
Giuseppe Sanchioli (married in 1802)
Antonio Negroni (married in 1809)
Gioanni Francesco Mellana (married in 1805)
Antonio Maria Gallone (married in 1805)
Spouse unknown (married in 1828)
Spouse unknown (married in 1818)
Marianna Sanchioli
Carolina Gallone †
Evasio Gallone
Giacoma Gallone

marriage if they were minors.[18] Both the consent given by Clara Sassi to her son's marriage and the fact that she received her daughter-in-law's dowry prove she was a widow. Although at that time the Napoleonic Code was in force in this area and excluded recourse to any other sources of law, people continued to resolve acts by referring to local statutes. Given the uncertain political and juridical situation, perhaps people preferred to resort to the legal system with which they were familiar, despite its many inconsistencies.

Two other daughters, Vincenza and Teresa, both married in 1805: Vincenza married Gioanni Francesco Mellana on 23 June and Teresa married Antonio Maria Gallone on 17 November. On the day of Teresa's marriage both sisters' dowry instruments were signed: their father Giuseppe gave them three thousand Milanese scudi each, while their mother Maria granted them 833 scudi each.[19] Both parents signed the dowry instruments after the marriages of the two girls, as did the girls' fathers-in-law, who in their turn promised the *controdote*, as was customary in that area.[20] These instruments were made on the basis of the Statutes of Vigevano, the town where the two sisters lived and would continue to live after their marriage.

---

moralmente lecita' [it constituted an obligation whenever the promise was morally lawful] (Pertile, *Storia del diritto italiano*, IV, 467–70). An oath was also meant to be an assertion of the truth 'invocando Dio come vindice della menzogna' [invoking God as the avenger of lies] (Antonio Lorenzoni, *Scelta di disposizioni del diritto romano* (Padua: Cartallier and Sicca, 1838), pp. 160–63). Further, it was also a confirmation of the truth ('colui che giura rende a Dio il diritto della verità' [the one who swears gives to God the right of truth]), hence an obligation which bound people who swore one, compelling them to fulfil this promise. The oath was 'un atto di religione col quale si prende Dio a testimonio delle cose che si affermano o si promettono' [an act of faith with which God is taken as a witness of the things that are affirmed or promised] (*Enciclopedia dell'ecclesiastico*, 4 vols (Naples: Ranucci, 1844), II, 241–44. Despite its decreasing use in the eighteenth century, the *Regie Costituzioni* describes the oath in great detail. See Artt. 1–20, Lib. III, Tit. XIV, in *Leggi, e costituzioni di Sua Maestà. Loix et constitutions de Sa Majesté*, 2 vols (Turin: Stamperia Reale, 1770), I, 350–58. In particular, Art. 11 mentions that anyone who perjured himself was considered 'ipso iure per infame, sarà privato d'ogni dignità, o altro pubblico uffizio' [by the law itself as infamous, [and] will be deprived of any rank, or other public office] (Art. 11, p. 354–55).

18 De Poenis, Lib. IV, *Constitutiones Mediolanensis* (Milan: Marelli, 1764), p. 255.

19 Luigi Malavasi, *La Metrologia Italiana, nei suoi scambievoli rapporti desunti dal confronto col sistema metrico-decimale* (Modena: Malavasi and Compagno, 1844), p. 284. The *scudo* or *scudo effettivo* of Milan roughly corresponded to six Milanese lire, 3.89 Piedmontese lire, 4.61 Piedmontese new lire and 4.56 Italian lire.

20 State Archive of Turin, Casale, Corte di Appello, First Quarter of 1849, n. 31.

At the turn of the century several new norms were enforced in the area where the Roncalli lived, which was then under French rule: in 1805, at the time of the girls' marriages, the *droit intermédiaire* was in force; in 1806 the Napoleonic Code would be applied. However, as Giuseppe and Maria Roncalli had already done with their first two daughters, the dowries of Vincenza and Teresa, too, were signed according to municipal statutes. In Vincenza's instrument, Filippo Mellana, father of Gioanni Francesco and acting on his behalf through a power of attorney, 'ha confessato, admesso, e dichiarato, avere avuto, e ricevuto [la dote e] tutta la scherpa, o fardello' [has acknowledged, admitted and declared to have had and received the dowry and all the trousseau]; and has promised that 'mai più né esso, né il suo signor padre, loro eredi, e successori gli chiederanno più cosa alcuna per quanto sopra, a pena dei danni, interessi e spese in giudicio e fuori' [never again will he, nor his father, nor their heirs and descendants ask anything more for the above, under penalty of damages, interest and costs both in and out of court].[21] The instrument also reports that, if Gioanni died before Vincenza, the dowry was to be returned with a twenty per cent increase (*controdote*). If, instead, she were to die before him and the couple had no children, only half the dowry was to be returned (this gain was known as *lucrum dotis* and is analysed in the next chapter). The *controdote* and the *lucrum dotis* were common customs of that area, whereas some statutes of the Italian Peninsula explicitly mentioned these provisions.

Interestingly, the act also states that Maria Longhi, Vincenza's mother, gave 833 scudi:

> coll'assenso, e pieno consenso del nominato di lei consorte signor Giuseppe Roncalli, quanto anche per ogni maggior abbondanza delli signori Cappellano in questa Regia cattedrale Pietro Paolo fu signor Gioanni Antonio, e Giacomo ambi Longhi del vivente Gioanni Battista, qui nati, ed abitanti, quali conoscendo utile il presente contratto le danno e prestano il loro assenso, e consenso.[22]
>
> [with the assent and full consent of her husband Giuseppe Roncalli; and also for further approval from the Chaplain of this Royal Cathedral, Pietro Paolo of the late Gioanni Antonio and Giacomo of Gioanni Battista, both Longhi, born here and inhabitants of this place, who, knowing that this contract is useful, give her their assent and consent.]

21 State Archive of Turin, Casale, Corte di Appello, First Quarter of 1849, n. 31.

22 State Archive of Turin, Casale, Corte di Appello, First Quarter of 1849, n. 31.

Pietro Paolo and Giacomo were cousins of Maria Longhi and were not required by law to authorise her to undertake this act, but, as written in the instrument, this was nevertheless done 'per ogni maggior abbondanza'. As we see in Chapter 3, male relatives were a sort of reference point from the family of origin to whom a woman could report in case of need. Their inclusion in the signature of these acts was also a way of insuring themselves against potential future disputes.

The act establishing Teresa's dowry was similar to that of Vincenza and was signed by Evasio Gallone on behalf of his son Antonio Maria.[23] On 30 March 1831 Maria Longhi died. In her will, dated 6 June 1817, she left all her patrimony to her only son Vincenzo. She added that a dowry equal to those of Vincenza and Teresa was to be given to the remaining daughters, Giuseppa and Rosa Anna, who at the time when she drew up her will were not yet married. She also pointed out that if Giuseppa and Rosa Anna wanted to become nuns, Vincenzo would have to give them 'vita loro natural durante un annuo livello di lire duecento cinquanta di Milano, eguali a lire cento novantuna, e centesimi ottantotto nuove di Piemonte da pagarsi a semestri maturati' [an annual allowance of two hundred and fifty Milanese lire, equal to one hundred and ninety-one lire and eighty-eight new cents of Piedmont, to be paid after each semester for the length of their natural life].[24] If they were to die unmarried, the 833 scudi they would otherwise receive should not be shared between the other daughters but should go to Vincenzo.[25] Giuseppa married in 1818, just a year after her mother's will was written, and Rosa Anna in 1828, but Maria had not made any change to her testament.

On 15 July 1834, three years after Maria's death, her husband also died. In his will, made on 24 September 1819, Giuseppe Roncalli 'supplement[ed] the rules of law concerning inheritance',[26] leaving all his patrimony to his son Vincenzo whilst bequeathing one hundred coins of pure gold to each of his daughters and to his grandchildren, Marianna Sanchioli, daughter of Giacoma, and Carolina, Evasio and Giacoma Gallone, children of Teresa, who by 1819 had already passed away. These legacies were to be paid out a year after his death and without any interest. Giuseppe also added that they could have these coins only if they did not bother Vincenzo with further

23 State Archive of Turin, Casale, Corte di Appello, First Quarter of 1849, n. 31.

24 State Archive of Turin, Casale, Corte di Appello, First Quarter of 1849, n. 31.

25 State Archive of Turin, Casale, Corte di Appello, First Quarter of 1849, n. 31.

26 Kuehn, *Family and Gender*, p. 225.

requests. To Rosa Anna, the only daughter who was not yet married at the time he drafted his will, he left the same amount of money he had given his other daughters as a dowry. Rosa Anna eventually married in 1828, but at the time of her father's death had already died. Giuseppe Roncalli could be described as 'an unchanging legal image of the father who knows best and always does right by his children and substance':[27] a typical *paterfamilias*, whose major concern was the transmission of his property to the right person, who, in this case, was his son. One might argue that Giuseppe's will favoured his daughters and grandchildren rather than his son Vincenzo: as we saw, according to the law in force (the *Regie Costituzioni*) women were excluded from inheriting and the price of their exclusion was a dowry. Hence, they were not entitled to receive any further goods or money if already dowered, contrary to what happened in this case. However, the fact that Giuseppe died fifteen years after drawing up his will and had not even considered the marriage and the death of his daughter Rosa Anna allows us to suppose that his major concern was to benefit his son, who would become the new *paterfamilias*, and to prevent the fragmentation of his patrimony, a dreadful scenario he had witnessed as a possibility during the French conquests just thirty years earlier.

Three months after his father's death Vincenzo gave the legacy of one hundred coins included in his father's testament to his four sisters, to his nephew Evasio and to his two nieces Marianna and Giacoma. The other niece, Carolina, was already dead. As we saw, in his will Giuseppe Roncalli stipulated that if in the meantime any of his daughters or grandchildren had died, their legacy should not be given to their surviving heirs. Vincenzo, however, decided to donate Carolina's legacy to Evasio and Giacoma rather than keeping it for himself. He did the same with his sister Rosa Anna's children, whose mother was already dead by then and who, based upon the will, were not entitled to receive any legacy. The recipients of the legacies signed an act by which they declared they would not ask for any more money. Vincenzo's generosity might have relied on the fact that the patrimony he inherited was so large that the two hundred gold coins involved were not much to him and, by being magnanimous, he might have been hoping to forestall any further disputes. The fact that he gave these legacies nine months earlier than the prescribed time also confirms this assumption.

27 Kuehn, *Family and Gender*, p. 346.

Despite formally renouncing any further claim, on 11 March 1842 Teresa's children and Vincenza sued Vincenzo before the court of Vigevano. Their claim was that both sisters (Teresa and Vincenza) had married under the *droit intermédiaire* and Law 6 Thermidor V (24 July 1797) stipulated that a dowry alone would not exclude women from further inheritance. In this case, Teresa's and Vincenza's parents had excluded them from their wills, but they were still entitled to obtain the *legitima portio*. Given that Maria and Giuseppe had seven children, the *legitima portio* was a fourteenth of their patrimony. Moreover, the claimants asserted that, at the time of their marriages, Vincenza and Teresa were not able validly to renounce their rights because they did not know the exact value of their parents' patrimony, which they now estimated to be worth two million lire.[28] Their brother Vincenzo Roncalli, by contrast, argued that both their parents had died at the time when the *Regie Costituzioni* and the Statutes of Vigevano were again in force and asserted that the sisters were entitled only to an appropriate dowry.

It took three years to obtain the first ruling; and on 14 June 1845 the tribunal of Vigevano directed that, although Law 6 Thermidor V allowed women to inherit, these rights were granted only if these norms were still in force at the time of their parents' death. Therefore, the case was to be decided on the basis of the *Regie Costituzioni*, in which, 'trattandosi d'escludere le femmine dalle successioni ab intestato, ravvisavano congrua quella dote, quand'anche tenuissima, purché fossevi susseguito l'onesto ricapito della dotata' [since it was a question of excluding females from *ab intestato* inheritances, they considered an appropriate dowry to be one which provided for the honest placement of the dowered woman, even if it was meagre].[29] In this particular case:

> in cui non trattasi di successione ab intestato, congrua devesi ritenere la dote costituita alle Vincenzina, e Teresa sorelle Roncalli, dacché tale venne dichiarata nel testamento paterno e tale venne pure riconosciuta dalli Mellana, e Gallone rispettivi mariti delle dette sorelle Vincenzina e Teresa, non che dai loro genitori dai quali vennero tali doti esatte senza punto muovere querela sulla incongruità loro.[30]
>
> [in which it is not about an intestate inheritance, the dowry given to Vincenzina and Teresa, Roncalli sisters, should be considered

28 Two million lire were worth 433,839 scudi.

29 State Archive of Turin, Casale, Corte di Appello, First Quarter of 1849, n. 31.

30 State Archive of Turin, Casale, Corte di Appello, First Quarter of 1849, n. 31.

> appropriate, since this was declared in the paternal will and also acknowledged by Mellana and Gallone, respectively the husbands of the said sisters Vincenzina and Teresa, and by their parents from whom these dowries came, without anyone complaining about these not being appropriate.]

The tribunal also argued that Giuseppe, the *paterfamilias*, had explicitly requested his daughters not to 'molestare l'erede' [harass the heir]: by accepting his legacy, Teresa's children and Vincenza had demonstrated a perfect understanding of the testator's will and had no reason to insist.[31]

However, the lawsuit was far from over: they appealed before the Senato of Casale, a Piedmontese high court, which, in order to reach a decision, evaluated all the documents presented by both parties. The lawyers of Vincenza and of Teresa's children maintained that there were some objections which could overturn the previous decision: first, as they had done in the previous instance before the court of Vigevano, they reasserted that Law 6 Thermidor V, which did not exclude women from inheritance, had been in force when the two women married; second, their dowries had not been established in the presence of Vincenza and Teresa and, particularly, at the time of the dowries' creation the two women were already married and 'queste circostanze bastano ad escludere li concetti di doti congrue, od incongrue' [these circumstances are sufficient to exclude the concepts of appropriateness or inappropriateness]; third, their dowry instruments were void because they had been drawn up on the basis of the Statutes of Vigevano, which could not be enforced since, at that time, the *Regie Costituzioni* had already been enacted. These were the laws of the whole Kingdom of Sardinia and could not be overridden by the law of a town, as municipal statutes were.[32] The appellants also insisted, once again, that they had not known the exact amount of the patrimony of Maria and Giuseppe Roncalli when they signed the acquittance after receiving the legacy of one hundred coins and offered to prove this by oath. They claimed that Maria's patrimony was worth 300,000 lire in estates; Giuseppe had properties in Vigevano and Novara worth 700,000 lire, twenty thousand lire in chattels and a further 800,000 lire in money and funds held in banks in Milan and Piedmont.

31 State Archive of Turin, Casale, Corte di Appello, First Quarter of 1849, n. 31.

32 State Archive of Turin, Casale, Corte di Appello, First Quarter of 1849, n. 31. On hierarchy of legal sources, see also Alberto Liva, *La gerarchia delle fonti di diritto nelle città dell'Italia settentrionale* (Milan: Giuffrè, 1976).

In the eyes of their parents the Roncalli daughters were going to enrich other families through their dowries and have children not bearing the Roncalli name: their son, by contrast, was going to 'preserve' and 'perpetuate' the Roncalli name and was worthy of an amount of wealth which would allow him to become a *paterfamilias*, that is, the head of a patriarchal and upstanding family, as his father had been. Accordingly, the daughters were deemed worthy of receiving 3,833 scudi each, while Vincenzo inherited roughly 410,000 scudi. Against the appellants' argument, Vincenzo's lawyer affirmed that the inherited patrimony was not particularly large, but any investigation to estimate its exact amount was 'superflua e senza scopo' [superfluous and without purpose] because the Statutes of Vigevano ruled that women could only obtain an appropriate dowry, no matter whether given before or after marriage.[33] The exact amount of an appropriate dowry was not mentioned in these Statutes but, as Vincenzo's lawyer claimed, it could be inferred from the sixteen documents he presented. These describe dowries given to 'femmine vigevanasche' [women from Vigevano] between 1795 and 1806 and from 1814 to 1836 and represent a further source of information about the customs of the town of Vigevano: alongside the value of dowries, they also allow us better to understand the social and economic fabric of the area. In 1795, for example, Francesca Mantegazza, a *femmina vigevanasca*, married the physician Ignazio Clerici with the consent of her father Pietro Giorgio Mantegazza and was given a dowry of eight thousand lire (1,735 Milanese scudi). Francesca considered this dowry appropriate as set out by the Statutes of Vigevano and accepted it with 'l'intervento, pieno consenso e approvazione del suo signor marito' [the intervention, full consent and approval of her husband].[34] Her husband authorised her to accept this dowry 'perché riconosce cedere le cose suddette in evidente utilità e vantaggio della detta sua moglie' [because he recognises that the aforesaid things will be of evident utility and advantage to his wife].[35] Maria Gusberti, another *vigevanasca*, married Federico Rainoldi in 1801 and, after her marriage, received a dowry of 21,000 Milanese lire (3,500 scudi) and a *fardello* worth three thousand lire (five hundred scudi). She confirmed that its creation was prescribed by the Statutes of Vigevano. Teresa Negroni, too, received her dowry after her marriage to Francesco Fusi in 1815: its value was 25,000 Milanese lire, while her *scherpa* was

33 State Archive of Turin, Casale, Corte di Appello, First Quarter of 1849, n. 31.

34 State Archive of Turin, Casale, Corte di Appello, First Quarter of 1849, n. 31.

35 State Archive of Turin, Casale, Corte di Appello, First Quarter of 1849, n. 31.

worth 2,800 lire. Lucia De Previde Massara married Cavalier Zeffirino Calleri di Sala in 1827 and received a dowry worth 25,328 lire (5,494 Milanese scudi) from her father Ignazio. The dowry was created a year later with an act dated 30 June 1828 and given to her father-in-law Francesco Zeffirino, who was a member of the Reggimento Cavalleggeri Savoia, a prominent cavalry unit.

These dowries had been given to women whose status – according to Vincenzo's claims – was comparable to that of the Roncalli family, who were landowners. However, only one of the sixteen documents produced, that concerning Lucia De Previde Massara's dowry, was regarding a dowry which exceeded the dowries of the Roncalli women. The other dowry instruments provided by Vincenzo's lawyer concerned families of lower status and were very meagre. Giovanna Carnevale, for example, married Felice Bassi in 1795 and received a dowry of 266.10 lire (57.7 scudi). In the same year, Maria Delbuono married Giovanni Battista Zorzoli. Her dowry, worth 133 Piedmontese lire, was paid by her brother on the basis of their father's will. The dowry of Maria Riva, who married Gioanni Acquotta in 1817, was small, too. She received only 380 lire. Finally, Regina Ornati married Pietro Dondena in 1838 and received her dowry of 740 lire from her brothers, as specified in their father's will.

Vincenzo's lawyer claimed that the cases of two other families, the Pellegrini and the Rabezzana, should also be taken into consideration as judicial precedents in order to reach a fair decision. The former case was cited to show that the Pellegrini sisters – Maria, Angelica and Maddalena – had won their cause against their brothers Michele and Bartolomeo because their dowry instruments lacked the formal requirements needed for this kind of act. As both their parents died *ab intestato*, the father in August 1833 and the mother in December 1829, the Pellegrini sisters asked their brothers to give 'una esatta e fedele consegna dell'eredità paterna e materna' [an exact and faithful inventory of the paternal and maternal inheritance]: this would allow them to assess their *dote congrua* based on their father's and mother's patrimony.[36] They maintained that their dowries had at least to be close to the value of the *legitima portio*, that is, an eighteenth of the patrimony, as there were seven daughters and two sons. They claimed that their father's assets were worth seventy thousand lire, while their mother's goods consisted of 3,400 lire. As the *Regie Costituzioni* excluded women from inheritance, they had to receive the 'price' of this exclusion, which was worth 'una congrua dote ragguagliata

36 State Archive of Turin, Casale, Corte di Appello, First Quarter of 1849, n. 31.

sulla legittima' [an appropriate dowry considering the legitime].[37] Moreover, they asserted that they had to obtain 'tante [...] le doti, quante le successioni, attesoché erano il prezzo dell'esclusione' [as many [...] dowries, as many inheritances, since these were the price of their exclusion],[38] a point contradicting the argument presented earlier in *Annali di giurisprudenza* which highlighted that a properly dowered woman was not entitled to obtain any addition to the amount which she had already received.

Michele and Bartolomeo Pellegrini produced three instruments, dated 21 September 1824, 21 September 1825 and 6 April 1832, which showed that their sisters' husbands had received 1,300 lire each and promised not to 'inferirli né permettere che loro venisse inferta molestia' [harass or allow others to harass them].[39] They added that their sisters' dowries were appropriate because they had allowed them to be *onestamente recapitate,* according to the status of their families and the customs of Boves, the village one hundred kilometres away from Turin where they lived. On 7 April 1843 the Senato of Piedmont directed that the three acts were not formally valid dowry instruments and that their contents did not explicitly recognise the dowries as *congrue*. The three instruments had been signed by Giacomo Peano, father-in-law of Maddalena, and by Giuseppe Cavallo and Giuseppe Pellegrini, husbands of Angelica and Maria respectively, but none of the women had been present. The father-in-law and the two husbands declared themselves satisfied with the amount of the dowries, but did not dismiss the possibility of future claims. Vincenzo Roncalli produced this case to demonstrate that the grounds for this judgement, made in favour of the women, was that these instruments had not been drawn up in the correct way. Conversely, Vincenzo maintained that in his own case all the formalities required by law had been observed.

The other case brought in by Vincenzo's lawyer was that of the Rabezzana family. The *paterfamilias*, Giuseppe, died on 9 November 1835 after making his will on 17 January of the same year. He bequeathed the sum of 1,500 lire to each of his two daughters: Teresa, married to Giuseppe Bonino; and Maria, married to Carlo Massa. All his other assets were to be inherited by his son Bartolomeo and his grandsons Giuseppe and Francesco, children of his deceased son Francesco. Since the two women had married under French laws,

37 State Archive of Turin, Casale, Corte di Appello, First Quarter of 1849, n. 31.

38 State Archive of Turin, Casale, Corte di Appello, First Quarter of 1849, n. 31.

39 State Archive of Turin, Casale, Corte di Appello, First Quarter of 1849, n. 31.

Teresa had not received any dowry, while Maria had received one thousand lire 'pour avancement d'hoire' [advance on the inheritance], together with a trousseau worth 1,300 lire, on 21 September 1810.[40] Maria, together with the heirs of Teresa, who died in 1839, asked for the *legitima portio* estimated at eight thousand lire over Giuseppe's patrimony, which was worth 100,000 lire. After the judgement made by the tribunal of Asti in favour of Teresa's heirs and Maria on 27 May 1843, Bartolomeo and Giuseppe's grandsons appealled before the Senato of Piedmont. On 30 January 1844 the court reversed the previous sentence by arguing that a dowry was not an indisputable hereditary right. Its amount was not certain, because 'non sempre il patrimonio del dotante è giusta norma per misurare la congruità' [the assets of the person who is providing the dowry are not always the right rule by which to measure the adequacy [of the dowry]].[41] The court maintained that Maria and Teresa were not able to produce any evidence to confirm they had not known the exact amount of their father's patrimony when they accepted the legacy of 1,500 lire. As they were 'assistite massimamente [...] sempre dai mariti loro' [always greatly assisted [...] by their husbands], they had consciously accepted the bequest, which would prevent them from undertaking any further act.[42] The women:

> non avendo [...] potuto ignorare il disposto del testamento del padre soprattutto nella parte che le concerneva, non potevano dubitare che il padre stesso non aveva riputata sufficiente la somma loro sborsata nell'atto del rispettivo matrimonio per dirle congruamente dotate, a segno di poterle senz'altro escludere dalla sua successione.[43]
>
> [not having [...] been able to ignore the disposition of the father's will, especially in the part that concerned them, could not doubt that the father himself had assessed that the sum paid to them in the act of their respective marriages was sufficient to provide them with an appropriate dowry and therefore was undoubtedly able to exclude them from his succession.]

This case was produced by Vincenzo as evidence that, by accepting the legacy of one hundred coins, his sisters had been aware of their father's patrimony and had thus legitimately renounced any further

40 State Archive of Turin, Casale, Corte di Appello, First Quarter of 1849, n. 31.

41 State Archive of Turin, Casale, Corte di Appello, First Quarter of 1849, n. 31.

42 State Archive of Turin, Casale, Corte di Appello, First Quarter of 1849, n. 31.

43 State Archive of Turin, Casale, Corte di Appello, First Quarter of 1849, n. 31.

claim. Despite all Vincenzo's efforts to support his argument, the judgement of the Senato of Casale was not in his favour. The tribunal maintained that the Statutes of Vigevano were valid only with regard to the norms not included in the *Regie Costituzioni* and 'furono solo mantenuti in quelle parti che non ripugnassero alle Costituzioni medesime' [were only retained in those parts which did not clash with the *Costituzioni*].[44] It was pointed out that, in order to exclude women from inheriting, these Statutes did not require a dowry to be *congrua*, whereas the *Regie Costituzioni* prescribed that a woman's exclusion was permitted only against an appropriate dowry, with Article 6 explicitly defining the requisites of this concept. The court added that, if forms of compensation other than an appropriate dowry were taken into account for the exclusion of women from inheritance, the provisions of the *Regie Costituzioni* would be overridden. In particular:

> non è sfuggito alla sapienza di Carlo Emmanuele III come l'eccessivo desiderio di conservazione delle famiglie che cotanto dominava in que' tempi si dovesse pure conciliare coll'amor naturale che nelle leggi di successioni era stato norma all'Imperator Giustiniano; non gli sfuggiva neppure come un soverchio concentramento di ricchezze possa talvolta tornar pregiudicevole, quindi con una apposita disposizione fissava i limiti dell'esclusione delle figlie dalla successione paterna, ossia quale dovesse essere il correspettivo di tale loro esclusione.[45]
>
> [it has not escaped Carlo Emmanuele III's wisdom that the excessive desire for the conservation of families so widespread in those times should also be reconciled with the natural love that had been the norm for the Emperor Justinian in succession laws; it had not even escaped him how an overwhelming concentration of wealth could sometimes be prejudicial; therefore he set the limits on daughters' exclusion from the paternal succession with a special provision, namely what the compensation for their exclusion should be.]

The Senato suggested that King Carlo Emmanuele III's 'wisdom' decreed rules favouring women, but what emerges from these words much more is the concern about a possible 'concentration of wealth', which had to be limited if not avoided altogether. The 'conservation of families' was considered crucial but had to be pursued within appropriate norms, such as those included in the

44 State Archive of Turin, Casale, Corte di Appello, First Quarter of 1849, n. 31.

45 State Archive of Turin, Casale, Corte di Appello, First Quarter of 1849, n. 31.

Regie Costituzioni. The preservation of families was a goal which was also taken into consideration by the Statutes of Vigevano, but 'la legge dominante esige come di rigore certi e determinati mezzi per conseguirlo; la legge particolare non li cura ed inumanamente li sprezza' [the prevailing law requires certain and determined means of rigour to achieve it; the individual law does not take care of them and inhumanly despises them].[46] Departing from the 'legge dominante', that is, the *Regie Costituzioni*, and asserting that the dowry instruments were valid private agreements could not be acceptable as even Roman law provided the maxim that 'ius publicum privatorum pactis mutari nequit' [the law could not be disregarded by private agreements].[47]

Even if 'non havvi contestazione sull'onesto recapito delle dotate' [the honest placement of the dowered women is not disputed], a father was obliged to provide his daughters not just with a dowry, regardless of its value, but with an appropriate one. The creation of a dowry was a formal act which had to be accepted by the dowered girl; and in this case no reference was made to any acceptance or consent given by Vincenza and Teresa. Indeed, 'si richiede che dallo stesso atto risulti non solamente dell'assegno di detta dote dal canto del padre, ma eziandio del consenso espresso o tacito per parte della figlia di accettare la dote medesima' [it is required that the act would show the dowry given by the father, but also the express or tacit consent by the daughter to accept the dowry]; and this consent was absolutely necessary and was to be 'almeno presunto' [at least presumed].[48] Chiara Saraceno points out that women's rights were difficult to assert before a court,[49] but their consent to acts which involved their rights was necessary. This is highly paradoxical: women were deemed able to understand the value of goods, that of their dowries in this case, a point strongly in conflict with the founding idea of marital authorisation or other kinds of authorisation needed by women to undertake legal acts.

The sixteen dowry instruments presented by Vincenzo's lawyer played in the appellants' favour. Given that no law defined the exact amount of a dowry, the court argued that a certain maxim quoted

46 State Archive of Turin, Casale, Corte di Appello, First Quarter of 1849, n. 31.

47 State Archive of Turin, Casale, Corte di Appello, First Quarter of 1849, n. 31.

48 State Archive of Turin, Casale, Corte di Appello, First Quarter of 1849, n. 31.

49 See, e.g., the analysis by Chiara Saraceno, 'Le donne nella famiglia: una complessa costruzione giuridica. 1750–1942', in *Storia della famiglia italiana, 1750–1950*, ed. by Barbagli and Kertzer, pp. 103–28 (pp. 105–10).

by jurisprudence and, in particular, by the influential Piedmontese jurist Tommaso Maurizio Richeri[50] allowed for the possibility of calculating the value of a dowry by considering the *legitima portio*, 'se non in modo rigoroso, almeno approssimativo' [if not accurately, at least roughly].[51] The maxim in question states that 'dos congrua illa dicitur quae respondet facultatibus mulieris atque utriusque coniugis dignitati: ratione quoque habita consuetudinis quae in regione seu familia servatur' [the appropriate dowry is one which corresponds to the wealth of the bride and to the dignity of the spouses; [and] also considers the customs followed both in the area and within their family].[52]

The Senato of Casale ruled that even if at the time of their parents' death the *Regie Costituzioni* had been in force again, the dowries of the two Roncalli sisters 'non valevano ad altro titolo che ad anticipazione di eredità' [were not valid in any way other than as an advance of inheritance], because Vincenza and Teresa were 'non presenti e non stipulanti' [not present and not stipulating] and had not signed any document in which they renounced their lawful portion of inheritance.[53] In other words, Vincenza and Teresa's heirs were entitled to receive an addition to the dowries given at the time of their marriages. There are no further archival documents which provide evidence of how the case was settled between Vincenzo and the appellants: we can assume that Vincenza and Teresa's heirs obtained a sum of money close to the *legitima portio*, 30,988 Milanese scudi or 142,857 lire, which corresponds to the fourteenth part of the Roncalli patrimony. As we saw, this was worth two million lire.

Negotiating their Exclusion: The Marchisone Sisters

The case of the Roncalli family did not stand alone and allowed similar decisions. Another case in point is that of the Marchisone family, from which we can again infer the considerable difference

50 Tommaso Maurizio Richeri (1733–1797) was a Piedmontese jurist. His major work, *Universa civilis et criminalis iurisprudentia iuxta seriem institutionum ex naturali et romano iure deprompta et ad usum fori perpetuo accomodata* (1774–82), was considered fundamental to the learning and understanding of Roman law.

51 State Archive of Turin, Casale, Corte di Appello, First Quarter of 1849, n. 31.

52 State Archive of Turin, Casale, Corte di Appello, First Quarter of 1849, n. 31.

53 State Archive of Turin, Casale, Corte di Appello, First Quarter of 1849, n. 31. See also *Giurisprudenza Italiana*, 2 (1849), 671–97 (p. 694).

The Marchisone Family in 1847

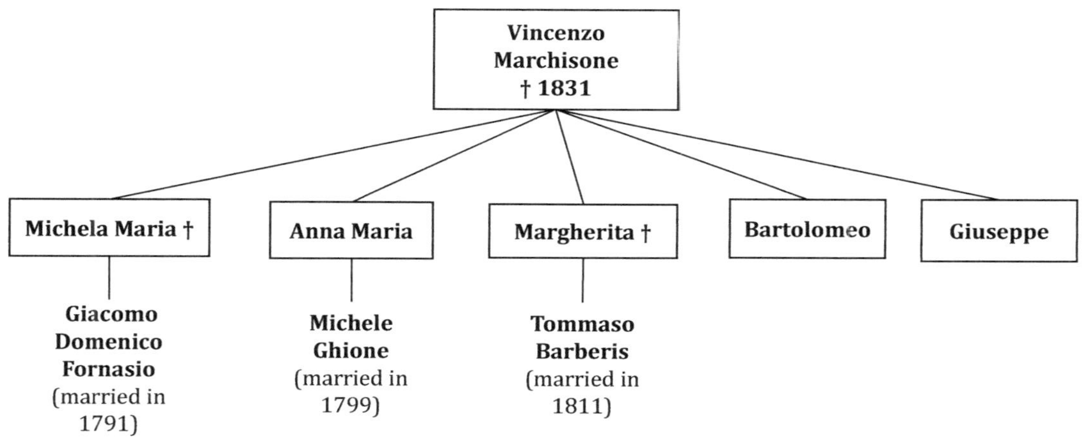

between women and men in matters of inheritance rights.[54] The members of the Marchisone family lived in the province of Turin, in the towns of Ajrasca (now Airasca), Orbassano and Villafranca. Vincenzo was the *paterfamilias* and had three daughters, Michela Maria, Anna Maria and Margherita, and two sons, Bartolomeo and Giuseppe. On 11 June 1791 Michela Maria Marchisone, together with Giacomo Domenico Fornasio from Ajrasca, whom she had married a few months earlier, appeared before a notary to receive her dowry from her father Vincenzo. She obtained the amount promised before her marriage, two thousand lire in cash, gold and silver, along with the *fardello*. The two spouses declared themselves to be 'soddisfatti tanto per la dotte quanto per il fardello che dichiarano di aver ricevuto nella conformità' [satisfied with both the dowry and the trousseau, which they claim to have received as per the agreement] and affirmed that they would not ask for any more money.[55] Giacomo Domenico also followed the 'lodevole consuetudine di questo luogo' [commendable custom of this place], which consisted of his promise to constitute a *controdote* worth a third of the dowry itself. He thus vowed that he would 'il tutto conservare, e custodire, rendere e restituire [...] in caso di soluzione di matrimonio o altro legittimo contrario evento il che Dio non voglia [e di confermare] la quota consuetudinaria quanto ai reciproci guadagni e lucri dotali' [preserve and keep, give back and return it all [...] in the event of a dissolution of the marriage or another valid adverse event that God would not wish and confirm the customary share as regards mutual earnings and gains from the dowry].[56] A few years later, in 1799, Anna Maria, the sister of Michela Maria, also married. On 10 Messidor IX (29 June 1801), as Piedmont was already under French rule, Anna Maria, her husband Michele Ghione and her father-in-law appeared before the same notary in order to receive the dowry. This time the *paterfamilias* provided a dowry of three thousand lire and the trousseau. This dowry, too, was given in cash, gold and silver; and was 'dalla stessa Anna Maria presso di se rittirata, e quindi col pieno consenso del suo marito *brevi manu* rimessa al suo suocero Felice Ghione di Orbassano' [collected by the same Anna Maria; and therefore with

54 A short summary of this case can also be found in *Giurisprudenza degli Stati Sardi* (1852), 141–43.

55 State Archive of Turin, Notaio Giovanni Pietro Ellena, 1791, n. 2262.

56 State Archive of Turin, Notaio Giovanni Pietro Ellena, 1791, n. 2262.

the full consent of her husband given by hand to her father-in-law Felice Ghione of Orbassano].[57] Like her sister, Anna Maria regarded herself 'sufficientemente dotata secondo il suo stato e qualità tanto per le ragioni paterne che materne, vi ha perciò a queste rinunciato' [sufficiently dowered according to her status and her quality based on both paternal and maternal [wealth] and she therefore renounced them].[58] Both her husband and her father-in-law promised the *aumento dotale* (*controdote*) of one third of the value of the dowry, as 'la lodevole consuetudine di questo comune' [the laudable custom of this municipality] provided.[59] Vincenzo Marchisone also established a dowry to his third daughter, Margherita, promised to Tommaso Barberis from Villafranca. Her dowry was worth three thousand lire and a trousseau worth 1,400 lire. This act was signed on 8 October 1811, before her actual wedding.[60]

On 10 March 1847 Anna Maria Marchisone and the heirs of her deceased sisters Michela Maria and Margherita initiated a cause before the Tribunal of Pinerolo, the court with jurisdiction for the area where they lived. They sued Bartolomeo and Giuseppe, sons of Vincenzo, who had died in 1831, leaving a patrimony of 100,000 lire. In his will, drawn up on 20 November 1828, Vincenzo had declared that, since his daughters were already dowered, his two sons Bartolomeo and Giuseppe were to be the sole heirs to all his assets. The Tribunal of Pinerolo ruled that the plaintiffs were not entitled to receive any portion of Vincenzo's patrimony, but requested further confirmation with regard to Margherita's case. Her dowry had been established before her marriage, when the *Civil Code of the Kingdom of Italy*, known as Napoleonic Code, had been in force. Nevertheless, as her father had died under the regime of the *Regie Costituzioni*, the appropriateness of her dowry was to be measured on this basis, which – as we have seen – ruled that women were not entitled to receive any further goods or money if already dowered. In addition, in the years from her marriage up to Vincenzo's death 'non fu mai elevato dubbio che la stessa famiglia non fosse pienamente soddisfatta di ogni sua ragione' [there was never any doubt that

57 State Archive of Turin, Notaio Giovanni Pietro Ellena, 1801, n. 2271.

58 State Archive of Turin, Tribunale di Pinerolo, Sentenze civili, First Quarter of 1847, n. 60.

59 State Archive of Turin, Tribunale di Pinerolo, Sentenze civili, First Quarter of 1847, n. 60.

60 State Archive of Turin, Tribunale di Pinerolo, Sentenze civili, First Quarter of 1847, n. 60.

the family itself was not fully satisfied with all its claims] and, furthermore, 'la querela d'inofficiosità contro il testamento paterno competendo ai figli ingiustamente diseredati dal padre, non presenta nemmeno una analogia alla domanda di supplemento di dote mossa dalli padre e figli Barberis' [the children unjustly disinherited by the father are entitled to initiate a complaint of injustice against the paternal will. This has no analogy to the demand for a supplement to a dowry made by the Barberis father and children].[61] However, because Margherita had not signed a receipt accepting the dowry as 'congrua' [appropriate], her brothers Bartolomeo and Giuseppe were ordered to present documents which would allow her heirs to assess its appropriateness. In the case of Michela Maria and Anna Maria, their dowries were formally established after, but had been promised before, their marriages, when the *Regie Costituzioni* had been in force. Therefore, the tribunal maintained that 'non si mosse neppur dubbio in atti, che queste due figlie Marchisone siano state onestamente ricapitate con quella rispettiva dote' [it was not even doubted in the proceedings that these two daughters Marchisone were honestly placed with their respective dowries].[62]

In the absence of any documents which testify to further actions taken against Bartolomeo and Giuseppe, we may assume that the issue regarding Margherita's dowry was somehow resolved through a private agreement. Anna Maria Marchisone and the heirs of her sister Michela Maria instead appealed to the court of Turin. On 26 April 1850 the court ordered Bartolomeo and Giuseppe to give an 'esatta e fedele consegna' [exact and faithful inventory] of the inherited patrimony.[63] This would allow the appellants to estimate whether the dowries given to the two sisters were appropriate, as showed in the disquisition described earlier in this chapter. The two brothers refused to execute this order and appealed to the Corte di Cassazione, the court of last appeal: in its decision of 5 January 1852 the court sentenced them to pay an appropriate dowry to Anna Maria and Michela Maria's heirs. The Corte di Cassazione explained that a

61 The *querela inofficiosi testamenti* was a means provided by Roman law which allowed an heir who had been disinherited or passed over without valid reason to initiate a lawsuit and request the annulment of a will (*Digest*, 5.2.1–32; *Codex*, 3.28.1–36). See also *Giurisprudenza romana ossia corpo del diritto civile romano volgarizzato col testo a fronte* (Milan: Baret, 1815), pp. 165–67.

62 State Archive of Turin, Tribunale di Pinerolo, Sentenze civili, First Quarter of 1847, n. 60.

63 State Archive of Turin, Giudice di Appello, Sentenza Civili, April 1850, n. 315.

women's exclusion from the right to co-succeed with their brothers to parental inheritance was compensated for by the right to an appropriate dowry and this right was to be guaranteed.[64] Indeed, for the sake of justice a daughter was entitled to discuss the compensation and the price for her exclusion from her relatives' inheritance:

> prima ancora di abbandonare la casa e famiglia paterna, per passare a far parte o ad essere origine di altra famiglia, prima di devenire ad un patto che importasse od involvesse in sé una rinuncia ad ogni diritto sulla successione dei propri ascendenti, se il matrimonio consideravasi come apertura della successione a di lei profitto.[65]
>
> [before leaving the paternal home and family, to become part of or give origin to another family, before coming to a pact which implied or involved in itself a renunciation of all rights on the succession of their parents, if the marriage was to be considered as the opening of the succession in her favour.]

This judgement relied upon the fact that the two sisters were already married when their dowries were established. In other words, their dowries were established *after* their marriages; and consequently they had not been given any chance to discuss compensation for their exclusion from inheritance before being involved in the lifelong and irrevocable bond that was wedlock.

These cases show that nineteenth-century law in action did not always have a self-evident outcome: judgements were often completely reversed by other courts and judges did not even feel morally bound to the judicial precedent. The dowry, the great importance of which has been demonstrated by the analysis of these cases, was intended to provide for the needs and decorum of the family. Hence, its value was carefully assessed by women as well as by their husbands and heirs, who tried to obtain as much money as they could and would not hesitate to resort to a judge and go through several proceedings before reaching a final and, they hoped, positive verdict. Even though they abided by the legal system and shared a common view of women's status, courts closely examined all circumstances and carefully considered women's rights to obtain further money from their parents' inheritance. The point that the Roncalli and Marchisone sisters had not been allowed to negotiate their exclusion from the inheritance because the former were absent when their dowries were established and the latter were already married highlights an

64 State Archive of Turin, Corte di Cassazione, 1852, 9, n. 242.

65 State Archive of Turin, Corte di Cassazione, 1852, 9, n. 242.

interesting issue: women did not just have to comply with someone else's decision but were given the chance to discuss and assess the value of their dowry. Although it is difficult to understand the extent of negotiations a woman could undertake before obtaining a dowry, the two cases demonstrate that courts allowed them to have a say. The nineteenth-century family, therefore, was still 'fondata su rapporti asimmetrici, generatrice di tensioni e di conflitti ma anche articolata in modo da offrire spazi alle figure "minori"' [founded on asymmetrical relationships, generating tensions and conflicts but also articulated in such a way as to offer spaces to 'minor' figures].[66] As Cesarina Casanova also argues: the real position of each member was the result of a continual negotiation.[67] This does not mean that women had the legal capacity of individualised choices and actions, but that the limits of their inclusion or exclusion could be fluid and negotiable. In 1837 the new Code promulgated in the Kingdom of Sardinia permitted all legitimate children or their descendants to succeed to their relatives' *ab intestato* inheritance. Nonetheless, by allowing the 'subingresso' (see Chapter 3) the code still marked a different hereditary regime between men and women. Although new ideas regarding women and their role in society began to spread along the Italian Peninsula, the heritage of the Ancien Régime remained strong and persistent; and the importance given to male heirs continued to be broadly accepted and praised by families.

Women and Wills in Lombardy-Venetia: Overriding the Law

Far from constituting a rational framework, the fluid boundaries of nineteenth-century law allowed room for discussion and legal disputes, which, nevertheless, did not always have a clear outcome. Alongside the co-existence of several laws in each state, courts often had to deal with cases regarding people, properties and laws from different states. In such a context people tried to tackle the issues which arose and in so doing often overrode the law. Moreover, in Lombardy-Venetia, where all children had the same inheritance rights regardless of their sex, some people tried not to comply with this rule by making wills that favoured sons. A case in point is that

66 Maria Antonietta Visceglia, 'Introduzione', in *Signori, patrizi, cavalieri in Italia centro-meridionale nell'età moderna*, ed. by Maria Antonietta Visceglia and Renata Ago (Rome: Laterza, 1992), pp. V-XXXIII (p. XXIII).

67 Casanova, *La famiglia italiana*, p. 148.

of Speranza Sacerdote, a woman who lived in Casale, a town in Piedmont, and sued her brothers to obtain a portion of the assets her deceased father owned in Lombardy-Venetia.[68] When she married Raffael Vita-Levi in 1808 her father gave her a sum of money as a dowry, explicitly stating that this was only an advance on her inheritance. On 19 May 1830 Speranza received from her father another thirteen thousand lire and subsequently declared herself to be 'onestamente ricapitata, congruamente dotata e sufficientemente provvista sul di lui patrimonio' [honestly placed, bestowed with an appropriate dowry and sufficiently provided for on his assets].[69] Her father, together with his sons, simulated a sale to ensure that his properties in Lombardy-Venetia would not be subject to the Austrian law which allowed daughters to have succession rights in addition to the dowry. Speranza initiated litigation, asking to inherit her lawful portion of her father's assets in Lombardy-Venetia. On 25 July 1853 the court of Casale stated that the act of sale registered on 13 October 1831 was a simulation and that Speranza was entitled to obtain a portion of those properties as provided by the Austrian Code.

Such a decision is extremely important because it was made by a Piedmontese court which exceeded its jurisdiction to rule over a contract affecting properties abroad, allowing a woman to obtain an additional amount of wealth. Despite her declaration of being 'honestly placed', Speranza could still ask for more goods by demonstrating that what she had received matched neither her father's patrimony nor the amount normally given to women by other families of similar status. The court concluded that the abdication of rights was always linked to the appropriateness of the dowry: if it was not appropriate, there was room for further claims. The contradiction between written law, law in action and jurisprudence is evident: even though she was married, and a married woman was always considered to be 'appropriately dowered', Speranza could inherit. One might argue that the court of Casale clearly agreed with the point made in the Roncalli case, that is, 'an overwhelming concentration of wealth could sometimes be prejudicial'. Its decision to allow a woman to obtain more money was therefore meant to split large patrimonies and impede the concentration of wealth into the

68 State Archive of Turin, Casale, Corte di Appello, Second Semester of 1853, n. 45. An overview of this case can also be found in *Giurisprudenza degli Stati sardi* (1853), 655–60.

69 *Giurisprudenza degli Stati sardi* (1853), p. 656.

hands of few people. In this case, even though these properties were abroad their income would have further improved the economic power of the Sacerdote family.

As previously mentioned, in Lombardy-Venetia the *Codice civile universale austriaco pel Regno Lombardo-Veneto* allowed all children to inherit equally from their parents. The creation of a dowry was permitted and considered an advance on parental inheritance. However, in this state, as elsewhere, the custom of making wills was widespread among all social classes and often aimed at granting more rights to sons, to the detriment of daughters. In other words, it was a way to circumvent the law and to allow testators to bequeath a large part of their patrimonies to those of their choice.

The next case was reported in *Giurisprudenza pratica secondo la legislazione austriaca*,[70] a journal of jurisprudence published in Milan. It describes a situation similar to many others in nineteenth-century Lombardy-Venetia in which a father, Giovanni Battista Guarrini, only bequeathed the *legitima portio* to his daughter. Giovanni Battista was a nobleman who lived in Crema, a town fifty kilometres away from Milan. He died on 22 July 1824 and left a will rogated by the notary Giovanni Battista Tensini. He bequeathed to his daughter, Marianna, what was due to her by law, namely a quarter of his patrimony, and pointed out that she should 'riunire alla mia eredità comprendere e computare nella di lei legittima la dote e schirpe da me testatore costituita all'atto del suo matrimonio, e da me per intiero pagata' [combine with my inheritance, include and count in her legitime the dowry and trousseau made up at the time of her marriage, by me, testator, and paid in full by me].[71] The remaining three quarters of his patrimony were given to his son Giacomo Antonio,[72] who had to guarantee the usufruct of a quarter of the whole patrimony, 'tutto compreso e niente eccettuato' [everything included and nothing

70 The journal *Giurisprudenza pratica secondo la legislazione austriaca attivata anche nel Regno Lombardo-Veneto o sia collezione di decisioni sentenze e decreti in materia civile commerciale criminale di diritto pubblico* was published in Milan from 1817 to 1833; its name then changed to *Giurisprudenza teorico-pratica secondo la legislazione austriaca o sia Collezione di decisioni sentenze e decreti in materia civile commerciale criminale e di diritto pubblico* (1836–45).

71 *Giurisprudenza pratica*, 10 (1829), pp. 93–94.

72 In the Kingdom of Lombardy-Venetia, 'la porzione legittima assegnata dalla legge a ciascuno de' figli è la metà di quello che sarebbe pervenuto ad essi nella successione intestate' [the legitimate portion assigned by law to each of the children is half of what would have come to them in an *ab intestate* inheritance] (Art. 765, in *Codice civile universale austriaco pel Regno Lombardo-Veneto*, p. 189).

excluded], to his mother, Paola Fracavalli. Paola was also entitled to be given her dowry back. The testator had another son, Alessandro, who had left Crema several years earlier and had not been heard of since. As in many other cases, fathers 'contavano tradizionalmente sul potere sanzionatorio riconosciutogli dal diritto successorio' [traditionally counted on the sanctioning power recognised to them by inheritance law],[73] thus punishing Alessandro by ordering that, should he come back, he could receive no more than a quarter of his father's wealth.[74]

Marianna was married to the wealthy Count Paolo Premoli and had six children. She was given 54,735 *lire austriache* as a dowry. At first, Marianna's brother Giacomo complied with the testament of his father and made the hotchpot by bringing his sister's dowry into the *legitima*.[75] Marianna was entitled to receive 13,683 *lire austriache*, which was also confirmed by the tribunal of Crema in 1826.[76] However, two years later, in 1828, Giacomo returned before the court to ask whether, by law, the hotchpot of his sister's dowry and trousseau was to be made by considering the hereditaments of their father, or just the forced heirship as their father had written in his will. The difference between reuniting the dowry with the *legitima portio* or with the entire patrimony was great. Indeed, if Marianna had to make the hotchpot by considering the legitime, she would receive the 13,683 *lire austriache* mentioned above; otherwise, she would not be entitled to obtain any further sum.

The tribunal of Crema ruled that the hotchpot was to be made considering the entire patrimony. This judgement was appealed before the tribunal of Milan, which refuted the decision; and then before the Supremo Tribunale of Verona, which abided by the decision made in Crema. Its outcome was described in the journal *Giurisprudenza pratica*, which claimed that 'la tesi negli atti d'appello e di revisione nei quali presero parte anche li più reputati Giureconsulti del Foro di Milano' [the thesis in the court of appeal and of second

73 Cavina, *Il padre spodestato*, pp. 242–43.

74 *Giurisprudenza pratica*, 10 (1829), p. 95.

75 In order to secure equal division among heirs in an *ab intestato* succession, properties are fictitiously reunited through the so-called hotchpot. As is widely known, civil law systems do not recognise the total freedom of testators to dispose of their hereditaments. Therefore, the inheritance is composed of the portion, which could be freely disposed of, the free estate or discretionary portion, and of the indefeasible portion or forced heirship or *legitima portio*.

76 *Giurisprudenza pratica*, 10 (1829), p. 98.

instance, in which the most reputed jurisconsults of Milan's forum took part] was that the hotchpot was to be made on the value of the hereditament.[77] The issue debated in this lawsuit was very common in the nineteenth century and was included in this journal in order to help judges in similar circumstances. Far from introducing anything new in nineteenth-century jurisprudence, it confirmed, instead, the ongoing habit of considering women as 'caput et finis' to their families and therefore worthy of aspiring only to a dowry, or little more.

Provisions that debarred daughters from inheriting portions larger than the legitime were not uncommon, even in wills drawn up by women. Indeed, their behaviour strongly endorsed the idea that the man was the indisputable head of a family and wealth was to revolve around him. Women's rights, therefore, could be neglected and even given up for the sake of the family's prestige and status. Several wills held in archives, for example, give evidence of mothers granting their entire patrimony (except for the *legitima portio,* to which heirs were lawfully entitled) to their sons. These mothers pointed out that their daughters had already been provided with good dowries and had no motive to ask for more goods or money. For example, Maria Teresa Albertini, a wealthy woman from Verona married to a nobleman, Bartolomeo Raffoni Morardo, made her will on 5 October 1818. She had three children: Giuseppe, Anna Maria, a former nun, and Elisabetta, married to the nobleman Francesco Cavazocca. Having made religious vows, Anna Maria could not inherit, even if she was no longer a nun.[78] Hence, her mother made her a bequest of three hundred lire a year, which she had to receive from Giuseppe. While the legitime was left to Elisabetta and Giuseppe, Maria Teresa bequeathed 'tuttociò che la legge mi permette di disporre' [all that

77 *Giurisprudenza pratica,* 10 (1829), pp. 107–12. On the hotchpot, see also the disquisitions of three prominent jurists of the Austrian Empire, Vitaliano Oldrado, Vincenzo Augusto Wagner and Francesco Foramiti, reported in *Giurisprudenza pratica,* 10 (1829), 188–306.

78 Having made religious vows, monks and nuns supposedly became dead to the world. Their status was considered that of a civil death; consequently, they were not allowed to inherit. On this status, see Anthony Molho, '*Tamquam vere mortua*: le professioni religiose femminili nella Firenze del tardo Medioevo', *Società e Storia,* 43 (1989), 1–44; Sperling, *Convents and the Body Politic,* p. 2; Mary Laven, *Virgins of Venice: Broken Vows and Cloistered Lives in the Renaissance Convent* (New York: Viking, 2003). For a disquisition from that time, see also *Quistione transitoria se un monaco professo suddito del regno Lombardo-Veneto possa succedere ad una eredità apertasi in quel regno 1817 per quanto riflette i bene situati in Piemonte* (Milan: Pogliani, 1819).

the law allows me to dispose of] to her only son, Giuseppe.[79] Another example is that of a widow also from Verona, Palma Naido, who, in her testament drawn up on 6 July 1819, left the property of the disposable portion of her goods to her sons Pietro and Giuseppe, while the legitime was divided between all her five children: two sons and three daughters.[80] Finally, in her will rogated on 25 September 1857, Margherita Boschetti from Milan bequeathed all her assets to her son Paolo Pizzi.[81] She ordered that her son had to pay a pension of two-and-a-half *lire austriache* per day to her husband, who also obtained the usufruct of the garden and the house where they used to live.[82] Margherita then made a bequest of seven thousand *lire austriache* to the three children of her deceased daughter and pointed out that her grandchildren had to accept her will 'nel suo integrale tenore' [in its full tenor],[83] as their mother had already obtained a dowry at the time of her marriage. If they failed to accept her will, they could only have the legitime over her patrimony, which, after having deducted their mother's dowry, was less than the bequest made by Margherita.

The examples of these women, who limited the portion their daughters would inherit in favour of their sons, are particularly significant as they were all from Lombardy-Venetia. If some women living in areas where the dowry was their only right struggled to obtain more from their parents' inheritance, other women seemed to comply strictly with the dowry system. This behaviour is even more striking in states where laws ruled that they could inherit equally. However, these co-existing attitudes could have been two sides of the same coin: women abided by the idea of entering *aliene famiglie* and sought to contribute to the improvement of the families' prestige. By limiting the amount of money and goods their daughters could obtain, they strongly accepted that the 'correct' way to improve a family's prestige was through the male line.

79 State Archive of Verona, 1865, Testamenti, n. 73, n. 2000.

80 State Archive of Verona, 1865, Testamenti, n. 73, n. 3260.

81 State Archive of Milan, Notaio Giulio Caimi, 1857, n. 1781.

82 State Archive of Milan, Notaio Giulio Caimi, 1857, n. 1781.

83 State Archive of Milan, Notaio Giulio Caimi, 1857, n. 1781.

6. Ending Wedlock

Marriage, the crucial institution of society in the Ottocento, was a lifelong bond that was contracted before the Church and deemed to last until the death of one of the spouses. This 'natural' ending often raised issues of wealth and inheritance which deeply affected women. Widowhood was a pivotal moment in women's lives, as it could entail a sudden and large change in wealth and might even throw them into poverty. The first section of this chapter is devoted to the analysis of lawsuits and legal provisions concerning widows. As we shall see, lawmakers and courts attempted to provide some protection to women and often enabled them to inherit from their deceased husband if they were at risk of falling into poverty. Marriage could also come to an end through consensual or non-consensual separation, which did not allow the spouses to remarry because divorce did not exist for Catholics. These situations are examined in the second and third sections of the chapter. Litigation relating to consensual separation mainly involved financial issues, whereas lawsuits related to non-consensual separation were thorny cases in which two people confronted each other before a court and tried their best to avoid separation.

Wealth, Poverty and Widowhood

As most marriages in the Ottocento came to an end with the death of one of the spouses, people often wrote wills to guarantee some rights to their surviving spouse. After the death of their husbands, women had no rights to their husbands' patrimony and were only entitled to ask for a scant portion of an inheritance if they were poor and without a dowry. As we saw in the previous chapter, the main purpose of a dowry was to bear the financial burden of the marriage. However, dowries had a second, perhaps even more important, purpose in that they were often a widow's only means of support.[1] Becoming a widow, already a difficult time of grief and solitude, had financial implications which required consideration. The Justinian *Corpus Iuris Civilis* defined the dowry as the property of the woman *naturaliter*,[2] even though it was in the possession of the husband's family. Therefore, a woman's in-laws were obliged to return her dowry,[3] but this was not always a smooth process: sometimes a woman and her family of origin had to face long negotiations and often the dowry was not returned in full. One example is the case of Costanza Monti Perticari, the daughter of the poet Vincenzo Monti, whose dowry was only returned after long and exhausting arbitration.[4]

Upon becoming a widow, a woman would normally return to her natal family or might decide to live alone if she were wealthy enough.[5] As previously mentioned, in the Italian Peninsula patrimonial

1 On widowhood, see in Maura Palazzi, 'Solitudini femminili e patrilignaggio. Nubili e vedove fra Sette e Ottocento', in *Storia della famiglia italiana, 1750–1950*, ed. by Barbagli and Kertzer, pp. 129–59; *Widowhood in Medieval and Early Modern Europe*, ed. by Sandra Cavallo and Lyndan Warner (Harlow: Longman, 1999); Ann Crabb, *The Strozzi of Florence: Widowhood and Family Solidarity in the Renaissance* (Ann Arbor, MI: University of Michigan Press, 2000). For a study on widows and conduct literature, see Helena Sanson, 'Widowhood and Conduct in Late Sixteenth-Century Italy: The Unusual Case of *La Vedova del Fusco* (1570)', *The Italianist*, 35 (2015), 1–26; Hosker, '"Donne sole" in Post-Unification Italy', pp. 33–52; Helena Sanson, 'Conduct for the *Real* Widow: Giulio Cesare Cabei's *Ornamenti della gentildonna vedova* (1574)', in *Conduct Literature for and about Women in Italy*, ed. by Sanson and Lucioli, pp. 41–62.

2 *Codex*, 5, 12, 30.

3 Until approximately the second century BC, the dowry, once paid, merged completely with the assets of the groom if he was *sui iuris*, or with those of his *paterfamilias* if he was not emancipated. Later an action known as the *Actio rei uxoriae* was introduced to ensure that the dowry would be returned to the woman or her natal family, if and when the marriage ended (Fayer, *La familia romana*, II, 698).

4 The case of Costanza Monti Perticari is described in Chiara Agostinelli, *"Per me sola". Biografia intellettuale e scrittura privata di Costanza Monti Perticari* (Rome: Carocci, 2006); and Luciano Baffioni Venturi, *Costanza Monti e Giulio Perticari. Amore e morte tra Marche e Romagna all'inizio dell'Ottocento* (Ancona: peQuod, 2008).

5 See, e.g., the case of Teresa Pucci, a woman from the Papal States who had always lived with her brother's family. Although she had a dowry, she could not afford to live alone and sustain her lifestyle solely on its interest. Even after the death of her brother Teresa continued to live with her sister-in-law (Sara Delmedico, 'Alimenti e dote alla periferia dello Stato Pontificio: La famiglia Pucci', *The Italianist*, 37 (2017), 50–68 (p. 58).

relationships between spouses were marked by a strict separation of goods and legal norms complied with the principle *paterna paternis, materna maternis*. A woman who lived alone on nothing more than her dowry, along with the interest it produced, might have to face significant changes in her lifestyle. Given the great importance of status in society, sometimes the easiest way to maintain a family's prestige was to 'ricollocare' – literally to 're-place' – the widow, i.e., to find her another husband. A new marriage would, it was hoped, ensure the widow's economic position was maintained while also creating further relations and connections which might prove profitable to the widow's brothers or other relatives.[6]

As we see in Chapter 3, having a dowry was not a prerequisite for marriage, but widows who were not dowered had no money or other goods on which to rely. To address this issue, some laws prescribed that, if poor and without a dowry, a widow was entitled to obtain a portion of her deceased spouse's assets, known as the *quarta uxoria*. This provision, which had been in force since the time of Justinian, implied that women were granted a quarter of the property. According to Novel 53 of the *Corpus Iuris Civilis*, women who had married without a dowry were to be supported by the property left by the decedent and share it with their children. This provision was further detailed in Novel 117, where it was explicitly stated that a wife had inheritance rights over her husband's property. These rights were usufruct if there were children and ownership if there were no children. In the Kingdom of Sardinia the *Regie Costituzioni* of 1770 made a generic reference to the 'Legge', meaning that Novels 53 and 117 of the *Corpus Iuris Civilis* were to be taken into account.[7]

6 Despite dealing with the Middle Ages and the Early Modern period, the following essays can also offer an interesting insight into widowhood and remarriage for the period we analyse: Calvi, 'Reconstructing the Family'; Chabot, 'Seconde nozze e identità materna'; Megan Moran, 'Motherhood and the Politics of Family Decisions in Early Modern Italy', *Journal of Family History*, 40 (2015), 351–72 (pp. 360–64).

7 Art. 17, Lib. V, Tit. 1, in *Leggi, e costituzioni di Sua Maestà*, 2 vols (Turin: Stamperia Reale, 1770), I, 301. The financial situation for the surviving spouse did not improve under the Napoleonic Code, which stipulated that, unless legally separated, he or she could obtain ownership of the inheritance only in the absence of relatives and natural children (Art. 767, in *Codice civile di Napoleone il Grande pel regno d'Italia* (Turin: Reale Stamperia, 1806), pp. 225–26). Similarly, according to the law in force in other states, such as in the Grand Duchy of Tuscany, poverty was a requirement for the surviving spouse to invoke the *quarta uxoria*. This right relied on the provisions of both Novel 117 and Article 27 of Law 18 August 1814, which — in the case of women — ensured

As we shall see in the following cases, the law and tribunals considered women worthy of protection and allowed them to have access to this *quarta uxoria*. The first case concerns Carlo Garello, a notary from Susa, Piedmont, who made his will on 16 November 1832. Carlo bequeathed to Ignazio, Teresa and Giuseppa, his three natural children, 'quel tanto che fosse loro dovuto a termini delle leggi' [only as much as was legally due to them].[8] The law stipulated that natural children were only entitled to receive alimony from their father or from his heirs. Carlo's patrimony was left to his sisters' children. Six days after making his will, Carlo married Cattarina Montabone, mother of his natural children. He had already been compelled to pay his children alimony after a judgement made by the Reale Senato on 10 February 1818. Another judgement, decreed by the Bishop's Curia, had ordered him to marry or dower Cattarina. However, he died a few hours after his marriage. Cattarina and his children, who were poor, initiated a lawsuit before the Regio Tribunale di Prefettura of Susa on 11 January 1835. Their poverty was already sufficiently substantiated for them to qualify for free legal aid from the lawyer of the poor. Since Ignazio, Teresa and Giuseppa were no longer considered natural children but became legitimate following their parents' marriage, they demanded the annulment of the will. Carlo's sisters, on the contrary, claimed that his children were still considered natural and not legitimate because his marriage with Cattarina was not valid. They argued that, in the marriage act:

> non costava sufficientemente della delegazione che dal Vescovo si fosse fatta al Parroco, e da questo al Sacerdote, dinanzi a cui si disse contratto il matrimonio. [...] tale delegazione non erasi fatta né in iscritti, né con parole; bensì il sacerdote Re circa le ore quattro del mattino del giorno stesso, in cui il testatore morì, spedì uno degli individui, che dovevano server di testimonio, al Parroco, onde ottenerne l'opportuna delegazione; [...] recatosi quegli alla

---

a *legitima portio* over the spouse's inheritance (see the discussion in the legal journal *La temi: giornale di legislazione e di giurisprudenza* (1847), 374–75). In the Duchy of Parma, the *Codice civile per gli stati parmensi* provided the usufruct of the fourth part of the inheritance to the impecunious surviving spouse (Art. 659, in *Codice civile per gli stati parmensi*, p. 412). The *Codice Civile per gli Stati Estensi* from 1851 had similar rules: it granted alimony to the impoverished spouse if there were children and ownership if the deceased did not have any offspring (Artt. 836 and 934, in *Codice Civile per gli Stati Estensi* (Modena: Eredi Tipografi Reali, 1851), p. 200). Last, the law in the Papal States did not make any reference to this kind of situation, which meant that Roman law was to be taken into consideration as a subsidiary source.

8 *Annali di giurisprudenza*, 2 (1838), 154–73 (p. 155).

casa parrocchiale ed esposta la sua commissione alla fantesca del Parroco, la medesima dettogli che ne avrebbe informato il Parroco stesso, dopo pochi istanti ritornò dicendo a quell'individuo, che il Parroco l'incaricava d'annunziargli che per ben fatto avrebbe avuto quanto sarebbe per fare il sacerdote Re.[9]

[the permission granted by the bishop to the parish priest, and from him to the priest before whom the marriage was said to have been contracted, [...] was not sufficient. [...] This permission was neither written nor verbal; at about four o'clock in the morning of the same day on which the testator died, the priest Re sent one of the individuals who had to serve as a witness to the parish priest in order to obtain the appropriate permission; [...] he went to the parish house and explained his commission to the maidservant of the parish priest, who said that she would inform the parish priest and after a few moments she returned, saying to that individual that the parish priest had instructed her to announce that the priest Re was allowed to proceed.]

The marriage was celebrated on 22 November 1822, at six in the morning, and, as becomes evident from this report, Carlo was near death when he decided to marry Cattarina. Given that the lawsuit concerned the validity of both a marriage and a will, the tribunal of Susa declared itself incompetent to judge the case and sent it to the Senato of Turin. The Senato argued that a superior court could more appropriately pass judgement on such a thorny issue, which encompassed both ecclesiastical and secular matters. After taking into consideration the assessment of the Office of the General Attorney, which considered that Cattarina and Carlo had contracted a valid marriage, the Senato decided that Cattarina and Carlo's son Ignazio were entitled to receive the 'porzione dalla legge riserbata a favore della moglie povera e indotata' [portion that the law granted to a wife who was poor and without a dowry] and the *legitima portio* respectively.[10] Thus, Ignazio obtained a third of his father's patrimony; Cattarina enjoyed the usufruct over a quarter of the assets; the two daughters, Teresa and Giuseppa, could obtain dowries. The amount that Carlo's sisters would inherit was, therefore, substantially reduced.

Carlo had made his will in favour of his sisters six days before dying and decided to marry Cattarina at 4 a.m. on the day of his death: arguably, his mind may not have been entirely lucid when he married, making his consent to the marriage defective. Moreover,

9 *Annali di giurisprudenza*, 2, p. 157.

10 *Annali di giurisprudenza*, 2, p. 172.

whilst a marriage was valid if celebrated *in facie ecclesiae*, and the 'priest Re' was a representative of the Church, the authorisation to marry the couple was given by the parish priest's maidservant, who reported the words of the parish priest. Given that Re did request authorisation, one might argue that obtaining permission was usually deemed necessary and thus the full validity of this oral authorisation might be questioned. Nonetheless, the Senato of Turin ruled in favour of Cattarina and her children, providing them with support. Through this judgement the court showed itself to be close to people and to understand their needs, acting not only within the boundaries of the law but also as an institution which was well rooted in society.

Another case in point is that of Maria Vandoni, which was brought before the Tribunale di Prefettura of Novara (Piedmont) in 1836 and then appealed to the Senato of Casale in 1839. Maria asked Pietro Valentino, brother and heir of her deceased husband, Giovanni Valentino, for the *quarta uxoria*, maintaining that she was poor and without a dowry.[11] Pietro tried to refute this claim by replying that she ran a small shop selling salt and tobacco in the village of Alzate and also a food shop not far from there, 'da cui [poteva] trarre una sussistenza adatta alla sua condizione di contadina' [from which she [could] draw a subsistence suited to her peasant status].[12] Furthermore, during her first marriage to Lorenzo Ballaro she had received a dowry of one thousand lire: Pietro assumed it had been reconstituted for her second marriage to Luigi Valbassora, as well as for her third marriage to Pietro's brother Giovanni in 1834.

The three marriages contracted by Maria are testament to the reliability of the model suggested by Lucetta Scaraffia and already mentioned in Chapter 1. Life in rural areas frequently necessitated living and working as a couple to carry out everyday tasks and household roles. Moreover, the economic support spouses could provide for each other was crucial among those with low incomes. This could explain why Maria married three times even though she was no longer young and only had a poor dowry at the time of her first marriage: what made her attractive on the marriage market were her personal attributes, such as her ability to carry out household tasks.

Pietro also added that Maria and Giovanni had lived together for some time without being married: extramarital relations, as we

11 State Archive of Turin, Casale, Corte di Appello, Second Semester, 1839, n. 4. This case can also be found in *Annali di giurisprudenza*, 4 (1839), 258–68.

12 *Annali di giurisprudenza*, 4, p. 258.

have seen, were both a sin and a crime which could have an impact on a woman's reputation and, in this case, they were mentioned in order to affect her request for a portion of the inheritance. Countering Pietro's first argument, Maria replied that the proceeds of her sales counter of salt and tobacco belonged to her son from her first marriage; and that the dowry brought to the first husband was no more than some house furniture she had then owned, as shown in the dowry instrument. Lorenzo Vandoni, Maria's brother, testified that he had created a dowry for his sister which was worth one thousand Milanese lire in house furniture, as requested by their father in his will of 11 January 1803. Maria's father, although not able to give his daughter any money as a dowry, wrote a testament to dispose of his poor goods, an act which demonstrates the extensive use of wills even among lower classes. The house furniture was worn-out and some of it had been used for the dowry of Maria's own daughter, who had married in 1825. Maria, who had married Giovanni three months before his death, maintained that she was able to demonstrate that his assets were worth nine thousand lire. On 2 September 1839 the Senato of Casale explained in its judgement that, to the demand of the *quarta uxoria*:

> non può opporsi in modo generico, che la donna, che vi aspira sia dotata, ma vuolsi di più, che questa dote sia effettiva, reale e sufficiente a torla da quell'inopia, cui l'Imperatore Giustiniano pensò e provvide, accordando al coniuge superstite questo benefizio.[13]
>
> [it is not possible to make a generalised objection [to a request for *quarta uxoria*], on the grounds that the woman who aspires to it has a dowry, but it is necessary that this dowry be existent, real and sufficient to remove her from poverty. It was to this end that the Emperor Justinian devised and enacted [the Code], granting this benefit to the surviving spouse.]

This benefit was granted to the surviving spouse, no matter whether they were a man or a woman. The *quarta* was not to be considered only *uxoria*: a poor husband could also obtain this portion from the inheritance of his wealthy, deceased wife.[14] The *ratio* of providing the *quarta uxoria* was to avoid that 'quella [persona] che aveva condotta consuetudine matrimoniale una vita commoda ed agiata, vedevasi costretta a mendicare quasi ne' tristi giorni della vedovanza' [the [person] who was used to a comfortable and

13 *Annali di giurisprudenza*, 4, p. 261.

14 See *Annali di giurisprudenza*, 4 (1839), 455–61.

prosperous married life would be practically forced to beg in the sad days of his/her widowhood].[15]

The court eventually assumed that Maria did not have a dowry at the time of her marriage to Giovanni and the proceeds of her food shop were deemed insufficient to support her financially. The judge maintained that jurisprudence had moved on from the view of the medieval jurist Bartolus of Saxoferrato, who had claimed that 'dos data in primo matrimonio intelligitur in secundo repetita' [a dowry given for the first marriage of a woman is also assumed to be reproduced for the second one].[16] The judge also emphasised that in current practice it was necessary for the person who gave the first dowry to consent to the creation of a new dowry in the event of a second marriage. In Maria's case no such consent had been given. Moreover, whilst it had been possible to create a dowry without registering it with a notary prior to the publication of the *Regie Costituzioni*, at the time of Maria's marriage registration was mandatory. Consequently, the court ruled that Maria did not have any dowry and was able to inherit from her deceased husband.

In 1837 poverty was removed as a prerequisite from the Civil Code of the Kingdom of Sardinia. The new law granted the surviving spouse the right of usufruct over the *quarta*; and if the deceased did not have any legitimate children, the quarter of the inheritance was fully given over to the spouse.[17] This provision was similar to that of the 1816 *Codice civile universale austriaco pel Regno Lombardo-Veneto*, by which the surviving spouse was granted the usufruct of a portion of the estate which was equal to that of the children if there were three or more; and was a third of the estate if there were fewer than three children. While property was always left to children, the usufruct of a portion could be enjoyed by the spouse, who did not need to be poor to receive these rights over the inheritance.[18] The introduction of this provision in nineteenth-century legal codes marked a crucial transition from the idea of marriage as a mere contract between two families, with women considered no more than childbearing vessels, to that of a relationship between two people which could also involve love and mutual support. Law-makers seemed to acknowledge that women actively contributed to the household; and allowing widows

15 *Annali di giurisprudenza*, 4, pp. 262–63.

16 Bartolus of Saxoferrato, *Ad legem 40*, cited in *Annali di giurisprudenza*, 4, pp. 264–65.

17 Artt. 959 and 960, in *Codice civile per gli Stati di S. M. il Re di Sardegna*, p. 652.

18 Art. 757, in *Codice civile universale austriaco pel Regno Lombardo-Veneto*, p. 189.

to inherit was, to some extent, a sort of 'compensation' for the wealth they had helped to build up during their marriage.

Annulment and Consensual Separation

According to the Catholic Church, a valid, sacramental and consummated marriage was a 'foedus a Deo institutum' [a pact instituted by God] which came to an end with the death of one of the spouses. However, if there were coherant reasons, the spouses could ask for an annulment. This was a dispensation given by the Pope, but only if the marriage was 'ratum sed non consummatum' [concluded but not consummated].[19] The declaration of annulment followed several examinations. First, the spouses should relate 'tutta la storia dei fatti occorsi nella consumazione del matrimonio, e specialmente quante volte, e da quanto tempo l'ha[nno] tentata con buon fede, e rimosso qualunque dolo' [the whole history of the events that occurred in the consummation of the marriage; and especially how many times and for how long they had tried it in good faith and without any malice].[20] The annulment process could involve gathering proof to ascertain that consummation had not taken place. The spouses might be ordered to live together for three years, undergo a physical inspection, or be asked for the deposition of the 'settima mano' [seventh hand], that is, seven kin would have to confirm they were morally convinced that the marriage had not been consummated. The annulment was a grace given by the Pope and nullified the marriage *ex nunc* [from now on].[21] A *ratum sed non consummatum* marriage was valid until the declaration of nullity was made. By contrast, a marriage could also be declared void *ex tunc* [from the outset]: this was the case if a marriage presented

19 'Dei Miseratione, 3 November 1741', in *Sanctissimi domini nostri Benedicti Papae XIV, Bullarium*, 4 vols (Venice: Occhi, 1768), I, 695–701. On marriage in canon law, see Adhémar Esmein, *Le Mariage en droit canonique*, 2 vols (Paris: Larose et Forcel, 1891); Gaudemet, *Le Mariage en Occident*; Arturo Carlo Jemolo, *Il matrimonio nel diritto canonico. Dal Concilio di Trento al Codice del 1917* (Bologna: Il Mulino, 1993).

20 Tommaso Michele Salzano, *Lezioni di diritto canonico pubblico, e privato considerato in sé stesso e secondo l'attual polizia del Regno delle Due Sicilie*, 4 vols (Naples: Giordano, 1843), IV, 90.

21 On annulment, see also Emilio Gentile, *Teorico-pratica secondo l'ecclesiastica, e la civil polizia*, 2 vols (Naples: Manfredi, 1794), II, 236–58; Ginesio Grimaldi, *Dissertazione di Ginesio Grimaldi sul punto dello scioglimento de' matrimoni per cagion d'impotenza* (Naples: Simoniana, 1765); Mercanti, *Compendio di diritto canonico*, II, 525–26; Salzano, *Lezioni di diritto canonico pubblico, e privato*, IV, 90–96.

formal defects, such as a failure to comply with the rules of form or procedure, or if it was based on a lie. A nullified *ex tunc* marriage was considered never to have been contracted from the outset.

Despite being 'principium, et fundamentum immortalitatis humani generis' [the principle and foundation of humankind's immortality], marriage could also come to an end through separation.[22] Separation did not allow remarriage because, as previously mentioned, the marriage bond between Catholics could only end with the death of one of the spouses.[23] This was also the case if only one of the spouses was Catholic at the time of the marriage. In the Kingdom of Lombardy-Venetia remarriage was only permitted for non-Catholic subjects if they had not been instrumental in causing the end of their previous marriage.[24] The process of ending a marriage through separation initially involved the Church. The authorisation of the parish priest, the bishop, or even the Pope, was necessary for a separation to be legally recognised. Whereas the *Codice civile per gli Stati di S. M. il Re di Sardegna* only mentioned that a separation was illicit without the authorisation of the ecclesiastic curia,[25] the *Codice civile universale austriaco pel Regno Lombardo-Veneto* described in detail how this approval was to be requested. The couple were required to report to the parish priest and explain what had motivated them to make this decision. The parish priest, in turn, had the duty to 'richiamare

22 Cristoforo Cosci, *De separatione tori conjugalis tam nullo existente seu soluto, quam salvo vinculo matrimonii, eiusque effectibus*, 3 vols (Rome: Salvioni, 1773–79), I (1773), 1. For an example of separation among lower class people, see D. Lombardi, 'L'odio capitale, ovvero l'incompatibilità di carattere: Maria Falcini e Andrea Lotti (Firenze 1773–1777)', in *Coniugi nemici*, ed. by Seidel Menchi and Quaglioni, pp. 335–67. An example of separation between nobles can be found in Irene Fosi, 'Da un tribunale all'altro: il divorzio fra Benedetta Pinelli e Girolamo Grimaldi, principe di Gerace (1609–1653)', in *Coniugi nemici*, ed. by Seidel Menchi and Quaglioni, pp. 417–52. See also, Palazzi, *Donne sole*; Linda Guzzetti, 'Separations and Separated Couples in Fourteenth-Century Venice', in *Marriage in Italy*, ed. by Dean and Lowe, pp. 249–74. For a study of separated women in conduct literature, see Hosker, '"Donne sole" in Post-Unification Italy', pp. 63–284.

23 Artt. 144 and 150, in *Codice civile per gli Stati di S. M. il Re di Sardegna*, p. 600; Art. 111, in *Codice civile universale austriaco pel Regno Lombardo-Veneto*, p. 153. See also Maria Rosa Di Simone, 'La condizione giuridica della donna nell'ABGB', *Historia et ius*, 9 (2016), paper 3, pp. 17–18. On marriage as a lifelong bond according to canon law, see Gaudemet, *Le Mariage en Occident*, pp. 284–89.

24 Artt. 116–119, in *Codice civile universale austriaco pel Regno Lombardo-Veneto*, p. 153.

25 Art. 140, in *Codice civile per gli Stati di S. M. il Re di Sardegna*, p. 600.

alla mente dei conjugi le promesse reciproche solennemente fatte al momento dell'unione in matrimonio, e l'inculcare loro energicamente le conseguenze dannose della separazione. Queste ammonizioni debbono ripetersi per tre diverse volte' [remind the couple of the mutual promises that had been solemnly made upon entering marriage; and strenuously to communicate the harmful consequences of separation. These admonitions must be repeated three different times].[26]

As explained in a civil law handbook of the time, the *Manuale sul Codice civile generale austriaco* (1844), the three warnings needed to be repeated 'in uno spazio di tempo competente a lasciare luogo alla riflessione' [over sufficient time to allow room for reflection].[27] If these attempts proved ineffective, the parish priest could produce a document in which he explained that, although extensively warned, the couple persisted in their will to separate. This document allowed the couple to report to the civil judge and ask to settle any patrimonial agreements relating to the marriage.[28] Despite being strictly interconnected, the ecclesiastic and secular judges defended their prerogatives. In 1854, for example, the court of Casale pointed out that if the Curia had not authorised a separation, the civil judge could not countermand this decision (as we shall see, exceptions could be made only in cases of torture).[29] Similarly, in a case brought to sentence in Turin in 1856 the tribunal stated that if an ecclesiastic court decided on alimony or other civil effects of separation, it would commit an abuse of power.[30] Separation had to be assessed by a court and could not be decided by the spouses: indeed, they could not autonomously decide to live in different houses because this behaviour would be illegal and would invalidate any demand for alimony.[31] Furthermore, a decision in 1859 defined the pact made by two married people to live separately as 'immorale e nullo' [immoral and void].[32] The use of the term immoral provides, once again, an insight into nineteenth-century attitudes: a woman and a man

26 Art. 104, in *Codice civile universale austriaco pel Regno Lombardo-Veneto*, p. 152.

27 Andrea Amati, *Manuale sul Codice civile generale austriaco* (Milan: Visaj, 1844), p. 49.

28 Art. 105, in *Codice civile universale austriaco pel Regno Lombardo-Veneto*, p. 152.

29 *Giurisprudenza degli Stati Sardi* (1854), 596–98.

30 *Giurisprudenza degli Stati Sardi* (1856), 232–35.

31 *Giurisprudenza degli Stati Sardi* (1848/1849), 346.

32 *Giurisprudenza degli Stati Sardi* (1859), 892.

married but living in two different households without a specific reason did not comply with the shared moral values of society.

Although separation did not dissolve the marriage bond, the spouses were allowed to live in separate houses and all other marital agreements continued to be in force unless explicitly stated. This meant that, as a dowry was *ad sustinenda onera matrimonii* – to bear the burden of marriage – the person who kept the dowry was obliged to provide alimony to the other spouse, even though they were separated. A case appealed before the tribunal of Turin in 1852 demonstrates this point. Giovanni Maria Gambone and Anna Paoletti requested and obtained separation from the Archbishop's Curia, but Giovanni Maria did not want to leave the house in which they used to live. The couple had a daughter aged nine, but Anna – a widow who had remarried – also had two other daughters from her previous marriage, to whom Giovanni Maria was co-guardian. He refused to leave the marital house because he was not able appropriately to perform his duties as co-guardian if he had to live somewhere else. The house where they lived was owned by his wife, as a paraphernal asset, and by the daughters from her first marriage. The court ruled that one of the effects of a separation was that the couple would have to live in two different places. Given that Anna was co-owner of the house, Giovanni Maria was obliged to move out, even though he was co-guardian of Anna's daughters.

Living in two different households, however, did not allow the spouses to disentangle themselves from other requirements of the marital bond: a husband would continue to have rights over his wife's dowry. Even after separation, a woman had to support her husband with the interest her dowry produced. Indeed:

> la legge accorda al marito la facoltà di amministrare la dote della moglie e di perceverne li frutti, e li interessi lo obbliga in pari tempo a somministrare alla moglie in proporzione delle sue sostanze e del suo stato, tutto ciò che è necessario ai bisogni della vita come pure sottostare alle spese di mantenimento ed educazione della prole.[33]
>
> [the law grants the husband the power to administer the dowry of his wife and to keep its revenue, at the same time the interest he receives obliges him to give his wife, in proportion to his means and status, all the necessities of life, as well as to bear the costs of maintenance and education of the offspring.]

33 *Giurisprudenza degli Stati Sardi*, 3 (1853), 275–78 (p. 277).

In this case, the dowry (established on 10 November 1841) was kept by Anna because it was part of the patrimony she shared with her daughters and could not be split. Theoretically, her husband was entitled to receive the interest and then return to his wife the amount necessary to support her and the daughter from their marriage. The tribunal instead ordered that Anna Paoletti was entitled to keep the interest and then return the rest to her husband. This was meant to 'evitare l'occasione di emulativi e contestazione tra le parti, o d'un pregiudizievole ritardo ogni qualvolta venisse il caso di pagamento della pensione alimentari dovuta dal Gambone alla moglie ed alla comune figlia' [avoid the possibility of competition and dispute between the parties, or of a prejudicial delay whenever Gambone was due to pay alimony to his wife and their daughter].[34] It is worth noting that Anna had a dowry of seventeen thousand lire, which produced interest of 850 lire, and the court ordered that she was only entitled to keep 550 lire to support herself and the daughter she had with Giovanni Maria.[35] This was a powerful reminder of exactly who bore the burden of the marriage: the dowry was meant to support not just the wife's expenses, but those of the entire family. Anna owned and held her dowry, yet she was not allowed to manage it and use its returns as she wished. An even more striking point was that a separated wife could not freely administer her non-dotal assets, as she still needed her husband's authorisation to sell or mortgage her estates, even after separation.[36]

Non-Consensual Separation: Adultery and *Saevitiae*

Adultery

Court trials regarding consensual separation were usually initiated because of a disagreement on financial matters, as we saw in the case of Giovanni Maria Gambone and Anna Paoletti. Non-consensual separation, by contrast, implied strong discord. Causes to demand a non-consensual separation were various, but adultery was one of the most sensitive issues: it was deemed to cause *disordine* within society, threatening a family's honour and also resulting in the birth

34 *Giurisprudenza degli Stati Sardi* (1853), p. 277.

35 *Giurisprudenza degli Stati Sardi* (1853), p. 278.

36 Art. 143, in *Codice civile per gli Stati di S. M. il Re di Sardegna*, p. 600.

of illegitimate children who would challenge the purity of the family lineage. Adultery was considered a crime and had been treated as such for many centuries. It was 'la prova oggettiva della differenza sessuale che fonda l'ordine maschile' [the objective proof of the difference between the sexes that gives rise to patriarchy] and was judged with varying degrees of harshness if committed by a man or a woman.[37] It thus confirmed the double standard by which society assessed men's and women's behaviour. Roman law defined adultery as a situation in which a married woman had sexual intercourse with a man who was not her spouse. In ancient times – under Augustus's laws, for example – the husband or the father of the adulterous woman had the *jus occidendi*, the right to slay, and the husband was entitled to retain a portion of his wife's dowry.[38] Canon law, too, addressed the issue and explained that only the *copula perfecta* was to be considered adultery.[39] The law of the Church prescribed that the adulterous woman would lose her dowry.[40] If the husband was the adulterous one, he would lose the right to hold and retain the interest generated by his wife's dowry.[41] Women's *imbecillitas* – Maurice Daumas points out – was not considered when handling adultery: 'al contrario, in quanto alleata naturale del Nemico, è molto spesso designata come la fonte stessa del male' [on the contrary, as a natural ally of the Enemy she is frequently blamed for being the true source of the evil].[42]

Medieval municipal statutes also punished those who committed adultery, especially from the early fourteenth century onwards, when they began first to impose financial penalties and, later on,

37 Daumas, *Adulteri e cornuti*, p. 70.

38 For an overview of adultery and *jus occidendi* in Roman law, see David Cohen, 'The Augustan Law on Adultery: The Social and Cultural Context', in *The Family in Italy*, ed. by Kertzer and Saller, pp. 109–26; Eva Cantarella, 'Homicides of Honor: The Development of Italian Adultery Law over Two Millennia', in *The Family in Italy*, ed. by Kertzer and Saller, pp. 229–44 (pp. 229–35); Fayer, *La familia romana*, III, 189–374; Andrea Massironi, 'The Father's Right to Kill his Adulterous Daughter in the Late Ius Commune', in *Family Law and Society in Europe*, ed. by Di Renzo Villata, pp. 187–215. See also F. Roberti, 'Adulterio (diritto canonico)', in *Novissimo Digesto Italiano*, 20 vols (Turin: Utet, 1957), I, 333–35; Giuseppe Branca, 'Adulterio (diritto antico)', in *Enciclopedia del diritto*, I (1958), 620–21.

39 The *copula perfecta* was sexual intercourse which led to procreation (Pietro D'Avack, 'La *copula perfecta* e la *consummatio coniugi* nelle fonti e nella dottrina canonistica classica', *Rivista italiana per le scienze giuridiche*, 86 (1949), 163–250).

40 Mercanti, *Compendio di diritto canonico*, II, 536–37.

41 Mercanti, *Compendio di diritto canonico*, II, 536–37.

42 Daumas, *Adulteri e cornuti*, p. 103.

corporal ones.[43] Some statutes of the Italian Peninsula prescribed mild penalties, such as a fine or the cutting of the adulterers' hair, while others had very harsh rules. According to the Statute of Tivoli of 1305, for example, the betrayed wife, or a person she nominated, could whip her husband's *amasia* (mistress) for as long as she wanted, providing that she avoided homicide or 'perdita di membro' [loss of a limb].[44] The Statute of Omegna (1384) went so far as to condemn to death those who committed adultery.[45] However, adultery was not considered a point of no return, because 'love as a disorienting or mad passion was of limited duration; thus, in cases of love it could be hoped that lovers would eventually return to their senses and their correct familial places'.[46] Bartolus of Saxoferrato suggested sending the adulterous wife to a nunnery. In this way, the husband could be reconciled with his adulterous wife because the time spent there was believed to remove any stain of sin.[47] As explained by Guido Ruggiero, adultery was 'perceived as loss of property for a husband and his household, [and] courts were largely concerned with marriage in term of property as were most of the husbands who sought justice against adulterers'.[48] This might further explain why men could be convicted of adultery only if they kept their *amasia* in the marital house.[49]

43 Dean, 'Fathers and Daughters', pp. 86–87.

44 Antonio Marongiu, 'Adulterio (diritto intermedio)', *Enciclopedia del diritto*, I (1958), 622.

45 Marongiu, 'Adulterio (diritto intermedio)', p. 622.

46 Ruggiero, *The Boundaries of Eros*, p. 66.

47 'Monasterium omnem maculam detergit [...] vir potest sibi reconciliare uxorem de adulterio damnatam, et in monasterium missam' [The monastery cleans every stain [and therefore] a man can reconcile with his wife, who was convicted of adultery and put into a monastery] (Bartolus of Saxoferrato, *Commentaria in Corpus iuris civilis. Super Authenticis, & Institutionibus* (Venice: Giunta, 1585), Collatio IX, 54).

48 Ruggiero, *The Boundaries of Eros*, p. 45.

49 Marongiu, 'Adulterio (diritto intermedio)', p. 623. On adultery, see also Ruggiero, *The Boundaries of Eros*, pp. 45–69. For some disputes regarding adultery and the demand for separation during the Early Modern period, see Guzzetti, 'Separations and Separated Couples', pp. 249–74; Stanley Chojnacki, 'Il divorzio di Cateruzza: rappresentazione femminile ed esito processuale (Venezia 1465)', in *Coniugi nemici*, ed. by Seidel Menchi and Quaglioni, pp. 371–416; Marco Bellabarba, 'I processi per adulterio nell'Archivio Diocesano Tridentino (XVII–XVIII secolo)', in *Trasgressioni*, ed. by Seidel Menchi and Quaglioni, pp. 185–227 (esp. pp. 193–94); Turchi, 'Adulterio, onere della prova e testimonianza'. For a comparison, see the study on adultery in England, David M. Turner, *Fashioning Adultery: Gender, Sex, and Civility in England, 1660–1740* (Cambridge: Cambridge University Press, 2002).

In the period from the Middle Ages to modern times the judicial approach to adultery changed in terms of punishment: explicit provisions of physical punishment were removed from eighteenth-century laws, even though, as we shall see, the sentence for the killing of an adulterous spouse was often mitigated. Over the course of time the double standard applied to men and women remained unchallenged and continued to be enshrined in law. Following the Napoleonic conquests and the promulgation of the Criminal Code in 1810,[50] the law ruled that only the husband was entitled to denounce his wife's adultery, which could be punished with imprisonment from three months up to two years. The husband could stop this punishment 'consentendo a riprendere la moglie' [by consenting to take the wife back].[51] These criminal-code provisions were already included in Napoleon's Civil Code.[52] Napoleonic criminal law stipulated that an adulterous husband could only be punished if he had brought his mistress to live in the spouses' house and that this punishment must be limited to a fine.[53] Adultery was an appropriate reason to demand divorce,[54] as it implied a breach of the right to mutual fidelity with which the spouses should comply and an even more crucial challenge to honour. However, even the right to ask for

50 The *Codice dei Delitti e delle Pene pel Regno d'Italia* (Milan: Reale Stamperia, 1810) was approved by decree 254 on 12 November 1810 and entered into force on 1 January 1811. On this code, see Andre Laingui, 'Il diritto penale della rivoluzione francese e dell'Impero', in *Diritto penale dell'Ottocento. I codici preunitari e il codice Zanardelli,* ed. by Sergio Vinciguerra (Padua: CEDAM, 1993), pp. 49–52; Adriano Cavanna, 'Il codice penale napoleonico. Qualche considerazione generalissima', in *Codice dei delitti e delle pene pel Regno d'Italia (1811),* ed. by Sergio Vinciguerra (Padua: Cedam, 2002), pp. XI–XXII (pp. XIV–XVI); Mario A. Cattaneo, 'L'autoritarismo penale napoleonico', in *Codice dei delitti e delle pene pel Regno d'Italia (1811),* ed. by Sergio Vinciguerra, pp. 23–32.

51 Artt. 336–337, in *Codice dei Delitti e delle Pene pel Regno d'Italia* (Milan: Reale Stamperia, 1810), p. 112.

52 Artt. 308 and 309, in *Codice Civile del Regno d'Italia,* in *Collezione Completa dei Moderni Codici Civili* (Turin: Minerva Subalpina, 1845), pp. 1–139 (p. 18).

53 Art. 339, in *Codice dei Delitti e delle Pene pel Regno d'Italia* (Milan: Reale Stamperia, 1810), p. 112.

54 Artt. 229 and 230, in *Codice Civile del Regno d'Italia,* p. 13. If there was no adultery implied, the Code allowed that both spouses could ask for divorce 'per eccessi, sevizie, o ingiurie gravi' (Art. 231, in *Codice Civile del Regno d'Italia,* p. 13). It is worth highlighting the fact that according to the Napoleonic Code a couple could ask for divorce and then remarry, while other legal systems in force after the Restoration only allowed separation. Divorce was introduced in the Italian legal system with Law 898 in 1970.

a divorce was granted to men and women to varying degrees, again confirming women's inferior status.

The work of the Dominican friar Faustino Scarpazza is representative of the thoughts regarding adultery, which were shared by many people in the Italian Peninsula and, as we have seen, confirmed by the law:

> L'adulterio non ha sempre la medesima gravità, [...] è più grave l'adulterio di una conjugata con un libero uomo, di quello di un conjugato, con una donna libera, poiché nel primo caso si ha l'incertezza sulla legittimità della prole. [...] Questa maggior gravità ci viene anche indicata dal Signore quando nei tempi antichi permise bensì la pluralità delle mogli, ma non mai la pluralità dei mariti. [Inoltre] la moglie non contrae infamia dall'adulterio del marito, niuno se ne scandalezza, e può ritenerla per complice del di lui peccato, purché dimostri il suo dispiacere pei vizj del marito, e si adoperi perché si emendi.[55]

> [Adultery does not always carry the same weight [...] when a married woman commits adultery with a single man it is more serious than when a married man commits adultery with a single woman, since in the first case there is doubt as to the legitimacy of any offspring. [...] The greater severity of this latter act has also been shown to us by the Lord, who allowed men to have may wives in ancient times, but never allowed women to have multiple husbands. [In addition] a wife is not disgraced by her husband's adultery, no one is scandalised by it, or considers her an accomplice in his sin, as long as she shows her displeasure at her husband's vices and strives to make him change his ways.]

Common views on marriage and the double standard relating to sexual behaviour were such that a wife's adultery was deemed to have a major impact on the honour of her husband and their families, especially because it could cause a breach in the family line. Adultery committed by a man, on the other hand, was not considered to be so significant, as long as the betrayed wife showed sorrow for her husband's vices and tried her best to assure society that she was not an accomplice. It is also worth noting that, according to Scarpazza, it was the wife who was asked to 'strive' to make her husband stop betraying her. Moreover, if a man had children born outside the family, it had a negligible effect on his standing and prestige, whereas for a woman having illegitimate children was a matter of the utmost dishonour.

55 Faustino Scarpazza, *Decisioni dei casi di coscienza e di dottrina canonica*, 14 vols (Naples: Nuovo Gabinetto Letterario, 1828–35), I, 24, 28.

The Criminal Code of the Kingdom of Sardinia from 1839 described adultery as a crime against 'l'ordine delle famiglie' [the order of the family] and confirmed the provisions of the Napoleonic Code.[56] This Code reduced the punishment of those who, in the grip of the 'justus dolor' [just rage], that is, uncontrollable passion, killed the adulterous spouse. This *justus dolor* was believed to erupt if, for example, a husband caught his wife in the act of committing adultery.[57] This reduction in sentence was also granted to a woman's parents if they caught their daughter committing adultery in their house and then killed her.[58] There was no provision set down for the case of a woman killing her adulterous husband because, as we saw, 'a wife is not disgraced by her husband's adultery'.

The Austrian Code of 1852 that was in force in Lombardy-Venetia ruled, on the other hand, that the adulterers were to be given a fine and imprisoned for between one and six months; and added that 'la donna deve punirsi con maggior rigore qualora, a motivo del commesso adulterio, possa insorger dubbio sulla legittimità del successivo parto' [the woman must be more harshly punished if the legitimacy of a subsequent birth is cast into question owing to her adultery]. The Austrian Code did not mention scandal and honour as reasons for the punishment of adultery: the adulterers were indicted for violating the right of the spouses to mutual fidelity.[59] With the Unification of Italy and the enactment of the new Civil Code (1865), legal provisions on adultery became similar to those enforced in the Napoleonic Code and the Code of the Kingdom of Sardinia, only permitting the wife to demand a separation if the husband had kept his mistress in the marital house, or – and the Napoleonic Code did not have this provision – 'notoriamente in altro luogo, oppure concorrano circostanze tali che il fatto costituisca una ingiuria grave alla moglie' [[he kept her] elsewhere in a flagrant manner, or in circumstances that would be deeply insulting to the wife].[60]

56 Artt. 523–529, in *Codice Penale per gli Stati di S. M. il Re di Sardegna* (Turin: Minerva Subalpina, 1840), pp. 90–91.

57 On this point, see Marco Cavina, *Nozze di sangue. Storia della violenza coniugale* (Rome: Laterza, 2011), pp. 68–81.

58 Art. 604, in *Codice Penale per gli Stati di S. M. il Re di Sardegna*, p. 102.

59 Oldrati, *Codice penale austriaco*, p. 428.

60 Art. 150, in *Codice civile del Regno d'Italia: corredato della relazione del Ministro Guardasigilli fatta a S. M. in udienza del 25 giugno 1865* (Turin: Botta, 1865), p. 30. See also Artt. 148–149.

Saevitiae

Adultery was not the only possible motivation behind a demand for a non-consensual separation. In Lombardy-Venetia, abuse, torture, or even only 'condotta sregolata in guisa che [...] i buoni costumi della famiglia siano posti in pericolo' [unregulated conduct that would endanger the family's good name] could serve as substantial reasons to initiate a claim.[61] It should be noted that not every kind of torture was considered harsh enough to initiate a claim and a wife had to bear a certain degree of abuse. As Marco Cavina observed, 'la violenza maritale fu un elemento fisiologico e accettato del matrimonio, legalmente fino a tutto l'Antico Regime, socialmente ben oltre' [domestic abuse was a physical reality of marriage that was legally acceptable for the entirety of the Old Regime and socially acceptable well beyond].[62] The collection of volumes written during the second half of the eighteenth century by Cristoforo Cosci, an apostolic prothonotary, clearly explains this point. Cosci writes that 'saevitia viri in uxorem est res pessima, [sed] percussio moderata uxoris ad correctionem non est causa separationis tori' [the torture of a woman by her husband is a very bad thing, [but] moderately beating the wife with the aim of correcting her is not a reason for conjugal separation].[63] The attitude of the time was that women – considered weak-headed and childish – needed to be guided and corrected by any possible means. By contrast, 'atroces saevitae' [atrocious tortures] could lead to separation and in order to determine the harshness of a *saevitia* 'semper attendenda est qualitas personae' [the status of the person involved should always be considered].[64] This meant that *saevitae* such as the denial of food and medicine were deemed to have differing impacts: 'in foeminis honestissimis et nobilibus illae saevitiae graviores sunt, [...] in humilioribus sunt leviores' [these methods of torture are more severe on honest and noble women, [...] and are less [severe] on the humble].[65] In a world which revolved around the ideas of status and prestige this statement

61 Art. 109, in *Codice civile universale austriaco pel Regno Lombardo-Veneto*, p. 152.

62 Cavina, *Nozze di sangue*, p. XII.

63 Cosci, *De separatione tori conjugalis*, I, 304–17. On domestic violence, see also Giovanni Minnucci, '"An mulier verberari possit": una "quaestio disputata" di argomento matrimoniale', in *Coniugi nemici*, ed. by Seidel Menchi and Quaglioni, pp. 491–98; Trevor Dean, 'Domestic Violence in Late-Medieval Bologna', *Renaissance Studies*, 18 (2004), 527–43; Cavina, *Nozze di sangue*.

64 Cosci, *De separatione tori conjugalis*, I, 317–27.

65 Cosci, *De separatione tori conjugalis*, I, 317–27.

is not surprising. The social, juridical and economic framework of the eighteenth- and nineteenth-century Italian Peninsula, with its legacy of 'soggezione di persona a persona' (see Chapter 3), easily accepted a worldview which linked the body to wealth, suggesting that the life of a noble, wealthy person was more important than that of a poor one.

The petition for separation due to *saevitia* suffered by one of the spouses was initiated in a similar way to those concerning other cases of separation. First, it was to be reported to the Curia, which had to release a document allowing the couple to report to the secular judge to assess their patrimonial matters. In the Kingdom of Sardinia the civil judge could also order a separation if the safety of the spouse who initiated the petition was at risk.[66] In Lombardy-Venetia, the civil judge could decide on the separation and on patrimonial matters if one of the spouses did not agree to appear before the Curia.[67] Non-consensual separation was not easy to obtain unless there were substantial reasons to petition for it. In two cases reported in legal journals (one in the *Giurisprudenza teorico-pratica secondo la legislazione austriaca* and the other in *Annali di Giurisprudenza*), the lawsuits were initiated because of the passing on of venereal disease, which was equated to a *saevitia*. For example, in a case which was brought before several tribunals of Lombardy-Venetia in 1835 a woman initiated a lawsuit against her husband, who, a few days after their marriage, had passed syphilis on to her.[68] The reported trials took place before secular judges, which leads us to believe that one of the spouses, the husband in this case, refused to appear before the Curia. Initially the wife was obliged to stay in bed although she was unaware of the nature of her sickness. Her uncle then invited her to his house for a few days, hoping for 'un miglioramento nel cambiamento dell'aria' [an improvement brought about by a change of air].[69] However,

66 Art. 140, in *Codice civile per gli Stati di S. M. il Re di Sardegna*, p. 600.

67 Artt. 107 and 108, in *Codice civile universale austriaco pel Regno Lombardo-Veneto*, p. 152.

68 *Giurisprudenza teorico-pratica secondo la legislazione austriaca*, 23 (1836), 173–94. Syphilis, often called 'lue celtica', 'lue venerea' or 'morbo gallico', was a widespread disease to which physicians gave much attention. Various nineteenth-century works also testified to the attempts to develop a vaccine through syphilisation, which, at that time, was deemed to be successful. See, e.g., Gaspare Federigo, *Osservazioni sugli effetti del gallico nel popolo, ed i metodi più facili di curarlo* (Venice: Andreola, 1791); Casimiro Sperino, *Sifilizzazione nell'uomo* ([n.p.]: Favale, 1851); Isacco Galligo, *Sulla vaccinazione celtica o meglio sulla sifilizzazione nell'uomo* (Florence: Cecchi, 1852).

69 *Giurisprudenza teorico-pratica*, 23 (1836), p. 173.

when she returned home her condition deteriorated to the extent that she was not able to do any housework. Her father was immediately informed and took her to his home, where 'le vennero prodigate tutte le possibili cure per rimetterla in salute' [they gave her every possible treatment to restore her to health].[70] The family even called a doctor from Milan, who confirmed that her sickness was due to the 'lue venerea dalla quale era gravemente attaccata' [serious attack of syphilis] and suggested sending her to the 'Ospedale Maggiore'.[71] The journal does not report the couple's names, or where they lived, but from the information given we can assume that they were from the province of Milan and the Ospedale Maggiore was probably that of Milan. There the wife was hospitalised, with the concomitant costs, for several months and, when she was able to return to her father's house, continued to be under medical attention for some time. All these vicissitudes were substantiated by two letters in which her husband admitted to being guilty of passing syphilis on to her and promised to bear the cost of his wife's medical treatment. She pointed out that the husband, perfectly aware of his sickness, had seriously undermined her health and her life. The records report her stating that:

> con medicozzi curavasi da sé già da qualche giorno [e] conscio della sua infezione, conscio per l'esperienza che il male era comunicabile, superò ogni riguardo, sciolse qualunque freno, usò con la sposa e con l'uso la rese inferma ed infetta di un malore pericoloso.[72]
>
> [he treated himself with medication for a few days and then, aware of his infection, aware from experience that the disease was contagious, he overcame any feelings of respect, he lost all restraint and had sex with his wife. In so doing he infected her with a dangerous illness and made her sick.]

The woman points out that her husband had come down with the *morbo gallico* by committing an illicit, prohibited action: as he himself had even confirmed, 'si era unito con una femmina da partito poco prima del matrimonio' [he had sexual intercourse with a prostitute shortly before his marriage].[73] As we saw earlier, extramarital sexual intercourse was not punished in Lombardy-Venetia. Hence, one might argue that the wife wanted to leverage the court's sense

70 *Giurisprudenza teorico-pratica* (1836), p. 173.

71 *Giurisprudenza teorico-pratica* (1836), p. 173.

72 *Giurisprudenza teorico-pratica* (1836), p. 178.

73 *Giurisprudenza teorico-pratica* (1836), p. 177.

of morality and show her husband in a bad light to facilitate her demand for a separation. According to Article 109 of the *Codice civile*, the wife asked the court to pronounce a sentence which declared their separation, the return of her dowry and her trousseau and the repayment of her medical expenses, which amounted to 252.2 *lire austriache*, as well as a daily alimony of 1.5 *lire austriache*.[74] The husband refuted his wife's argument by pointing out that syphilis was not among the diseases that allowed separation according to Article 109. In particular, he claimed that the *morbo gallico* was not strictly considered to be contagious: transmittable diseases were only those which were passed on 'con l'alito e con la semplice vicinanza, come sarebbe la febbre gialla, il morbo nero, le scrofole e simili' [via the breath of, or simply proximity to [an infected person], as are yellow fever, the black disease, scrofula and similar diseases].[75] He also claimed that he had not known he was sick; this explained why he took part 'nelle allegrezze nuziali non si astenne di valersi né di vitto, né di bibite eccitanti' [in the nuptial celebrations, where he did not refrain from availing himself of either food or stimulating drinks] and even consummated the marriage.[76] He added that, had he been aware of his condition, he would have postponed their marriage until after his complete recovery. There was no actual malice in his actions – he maintained – and the two letters presented to court were by no means evidence of his guilt and only showed 'l'umiliazione dell'innocente marito, che afflitto dall'avvenuto sinistro ne chiede scusa alla moglie' [the humiliation of an innocent husband who, afflicted by accident, begs for forgiveness from his wife].[77] He also asked the court to order his wife to return to the marital house within fourteen days, 'sotto la comminatoria d'esservi astretta anche con i mezzi compulsivi di giustizia' [under the order, which is to be carried out with the full force of the law].

In line with the prevailing ideas of the time, the tribunal of first instance assumed that a wife needed to bear a certain degree of *saevitiae* and ruled that there were insufficient reasons for the couple to separate. At most the wife could ask for a reimbursement for the medical expenses she had incurred. Passing on chronic syphilis was definitely a valid reason to ask for separation, but – the court ruled – only if this

74 *Giurisprudenza teorico-pratica* (1836), p. 174.

75 *Giurisprudenza teorico-pratica* (1836), p. 175.

76 *Giurisprudenza teorico-pratica* (1836), p. 175.

77 *Giurisprudenza teorico-pratica* (1836), p. 176.

was done consciously and if the syphilis was incurable.[78] As the couple married on 5 June and the husband sought medical help on 24 June, the court argued that it was unlikely that he could have been aware of his disease. This proved that there was no actual malice.[79] The court also rejected the point that the passing on of a disease could be equated to mistreatment. On the contrary:

> coll'avere inscientemente comunicato il male alla moglie non può dirsi che abbia il marito tese insidie alla di lei vita e salute né vuolsi parificare un tal fatto ad una propinazione di veleno: la visita fatta eseguire alla moglie dal medico e le istanze per sottoporla ad una cura escludono ogni idea di insidia.[80]
>
> [having unknowingly given the disease to his wife, it cannot be said that the husband has made an attempt on her life and health, nor can such an act be equated to having administered poison: the doctor's visit to the wife and [the husband's] requests that she be admitted for treatment precludes any will [on his part] to endanger her health.]

In the court's opinion, the husband's fairness and innocence could undoubtedly be inferred by his having called a doctor and provided his wife with medical treatment. Admittedly the woman's life could have been at risk, but no deadly event had occured and her suffering was not directly caused by her husband, as in the case, for example, of 'percosse, minacce, mancanza di alimenti e simili' [beatings, threats, lack of food and similar behaviour].[81] The court of first instance ruled that the spouses should reunite and that the wife, given that she had recovered, could 'quindi superare il ribrezzo che la ricordanza del male sofferto poteva ispirare' [therefore overcome the disgust that the memory of this suffering might inspire].[82]

The wife appealed the sentence and protested 'contro il disordine di voler constringere una infelice ed innocente giovane a nuovamente giacere su di un talamo che il marito le preparò coperto di veleno' [against the injustice of trying to force an unhappy and innocent young woman to again lie in a marriage bed which her husband had prepared for her by covering it in poison].[83] She even suggested that her husband's disease could have been caused by a 'commercio con

78 *Giurisprudenza teorico-pratica* (1836), p. 182.

79 *Giurisprudenza teorico-pratica* (1836), p. 184.

80 *Giurisprudenza teorico-pratica* (1836), p. 184.

81 *Giurisprudenza teorico-pratica* (1836), p. 184.

82 *Giurisprudenza teorico-pratica* (1836), p. 184.

83 *Giurisprudenza teorico-pratica* (1836), p. 186.

una *bagascia*' [interaction with a *prostitute*] after their marriage, which would make him culpable of adultery, according to Article 109. His fault was not excusable even if he had enjoyed this 'meretricio suo congiungimento' [association with a harlot] before their marriage, because he could have waited the time required for the disease to take its course.[84] The Eccelso Tribunale superiore d'Appello conceded the separation of bed and board because the wrong that the husband had committed was prodigious. The court argued that this woman, 'zitella onesta e nel fiore degli anni' [honest woman in her prime of life], had been offended 'nell'atto stesso di ascendere quel talamo che immacolato attendeva, e trovava contaminato; quell'animo non poteva non essere lacerato da amarissima afflizione' [in the very act of ascending that marriage bed, which she anticipated to be spotless and found to be defiled; her spirit could not help being torn by bitter affliction].[85]

The sentence was again appealed. This time the husband argued that this was not a cause which affected merely their own interests but was also a matter of public order. By enlarging upon ideas about marriage being a key institution on which society rested, the defendant won the favour of the court: the Supremo Senato of Verona, the tribunal of final instance, confirmed the first judgement and denied the petition for separation. However, the husband was required to refund the expenses incurred by his wife due to her disease. Despite appearances, this was an achievement for the wife, given that expenses for her sickness would usually have been paid out of her dowry. A marriage was a lifelong bond which could not be dissolved because one of the spouses had transmitted a disease, a judgement denying any significance to personal feelings and psychological issues. Although sexual intercourse outside wedlock was not looked upon favourably, it was socially accepted for men, who were not expected to abide by the same sexual rules as women. As a woman's goal was to marry, society required her to comply with behaviour which was seen as positive and womanly, such as being a good daughter, wife and then mother, being sexually virtuous and compliant in her role as an angel of the hearth. Furthermore, in this case, the wife asked for the separation, but at the same time seemed to share society's perspective on men and women. The wife's arguments revolved around the disease and her sickness; and although she mentioned that her husband might have committed a

84 *Giurisprudenza teorico-pratica* (1836), p. 186.

85 *Giurisprudenza teorico-pratica* (1836), pp. 190–91.

prohibited action, she neglected to refer to his morality. The syphilis had supposedly developed after an 'interaction with a prostitute', but this detail was revealed to explain the demand for a separation, not in order to stigmatise the act. We may assume that the 'marriage bed which she anticipated to be spotless and found to be defiled' only refers to the disease, as honesty and virginity were considered only womanly values.

Another interesting example of the law in action is a case discussed in the Kingdom of Sardinia which also dealt with a sexually transmitted disease, but this time the consequences were fatal, even though the case itself was about patrimonial matters.[86] The relatives of a deceased woman (names are not mentioned) asked the court to confirm that they were entitled to initiate legal proceedings against her widower in order to claim his forfeiture of the right to obtain the *lucrum dotis*, the share a man was entitled to keep before returning the dowry to his wife's heirs after her death. Alongside the amount of the dowry and the trousseau, wedding agreements signed before notaries also regulated issues such as the place where the couple would settle after the marriage and often confirmed the amount of the *lucrum dotis*. The value of the *lucrum dotis* was usually stipulated by the law, especially by municipal statutes, to which people still referred in many areas of the nineteenth-century Italian Peninsula. A husband could obtain this share only if the marriage was still in force at the time of his wife's death. The question around which this lawsuit revolved was whether the couple were separated or not, given that the woman had initiated a cause against her husband but had died before a verdict had been reached.

At the time of their wedding in 1836 the wife had obtained a dowry of forty thousand lire. More than half of this dowry (25,000 lire) was paid in cash, while the remaining portion was used to cancel a mortgage the husband had taken out on his own patrimony. In the dowry instrument the spouses referred to the Statute of Turin to determine the *lucrum dotis*. Shortly after their marriage the wife left the marital house and went before the Bishop of Turin to ask for the 'separazione di toro' [separation of bed], because she had discovered that she had been infected with syphilis by her husband, presumably after extramarital intercourse on his part. The husband claimed that neither he nor his wife had syphilis and demanded that his wife return to their house. Both presented documents drawn up by their respective physicians to support their claims but

86 *Annali di Giurisprudenza*, 3 (1839), 292–308.

shortly thereafter the woman died. The husband sued his wife's brother and mother, asking them to cancel the mortgage taken out on his property to guarantee the dowry and claimed he was entitled to keep twenty thousand lire for himself as *lucrum dotis*. They questioned his claims by maintaining he did not deserve any *lucrum dotis* because he had committed adultery; and presented a statement from a doctor showing that his wife's death was caused by a 'subdola infiammazione intestinale a cui la causa sifilitica [aveva] servito di avviamento ed accidentali cause atmosferiche [avevano] indi procacciato incremento ed acutizzazione' [insidious intestinal inflammation which the syphilis had brought about and that unforseeable environmental factors had then enhanced and exacerbated].[87] The husband, by contrast, argued that the autopsy did not report any traces of syphilis and that the cause of death was deemed to be inflammatory bowel disease.

In June 1837 the tribunal in Turin ruled that the husband was entitled to keep the *lucrum dotis* because, if the passing on of syphilis could have been equated to a *saevitia* –therefore allowing separation – this was to be done 'scientemente, e [...] il risultato di dolo, e di animo pravo, e che ebbe luogo con premeditazione, o con volontà deliberata di nuocere gravemente' [knowingly, as a result of deception, with a spirit of malice and which was done with premeditation, or with the deliberate will to inflict serious harm].[88] However, the court judged that this had not happened in this case and added that the documents presented allowed room for doubt as to whether the husband had passed on the disease deliberately or not.

The case was not over. Basing their claims on 'la legge, [...] la giurisprudenza, [...] e la sana ragione' [the law, [...] jurisprudence [...] and sound reason], the wife's brother and mother appealed the judgement, arguing that the couple were in fact separated at the time of the wife's death because of the husband's 'inosservanza di fede coniugale, e [...] mali trattamenti' [breach of marital fidelity, and [...] bad conduct].[89] The appellants' lawyer argued that the husband should lose the *lucrum dotis*, not because of the separation *per se*, but because of his behaviour. He had caused the separation 'malamente governandosi' [by behaving badly] and, if the death of his wife made the sentence of separation 'inutile, ed anzi impossibile' [useless and even impossible], the behaviour of the surviving spouse could not

87 *Annali di Giurisprudenza* (1839), p. 296.

88 *Annali di Giurisprudenza* (1839), p. 296.

89 *Annali di Giurisprudenza* (1839), p. 297.

be left unpunished.[90] Since jurisprudence suggested that 'le sevizie, le insidie tramate alla vita, le ingiuste diffamazioni' [torture, plots that threatened lives [and] unjust defamations] were valid reasons to ask for a separation, how much more was this the case for the transmission of such a disease.[91] Although one could argue that the syphilis was not passed on intentionally, jurisprudence maintained that a husband's duty was not to harm but to defend and protect his wife; therefore, the gross negligence which had made the woman ill could be equated to actual malice.[92] The appellants also pointed out that the *lucrum dotis* was a sort of reward, a sign of gratitude for a good marriage and the spouse, who had put the couple in such a deadly situation, could not aspire to profit by it.[93]

The husband's counterargument focused on the very intimate nature of the demand for a separation, suggesting that such a request could not be passed on to any heir and therefore his wife's relatives had no power to initiate any claim.[94] He also stated that he and his wife had reconciled and that she had even given him a gift for his name day in April 1836. He added that on the following 10 June his mother-in-law had given him the remaining five thousand lire to which he was entitled as part of his wife's dowry. Nonetheless, the husband's arguments were not enough to convince the Real Senato, which on 22 March 1839 decided in favour of the wife's relatives and claimed that the outcome of the case was not only crucial for the appellants' own interests but was particularly important for public morals. Although the woman's relatives had to move through several judicial stages, the Real Senato ruled that the appellants were entitled to make a claim to prohibit the widower from keeping the *lucrum dotis*. The couple had not been reconciled as the husband had claimed; and the gift for the name day, as well as the missing five thousand lire, were given before the cause for separation was presented to the Bishop of Turin (22 July 1836). The Real Senato also pointed out that it was not the sentence of separation itself that could have rendered him unworthy to obtain the *lucrum dotis*, but the facts that had led to such a sentence.[95] Although it is not clearly reported in the decision, one can argue that adultery and the passing on of syphilis were not

90 *Annali di Giurisprudenza* (1839), pp. 300–01.

91 *Annali di Giurisprudenza* (1839), p. 301.

92 *Annali di Giurisprudenza* (1839), p. 302.

93 *Annali di Giurisprudenza* (1839), p. 303.

94 *Annali di Giurisprudenza* (1839), p. 304.

95 *Annali di Giurisprudenza* (1839), pp. 305–08.

the only acts that made the husband unworthy of the *lucrum dotis*: the subsequent death of his wife made public his betrayal of the family's honour and this was strongly censurable.

In a world that revolved around marriage, which was considered indissoluble, any challenge to the legitimate family was of major concern. A marriage should only end with the death of one of the spouses and cases regarding adultery and separation were few. Despite adultery being largely acceptable when committed by men, courts nevertheless did take into consideration the threat it presented to the honour of the wife's family. If a woman in the private sphere was asked to bear *saevitae* and adultery to some extent, things changed once these injuries were made public. Women, who entered another *famiglia* through marriage, were not entitled to bring with them large amounts of their original family's wealth; they were entrusted instead with the task of preserving their status and honour. As their morality was deemed to have an impact on their natal family, a breach of their personal honour, if made public, was similarly considered an offence to their family as a whole.

Conclusion

The Ottocento was a crucial period for women in the Italian Peninsula. Both men and women acknowledged, and often shared, the new ideals of the Enlightenment, but changes were handled with extreme caution. This was reflected in the law, resulting in a legal framework with judges, jurists and lawmakers who praised institutions such as marital authorisation but at the same time included women among those entitled to access parental inheritance. Some interesting points can be inferred from the legal documents analysed in this study. First, the nineteenth-century family still bears significant traces of the Old Regime's idea of a choral and collective moral body which deployed its standing in society as a group. Within a context which relied on obedience and valued it as a major virtue, what Luciano Guerci called a 'crisi dell'obbedienza' emerged. Women questioned men's authority, sons disputed that of their fathers, challenging not only the family's peace but also the hierarchical set-up of society. This crisis of obedience came together with, or – one might argue – was the cause of, the decline of the patriarchal family, a process which possibly began with the Enlightenment and found its embodiment in the individualism of the Napoleonic Code.

Women initiating lawsuits had a salient role in this process. They showed a certain degree of consciousness about their rights and, when reporting their cases, also seemed to know how the law functioned in practice and how to seek advice. Although the rulings examined in this study were not always made in women's favour, they could be interpreted in several ways. Poised between the Ancien Régime and the disrupting novelties of the Napoleonic Code and with an eye to the future, judges and jurists bore in mind the ways people could be affected by the output of the law in action and how their decisions were understood in society. A possible conclusion which emerges from the analysis of these rulings is their aim to avoid discord and disruption by attempting, often awkwardly, not to neglect anyone and by always keeping in mind the importance of the family.

In particular, courts – both ecclesiastical and secular – specifically ruled in *favor matrimonii*. For example, the Bishop of Verona's court rejected the claim of Andrea Buttarini because he only wanted to carry out a 'leggiadra vendetta', but in the case of Giovanni Battista Civieri things were different: he had solid reasons to ask Luigia to keep her promise, not to mention that a breach of his honour before society was to be prevented. With regard to cases concerning money, decisions were often made so as to provide women with an addition to their dowries or to allow widows to access the *quarta uxoria*. In the cases described in Chapter 5 the courts ruled in women's favour, even though the value of their dowries was still far from the patrimony obtained by their brothers. The claims of Cattarina Montabone (Chapter 6) were met and her family was able to access part of her deceased husband's patrimony. Similarly, Maria Vandoni was granted a portion of her third husband's patrimony because she was poor and without dowry. This could imply an inclination to protect the weaker strata of society often represented by women. Cases regarding separation, by contrast, were thorny and their outcome often unexpected to the extent that a woman whose husband had infected her with syphilis was not allowed to separate from him, but only granted a refund for the expenses she had incurred through her illness: although her sufferings were acknowledged, there was something higher in play, that is, marriage, a 'foedus a Deo institutum'.

These general positions could, however, also be read from a different perspective. One could suggest that society did not aim to be inclusive but to preserve its own stratification and its own static, hierarchical, male-dominated structure. Thus, in the abovementioned case the efforts of the Bishop of Verona, rather than trying to satisfy the plaintiffs and safeguard the promise, may have been a means of conveying his persuasive force. Indeed, the force of ecclesiastical courts in cases concerning marriage promises was mainly moral; and marrying or not relied primarily on a person's will rather than on the sentence. Secular tribunals may have operated according to similar principles, thereby redistributing wealth among children and widows – not necessarily in an attempt to be fair, but rather aiming to avoid the concentration of goods and money in few hands. One might also argue that courts denied separation because within marriage a woman was in the place where nature had destined her to be, not to mention the fact that separated women were a challenge to society and to the institution of marriage.

However, the Ottocento was a period of transition: no matter how we read the outcome of lawsuits, changes were taking place and people had to establish a relationship with these transformations. If, after the Restoration, the feudal 'soggezione di persona a persona' was formally abolished, nineteenth-century society refrained from removing this *soggezione* from everyday interpersonal relations, confirming the subordinate status of women. With the Unification of Italy, institutions such as marital authorisation were enshrined in the law also in the territories of the former Lombardy-Venetia: from being able freely to manage their assets if married, women became dependent on men. After the drafting of the Pisanelli Code, some voices against women's inferior status began to be raised by members of the Parliament who noticed that the new legal system was taking Italy back into the past.[1] After its enactment, both men and women intervened in public debates, highlighting the anachronism of those new rules, which confined women to a lesser status at a time when their contribution to the building of the nation, and to society as a whole, was widely acknowledged. A slow but unrestrainable process had been triggered. Especially from the turn of the century onwards, legal drafts calling for the removal of marital authorisation from the legal system, for example, were presented to Parliament, leading eventually to its abrogation in 1919 with the passing of Law n. 1176. Nonetheless, marital authorisation was not the only means of defining women's subordinate status and there was still a long way to go. The right to vote, which until 1918 was not even granted to all men, was only given to women with the *Decreto legislativo luogotenenziale* of 1 February 1945, n. 23. The dowry, the physical representation of inequality, was still included in the Civil Code of 1942 and then formally abolished only with Law n. 151 in 1975.

One might argue that in the present the path towards equality is not yet completed at the cultural level. With prejudices and stereotypes heavily persisting in and influencing Italian society, together with a considerable pay gap and the lack of adequate female representation in key private and public institutions, there is still much to do. However, formally and legally men and women are equal. If the contribution of women and men such as Anna Maria Mozzoni, Anna Kuliscioff and Salvatore Morelli is known and has been extensively analysed, the steps of ordinary people should also be acknowledged.

These people were the women – and sometimes the men – who in their everyday lives contributed to changing history through small, ordinary actions. Some of them have been described in this study: they were those who initiated lawsuits asking for larger dowries or to end

1 On the discussion before the approval of the Pisanelli code, see *Codice civile del Regno d'Italia*, ed. by Galdi, pp. 231–32.

their marriage to an adulterous husband. They not only attempted to improve their situation, but also challenged commonplaces and society, thereby demonstrating a strong consciousness of self which theorists and moralists could no longer ignore. Although their encounter with the male-dominated, and often male-oriented, justice system did not always have a favourable outcome, it should be noted that in many cases verdicts were reached in women's favour. These women and these men, these anonymous and ordinary people, might not have had a prominent role in their world during their lifetimes; they left few historical traces but, nevertheless, contributed to the making of our present.

Table 1. Nineteenth-Century Coinage*

	Elaboration based on years	Coinage	Equivalent in lira italiana
Kingdom of Sardinia	1830–1844	Lira piemontese	1.17
Lombardy-Venetia	1830–1844	Lira Milanese	0.76
	1830–1844	Lira austriaca	0.87
	1830–1844	Lira veneta	0.71
Grand-Duchy of Tuscany	1830–1844	Scudo	6.3
	1830–1844	Lira	0.84
	1830–1844	Paolo	0.56
	1830–1844	Fiorino	1.4
Papal States	1830–1844	Scudo romano	5.38
	1830–1844	Lira bolognese	1.07
Duchy of Parma	1830–1844	Lira	0.24
Duchy of Modena	1830–1844	Lira of Modena	0.38
Kingdom of Two Sicilies	1861	Ducato	4.30

*This table is based on data included in Donino Donini, *La metrologia europea comparata con quella di Roma, di Bologna, e di Parigi, e viceversa* (Terni: Possenti, 1833); Luigi Malavasi, *La Metrologia Italiana, nei suoi scambievoli rapporti desunti dal confronto col sistema metrico-decimale* (Modena: Malavasi, 1844); *A Handbook for Travellers in Southern Italy: Being a Guide for the Provinces Formerly Constituting the Continental Portion of the Kingdom of the Two Sicilies* (London: Murray, 1868); and on legal documents analysed in this study.

Glossary

Ad sustinenda onera: to bear the burden. Usually it refers to the dowry, which is designed to bear the burden, or the expenses, of marriage.

Bona extra dotalia: goods which were not part of the dowry and were not secured against a mortgage. A woman could dispose of these goods without having to ask for permission from a judge.

Commune or *commune civitatis*: medieval city-state.

Controdote or *antifactum* or *antefactum*: counterdowry, a marriage gift of Roman origin given by the groom to the bride; usually its value was half that of the dowry.

Dowry instrument: a written instrument concerning the dowry and containing dotal agreement, normally rogated by a notary.

Familia: all people descending from the same ancestor. In a broader sense, *familia* is the whole household. It may also include servants and other co-workers.

Fideicommissum: a testamentary disposition by which a testator imposes on a person the obligation to hold and transfer the goods in question to a third person. This institution was used to preserve the patrimony and transmit it within the members of a family.

Filiusfamilia or filiafamilia: literally son/daughter of a family, he/she was under the authority (guardianship) of his/her father or of the *paterfamilias* until his death or his/her emancipation.

Hereditament: the property of a testator composed of a portion which could be freely disposed of (the free estate or discretionary portion) and an indefeasible portion (forced heirship or *legitima portio*).

Hotchpot: a fictious reunion of properties in order to secure equal division among heirs in an *ab intestato* succession.

Inter vivos donation: a donation which produces legal effects while the interested parties are still alive.

Ius commune: literally 'common law'; used to define Roman and canon law. The term *commune* meant that it was in use in several states.

Ius proprium: used in opposition to *ius commune* to indicate the law of a specific state.

Lucrum dotis: the gain a man was entitled to keep before returning the dowry to his wife's heirs after her death.

Majorat: the right of succession to property accorded to first-born sons.

Odium quartae: aversion to the wife's traditional claim to one-quarter of her husband's property as her marriage gift.

Paterfamilias: father or other male ancestor. He was the head of the family and could have under his power children and grand-children *ex filio* (from the side of his own son) but not *ex filia*.

Paterna paternis, materna maternis: this expression was used to signify that goods coming from the father of a deceased person descended to his paternal relations and those from the mother to the maternal side.

Peculium: the wealth that the *filiusfamilia* or *filiafamilia* could have which was not part of the patrimony of the *familia*.

Portio legitima or *legitima portio*: the portion of inheritance that could not be bequeathed by will.

Propter dotem: literally 'because of the dowry'. Usually used to mean the exclusion of a woman from inheritance because she already had a dowry.

Quarta: marriage gift of Lombard origin used in many Italian cities. The wife was granted the right to obtain a quarter of her husband's property after his death.

Successione ab intestato: an inheritance by intestacy, or the succession to the property of a person who dies without a valid will.

Sui juris: of one's own right. It defines an emancipated person who is not under the guardianship of someone else.

Tertia: marriage gift of Frankish origin used in many Italian cities. The wife was granted the right to obtain one-third of her husband's property after his death.

Bibliography

Primary Sources

Manuscripts

Fano, Archivio della Biblioteca Federiciana, 1846, Documenti vari
— Registro delle persone di Fano e suo distretto pregiudicate in opinione politica
Macerata, State Archive of Macerata, Processi Penali, 1891, 164
Milan, Archivio Diocesano, Carteggio Ufficiale, April 1855, 472
Milan, State Archive of Milan (SAM), Processi Politici, 43
— Processi Politici, 1112
— Processi Politici, 1127
Pesaro, State Archive of Pesaro, Notaio Luigi Perotti, 1854
Turin, State Archive of Turin, Casale, Corte di Appello, Second Semester, 1839, n. 4
— Casale, Corte di Appello, First Quarter of 1849, n. 31
— Casale, Corte di Appello, Second Semester of 1853, n. 45
— Corte di Cassazione, 1852, 9, n. 242
— Giudice di Appello, Sentenza Civili, April 1850, n. 315
— Notaio Giovanni Pietro Ellena, 1791, n. 2262
— Notaio Giovanni Pietro Ellena, 1801, n. 2271
— Tribunale di Pinerolo, Sentenze civili, First Quarter of 1847, n. 60
Verona, Bishop's Curia of Verona, Matrimoniorum, Processi, 1830–1844, 26
— Matrimoniorum, Dipense, 1863
Verona, State Archive of Verona, 1865, Testamenti, n. 73, n. 2000
— 1865, Testamenti, n. 73, n. 3260

Printed Sources

Periodicals

Annali di giurisprudenza raccolta mensile pubblicata da una società di avvocati e causidici (1838–45)
Archivio Giuridico (1868–97)
Corriere delle dame (1804–74)
Giornale del Foro (1817–75)
Giornale di giurisprudenza austriaca, ossia raccolta di memorie e dissertazioni sulle più importanti questioni del diritto austriaco (1839–46)
Giornale di giurisprudenza pratica (1846–62)
Giornale di giurisprudenza universale (1811–14)
Giurisprudenza del codice civile e delle altre leggi dei regj stati ossia collezione metodica e progressiva delle decisioni e sentenze pronunciate dai supremi magistrati sia dello stato che stranieri (1839–47); then *Giurisprudenza degli Stati Sardi* (1848–59); then *Giurisprudenza del Regno* (1860–61); then *Giurisprudenza italiana* (1862)
Giurisprudenza pratica secondo la legislazione austriaca attivata anche nel Regno Lombardo-Veneto o sia collezione di decisioni sentenze e decreti in materia civile commerciale criminale di diritto pubblico (1817–33); then *Giurisprudenza teorico-pratica secondo la legislazione austriaca o sia Collezione di decisioni sentenze e decreti in materia civile commerciale criminale e di diritto pubblico* (1836–45)
Guida dell'educatore (1836–42)
La donna italiana: giornale politico-letterario (1848)
La temi: giornale di legislazione e di giurisprudenza (1847–64)
Studii per le donne italiane (1836–43)

Articles and Books

Anon., *A Handbook for Travellers in Southern Italy: Being a Guide for the Provinces Formerly Constituting the Continental Portion of the Kingdom of the Two Sicilies* (London: Murray, 1868)
Anon., *Del patto di Capuana e Nido, e de' suoi effetti. Dissertazione* (Naples: Trani, 1823)
Anon., *Quistione transitoria se un monaco professo suddito del regno Lombardo-Veneto possa succedere ad una eredità apertasi in quel regno 1817 per quanto riflette i bene situati in Piemonte* (Milan: Pogliani, 1819)
Acta causae. Romana. Praetensae mercedis, coram Seraphino Olivier-Razali (1538–1609) ([n.p.]: [n. pub.], 1566)

Albericus of Rosciate, *Dictionarium iuri tam civilis quam canonici* (Venice: [n. pub.], 1581)
Albertazzi, Jacopo Antonio, *Il padre di famiglia in casa ed in campagna* (Lucca: Bertini, 1812)
Alessandrini, Alessandro, *I fatti politici delle Marche dal 1 gennaio 1859 all'epoca del plebiscito* (Macerata: Libreria editrice marchigiana, 1910)
Alighieri, Dante, *La Divina Commedia*, ed. by Giorgio Petrocchi (Turin: Einaudi, 1975)
Amati, Andrea, *Manuale sul Codice civile generale austriaco* (Milan: Visaj, 1844)
Aquinas, Thomas, *La somma teologica. Testo latino e italiano* (Bologna: Edizioni Studio Domenicano, 1985)
Archini, Francesco Ignazio, *Dei diritti acquistati in forza delle leggi civili abrogate al primo gennaio 1816* (Milan: Baret, 1816)
Atti del governo di Lombardia. Parte prima dal 1° gennajo al 30 giugno 1816 (Milan: Imperiale Regia Stamperia, 1816)
Balbo, Cesare, *Delle speranze d'Italia* (Capolago: Tipografia Elvetica, 1844)
— *Pensieri ed esempi: opera postuma; con l'aggiunta dei Dialoghi di un maestro di scuola pure inediti* (Florence: Le Monnier, 1856)
Bartolus of Saxoferrato, *Commentaria in primam infortiati partem* (Lyon: Fradin, 1551)
— *Commentaria in Corpus iuris civilis. Super Authenticis, & Institutionibus* (Venice: Giunta, 1585)
Beccaria, Cesare, *Dei delitti e delle pene* (Paris: Cazin, 1786)
Bellati, Alessandro, *Il diritto della donna alla sua emancipazione provato dalla ragione, dalla storia, dalla fisiologia e dall'anatomia* (Ferrara: Tipografia Sociale, 1874)
Bellomo, Giovanni, *Saggio sopra il più conveniente sistema di femminile educazione* (Venice: Tasso, 1832)
Bernini, Domenico, *Il tribunale della Sacra Rota Romana* (Rome: Bernabò, 1717)
Bianchi, Emilio, 'La inabilitazione e l'assenza del marito in materia di autorizzazione maritale, osservazioni sull'art. 135 N.° 1 del Codice civile italiano', *Archivio giuridico*, 40 (1888), 552–66
Bollati, Emanuele, *Fasti legislativi e parlamentari delle rivoluzioni italiane nel secolo XIX*, 5 vols (Milan: Giuseppe Civelli, 1863–66)
Bowring, John, *Statistica della Toscana, di Lucca, degli Stati Pontifici e Lombardo-Veneti e specialmente nelle loro relazioni commerciali* (London: Clowes, 1838)

Browne, Thomas, *Religio Medici: Or, the Christian Religion, as Professed by a Physician; Freed from Priest-Craft and the Jargon of Schools*, 2 vols (London: Curll, 1736 [1643])

Bruno, Giuseppe Antonio, *Introduzione alla canonica giurisprudenza* (Bologna: Rocchi, 1837)

Buniva, Giuseppe, *Delle leggi in generale e del diritto delle persone: sunti delle lezioni di diritto civile* (Turin: Tipografia Economica, 1858)

— *Del diritto delle persone secondo il Codice Civile del Regno d'Italia*, 2 vols (Turin: Arnaldi, 1871)

Buzzi Bonfichi, Francesca, *Vantaggi della donna istruita* (Turin: Fontana, 1841)

Cabanis, Pierre-Jean Georges, *Rapports du physique et du moral de l'homme*, 2 vols (Paris: Fortin, Masson, 1843 [1802])

Califronia, Rosa, *Breve difesa dei diritti delle donne scritta da Rosa Califronia contessa romana* (Assisi: Taglioretti, 1794)

Campan, Jeanne Louise Henriette [Madame Campan], *Dell'educazione*, 2 vols (Milan: Rezzi, 1827)

Canonici Fachini, Ginevra, *Prospetto biografico delle donne italiane rinomate in letteratura dal secolo decimoquarto fino a' giorni nostri, di Ginevra Canonici Fachini: con una risposta a lady Morgan risguardante alcune accuse da lei date alle donne italiane nella sua opera "L'Italie"* (Venice: Alvisopoli, 1834)

Capponi, Gino, *Pensieri sull'educazione. Frammento inedito 1841* (Lugano: Tipografia della Svizzera Italiana, 1845)

Caramelli, Giuseppe, *Sulla riforma della organizzazione giudiziaria negli stati Pontifici. Brevi cenni* (Rome: Ajani, 1847)

Carcano, Giovanni, *Il codice civile austriaco ed i suoi caratteri* (Milan: Manini, 1860)

Carmignani, Giovanni, *Teoria delle leggi della sicurezza sociale*, 3 vols (Pisa: Nistri, 1831)

— *Juris criminalis elementa* (Pisa: Nistri, 1833)

Casanova, Giacomo, *Lana Caprina: Lettre d'un lycanthrope* (Paris: Librairie de la société casanovienne, 1926 [1772])

Castellari, Giovanni, *Della condizione giuridica della donna secondo il Codice civile italiano* (Turin: Bona, 1877)

Cattaneo, Carlo, *D'alcune instituzioni agrarie dell'alta Italia applicabili a sollievo dell'Irlanda* (Milan: di Giovanni, 1847)

— *Scritti sulla Lombardia*, ed. by Giuseppe Anceschi and Giuseppe Armani (Milan: Ceschina, 1971)

Cavallari Cantalamessa, Giulia, *La donna nel Risorgimento nazionale* (Bologna: Zanichelli, 1893)

Chardon, Olivier Jacques, Antonino Lombardi and Fortunato Cafaro, *Trattato delle tre potestà maritale, patria e tutelare* (Naples: Pedone Lauriel, 1848)

Chassay, Frédéric-Edouard, *I doveri delle donne nella famiglia* (Milan: Volpato, 1856)

Cioffi, Alfredo, *Esame critico-storico sul diritto delle donne alla successione intestata* (Turin: Pelazza, 1853)

Code civil des Français: édition originale et seule officielle (Paris: Imprimerie de la République, 1804)

Codice civile di Napoleone il Grande pel regno d'Italia (Turin: Reale Stamperia, 1806)

Codice civile del Regno d'Italia, ed. by Domenicantonio Galdi (Naples: Marghieri and Perrotti, 1865)

Codice civile del Regno d'Italia: corredato della relazione del Ministro Guardasigilli fatta a S. M. in udienza del 25 giugno 1865 (Turin: Botta, 1865)

Il Codice Civile spiegato in ciascuno de' suoi articoli con annotazioni ed esempi (Turin: Cassone, Marzorati, Vercellotti, 1839)

Codice Civile per gli Stati Estensi (Modena: Eredi Tipografi Reali, 1851)

Codice civile per gli Stati di S. M. il re di Sardegna (Turin: Stamperia reale, 1837)

Codice criminale e di procedura criminale per gli Stati Estensi (Modena: Eredi Soliani Tipografi Reali, 1855)

Codice de' delitti e delle gravi trasgressioni politiche (Vienna: Stamperia Reale, 1803)

Codice dei Delitti e delle Pene pel Regno d'Italia (Milan: Reale Stamperia, 1810)

Il codice penale per il Regno d'Italia, ed. by Giulio Crivellari (Rome: Unione Tipografica, 1889)

Codice di procedura civile per gli stati di S. M. il Re di Sardegna (Turin: Stamperia reale, 1859)

Codice di procedura civile per gli Stati estensi (Modena: Eredi Soliani, 1852)

Codice di procedura penale per gli Stati di S. M. il re di Sardegna (Turin: Stamperia reale, 1859)

Codice penale dei crimini, dei delitti e delle contravvenzioni, e regolamento sulla stampa del 27 maggio 1852 (Vienna: Manz, 1869)

Codice penale pel Granducato di Toscana (Florence: Stamperia granducale, 1853)

Codice Penale per gli Stati di S. M. il Re di Sardegna (Turin: Minerva Subalpina, 1840)

Collezione Completa dei Moderni Codici Civili (Turin: Minerva Subalpina, 1845)

Il sacrosanto Concilio di Trento co' canoni e decreti emanati sotto Paolo III, Giulio III e Pio IV Sommi Pontefici con aggiunta di altre Bolle, Costituzioni Pontificie ec. ec. (Naples: Marotta, 1834)

Concone, Francesco, *Giurisprudenza femminile* (Turin: Fumero Maggiore, 1839)

Condorcet, Marie-Jean-Antoine-Nicolas de Caritat, *Sur l'admission des femmes au droit de cité* (Paris: Firmin Didot, 1790)

Constitutiones Mediolanensis (Milan: Marelli, 1764)

Corpus Iuris Civilis Romani, ed. by Denis Godefrey, 4 vols (Lyon: Vincenti, 1583)

Corso, Raffaele, *Di un preteso avanzo di matrimonio per ratto* (Scansano: Olmi, 1919)

Cosci, Cristoforo, *De separatione tori conjugalis tam nullo existente seu soluto, quam salvo vinculo matrimonii, eiusque effectibus*, 3 vols (Rome: Salvioni, 1773–79), I

Criscuolo, Federico, *La donna nella storia del diritto privato italiano* (Palermo: Carini, Caronna and Macoclin, 1885)

Cristoforis, Giovan Battista de, 'Filosofia pratica', *Studii per le donne italiane*, 1 (1837), 35–43

Cubain, Romain, *Trattato dei diritti delle donne: in materia civile e commerciale* (Palermo: Amenta, 1856)

Darwin, Charles, *The Descent of Man, and Selection in Relation to Sex* (London: Murray, 1871)

Decisiones S. Rotae Romanae coram Cosmae de Cursiis, eiusdem S. Rotae olim Decano, modo S. R. E. cardinali emeritissimo, ed. by A. Cavallini, 5 vols (Rome: Cajetani Chiassi, 1855)

Decisioni del Foro Toscano inedite dall'anno 1815, all'anno 1819, ed. by Lorenzo Cantini and Domenico Nenci, 5 vols (Florence: Stamperia del Giglio, 1821–28)

Decisiones Sacrae Rotae Romanae coram Josepho Alphonso de Véri (Rome: Fulgoni, 1787)

Decisioni del Supremo tribunale di revisione con note ed opuscoli relativi del cavaliere Francesco Melegari: Dal 27 aprile al 28 dicembre 1829 (Parma: Carmignani, 1832)

'Dei Miseratione, 3 November 1741', in *Sanctissimi domini nostri Benedicti Papae XIV, Bullarium*, 4 vols (Venice: Occhi, 1768), I, 695–701

Delacoux, Alexis, *Igiene delle donne, ossia Precetti di salute all'uso loro nella vita privata traduzione dal francese di N.P.* (Milan: Pirotta, 1830)

Del Forno, Nicola, *La storia civile del Regno di Napoli in compendio* (Naples: De Dominicis, 1841)

Della Porta, Giovan Battista, *De humana physiognomonia libri sex*, ed. by Alfonso Paolella (Naples: Edizioni scientifiche italiane, 2013)

Devincenzi, Giuseppe, 'Relazione sull'agricoltura dell'Alto e del Basso Milanese', *Annali universali di statistica*, 81 (1844), 329–38

Il digesto italiano: enciclopedia metodica comparata e alfabetica di legislazione, dottrina e giurisprudenza (diritto civile, commerciale, penale, giudiziario, costituzionale, amministrativo, internazionale, pubblico e privato, ecclesiastico, militare, marittimo, storia del diritto, diritto romano, legislazione comparata) (Turin: Unione tipografico-editoriale, 1894)

Donini, Donino, *La metrologia europea comparata con quella di Roma, di Bologna, e di Parigi, e viceversa* (Terni: Possenti, 1833)

D'Oria, Paolo-Mattia, *Ragionamenti di Paolo-Mattia D'Oria indirizzati alla signora d. Aurelia d'Este duchessa di Limatola ne' quali si dimostra la donna, in quasi che tutte le virtù più grandi, non essere all'uomo inferiore* (Frankfurt: [n. pub.], 1716)

Enciclopedia dell'ecclesiastico, 4 vols (Naples: Ranucci, 1844)

Ermini, Filippo, *Gli ordinamenti politici e amministrativi nelle "Constitutiones Aegidianae"* (Florence: Bocca, 1893)

Farini, Luigi Carlo, *Lo Stato romano dall'anno 1815 al 1850*, 4 vols (Florence: Le Monnier, 1853)

Federigo, Gaspare, *Osservazioni sugli effetti del gallico nel popolo, ed i metodi più facili di curarlo* (Venice: Andreola, 1791)

Ferriani, Lino, *La infanticida nel codice penale e nella vita sociale: Considerazioni* (Milan: Dumolard, 1886)

Filangieri, Gaetano, *La scienza della legislazione*, 8 vols (Genoa: Gravier, 1798 [1780])

Filomusi Guelfi, Francesco, *Enciclopedia giuridica ad uso di lezioni* (Naples: Jovene, 1873)

Finali, Gaspare, *Le Marche: ricordanze* (Ancona: Morelli, 1896)

Finotti, Guglielmo, *Della educazione intellettuale e morale della donna* (Caserta: Saccone, 1894)

Fontana, Antonio, *Manuale per l'educazione umana* (Milan: Fontana, 1834)

Foramiti, Francesco, *Enciclopedia, legale; ovvero Lessico ragionato di gius naturale, civile, canonico, mercantile-cambiario marittimo, feudale, penale, pubblico-interno e delle genti* (Venice: Gondoliere, 1842)

Fornasotto, Enrico, *La condizione giuridica della donna nella storia del diritto romano, con riguardo alla questione dell'emancipazione della donna* (Conegliano: Nardi, 1902)

Forti, Francesco, *Trattati inediti di giurisprudenza* (Florence: Viessieux, 1854)
Franceschi Ferrucci, Caterina, *Della educazione morale della donna italiana: libri tre* (Turin: Pomba, 1847)
— *Della educazione intellettuale: libri quattro indirizzati alle madri italiane* (Turin: Pomba, 1849–51)
— *Letture morali ad uso delle fanciulle – Alle alunne dell'Istituto italiano in Genova*, 3 vols (Genua: Tipografia del R. I. de' sordo-muti, 1851–52)
— *Degli studi delle donne: libri quattro* (Turin: Pomba, 1853)
— *Degli studi delle donne italiane* (Florence: Le Monnier, 1876)
— *Ai giovani italiani: ammaestramenti religiosi e morali* (Florence: Le Monnier, 1877)
— *Epistolario di Caterina Franceschi Ferrucci: edito ora la prima volta, con lettere di scrittori illustri a lei* (Reggio Emilia: Guidetti, 1910)
Franchetti, Leopoldo, *Condizioni economiche e amministrative delle provincie napoletane* (Florence: Gazzetta d'Italia, 1875)
Gabba, Carlo Francesco, *Della condizione giuridica delle donne nelle legislazioni francese, austriaca e sarda* (Milan: Radaelli, 1861)
— *La questione femminile e la principessa Dora d'Istria: considerazioni* (Florence: Le Monnier, 1865)
Galdi, Domenicantonio, *Enciclopedia legale, ovvero Repertorio alfabetico di legislazione, giurisprudenza e dottrina in materia di dritto civile, commerciale, criminale, amministrativo, canonico, pubblico, naturale e delle genti*, 5 vols (Naples: Marghieri, 1864–68)
Galeotti, Amilcare, *La patria potestà: tesi di laurea del dott. Amilcare Galeotti* (Siena: Lazzeri, 1872)
Galligo, Isacco, *Sulla vaccinazione celtica o meglio sulla sifilizzazione nell'uomo* (Florence: Cecchi, 1852)
Gallini, Carlo, *La donna e la legge: studi sulla condizione sociale e giuridica della donna* (Rome: Civelli, 1872)
Galluppi, Enrico, *La successione dei conjugi nella storia interna del diritto italiano* (Rome: Civelli, 1873)
Galton, Francis, *Hereditary Genius: An Inquiry into its Laws and Consequences* (New York, NY: Appleton, 1870)
Gentile, Emilio, *Teorico-pratica secondo l'ecclesiastica, e la civil polizia*, 2 vols (Naples: Manfredi, 1794)
Gioberti, Vincenzo, *Apologia del libro intitolato Il gesuita moderno con alcune considerazioni intorno al Risorgimento Italiano* (Brussels and Livorno: Meline and Cans, 1848)
— *Delle condizioni presenti e future d'Italia* (London: [n. pub.], 1848)
— *Il gesuita moderno*, 5 vols (Naples: Batelli, 1849)

— *Pensieri di Vincenzo Gioberti: miscellanee* (Turin: Eredi Botta, 1859–60)
— *Del rinnovamento civile d'Italia*, ed. by Fausto Nicolini (Bari: Laterza, 1911–12)
Giuriati, Domenico, *Le leggi dell'amore* (Turin: Roux Frassati, 1895)
Giurisprudenza romana ossia corpo del diritto civile romano volgarizzato col testo a fronte (Milan: Baret, 1815)
Gouges, Olympe, *Déclaration des droits de la femme et de la citoyenne*, ed. by Emanuèle Gaulier (Paris: Mille et une nuits, 2003)
Grimaldi, Ginesio, *Dissertazione di Ginesio Grimaldi sul punto dello scioglimento de' matrimoni per cagion d'impotenza* (Naples: Simoniana, 1765)
Guerrazzi, Francesco Domenico, *Amelia Calani ed altri scritti* (Milan: Guigoni, 1868)
Ippocrate, *Natura della donna*, ed. by Valeria Andò (Milan: Rizzoli, 2000)
Jacini, Stefano, *La proprietà fondiaria e le popolazioni agricole in Lombardia: studj economici* (Milan: Borroni e Scotti, 1854)
— *Atti della Giunta per la Inchiesta Agraria e sulle condizioni della classe agricola*, 15 vols (Rome: Forzani, 1885)
— *L'inchiesta agraria: proemio, relazione finale, conclusioni dell'inchiesta sulla Lombardia interpellanza al Senato* (Piacenza: Federazione italiana dei consorzi agrari, 1926)
Kant, Immanuel, *On the Old Saw. That May Be Right in Theory but it Won't Work in Practice*, trans. by E. B. Ashton, intro. by George Miller (Philadelphia, PA: University of Pennsylvania Press, 1974)
Klenze, Clemens August Carl and Eduard Böcking, *Gaii et Iustiniani, Institutiones iuris romani* (Berlin: Imbensis, 1829)
La Mantia, Vito, *Storia della legislazione italiana* (Rome: Bocca, 1884)
Lambruschini, Raffaello, *Sull'utilità della cooperazione delle donne bennate al buon andamento delle scuole infantili per il popolo* (Milan: Stella, 1834)
— 'I piaceri delle madri', in *Florilegio femminile*, ed. by Emanuele Rossi (Genua: Ferrando, 1840), pp. 363–70
Lattanzi, Carolina, *Schiavitù delle donne*, ed. by Gilberto Zacchè (Mantua: Edizioni Lombarde, 1976)
Lavater, Johann Kaspar, *Physiognomy: Or the Corresponding Analogy between the Conformation of the Features, and the Ruling Passions of the Mind* (London: Tegg, 1866)
Leggi, e costituzioni di Sua Maestà. Loix et constitutions du Roi (Turin: Valletta, 1723)

Leggi, e costituzioni di Sua Maestà. Loix et constitutions de Sa Majesté, 2 vols (Turin: Accademia Reale, 1729)

Leggi, e costituzioni di Sua Maestà. Loix et constitutions de Sa Majesté, 2 vols (Turin: Stamperia Reale, 1770)

Leopold, *Il mentore dei mariti e delle mogli o sia sposizione dei mezzi di essere felici nel matrimonio in tutte le classi diverse della società* (Milan: Giegler, 1819)

Le Play, Frederic, *L'Organisation de la famille, selon le vrai modèle signalé par l'histoire de toutes les races et de tous les temps* (Paris: Tequi, 1871)

— *La Réforme sociale en France déduite de l'observation comparée des peuples européens* (Paris: Dentu, 1887)

Letizia di, Alfonso, *Degli usi de' proceri, e magnati e di Capuana, e Nido* (Naples: Perger, 1786)

Lombroso, Cesare, *L'uomo delinquente* (Milan: Hoepli, 1876)

Lombroso, Cesare and Guglielmo Ferrero, *La donna delinquente: La prostituta e la donna normale* (Turin: Bocca, 1903)

Lomonaco, Vincenzo, *Storia de principii della legislazione* (Naples: Azzolino, 1844)

Luca, Giovanni Battista de, *Il dottor volgare, ovvero Il compendio di tutta la legge civile, canonica, feudale e municipale, nelle cose più ricevute in pratica, moralizzato in lingua italiana*, 6 vols ([n.p.]: [n. pub.], 1673)

— *Il cavaliere e la dama, overo Discorsi familiari nell'ozio tusculano* (Pavia: Magri, 1700 [1675])

Malavasi, Luigi, *La Metrologia Italiana, nei suoi scambievoli rapporti desunti dal confronto col sistema metrico-decimale* (Modena: Malavasi and Compagno, 1844)

Maranta, Roberto, *Speculum aureum et lumen aduocatorum praxis ciuilis* (London: Symphorianum Beraud, 1573)

Marcadé, Victor-Napoléon, *Éléments du droit civil français ou explication méthodique et raisonnée du Code Civil*, 5 vols (Paris: Cotillon, 1842)

Marini, Cesare, *Lezioni di dritto civile novissimo*, 4 vols (Naples: Osservatore medico, 1830–32)

Mazzini, Giuseppe, *Scritti editi e inediti*, 25 vols (Milan: Daelli, 1886)

— *Dei doveri dell'uomo* (Milan: RCS, 2010 [1860])

Merlin, Philippe-Antoine, *Dizionario universale ossia repertorio ragionato di giurisprudenza e quistioni di diritto*, trans. by Filippo Carillo, 14 vols (Venice: Antonelli, 1834–42)

Menestrina, Francesco, *Il processo civile nello Stato Pontificio* (Turin: Bocca, 1908)

Mercanti, Francesco, *Compendio di diritto canonico con illustrazioni istorico-dogmatiche*, 4 vols (Prato: Guasti, 1832)
Molino Colombini, Giulia, *Sulla educazione della donna: pensieri* (Turin: Fory and Dalmazzo, 1851)
Monnier, Marc, *Garibaldi: histoire de la conquête des Deux-Siciles* (Paris: Lévy frères, 1861)
Morardo, Gaspare, *L'arte di conservare ed accrescere la bellezza delle donne* (Turin: Morano, 1800–01)
Morelli, Salvatore, *La donna e la scienza considerate come soli mezzi atti a risolvere il problema dell'avvenire* (Naples: Stabilimento tipografico delle belle arti, 1861)
— *La donna e la scienza o La soluzione del problema sociale* (Naples: Tipografico dell'Ancora, 1863)
— *Lettera politica del deputato Salvatore Morelli ai suoi elettori del collegio di Sessa Aurunca* (Naples: De Angelis, 1868)
— *Riforme legislative proposte al Parlamento italiano dal deputato Salvatore Morelli il giorno 26 maggio 1875 per assicurare con nuove guarentigie giuridiche la sorte dei fanciulli e delle donne* ([n.p.]: [n. pub.], 1875)
Mozzoni, Anna Maria, *La donna e i suoi rapporti sociali* (Milan: Tipografia Sociale, 1864)
— *La donna in faccia al progetto del nuovo Codice civile italiano* (Milan: Tipografia Sociale, 1865)
Muratori, Ludovico Antonio, *Dei difetti della giurisprudenza* (Venice: Pasquali, 1742)
— *Della pubblica felicità, oggetto de' buoni principi* (Lucca: [n. pub.], 1749)
Negri, Giovanni Maria, *Dei difetti del Codice Civile Italico, che porta il titolo di Codice Napoleone e dei pregj del Codice Civile Austriaco* (Vicenza: Parise, 1815)
Niceforo, Alfredo, *L'Italia barbara contemporanea: Studi e appunti* (Milan: Sandron, 1898)
Oldrati, Luigi, *Codice penale austriaco attualmente in vigore nel regno Lombardo-Veneto con osservazioni teorico-pratiche e confronto coll'antecedente abrogato* (Milan: Manini, 1852)
Oriani, Alfredo, *Il matrimonio* (Bologna: Cappelli, 1923 [1886])
Pacifici Mazzoni, Emidio, *Studio storico sulla successione legittima dalle XII tavole al Codice civile italiano* (Modena: Vincenzi, 1870)
— *Il codice civile italiano commentato con la legge romana, le sentenze dei dottori e la giurisprudenza*, 14 vols (Florence: Cammelli, 1873)
Paladini, Luisa Amalia, *Manuale per le giovinette italiane* (Florence: Le Monnier, 1866 [1851])

Pani Rossi, Enrico, *La Basilicata libri tre. Studi politici, amministrativi e di economia pubblica* (Verona: Civelli, 1868)

Pepoli Sampieri, Anna, *La donna saggia ed amabile. Libri tre* (Capolago: Elvetica, 1838)

Peraldi, Mario Felice, *Considerazioni politiche sul governo dello Stato pontificio* (Pesaro: Nobili, 1832)

— *Conferenza sul temporal governo degli ecclesiastici* (Bastia: Fabiani, 1840)

Pertile, Antonio, *Storia del diritto italiano: dalla caduta dell'Impero Romano alla codificazione*, 6 vols (Padua: Salmin, 1874)

Piano, Michele and Giovanni Labus, 'Meditazione VI, Sul vizio della disonestà. *A spiritu fornicationis libera nos, Domine*', in Michele Piano and Giovanni Labus, *Istruzioni dogmatiche parrocchiali e discorsi evangelici; coll'aggiunta di due ragionamenti* (Milan: Manini, 1839), pp. 691–94

Pierozzi, Antonino, *Defecerunt Summula confessionalis utilissima* (Venice: Bindoni and Maffei Pasini, 1538)

Pisani, Emanuele, *La condizione giuridica della donna: disegno di legge Gallini* (Rome: Tipografia della Camera dei deputati, 1911)

Polatti, Girolamo, *Della protezione accordata alla donna dal cristianesimo* (Vicenza: Paroni, 1844)

Pouget, Firmin, *La buona madre, o sia vita di Teresa di Lamourous fondatrice e prima superiora della casa di misericordia di Bordeaux* (Milan: Boniardi-Pogliani, 1846)

Processi segreti della Sacra Consulta di Roma contro i liberali d'Italia (Milan: Colombo, 1860)

Puccinotti, Francesco, *Lezioni di medicina legale* (Macerata: Mancini-Cortesi, 1835)

Raccolta di alcune leggi aventi stretta relazione col codice civile per gli Stati Estensi (Modena: Eredi Soliani, 1852)

Raccolta di alcune notificazioni, editti, ed istruzioni: opera vtilissima a tutti gli ecclesiastici, 5 vols (Venice: Pitteri, 1740)

Raccolta degli atti del governo di Sua Maestà il Re di Sardegna dall'anno 1814 a tutto il 1832, 22 vols (Turin: Pignetti and Carena, 1842)

Raccolta delle Leggi e Disposizioni di pubblica amministrazione nello Stato Pontificio (Rome: Stamperia della R.C.A., 1850)

Raccolta delle leggi del 3 marzo e 26 aprile 1848 e successive 15 e 16 luglio 1859 per la formazione delle liste elettorali (Florence: Stamperia Governativa, 1859)

Raccolta delle leggi, decreti, ordinanze e regolamenti del governo dello Stato Romano, 3 vols (Bologna: Tiocchi, 1849)

Ravizza, Carlo, *Un curato di campagna: schizzi morali* (Milan: Pirola, 1841)

Re, Filippo, *Nuovi elementi di agricoltura* (Milan: Silvestri, 1837)
Registro di Pesaro e suo distretto pregiudicate in opinione politica (12-6-1835), published in *Studia Oliveriana*, 10 (1990)
Regolamento generale di procedura penale del 29 luglio 1853 per l'Impero d'Austria (Milan: Imperiale Regia Stamperia, 1853)
Regolamento generale del processo civile del regno lombardo veneto (Milan: Regia Stamperia, 1854)
Renazzi, Filippo Maria, *Elementa juris criminalis. Liber primus. De delictis generatim* (Bologna: Francisci Cardinali et Caroli Frulli, 1826)
Repetti, Emanuele, *Compendio storico della città Firenze, sua comunità, diocesi e compartimento fino all'anno 1849* (Florence: Tofani, 1849)
Rinuccini, Eleonora, *Ti lascio con la penna, non col cuore: lettere di Eleonora Rinuccini al marito Neri dei principi Corsini: 1835–1858*, ed. by Cristina Badon (Florence: Firenze University Press, 2012)
Roberto, Domenico de, *La dote di paraggio del diritto patrio* (Bari: Laterza, 1897)
Romagnosi, Gian Domenico, *Discorso sull'amore delle donne: considerato come motore precipuo della legislazione* (Trento: Monauni, 1792)
— *Opere. Istituzioni di civile filosofia ossia di giurisprudenza teorica* (Florence: Piatti, 1832–39)
— *Opere del professore G. D. Romagnosi* (Florence: Piatti, 1832–39)
— *Opere* (Milan: Perelli and Mariani, 1845)
Rösler, Augustin, *La condizione della donna nell'umana convivenza* (Turin: Marietti, 1915)
Rossi, Gabriello, *Sulla condizione economica e sociale dello Stato Pontificio confrontata specialmente con quella della Francia e della Inghilterra* (Bologna: Società Tipografica Bolognese, 1848)
Rossi, Pellegrino, *Trattato di diritto penale* (Milan: Borroni and Scotti, 1832)
Rousseau, Jean Jacques, *Émile, ou de l'éducation*, ed. by François Richard and Pierre Richard (Paris: Garnier, 1951)
Roussel, Pierre, *Sistema fisico e morale della donna seguito dal Sistema fisico e morale dell'uomo e da un frammento sulla sensibilità*, 2 vols (Naples: Manzi, 1829)
Rusconi, Carlo, *La Repubblica romana del 1849*, 2 vols (Turin: Cassone, 1850)
Sacrae rotae romanae decisiones coram Josepho Molines (Rome: Zinghi and Monaldi, 1728)
Salvatori, Filippo Maria, *Istruzione pratica per i confessori novelli: divisa in due parti* (Turin: Marietti, 1832)

Salzano, Tommaso Michele, *Lezioni di diritto canonico pubblico, e privato considerato in sé stesso e secondo l'attual polizia del Regno delle Due Sicilie*, 4 vols (Naples: Giordano, 1843)
Scarpazza, Faustino, *Decisioni dei casi di coscienza e di dottrina canonica*, 14 vols (Naples: Nuovo Gabinetto Letterario, 1828–35)
Scevola, Antonio, *L'autorizzazione maritale ed il mandato conferto dalla moglie al marito* (Turin: Unione Tipografico-Editrice, 1888)
Sclopis, Federigo, *Della legislazione civile: discorsi* (Turin: Bocca, 1835)
— *Storia della legislazione italiana*, 5 vols (Turin: Unione Tipografico-Editrice, 1863–64)
Scotton, Andrea, *Alla donna italiana intorno le cose d'Italia* (Venice: Merlo, 1863)
Serristori, Luigi, 'Dell'attuale condizione dell'industria in Italia', *Annali universali di statistica*, 85 (1845), 9–19
Sieyès, Emmanuel Joseph, *Observations sur le rapport du Comité de constitution concernant la nouvelle organisation de la France* (Versailles: Baudouin, 1789)
— *Qu'est-ce que le Tiers-État?* (Paris: [n. pub.], 1789)
Sperino, Casimiro, *Sifilizzazione nell'uomo* ([n.p.]: Favale, 1851)
Stato degli inquisiti dalla S. Consulta per la rivoluzione del 1849 (Rome: Vittoriano, 1937)
Statuti di Milano: volgarizzati con note, e spiegazioni (Milan: Galeazzi, 1773)
Statuto fondamentale del Regno d'Italia, 4 marzo 1848 (Padua: Salmin, 1866)
Stella, Luigi, 'Alcune considerazioni sulla minore responsabilità penale della donna', *Archivio Giuridico*, 4 (1869), 76–83
Sterlich, Alessandro de, *Annotazioni alla legge sull'amministrazione comunale e provinciale del 20 marzo 1865* (Naples: Trani, 1865)
Tarabotti, Arcangela, *L'Inferno monacale di Arcangela Tarabotti*, ed. by Francesca Medioli (Turin: Rosenberg and Sellier, 1990)
Tassoni, Alessandro Maria, *La religione, dimostrata e difesa* (Naples: Società Editrice, 1854 [1805])
Tesoro del foro toscano o sia Raccolta delle decisioni del Supremo Consiglio e delle Regie Ruote civili delle prime appellazioni di Toscana, ed. by Lorenzo Cantini (Florence: Stamperia del giglio, 1820–41)
Tommaseo, Niccolò, *Dell'educazione. Osservazioni e saggi pratici* (Venice: Andruzzi, 1842)
— *Delle nuove speranze d'Italia, presentimenti da un'opera di Niccolò Tommaseo* (Florence: Le Monnier, 1848)
— *Sull'educazione, desiderii* (Florence: Le Monnier, 1851 [1846])
— *La donna: scritti varii* (Milan: Agnelli, 1872 [1868])

Trivulzio di Belgioioso, Cristina, 'Della presente condizione delle donne e del loro avvenire' [1860], in *Il 1848 a Milano e Venezia: con uno scritto sulla condizione della donna*, ed. by Sandro Bortone (Milan: Feltrinelli, 1977), pp. 169–85

Tutini, Camillo, *Dell'origine e fundazione de' seggi di Napoli, del tempo in che furono istituiti* (Naples: Gessari, 1754)

Vanni, Icilio, *I progressi della legislazione civile in Italia dopo la rivoluzione* (Perugia: Santucci, 1878)

Vescia, Aniello, 'Se l'autorizzazione maritale sia necessaria alla moglie il cui marito è inabilitato', *Archivio giuridico*, 38 (1887), 33–43

Vicat, Béat Philippe, *Vocabularium juris utriusque*, 2 vols ([n.p.]: Ex officina Bousquetiana, 1759)

Voet, Johann, *Commentario alle Pandette*, 6 vols (Venice: Bazzarini, 1843 [1698])

Volpi, Gioanni Antonio, *Che non debbono ammettersi le donne allo studio delle scienze, e delle belle arti* ([n.p.]: [n. pub.], 1723)

Von Zallinger, Jakob Anton, *Institutiones juris ecclesiastici, maxime privati, ordine Decretalium*, 5 vols (Augsburg: Sons of Matthäus Rieger, 1793)

Waterworth, James (ed. and trans.), 'The Council of Trent. The Twenty-Fourth Session', in *The Canons and Decrees of the Sacred and Oecumenical Council of Trent* (London: Dolman, 1848) <https://history.hanover.edu/texts/trent/ct24.html> [accessed 30 April 2020]

Wollstonecraft, Mary, *A Vindication of the Rights of Woman: With Strictures on Political and Moral Subjects* (New York: Matsell, 1833)

Young, Arthur, *Travels during the Years 1787, 1788 and 1789* (London: Richardson, 1792)

Zecchini, Petronio Ignazio, *Dì geniali della dialettica delle donne ridotta al suo vero principio* (Bologna: S. Tommaso D'Aquino, 1771)

Secondary Literature

Anon., *Pensieri della libera cittadina I. P. M. alle sue concittadine* (Venice: Zatta, 1797)

Ago, Renata, 'Ruoli familiari e statuto giuridico', *Quaderni Storici*, 88 (1995), 111–33

— *Economia barocca. Mercato e istituzioni nella Roma del Seicento* (Rome: Donzelli, 1998)

Agostinelli, Chiara, *"Per me sola". Biografia intellettuale e scrittura privata di Costanza Monti Perticari* (Rome: Carocci, 2006)

Aimerito, Francesco, *La codificazione della procedura civile nel Regno di Sardegna* (Milan: Giuffrè, 2008)

Alessi, Giorgia, *Processo per seduzione: piacere e castigo nella Toscana leopoldina* (Catania: [n. pub.], 1988)

— 'Il gioco degli scambi: seduzione e risarcimento nella casistica cattolica del XVI e XVII secolo', *Quaderni storici*, 75 (1990), 805–31

— 'Stupro non violento e matrimonio riparatore. Le inquiete peregrinazioni dogmatiche della seduzione', in *I tribunali del matrimonio (secoli XV–XVIII)*, ed. by Silvana Seidel Menchi and Diego Quaglioni (Bologna: Il Mulino, 2006), pp. 609–40

Alessi, Maria Luisa, *Una giardiniera del Risorgimento italiano: Bianca Milesi* (Genoa: Streglio, 1906)

Anderson, Benedict, *Imagined Communities: Reflections on the Origin and Spread of Nationalism* (London: Verso, 1983)

Aquarone, Alberto, 'La restaurazione nello Stato Pontificio e i suoi indirizzi legislativi', *Archivio della Società romana di storia patria*, 78 (1955), 119–88

— 'Aspetti legislativi della Restaurazione in Toscana', *Rassegna storica del Risorgimento: organo della Società Nazionale per la Storia del Risorgimento Italiano*, 43 (1956), 3–34

— *L'unificazione legislativa e i codici del 1865* (Milan: Giuffrè, 1960)

Aquarone, Alberto, Mario D'Addio and Guglielmo Negri (eds), *Le Costituzioni italiane* (Milan: Edizioni di Comunità, 1958)

Ara, Angelo, *Lo statuto fondamentale dello Stato della Chiesa (14 marzo 1848). Contributo ad uno studio delle idee costituzionali nello Stato pontificio nel periodo delle riforme di Pio IX* (Milan: Giuffrè, 1966)

Ariès, Philippe, *L'Enfant et la vie familiale sous l'Ancien Régime* (Paris: Plon, 1960)

— *Padri e figli nell'Europa medievale e moderna* (Bari: Laterza, 1968)

— *Western Attitudes toward Death: From the Middle Ages to the Present*, trans. by Patricia M. Ranum (London: Marion Boyars, 1994 [1976])

Arrivo, Georgia, *Seduzioni, promesse, matrimoni. Il processo per stupro nella Toscana del Settecento* (Rome: Edizioni di Storia e Letteratura, 2006)

Ascenzi, Anna, *Il Plutarco delle donne. Repertorio della pubblicistica educativa e scolastica e della letteratura amena destinata al mondo femminile nell'Italia dell'Ottocento* (Macerata: EUM, 2009)

Ascheri, Mario, 'Il *Consilium* dei giuristi medievali', in *Consilium. Teorie e pratiche del consigliare nella cultura medievale*, ed. by Carla Casagrande, Chiara Crisciani and Silvana Vecchio (Florence: Edizioni del Galluzzo, 2004), pp. 243–58

— *The Laws of Late Medieval Italy (1000–1500): Foundations for a European Legal System* (Leiden: Brill, 2013)

Astuti, Guido, 'Gli ordinamenti giuridici degli Stati Sabaudi', in *Storia del Piemonte*, ed. by Dino Gribaudi (Turin: Casanova, 1960), pp. 487–562

— 'Il Code Napoléon in Italia e la sua influenza sui codici degli stati italiani successori', *Accademia nazionale dei Lincei*, 179 (1973), 176–237

Badinter, Élisabeth, *L'Amour en plus: histoire de l'amour maternel (XVIIe–XXe siècle)* (Paris: Flammarion, 1981)

— *L'Un est l'autre: des relations entre hommes et femmes* (Paris: Jacob, 1992 [1986])

— 'Préface', in *Qu'Est-ce qu'une femme? Antoine Léonard Thomas, Diderot, Madame d'Épinay*, ed. by Élisabeth Badinter (Paris: P.O.L., 1989), pp. 9–47

— (ed.), *Qu'Est-ce qu'une femme? Antoine Léonard Thomas, Diderot, Madame d'Épinay* (Paris: P.O.L., 1989)

Baffioni Venturi, Luciano, *Costanza Monti e Giulio Perticari. Amore e morte tra Marche e Romagna all'inizio dell'Ottocento* (Ancona: peQuod, 2008)

Balestracci, Duccio, *Medioevo e Risorgimento. L'invenzione dell'identità italiana nell'Ottocento* (Bologna: Il Mulino, 2015)

Banti, Alberto Mario, 'Ricchezza e potere. Le dinamiche patrimoniali nella società lucchese del XIX secolo', *Quaderni Storici*, 50 (1982), 629–61

— *Terra e denaro. Una borghesia padana dell'Ottocento* (Venice: Marsilio, 1989)

— 'I proprietari terrieri nell'Italia centro-settentrionale', in *Storia dell'agricoltura italiana in età contemporanea*, ed. by Piero Bevilacqua, 3 vols (Venice: Marsilio, 1992), III, 45–103

— *La nazione del Risorgimento. Parentela, santità e onore alle origini dell'Italia unita* (Turin: Einaudi, 2000)

— *Il Risorgimento italiano* (Rome: Laterza, 2004)

— *L'onore della Nazione. Identità sessuali e violenza nel nazionalismo europeo dal XVIII secolo alla Grande Guerra* (Turin: Einaudi, 2005)

— *Sublime madre nostra. La nazione italiana dal Risorgimento al fascismo* (Rome: Laterza, 2011)

Banti, Alberto Mario and R. Bizzocchi (eds), *Immagini della nazione nell'Italia del Risorgimento* (Rome: Carocci, 2002)

Banti, Alberto Mario and Paul Ginsborg (eds), *Storia d'Italia. Annali 22. Il Risorgimento* (Turin: Einaudi, 2007)

Banti, Alberto Mario and others (eds), *Atlante culturale del Risorgimento. Lessico del linguaggio politico dal Settecento all'Unità* (Rome: Laterza, 2011)

Baranski, Zygmunt G. and Shirley W. Vinall (eds), *Women and Italy: Essays on Gender, Culture and History* (Basingstoke: Macmillan, 1991)

Barbagli, Marzio (ed.), *Famiglia e mutamento sociale* (Bologna: Il Mulino, 1977)

— *Sotto lo stesso tetto. Mutamenti della famiglia in Italia dal XV al XX secolo* (Bologna: Il Mulino, 1984)

Barbagli, Marzio and David I. Kertzer (eds), *Storia della famiglia italiana, 1750–1950* (Bologna: Il Mulino, 1992)

Baritono, Raffaella, 'Il pensiero politico delle donne', in *Il pensiero politico. Idee. Teorie. Dottrine*, ed. by Alberto Andreatta and others, 4 vols (Turin: UTET, 1999), III.II, *Ottocento e Novecento*, pp. 153–70

— (ed.), *Il sentimento delle libertà: la dichiarazione di Seneca Falls e il dibattito sui diritti delle donne negli Stati Uniti di metà Ottocento* (Turin: La Rosa, 2001)

Battaglia, Salvatore, *Grande dizionario della lingua italiana*, 21 vols (Turin: UTET, 1961–2002)

— 'Zitella', in *Grande dizionario della lingua italiana*, 21 vols (Turin: UTET, 1961–2002), XXI (2002), 1083

Beales, Derek and Eugenio F. Biagini, *The Risorgimento and the Unification of Italy* (London: Longman, 2002)

Bellabarba, Marco, 'I processi per adulterio nell'Archivio Diocesano Tridentino (XVII–XVIII secolo)', in *Trasgressioni. Seduzione, concubinato, adulterio, bigamia (XIV–XVIII secolo)*, ed. by Silvana Seidel Menchi and Diego Quaglioni (Bologna: Il Mulino, 2004), pp. 185–227

Bellamy, Richard (ed.), *Cesare Beccaria: On Crimes and Punishments, and Other Writings*, trans. by Richard Davies (Cambridge: Cambridge University Press, 1995)

Bellettini, Athos, 'La popolazione italiana dall'inizio dell'era volgare ai giorni nostri. Valutazioni e tendenze', in *Storia d'Italia*, ed. by Ruggiero Romano and Corrado Vivanti, 6 vols (Turin: Einaudi, 1973), V, *I documenti*, pp. 489–532

— 'Les Remariages dans la ville et dans la campagne de Bologne au dix-neuvième siècle', in *Marriage and Remarriage in Populations of the Past*, ed. by Jacques Dupâquier and others (London: Academic Press, 1981), pp. 259–72

Bellomo, Manlio, 'Dote (diritto intermedio)', in *Enciclopedia del diritto*, 16 vols (Milan: Giuffrè, 1958–65), IV (1959), 8–32

— *Ricerche sui rapporti patrimoniali tra coniugi* (Milan: Giuffrè, 1960)
— *Società e istituzioni in Italia tra medioevo ed età moderna* (Catania: Giannotta, 1977)
— *The Common Legal Past of Europe: 1000–1800* (Washington, DC: The Catholic University of America press, 1995)
— *La condizione giuridica della donna in Italia. Vicende antiche e moderne* (Rome: Il Cigno, 1996 [1970])
Berkner, Lutz K. and Franklin F. Mendels, 'Sistemi di eredità, struttura familiare e modelli demografici in Europa (1700–1900)', in *Famiglia e mutamento sociale*, ed. by Marzio Barbagli (Bologna: Il Mulino, 1977), pp. 216–34
Bernal Palacios, Arturo, 'La condiciòn de la mujer en sancto Tomàs de Aquino', *Escritos del Vedat*, 4 (1974), 285–355
Bertelli, Sergio and Monica Centanni (eds), *Il gesto nel rito e nel cerimoniale dal mondo antico ad oggi* (Florence: Ponte alle Grazie, 1995)
Bertolo, Bruna, *Donne del Risorgimento. Le eroine invisibili dell'Unità d'Italia* (Rome: Ananke, 2011)
Bertoni Jovine, Dina, *I periodici popolari del Risorgimento* (Milan: Feltrinelli, 1959)
Besta, Enrico, *Le persone nella storia del diritto italiano* (Padua: CEDAM, 1931)
— *La famiglia nella storia del diritto italiano* (Milan: Giuffrè, 1962)
Betti, Emilio, *Teoria generale della interpretazione*, 2 vols (Milan: Giuffrè, 1955)
Bevilacqua, Piero (ed.), *Storia dell'agricoltura italiana in età contemporanea*, 3 vols (Venice: Marsilio, 1992)
Biagioli, Giuliana, 'Patrimoni e congiuntura: crescita, crisi e ripresa di una famiglia nobile toscana fra Sette e Ottocento', in *Ricerche di storia moderna*, ed. by Elsa Luttazzi Gregori and others, 4 vols (Pisa: Pacini, 1976–95), II (1979), *Aziende e patrimoni di grandi famiglie (sec. XV–XIX)*, 297–377
Bigaran, Mariapia, 'Progetti e dibattiti sul suffragio femminile: da Peruzzi a Giolitti', *Rivista di storia contemporanea*, 1 (1985), 50–82
Bizzocchi, Roberto, 'Una nuova morale per la donna e la famiglia', in *Storia d'Italia. Annali 22. Il Risorgimento*, ed. by Alberto Mario Banti and Paul Ginsborg (Turin: Einaudi, 2007), pp. 69–96
Black, Christopher F., *Church, Religion and Society in Early Modern Italy* (Basingstoke: Palgrave Macmillan, 2004)
Bock, Gisela, *Le donne nella storia europea. Dal Medioevo ai giorni nostri* (Rome: Laterza, 2001)

Bonacchi, Gabriella, *Legge e peccato. Anime, corpi, giustizia alla corte dei papi* (Rome: Laterza, 1995)

Bonacchi, Gabriella and Angela Groppi, *Il dilemma della cittadinanza: diritti e doveri delle donne* (Rome: Laterza, 1993)

Boneschi, Marta, *La donna segreta. Storia di Metilde Viscontini Dembowski* (Venice: Marsilio, 2010)

Boureau, Alain, 'L'imene e l'ulivo. La verginità femminile nel discorso della Chiesa nel XIII secolo', *Quaderni storici*, 25 (1990), 791–803

— *The Lord's First Night: The Myth of the Droit de Cuissage* (Chicago, IL: University of Chicago Press, 1998)

Branca, Giuseppe, 'Adulterio (diritto antico)', *Enciclopedia del diritto*, 16 vols (Milan: Giuffrè, 1958–65), I (1958), 620–21

Brandileone, Francesco, 'Studi preliminari sullo svolgimento dei rapporti patrimoniali fra coniugi in Italia', *Archivio giuridico*, 67 (1901), 201–81

— *Saggi sulla storia della celebrazione del matrimonio in Italia* (Milan: Hoepli, 1906)

Breschi, Marco, *La popolazione della Toscana dal 1640 al 1940. Un'ipotesi di ricostruzione* (Florence: Dipartimento Statistico, 1990)

Breschi, Marco and others, 'Family Composition and Remarriage in Pre-Transitional Italy: A Comparative Study', *European Journal of Population*, 25 (2009), 277–96

Bronzuoli, Daniele, *Matrimoni e patrimoni. La dote di Anna Bonaccorsi e la strategia imprenditoriale di Bettino Ricasoli* (Florence: Polistampa, 2013)

Brooks, Peter, *Troubling Confessions: Speaking Guilt in Law and Literature* (Chicago, IL: University of Chicago Press, 2000)

Brown, Judith C. and Robert C. Davis (eds), *Gender and Society in Renaissance Italy* (London: Longman, 1998)

Brundage, James A., *Law, Sex and Christian Society in Medieval Europe* (Chicago, IL: University of Chicago Press, 1987)

Bruni, Emanuela, Patrizia Foglia and Marina Messina (eds), *La donna in Italia: 1848–1914: unite per unire* (Cinisello Balsamo: Silvana, 2011)

Bruni, Francesco, *Italia. Vita e avventure di un'idea* (Bologna: Il Mulino, 2010)

Buckley, Rhonda R., 'Hypergamy', in *The Wiley Blackwell Encyclopedia of Family Studies*, ed. by Constance L. Shehan, 4 vols (Chichester: Wiley Blackwell, 2016), II, 1085–86

Burguière, André and François Lebrun, 'The One Hundred and One Families of Europe', in *A History of the Family*, ed. by André

Burguière and others, 2 vols (Cambridge: Polity Press, 1996), II, 11–94

Buttafuoco, Annarita, 'Straniere in patria. Temi e momenti dell'emancipazione femminile italiana dalle Repubbliche giacobine al fascismo', in *Esperienza storica femminile nell'età moderna e contemporanea: Atti del seminario*, ed. by Anna Maria Crispino, 2 vols (Rome: Unione donne italiane circolo "La Goccia", 1988), II, 91–124

— 'La causa delle donne. Cittadinanza e genere nel triennio "giacobino" italiano', in *Modi di essere. Studi, riflessioni, interventi sulla cultura e la politica delle donne in onore di Elvira Badaracco*, ed. by Annarita Buttafuoco (Bologna: EM, 1991), pp. 79–106

— (ed.), *Modi di essere. Studi, riflessioni, interventi sulla cultura e la politica delle donne in onore di Elvira Badaracco* (Bologna: EM, 1991)

Cafagna, Luciano, *The Industrial Revolution in Italy, 1830–1914*, trans. by Muriel Grindrod (London: Collins, 1971)

Calasso, Francesco, *Medio Evo del diritto* (Milan: Giuffrè, 1954)

Calvi, Giulia, 'Reconstructing the Family: Widowhood and Remarriage in Tuscany in the Early Modern Period', in *Marriage in Italy, 1300–1650*, ed. by Trevor Dean and Katherine J. P. Lowe (Cambridge: Cambridge University Press, 1998), pp. 275–96

Calvi, Giulia and Isabelle Chabot (eds), *Le ricchezze delle donne. Diritti patrimoniali e poteri familiari in Italia* (Turin: Rosenberg and Sellier, 1998)

Cantarella, Eva, 'Homicides of Honor: The Development of Italian Adultery Law over Two Millennia', in *The Family in Italy: From Antiquity to the Present*, ed. by David I. Kertzer and Richard P. Saller (New Haven, CT; London: Yale University Press, 1991), pp. 229–44

Carteny, Andrea, 'Il brigantaggio in Italia tra Risorgimento e questione meridionale: un'introduzione al tema', *Chronica Mundi*, 11 (2016), 249–71

Casanova, Cesarina, *La famiglia italiana in età moderna. Ricerche e modelli* (Rome: Carocci, 2000)

Cattaneo, Mario A., 'L'autoritarismo penale napoleonico', in *Codice dei delitti e delle pene pel Regno d'Italia (1811)*, ed. by Sergio Vinciguerra (Padua: CEDAM, 1993), pp. 23–32

Cavallo, Sandra and Lyndan Warner (eds), *Widowhood in Medieval and Early Modern Europe* (Harlow: Longman, 1999)

Cavanna, Adriano, *Storia del diritto moderno in Europa*, 2 vols (Milan: Giuffrè, 1979)

— 'Il codice penale napoleonico. Qualche considerazione generalissima', in *Codice dei delitti e delle pene pel Regno d'Italia*

(1811), ed. by Sergio Vinciguerra (Padua: CEDAM, 1993), pp. XI–XXII

Cavazza, Marta, 'Women's Dialectics, or the Thinking Uterus: An Eighteenth-Century Controversy on Gender and Education', in *The Faces of Nature in Enlightenment Europe*, ed. by Lorraine Daston and Gianna Pomata (Berlin: BWV, 2003), pp. 237–57

Cavina, Marco, *Il padre spodestato. L'autorità paterna dall'antichità a oggi* (Rome: Laterza, 2007)

— *Nozze di sangue. Storia della violenza coniugale* (Rome: Laterza, 2011)

Cazzetta, Giovanni, *Praesumitur seducta. Onestà e consenso femminile nella cultura giuridica moderna* (Milan: Giuffrè, 1999)

Chabot, Isabelle, 'Seconde nozze e identità materna nella Firenze del tardo medioevo', in *Tempi e spazi di vita femminile tra medioevo ed età moderna*, ed. by Silvana Seidel Menchi, Anne Jacobson Schutte and Thomas Kuehn (Bologna: Il Mulino, 1999), pp. 493–523

Chabot, Isabelle and Massimo Fornasari, *L'economia della carità. Le doti del Monte di pietà di Bologna (secoli XVI–XX)* (Bologna: Il Mulino, 1997)

Chiavistelli, Antonio, 'Rappresentanza', in *Atlante culturale del Risorgimento. Lessico del linguaggio politico dal Settecento all'Unità*, ed. by Alberto Mario Banti and others (Rome: Laterza, 2011), pp. 343–58

Chojnacki, Stanley, 'Dowries and Kinsmen in Early Renaissance Venice', *The Journal of Interdisciplinary History*, 5 (1975), 571–600

— 'Il divorzio di Cateruzza: rappresentazione femminile ed esito processuale (Venezia 1465)', in *Coniugi nemici. La separazione in Italia dal XII al XVIII secolo*, ed. by Silvana Seidel Menchi and Diego Quaglioni (Bologna: il Mulino, 2000), pp. 371–416

— *Women and Men in Renaissance Venice* (Baltimore, MD: Johns Hopkins University Press, 2000)

Cohen, David, 'The Augustan Law on Adultery: The Social and Cultural Context', in *The Family in Italy: From Antiquity to the Present*, ed. by David I. Kertzer and Richard P. Saller (New Haven, CT; London: Yale University Press, 1991), pp. 109–26

Conti Odorisio, Ginevra, Cristina Giorcelli and Giuseppe Monsagrati (eds), *Cristina di Belgiojoso: politica e cultura nell'Europa dell'Ottocento* (Casoria: Loffredo, 2010)

Corradi, Morena, '"Un esercito femminile": educazione e nation-building nell'Italia del secondo Ottocento', *Chronica Mundi*, 14 (2019/2020), forthcoming

Corsini, Carlo Alberto, 'Why is Remarriage a Male Affair? Some Evidence from Tuscan Villages during the Eighteenth Century', in *Marriage and Remarriage in Populations of the Past*, ed. by Jacques Dupâquier and others (London: Academic Press, 1981), pp. 385–95

Cortellazzo, Manlio and Paolo Zolli, *Dizionario etimologico della lingua italiana*, 5 vols (Bologna: Zanichelli, 1979–88)

— 'Zitella', in *Dizionario etimologico della lingua italiana*, 5 vols (Bologna: Zanichelli, 1979–88), v (1988)

Cortese, Ennio, 'Per la storia del mundio in Italia', *Rivista italiana per le scienze giuridiche*, 3 (1955/1956), 323–474

— *Appunti di storia giuridica sarda* (Milan: Giuffrè, 1964)

— *Il Rinascimento giuridico medievale* (Rome: Bulzoni, 1992)

— *Le grandi linee della storia giuridica medievale* (Rome: Il cigno Galileo Galilei, 2001)

Costa, Pietro, *Cittadinanza* (Rome and Bari: Laterza, 2005)

— 'Diritti/Doveri', in *Atlante culturale del Risorgimento. Lessico del linguaggio politico dal Settecento all'Unità*, ed. by Alberto Mario Banti and others (Rome: Laterza, 2011), pp. 270–84

Costa, Pietro and Danilo Zolo (eds), *The Rule of Law: History, Theory and Criticism* (Dordrecht: Springer, 2007)

Covato, Carmela, 'Educata a non istruirsi: un'introduzione al problema', in *E l'uomo educò la donna*, ed. by Carmela Covato and Maria Cristina Leuzzi (Rome: Editori riuniti, 1989), pp. 25–45

— *Sapere e pregiudizio: l'educazione delle donne fra '700 e '800* (Rome: Archivio Guido Izzi, 1998)

— 'Educare bambine dell'Ottocento', in *Le bambine nella storia dell'educazione*, ed. by Simonetta Ulivieri (Rome and Bari: Laterza, 2003), pp. 215–46

— 'Istruzione femminile e metamorfosi dell'identità in Italia fra Ottocento e Novecento', in *Conduct Literature for and about Women in Italy, 1470–1900: Prescribing and Describing Life*, ed. by Helena Sanson and Francesco Lucioli (Paris: Classiques Garnier, 2016), pp. 283–99

Cox, Virginia, 'The Single Self: Feminist Thought and the Marriage Market in Early-Modern Venice', *Renaissance Quarterly*, 48 (1995), 513–81

Cozzi, Gaetano, *La società veneta e il suo diritto. Saggi su questioni matrimoniali, giustizia penale, politica del diritto, sopravvivenza del diritto veneto nell'Ottocento* (Venice: Marsilio, 2000)

Crabb, Ann, *The Strozzi of Florence: Widowhood and Family Solidarity in the Renaissance* (Ann Arbor, MI: University of Michigan Press, 2000)

Crescenzi, Victor, 'Problemi dell'interpretatio nel diritto comune classico', in *El Dret Comù i Catalunya, Actes del II Simposi Internacional, Barcelona, 31 maig 1 juny del 1991*, ed. by Aquilino Iglesia Ferreiròs (Barcelona: [n. pub.], 1992), pp. 167–206

— 'Per una semantica della famiglia (ovvero: di cosa si parla, quando si parla di famiglia?)', in *Il giurista e il diritto: studi per Federico Spantigati*, ed. by Andrea Bixio and Giuliano Crifò (Milan: FrancoAngeli, 2010), pp. 3–31

— 'L'autorizzazione maritale e il problema storico della capacità della donna coniugata di disporre dei propri beni', in *Mujeres y derecho. Una perspectiva histórico-jurídica. Encuentro de historiadores del derecho. Actas*, ed. by Francisco L. Pacheco Caballero (Barcellona: Associació Catalana d'História del Dret, 2015), pp. 127–85

Crispino, Anna Maria (ed.), *Esperienza storica femminile nell'età moderna e contemporanea: Atti del seminario*, 2 vols (Rome: Unione donne italiane circolo "La Goccia", 1988)

D'Amelia, Marina, 'La conquista di una dote. Regole del gioco e scambi femminili alla Confraternita dell'Annunziata (secc. XVII–XVIII)', in *Ragnatele di rapporti. Patronage e reti di relazione nella storia delle donne*, ed. by Lucia Ferrante, Maura Palazzi and Gianna Pomata (Turin: Rosenberg and Sellier, 1988), pp. 305–43

D'Antonio, Mario, *Ricerca sul diritto di famiglia* (Rome: Servizio Studi, Legislazione e Inchieste Parlamentari, 1969)

D'Avack, Pietro, 'La *copula perfecta* e la *consummatio coniugi* nelle fonti e nella dottrina canonistica classica', *Rivista italiana per le scienze giuridiche*, 86 (1949), 163–250

Dalton, Susan, *Engendering the Republic of Letters: Reconnecting Public and Private Spheres in Eighteenth-Century Europe* (Montreal; London: McGill-Queen's University Press, 2003)

Danelon Vasoli, Nidia, *Il plebiscito in Toscana nel 1860* (Florence: Olschki, 1968)

Daston, Lorraine and Gianna Pomata (eds), *The Faces of Nature in Enlightenment Europe* (Berlin: BWV, 2003)

Daumas, Maurice, *Adulteri e cornuti. Storia della sessualità maschile tra Medioevo e modernità* (Bari: Dedalo, 2008)

Davidson, Ian, *The French Revolution: From Enlightenment to Tyranny* (London: Profile Books, 2016)

Davidson, Nicholas, 'Theology, Nature and the Law: Sexual Sin and Sexual Crime in Italy from the Fourteenth to the Seventeenth Century', in *Crime, Society and the Law in Renaissance Italy*, ed.

by Trevor Dean and K. J. P. Lowe (Cambridge: Cambridge University Press, 1994), pp. 74–98

Davis, James C., *The Decline of the Venetian Nobility as a Ruling Class* (Baltimore, MD: Johns Hopkins University Press, 1962)

— *A Venetian Family and Its Fortune, 1500–1900: The Donà and the Conservation of Their Wealth* (Philadelphia, PA: American Philosophical Society, 1975)

Davis, John A. and Paul Ginsborg, *Society and Politics in the Age of the Risorgimento: Essays in Honour of Denis Mack Smith* (Cambridge: Cambridge University Press, 2002)

Dean, Trevor, 'Fathers and Daughters: Marriage Laws and Marriage Disputes in Bologna and Italy, 1200–1500', in *Crime, Society and the Law in Renaissance Italy*, ed. by Trevor Dean and K. J. P. Lowe (Cambridge: Cambridge University Press, 1994), pp. 85–106

— 'Marriage and Mutilation: Vendetta in Late Medieval Italy', *Past and Present*, 157 (1997), 3–36

— 'Domestic Violence in Late-Medieval Bologna', *Renaissance Studies*, 18 (2004), 527–43

— *Crime and Justice in Late Medieval Italy* (Cambridge: Cambridge University Press, 2007)

Dean, Trevor and Katherine J. P. Lowe, 'Introduction: Issues in the History of Marriage', in *Marriage in Italy, 1300–1650*, ed. by Trevor Dean and Katherine J. P. Lowe (Cambridge: Cambridge University Press, 1998), pp. 1–21

— (eds), *Crime, Society and the Law in Renaissance Italy* (Cambridge: Cambridge University Press, 1994)

— (eds), *Marriage in Italy, 1300–1650* (Cambridge: Cambridge University Press, 1998)

De Bernardi, Alberto, 'Città e campagna nella storia contemporanea', in *Storia dell'economia italiana*, ed. by Ruggiero Romano, 3 vols (Turin: Einaudi, 1990–91), III (1991), *L'età contemporanea: un paese nuovo*, 252–78

De Giorgio, Michela, 'Raccontare un matrimonio moderno', in *Storia del matrimonio*, ed. by Michela De Giorgio and Christiane Klapisch-Zuber (Rome: Laterza, 1996), pp. 307–90.

De Giorgio, Michela and Christiane Klapisch-Zuber (eds), *Storia del matrimonio* (Rome: Laterza, 1996)

Delille, Gérard, *Agricoltura e demografia nel Regno di Napoli nei secoli XVIII e XIX* (Naples: Guida, 1977)

— 'Un esempio di assistenza privata: I monti di maritaggio del Regno di Napoli (secoli XVI–XVIII)', in *Timore e carità. I poveri nell'Italia moderna*, ed. by Giorgio Politi, Mario Rosa and Franco Della Peruta (Cremona: Libreria del Convegno, 1982), pp. 227–81

— 'Strategie di alleanza e demografia del matrimonio', in *Storia del matrimonio*, ed. by Michela De Giorgio and Christiane Klapisch-Zuber (Rome: Laterza, 1996), pp. 283–306

Delmedico, Sara, *Breve studio sulla condizione giuridica della donna nello Stato Pontificio dell'Ottocento* ([n.p.]: Lulu, 2014)

— 'Alimenti e dote alla periferia dello Stato Pontificio: la famiglia Pucci', *The Italianist*, 37 (2017), 50–68

— 'The Dowry in Mid-Nineteenth-Century Papal States: The Case of Umbellina Livi', in *Gender and Generations: Spaces, Times, Identity*, ed. by Ekaterina Lung, Gabriella Valera and Christopher Heath (= *Chronica Mundi*, 13 (2018)), pp. 92–106

De Marchi, Elena, *Dai campi alle filande. Famiglia, matrimonio e lavoro nella "pianura dell'Olona" 1750–1850* (Milan: FrancoAngeli, 2009)

Del Panta, Lorenzo, *Evoluzione demografica e popolamento nell'Italia dell'Ottocento: 1796–1914* (Bologna: CLUEB, 1984)

Delumeau, Jean, *Sin and Fear: The Emergence of a Western Guilt Culture, XIII–XVIII Centuries* (New York: St. Martin's Press, 1990)

Dezza, Ettore, *Lezioni di storia della codificazione civile: il Code civil (1804) e l'Allgemeines Bürgerliches Gesetzbuch (ABGB, 1812)* (Turin: Giappichelli, 1998)

Dezza, Ettore and Pio Caroni (eds), *L'ABGB e la codificazione asburgica in Italia e in Europa: atti del Convegno internazionale, Pavia, 11–12 ottobre 2002* (Padua: CEDAM, 2006)

Dickie, John, 'A World at War: The Italian Army and the Brigandage 1860–1870', *History Workshop Journal*, 33 (1992), 1–24

Di Renzo Villata, Maria Gigliola (ed.), *Family Law and Society in Europe from the Middle Ages to the Contemporary Era* (Cham, NY: Springer International Publishing, 2016)

Di Simone, Maria Rosa, 'La donna nella storia del diritto austriaco: tradizione e innovazione tra medioevo e Settecento', in *Donne tra storia e politica*, ed. by Agata Cecilia Amato Mangiameli (Turin: Giappichelli, 2012), pp. 24–43

— 'Le discussioni sui diritti delle donne per il Codice civile unitario', in *Avvocati protagonisti e rinnovatori del primo diritto unitario*, ed. by Stefano Borsacchi and Gian Savino Pene Vidari (Bologna: Il Mulino, 2014), pp. 95–121

— 'La condizione giuridica della donna nell'ABGB', *Historia et ius*, 9 (2016), paper 3, 1–29

Di Simplicio, Oscar, *Peccato penitenza perdono. Siena 1575–1800. La formazione della coscienza nell'Italia moderna* (Milan: FrancoAngeli, 1994)

Donahue, Charles, *Law, Marriage, and Society in the Later Middle Ages: Arguments about Marriage in Five Courts* (Cambridge: Cambridge University Press, 2007)

Doni, Elena, 'Rose bianche per un soldato. Colomba Antonietti', in *Donne del Risorgimento*, ed. by Elena Doni and others (Bologna: Il Mulino, 2011), pp. 25–33

Doni, Elena and others (eds), *Donne del Risorgimento* (Bologna: Il Mulino, 2011)

Duby, Georges and Michelle Perrot (eds), *Storia delle donne. L'Ottocento* (Rome and Bari: Laterza, 1991)

Dupâquier, Jacques and others, *Marriage and Remarriage in Populations of the Past* (London: Academic Press, 1981)

Enciclopedia del diritto, 16 vols (Milan: Giuffrè, 1958–65)

Ercole, Francesco, 'L'istituto dotale nella pratica e nella legislazione statutaria dell'Italia superiore', *Rivista italiana per le scienze giuridiche*, 45 (1909), 191–302 and 46 (1910), 167–257

Esmein, Adhémar, *Le Mariage en droit canonique*, 2 vols (Paris: Larose et Forcel, 1891)

Evans, Richard J., *The Feminists: Women's Emancipation Movements in Europe, America and Australasia, 1840–1920* (London: Routledge, 2013)

Faoro, Luca, '"Nefandum dogma". Seduzione e promessa di matrimonio in una comparsa trentina del XVII secolo', in *Matrimoni in dubbio. Unioni controverse e nozze clandestine in Italia dal XIV al XVIII secolo*, ed. by Silvana Seidel Menchi and Diego Quaglioni (Bologna: Il Mulino, 2001), pp. 431–528

Fayer, Carla, *La familia romana: aspetti giuridici ed antiquari*, 3 vols (Rome: "L'Erma" di Bretschneider, 1994)

Fazio, Ida, 'La Signora dell'Oro. Carità femminile, potere e controllo sociale in una comunità siciliana tra Sette e Ottocento', in *Ragnatele di rapporti: patronage e reti di relazione nella storia delle donne*, ed. by Lucia Ferrante, Maura Palazzi and Gianna Pomata (Turin: Rosenberg and Sellier, 1988), pp. 80–98

— 'Valori economici e valori simbolici. Il declino della dote nell'Italia dell'Ottocento', *Quaderni storici*, 78 (1992), 291–317

Ferrante, Lucia, 'Patronesse e patroni in un'istituzione assistenziale femminile (Bologna sec. XVII)', in *Ragnatele di rapporti. Patronage e reti di relazione nella storia delle donne*, ed. by Lucia Ferrante, Maura Palazzi and Gianna Pomata (Turin: Rosenberg and Sellier, 1988), pp. 59–79

Ferrante, Lucia, Maura Palazzi and Gianna Pomata (eds), *Ragnatele di rapporti. Patronage e reti di relazione nella storia delle donne* (Turin: Rosenberg and Sellier, 1988)

Filippini, Nadia M., 'Donne sulla scena politica: dalle Municipalità del 1797 al Risorgimento', in *Donne sulla scena pubblica. Società e politica in Veneto tra Sette e Ottocento*, ed. by Nadia M. Filippini and others (Milan: FrancoAngeli, 2006), pp. 81–137

Filippini, Nadia M. and others (eds), *Donne sulla scena pubblica. Società e politica in Veneto tra Sette e Ottocento* (Milan: FrancoAngeli, 2006)

Fioravanzo, Monica, 'Sull'autorizzazione maritale. Ricerche attorno alla condizione giuridica della donna nell'Italia unita', *Clio*, 30 (1994), 641–725

Fisher, Kate, 'Marriage and Companionate Ideals since 1750', in *The Routledge History of Sex and the Body: 1500 to the Present*, ed. by Sarah Toulalan and Kate Fisher (London and New York: Routledge, 2013), pp. 328–48

Fosi, Irene, 'Da un tribunale all'altro: il divorzio fra Benedetta Pinelli e Girolamo Grimaldi, principe di Gerace (1609–1653)', in *Coniugi nemici. La separazione in Italia dal XII al XVIII secolo*, ed. by Silvana Seidel Menchi and Diego Quaglioni (Bologna: il Mulino, 2000), pp. 417–52

— *La giustizia del papa. Sudditi e tribunali nello Stato Pontificio in età moderna* (Rome and Bari: Laterza, 2007)

Franchini, Silvia, *Élites ed educazione femminile nell'Italia dell'Ottocento. L'Istituto della SS. Annunziata di Firenze* (Florence: Olschki, 1993)

Fruci, Gian Luca, 'Cittadine senza cittadinanza. La mobilitazione femminile nei plebisciti del Risorgimento (1848–1870)', *Genesis*, 5 (2006), 21–55

— 'Il sacramento dell'unità nazionale: linguaggi, iconografia e pratiche dei plebisciti risorgimentali (1848–70)', in *Storia d'Italia. Annali 22. Il Risorgimento*, ed. by Alberto Mario Banti and Paul Ginsborg (Turin: Einaudi, 2007), pp. 567–605

— 'Alle origini del momento plebiscitario risorgimentale (1797–1870)', in *Verso l'Unità. Conferenze e laboratori didattici organizzati con la collaborazione della Domus Mazziniana: Pisa, ottobre-novembre 2010* (Ospedaletto: Pacini, 2011), pp. 43–56

Fugazza, Mariachiara, 'Il lungo cammino dei diritti', in *La donna in Italia: 1848–1914: unite per unire*, ed. by Emanuela Bruni, Patrizia Foglia and Marina Messina (Cinisello Balsamo: Silvana, 2011), pp. 67–78

Fugazza, Mariachiara and Karoline Rörig (eds), *"La prima donna d'Italia". Cristina Trivulzio di Belgiojoso tra politica e giornalismo* (Milan: FrancoAngeli, 2010)

Fumagalli, Camillo, *Il diritto di fraterna nella giurisprudenza da Accursio alla codificazione* (Turin: Bocca, 1912)

Galasso, Giuseppe, 'Il contesto storico: l'età del *Codice*', *Il bicentenario del codice napoleonico: Convegno. Roma 20 dicembre 2004. Atti dei convegni lincei*, 221 (2004), 9–18

Galeotti, Giulia, 'L'autorizzazione maritale nel primo codice civile unitario: un istituto "estraneo" alla tradizione italiana?', *Dimensioni e problemi della ricerca storica*, 2 (2005), 155–82

— *Storia del voto alle donne in Italia. Alle radici del difficile rapporto tra donne e politica* (Rome: Biblink, 2006)

Gardner, Jane F., *Family and Familia in Roman Law and Life* (Oxford: Clarendon Press, 1998)

Garlati, Loredana, 'La famiglia tra passato e presente', in *Diritto della famiglia*, ed. by Salvatore Patti and Maria Giovanna Cubeddu (Milan: Giuffrè, 2011), pp. 1–48

— 'Honour and Guilt. A Comparative Study on Regulations on Infanticide between the Nineteenth and Twentieth Century', in *Family Law and Society in Europe from the Middle Ages to the Contemporary Era*, ed. by Maria Gigliola Di Renzo Villata (Cham, NY: Springer International Publishing, 2016), pp. 257–81

Gastel Chiarelli, Cristina, *Niente zucchero nel calamajo: lettere di Giuseppe Verdi a Clara Maffei* (Milan: Archinto, 2005)

Gaudemet, Jean, *La Formation du droit canonique médiéval* (London: Variorum, 1980)

— *Sociétés et marriage* (Strasbourg: Cerdic, 1980)

— *Le Mariage en occident. Les mœurs et le droit* (Paris: Cerf, 1987)

— *Le Droit canonique* (Paris: Fides, 1989)

— *Storia del diritto canonico: ecclesia et civitas* (Milan: San Paolo Edizioni, 1998)

— 'L'Apport de la doctrine canonique aux droits occidentaux en matière de mariage', in *Ius canonicum in Oriente et Occidente*, ed. by Stefan Korta and others (Frankfurt: Peter Lang, 2003), pp. 167–95

Ghisalberti, Carlo, *Le costituzioni giacobine (1796–1799)* (Milan: Giuffrè, 1973)

— *Dall'antico regime al 1848. Le origini costituzionali dell'Italia moderna* (Rome: Laterza, 1974)

— *Unità nazionale e unificazione giuridica in Italia* (Rome: Laterza, 1988)

— *Istituzioni e società civile nell'età del Risorgimento* (Rome and Bari: Laterza, 2005)

Goldthwaite, Richard A., *Private Wealth in Renaissance Florence: A Study of Four Families* (Princeton, NJ: Princeton University Press, 1968)

Goody, Jack, 'Dowry and the Rights of Women to Property', in *Property Relations: Renewing the Anthropological Tradition*, ed. by

C. M. Hann (Cambridge: Cambridge University Press, 1998), pp. 201–13

Gordley, James, 'Myths of the French Civil Code', *The American Journal of Comparative Law*, 42 (1994), 459–505

Gouges, Olympe de, *Déclaration des droits de la femme et de la citoyenne*, ed. by Emanuèle Gaulier (Paris: Mille et une nuits, 2003)

Green, David R. and Alastair Owens (eds), *Family Welfare: Gender, Property, and Inheritance since the Seventeenth Century* (London: Praeger, 2004)

Greenfield, Kent R., *Economia e liberalismo nel Risorgimento. Il movimento nazionale in Lombardia dal 1814 al 1848* (Bari: Laterza, 1964)

Groppi, Angela, 'Una gestione collettiva di equilibri emozionali e materiali. La reclusione delle donne nella Roma dell'Ottocento', in *Ragnatele di rapporti. Patronage e reti di relazione nella storia delle donne*, ed. by Lucia Ferrante, Maura Palazzi and Gianna Pomata (Turin: Rosenberg and Sellier, 1988), pp. 130–47

Grossi, Paolo, 'Per la storia della legislazione sabauda in Sardegna: il Censore dell'agricoltura', *Annali della Facoltà Giuridica dell'Università di Macerata*, 26 (1963), 197–240

— 'Tradizione e modelli nella sistemazione post-unitaria della proprietà', *Quaderni Fiorentini per la storia del pensiero giuridico moderno*, 5/6 (1976/1977), 202–338

— 'Assolutismo giuridico e diritto privato nel secolo XIX', *Rivista di storia del diritto italiano*, 64 (1991), 5–17

— '*Code Civil*: una fonte nuovissima per la nuova civiltà giuridica', *Atti dei Convegni Lincei*, 221 (2006), 19–42

— *A History of European Law* (Chichester: Wiley-Blackwell, 2010)

Grosso, Maria and Loredana Rotondo, '"Sempre tornerò a prendere cura del mio paese e a rivedere te". Cristina Trivulzio di Belgiojoso', in *Donne del Risorgimento*, ed. by Elena Doni and others (Bologna: Il Mulino, 2011), pp. 65–94

Guerci, Luciano, *La discussione sulla donna nell'Italia del Settecento: aspetti e problemi* (Turin: Tirrenia Stampatori, 1987)

— *La sposa obbediente: donna e matrimonio nella discussione dell'Italia del Settecento* (Turin: Tirrenia Stampatori, 1988)

Guerra Medici, Maria Teresa, 'Diritto statutario e condizione della donna nella città medievale dei secc. XII–XIV', *Rivista di storia del diritto italiano*, 65 (1992), 319–36

— *La cittadinanza difficile* (Camerino: Università di Camerino, 2000)

Guidi, Laura, 'La "passione governata dalla virtù": benefattrici nella Napoli ottocentesca', in *Ragnatele di rapporti. Patronage e reti di relazione nella storia delle donne*, ed. by Lucia Ferrante, Maura

Palazzi and Gianna Pomata (Turin: Rosenberg and Sellier, 1988), pp. 148–65

Guidi, Laura, Angela Russo and Marcella Varriale, *Il Risorgimento invisibile. Patriote del Mezzogiorno d'Italia* (Naples: Comune di Napoli Edizioni, 2011)

Guzzetti, Linda, 'Separations and Separated Couples in Fourteenth-Century Venice', in *Marriage in Italy, 1300–1650*, ed. by Trevor Dean and Katherine J. P. Lowe (Cambridge: Cambridge University Press, 1998), pp. 249–74

Habermas, Jürgen, *The Structural Transformation of the Public Sphere: An Inquiry into a Category of Bourgeois Society*, trans. by Thomas Burger and Frederick Lawrence (Cambridge, MA: MIT Press, 1996)

Hacke, Daniela, 'La promessa disattesa: il caso di Perina Gabrieli (Venezia 1620)', in *Matrimoni in dubbio. Unioni controverse e nozze clandestine in Italia dal XIV al XVIII secolo*, ed. by Silvana Seidel Menchi and Diego Quaglioni (Bologna: Il Mulino, 2001), pp. 395–413

Hallamore Caesar, Ann, 'Gender, Genre and Education. Writing about Conduct in Eighteenth-Century Venice', in *Conduct Literature for and about Women in Italy, 1470–1900: Prescribing and Describing Life*, ed. by Helena Sanson and Francesco Lucioli (Paris: Classiques Garnier, 2016), pp. 119–34

Halpérin, Jean Louis, *L'Impossible Code Civil* (Paris: Presses universitaires de France, 1992)

Hardman, John, *The French Revolution: The Fall of the Ancien Régime to the Thermidorian Reaction, 1785–1795* (London: Arnold, 1981)

Herlihy, David, 'Family Solidarity in Medieval Italian History', *Exploration in Economic History*, 7 (1969), 173–84

— 'The Medieval Marriage Market', *Medieval and Renaissance Studies*, 6 (1976), 3–27

Hoffman, Paul, *La Femme dans la pensée des lumières* (Paris: Ophrys, 1977)

Hosker, Lucy, '"Donne sole" in Post-Unification Italy: The Works of Tommasina Guidi and Emilia Nevers' (unpublished doctoral thesis, University of Cambridge, 2015)

Hufton, Olwen H., *The Prospect before Her: A History of Women in Western Europe 1500–1800* (London: HarperCollins, 1995)

Ibbetson, David, 'Comparative Legal History: A Methodology', in *Making Legal History: Approaches and Methodologies*, ed. by Anthony Musson and Chantal Stebbings (Cambridge: Cambridge University Press, 2012), pp. 131–45

Irti, Natalino and Francesco Santoro-Passarelli, 'Consolidazioni e codificazioni delle leggi civili', *Atti Dei Convegni Lincei*, 106 (1994), 245–52

Isastia, Anna Maria, *Storia di una famiglia del Risorgimento. Sarina, Giuseppe, Ernesto Nathan* (Turin: Università Popolare di Torino, 2010)

Isnenghi, Mario and Eva Cecchinato (eds), *Fare l'Italia: unità e disunità nel Risorgimento* (Turin: UTET, 2008)

Jemolo, Arturo Carlo, *Il matrimonio nel diritto canonico. Dal Concilio di Trento al Codice del 1917* (Bologna: Il Mulino, 1993)

Jones, Verina R., 'Journalism, 1750–1850', in *A History of Women's Writing in Italy*, ed. by Letizia Panizza and Sharon Wood (Cambridge: Cambridge University Press, 2000), pp. 120–34

Kantorowicz, Hermann and William Warwick Buckland (eds), *Studies in the Glossators of the Roman Law: Newly Discovered Writings of the Twelfth Century* (Cambridge: Cambridge University Press, 1938)

Kelly, Joan, *Women, History and Theory: The Essays of Joan Kelly* (Chicago, IL; London: University of Chicago Press, 1984)

Kelly-Gadol, Joan, 'The Social Relation of the Sexes: Methodological Implications of Women's History', *Signs*, 1 (1976), 809–23

Kelso, Ruth, *Doctrine for the Lady of the Renaissance* (Urbana, IL: University of Illinois Press, 1956)

Kent, Francis William, *Household and Lineage in Renaissance Florence: The Family Life of the Capponi, Ginori, and Rucellai* (Princeton, NJ: Princeton University Press, 1977)

Kertzer, David I. and Wendy Sigle, 'The Marriage of Female Foundlings in Nineteenth-Century Italy', *Continuity and Change*, 13 (1998), 201–20

Kertzer, David I. and Richard P. Saller (eds), *The Family in Italy: From Antiquity to the Present* (New Haven, CT; London: Yale University Press, 1991)

King, Helen, *Hippocrates' Woman: Reading the Female Body in Ancient Greece* (London: Routledge, 1998)

King, Margaret L. and Albert Rabil Jr., 'The Other Voice in Early Modern Europe: Introduction to the Series', in *The Contest for Knowledge: Debates over Women's Learning in Eighteenth-Century Italy*, ed. by Rebecca Messbarger and Paula Findlen (Chicago, IL: University of Chicago Press, 2005), pp. xi-xxxi

Kirshner, Julius, 'Pursuing Honor While Avoiding Sin: The "Monte Delle Doti" of Florence', *Quaderni di studi senesi*, 41 (1978), 1–82

— 'Materials for a Gilded Cage: Non-Dotal Assets in Florence, 1300– 1500', in *The Family in Italy: From Antiquity to the Present*, ed. by David I. Kertzer and Richard P. Saller (New Haven, CT; London: Yale University Press, 1991), pp. 184–207

— *Marriage, Dowry, and Citizenship in Late Medieval and Renaissance Italy* (Toronto: University of Toronto Press, 2015)

Klein, Lawrence E., 'Gender and the Public/Private Distinction in the Eighteenth Century: Some Questions about Evidence and Analytic Procedure', *Eighteenth-Century Studies*, 29 (1995): *The Public and the Nation*, 97–109

Kuehn, Thomas J., *Law, Family and Women: Toward a Legal Anthropology of Renaissance Italy* (Chicago, IL: University of Chicago Press, 1991)

— 'Household and Family in Ius Commune and Ius Proprium', in *The Household in Late Medieval Cities: Italy and Northwestern Europe Compared*, ed. by Myriam Carlier and Tim Soens (Leuven: Garant, 2001), pp. 37–50

— *Family and Gender in Renaissance Italy, 1300–1600* (Cambridge: Cambridge University Press, 2017)

Laingui, Andre, 'Il diritto penale della rivoluzione francese e dell'Impero', in *Diritto penale dell'Ottocento. I codici preunitari e il codice Zanardelli*, ed. by Sergio Vinciguerra (Padua: CEDAM, 1993), pp. 49–52

Lane, Frederic C., *Andrea Barbarigo: Merchant of Venice, 1418–1449* (Baltimore, MD: Johns Hopkins University Press, 1944)

Laqueur, Thomas, *Making Sex: Body and Gender from the Greeks to Freud* (Cambridge, MA; London: Harvard University Press, 1992)

Laslett, Peter, 'Family and Household as Work Group and Kin Group: Areas of Traditional Europe Compared', in *Family Forms in Historic Europe*, ed. by Richard Wall, Jean Robin and Peter Laslett (Cambridge: Cambridge University Press, 1983), pp. 513–64

Lattes, Alessandro, 'Le leggi civili e criminali di Carlo Felice pel Regno di Sardegna', in *La Sardegna di Carlo Felice e il problema della terra*, ed. by Carlino Sole (Cagliari: Editrice sarda Fossataro, 1967), pp. 403–509

Laven, David, *Venice and Venetia under the Habsburgs, 1815–1835* (Oxford: Oxford University Press, 2002)

Laven, Mary, *Virgins of Venice: Broken Vows and Cloistered Lives in the Renaissance Convent* (New York: Viking, 2003)

Lenci, Mauro, 'The Battle over "Democracy" in Italian Political Thought during the Revolutionary *Triennio*, 1796–1799', in *The Political Culture of the Sister Republics, 1794–1806*, ed. by Joris Oddens, Erik Jacobs and Mart Rutjes (Amsterdam: Amsterdam University Press, 2015), pp. 97–106

Lerner, Gerda, 'Placing Women in History: A 1975 Perspective', in *Liberating Women's History: Theoretical and Critical Essays*, ed. by Berenice A. Carroll (Urbana, IL: University of Illinois, 1976), pp. 358–67

Lewis, David, *Jessie White Mario: An English Heroine in the Liberation of Italy* (Oxford: Eureka, 2006)

Litchfield, Robert B., 'Caratteristiche demografiche delle famiglie patrizie fiorentine dal sedicesimo al diciannovesimo secolo', in *Saggi di demografia storica*, ed. by Carlo Alberto Corsini and others (Florence: Università di Firenze, 1969), pp. 17–34

Liva, Alberto, *La gerarchia delle fonti di diritto nelle città dell'Italia settentrionale* (Milan: Giuffrè, 1976)

Livi-Bacci, Massimo, *A History of Italian Fertility during the Last Two Centuries* (Princeton, NJ: Princeton University Press, 1977)

— 'On the Frequency of Remarriage in Nineteenth Century Italy: Methods and Results', in *Marriage and Remarriage in Populations of the Past*, ed. by Jacques Dupâquier and others (London: Academic Press, 1981), pp. 347–61

Lobrano, Giovanni, *Pater et filius eadem persona: per lo studio della 'patria potestas'* (Milan: Giuffrè, 1984)

Lombardi, Daniela, 'Intervention by Church and State in Marriage Disputes in Sixteenth- and Seventeenth-Century Florence', in *Crime, Society and the Law in Renaissance Italy*, ed. by Trevor Dean and K. J. P. Lowe (Cambridge: Cambridge University Press, 1994), pp. 142–56

— 'Fidanzamenti e matrimoni dal Concilio di Trento alle riforme settecentesche', in *Storia del matrimonio*, ed. by Michela De Giorgio and Christiane Klapisch-Zuber (Rome: Laterza, 1996), pp. 215–50

— 'L'odio capitale, ovvero l'incompatibilità di carattere: Maria Falcini e Andrea Lotti (Firenze 1773–1777)', in *Coniugi nemici. La separazione in Italia dal XII al XVIII secolo*, ed. by Silvana Seidel Menchi and Diego Quaglioni (Bologna: Il Mulino, 2000), pp. 335–67

— *Matrimoni di antico regime* (Bologna: Il Mulino, 2001)

— *Storia del matrimonio dal Medioevo a oggi* (Bologna: Il Mulino, 2008)

Lorenzoni, Antonio, *Scelta di disposizioni del diritto romano* (Padua: Cartallier and Sicca, 1838)

Lowe, Katherine J. P., *Nuns' Chronicles and Convent Culture in Renaissance and Counter-Reformation Italy* (Cambridge: Cambridge University Press, 2003)

Luise, Flavia, 'Famiglia e società a Solofra tra il 1640 e il 1676 nei capitoli matrimoniali e nei testamenti', *Mélanges de l'Ecole française de Rome. Moyen-Age–Temps modernes*, 95 (1983), 299–338

Lussana, Fiamma, 'Misoginia e adulazione: ambiguità dell'immagine femminile nel secolo dei Lumi', *Studi Storici*, 2 (1984), 547–58

Luzzatto, Gino, *Per una storia economica d'Italia. Progressi e lacune* (Bari: Laterza, 1957)

McDougall, Sara, 'Women and Gender in Canon Law', in *The Oxford Handbook of Women and Gender in Medieval Europe*, ed. by Judith M. Bennett and Ruth Mazo Karras (Oxford; New York: Oxford University Press, 2013), pp. 163–80

Maclean, Ian, *The Renaissance Notion of Woman: A Study in the Fortunes of Scholasticism and Medical Science in European Intellectual Life* (Cambridge: Cambridge University Press, 1980)

Macry, Paolo, *Ottocento. Famiglia, élites e patrimoni a Napoli* (Turin: Einaudi, 1988)

Marchetto, Giuliano, 'Il volto terribile del padre. "Metus reverentialis" e matrimonio nell'opera di Tomás Sánchez', in *I tribunali del matrimonio (secoli XV–XVIII)*, ed. by Silvana Seidel Menchi and Diego Quaglioni (Bologna: Il Mulino, 2006), pp. 269–88

Marcucci, Maria Chiara, 'Le "zitelle" e il gioco del lotto a Fano (1857–1860)', *Nuovi Studi Fanesi*, 10 (1995), 169–94

Mari, Eric de, 'Le Droit intermédiaire. Posture juridique, imposture politique et vacuité d'une convention', *La Révolution française, Rupture(s) en Révolution*, 5 (2011) <http://lrf.revues.org/340> [accessed 22 September 2020]

Marongiu, Antonio, 'Adulterio (diritto intermedio)', *Enciclopedia del diritto*, 16 vols (Milan: Giuffrè, 1958–65), I (1958), 622

— *Saggi di storia giuridica e politica sarda* (Padua: CEDAM, 1975)

— 'Il matrimonio "alla sardesca"', *Archivio Storico Sardo di Sassari*, 7 (1981), 85–93

Martines, Lauro, *The Social World of the Florentine Humanists, 1390–1460* (London: Routledge and Kegan Paul, 1963)

Martucci, Roberto, *L'invenzione dell'Italia unita: 1855–1864* (Milan: Sansoni, 1999)

Massironi, Andrea, 'The Father's Right to Kill his Adulterous Daughter in the Late Ius Commune', in *Family Law and Society in Europe from the Middle Ages to the Contemporary Era*, ed. by Maria Gigliola Di Renzo Villata (Cham, NY: Springer International Publishing, 2016), pp. 187–215

Mattone, Antonello, 'Assolutismo e tradizione statutaria. Il governo sabaudo e il diritto consuetudinario del Regno di Sardegna (1720–1827)', *Rivista storica italiana*, 116 (2004), 926–1007

Mazza, Gaetana, *Tra storia e storie. Banditismo, brigantaggio e milizie civili nel meridione d'Italia dal XVI al XIX secolo* (Rome: Aracne, 2015)

Mazzotti, Massimo, *The World of Maria Gaetana Agnesi, Mathematician of God* (Baltimore, MD: Johns Hopkins University Press, 2007)

Melograni, Piero and Lucetta Scaraffia (eds), *La famiglia italiana dall'Ottocento a oggi* (Rome and Bari: Laterza, 1988)

Meriggi, Marco, *Amministrazione e classi sociali nel Lombardo-Veneto (1814–1848)* (Bologna: Il Mulino, 1983)

— *Milano borghese. Circoli ed élites nell'Ottocento* (Venice: Marsilio, 1992)

— 'Società, istituzioni e ceti dirigenti', in *Storia d'Italia*, ed. by Giovanni Sabbatucci and Vittorio Vidotto, 6 vols (Rome and Bari: Laterza, 1994), I, *Le premesse dell'unità*, 119–228

Merzario, Raul, *Il paese stretto. Strategie matrimoniali nella diocesi di Como, secoli XVI–XVIII* (Turin: Einaudi, 1981)

Messbarger, Rebecca, *The Century of Women: Representations of Women in Eighteenth-Century Italian Public Discourse* (Toronto: University of Toronto Press, 2002)

Minnucci, Giovanni, '"An mulier verberari possit": una "quaestio disputata" di argomento matrimoniale', in *Coniugi nemici. La separazione in Italia dal XII al XVIII secolo*, ed. by Silvana Seidel Menchi and Diego Quaglioni (Bologna: il Mulino, 2000), pp. 491–98

Mitchell, Katherine and Helena Sanson, 'Introduction', in *Women and Gender in Post-Unification Italy: Between Private and Public Spheres*, ed. by Katherine Mitchell and Helena Sanson (Oxford: Peter Lang, 2013), pp. 1–9

Mitchell, Katherine and Helena Sanson (eds), *Women and Gender in Post-Unification Italy: Between Private and Public Spheres* (Oxford: Peter Lang, 2013)

Molho, Anthony, '*Tamquam vere mortua*: le professioni religiose femminili nella Firenze del tardo Medioevo', *Società e Storia*, 43 (1989), 1–44

— *Marriage Alliance in Late Medieval Florence* (Cambridge, MA: Harvard University Press, 1994)

Moran, Megan, 'Motherhood and the Politics of Family Decisions in Early Modern Italy', *Journal of Family History*, 40 (2015), 351–72

Morello, Maria, 'Per una ricostruzione giuridica dello *stupro* e della violenza sulle donne nell'età dello *ius commune*', *Studi Urbinati. Scienze giuridiche, politiche ed economiche*, 64 (2013), 101–29

Mori, Maria Teresa, *Salotti. La sociabilità delle élite nell'Italia dell'Ottocento* (Rome: Carocci, 2000)

Moroni, Andrea, 'Antica gente e subiti guadagni. Patrimoni aristocratici fiorentini nell'800', *Biblioteca di storia toscana moderna e contemporanea*, 44 (1997), 1–364

Mousset, Sophie, *Olympe de Gouges et les droits de la femme* (Paris: Félin, 2003)

— *Women's Rights and the French Revolution: A Biography of Olympe de Gouges* (New Brunswick, NJ; London: Transaction, 2007)

Nardi, Carlo, 'Una legislazione egualitaria d'un re assolutista: il codice della colonia di S. Leucio', *L'Eloquenza*, 49 (1959), 96–111

Neri, Valerio and Beatrice Girotti (eds), *La famiglia tardoantica. Società, diritto, religione* (Milan: LED, 2016)

Niccoli, Ottavia, 'Baci rubati. Gesti e riti nuziali in Italia prima e dopo il Concilio di Trento', in *Il gesto nel rito e nel cerimoniale dal mondo antico ad oggi*, ed. by Sergio Bertelli and Monica Centanni (Florence: Ponte alle Grazie, 1995), pp. 224–47

Okin, Susan M., *Women in Western Political Thought* (Princeton, NJ: Princeton University Press, 1992)

Padoa-Schioppa, Antonio, *A History of Law in Europe: From the Early Middle Ages to the Twentieth Century* (Cambridge: Cambridge University Press, 2017)

Palazzi, Maura, 'Solitudini femminili e patrilignaggio. Nubili e vedove fra Sette e Ottocento', in *Storia della famiglia italiana, 1750–1950*, ed. by Marzio Barbagli and David I. Kertzer (Bologna: Il Mulino, 1992), pp. 129–59

— *Donne sole. Storie dell'altra faccia dell'Italia tra antico regime e società contemporanea* (Milan: Mondadori, 1997)

Pallunto, Stefania, *Sara Levi Nathan* (Pesaro: Comune di Pesaro, 1993)

Pancera, Carlo, 'Figlie del Settecento', in *Le bambine nella storia dell'educazione*, ed. by Simonetta Ulivieri (Rome and Bari: Laterza, 2003), pp. 189–213

Panizza, Letizia and Sharon Wood (eds), *A History of Women's Writing in Italy* (Cambridge: Cambridge University Press, 2000)

Papagna, Elena, 'Storie comuni di sposi promessi. I processi della curia arcivescovile di Trani nel tardo Settecento', in *I tribunali del matrimonio (secoli XV–XVIII)*, ed. by Silvana Seidel Menchi and Diego Quaglioni (Bologna: Il Mulino, 2006), pp. 459–95

Passaniti, Paolo, *Diritto di famiglia e ordine sociale. Il percorso storico della società coniugale in Italia* (Milan: Giuffrè, 2011)

Paster, Gail Kern, 'Unbearable Coldness of Female Being: Women's Imperfection and the Humoral Economy', *English Literary Renaissance*, 28 (1998), 416–40

Patriarca, Silvana, *Italianità. La costruzione del carattere nazionale* (Rome: GLF editori Laterza, 2010)
— 'Italiani/Italiane', in *Atlante culturale del Risorgimento. Lessico del linguaggio politico dal Settecento all'Unità*, ed. by A. M. Banti and others (Rome: Laterza, 2011), pp. 199–213
Pedìo, Tommaso, *La soppressione del neonato per causa di onore* (Milan: Giuffrè, 1954)
Pelaja, Margherita, 'La promessa', in *Storia del matrimonio*, ed. by Michela De Giorgio and Christiane Klapisch-Zuber (Rome: Laterza, 1996), pp. 391–416
— *Matrimonio e sessualità a Roma nell'Ottocento* (Rome and Bari: Laterza, 1994)
— *Scandali. Sessualità e violenza nella Roma dell'Ottocento* (Rome: Biblink, 2001)
Pelaja, Margherita and Lucetta Scaraffia, *Due in una carne. Chiesa e sessualità nella storia* (Rome: Laterza, 2008)
Pellizer, Ezio, Nevio Zorzetti and Alberto Maffi (eds), *La paura dei padri nella società antica e medievale* (Rome: Laterza, 1983)
Pene Vidari, Gian Savino, *Ricerche sul diritto agli alimenti* (Turin: Giappichelli, 1970)
— 'L'attesa dei codici nello Stato Sabaudo della Restaurazione', *Rivista di storia del diritto italiano*, 68 (1995), 107–52
Peretti, Alessandra (ed.), *Verso l'unità. Conferenze e laboratori didattici organizzati con la collaborazione della Domus Mazziniana: Pisa, ottobre – novembre 2010* (Ospedaletto: Pacini, 2011)
Pertile, Antonio, *Storia del diritto italiano: dalla caduta dell'Impero Romano alla codificazione*, 8 vols (Turin: Unione tipografico-editrice, 1892)
Pescanti Botti, Renata, *Donne nel Risorgimento italiano* (Milan: Ceschina, 1966)
Pescosolido, Guido, 'L'economia e la vita materiale', in *Storia d'Italia*, ed. by Giovanni Sabbatucci and Vittorio Vidotto, 6 vols (Rome and Bari: Laterza, 1994), I, *Le premesse dell'unità*, 3–118
Petronio, Ugo, 'Una categoria storiografica da rivedere', in *Quaderni Fiorentini per la storia del pensiero giuridico moderno*, 13 (1984), 705–17
Petrusewicz, Marta, *Latifondo. Economia morale e vita materiale in una periferia dell'Ottocento* (Venice: Marsilio, 1990)
— 'Agronomia: innovatori agrari nelle periferie europee dell'Ottocento', in *Storia dell'agricoltura italiana in età contemporanea*, ed. by Piero Bevilacqua, 3 vols (Venice: Marsilio, 1992), III, *Mercati* e *istituzioni*, 295–344

Piccialuti, Maura, *L'immortalità dei beni. Fedecommessi e primogeniture a Roma nei secoli XVII e XVIII* (Rome: Viella, 1999)
Pizzini, Franca (ed.), *Profili di donne lombarde: quattro protagoniste dell'aristocrazia nel XIX e XX secolo* (Milan: Mazzotta, 2009)
Pocar, Valeria and Paola Ronfani, *La famiglia e il diritto* (Rome: Laterza, 1998)
Politi, Giorgio, Mario Rosa and Franco Della Peruta (eds), *Timore e carità. I poveri nell'Italia moderna* (Cremona: Libreria del Convegno, 1982)
Porciani, Ilaria, 'Famiglia e nazione nel lungo Ottocento', in *Famiglia e nazione nel lungo Ottocento italiano. Modelli, strategie, reti di relazioni*, ed. by Ilaria Porciani (Rome: Viella, 2006), pp. 15–54
— (ed.), *Famiglia e nazione nel lungo Ottocento italiano. Modelli, strategie, reti di relazioni* (Rome: Viella, 2006)
Proia, Gianna, *Cristina di Belgiojoso. Dal salotto alla politica* (Rome: Aracne, 2010)
Prosperi, Adriano, *Dare l'anima. Storia di un infanticidio* (Turin: Einaudi, 2005)
— *Infanticide, Secular Justice, and Religious Debate in Early Modern Europe* (Turnhout: Brepols, 2016)
Quaglioni, Diego, '"Sacramenti detestabili". La forma del matrimonio prima e dopo Trento', in *Matrimoni in dubbio. Unioni controverse e nozze clandestine in Italia dal XIV al XVIII secolo*, ed. by Silvana Seidel Menchi and Diego Quaglioni (Bologna: Il Mulino, 2001), pp. 61–79
— 'Segni, rituali e simboli nuziali nel diritto', in *I tribunali del matrimonio (secoli XV–XVIII)*, ed. by Silvana Seidel Menchi and Diego Quaglioni (Bologna: Il Mulino, 2006), pp. 43–63.
Rao, Anna Maria, 'Il sapere velato. L'educazione delle donne nel dibattito italiano di fine Settecento', in *Misoginia: la donna vista e malvista nella cultura occidentale*, ed. by Andrea Milano (Rome: Dehoniane, 1992), pp. 243–310
Ravera, Camilla, *La donna italiana dal primo al secondo Risorgimento* (Rome: Editori Riuniti, 1951)
Rendall, Jane, 'Women and the Public Sphere', *Gender and History*, 11 (1999), 475–88
Riall, Lucy, *Risorgimento: The History of Italy from Napoleon to Nation State* (New York: Palgrave Macmillan, 2009)
Ricaldone, Luisa, 'Eighteenth-century Literature', in *A History of Women's Writing in Italy*, ed. by Letizia Panizza and Sharon Wood (Cambridge: Cambridge University Press, 2000), pp. 95–106

Roberti, Francesco, 'Adulterio (diritto canonico)', *Novissimo Digesto Italiano*, 20 vols (Turin: Utet, 1957), I, 333–35

Roberti, Melchiorre, 'Per la storia dei rapporti patrimoniali fra coniugi', *Archivio Storico Sardo*, 1 (1908/1909), 273–92

— *Milano capitale napoleonica: la formazione di uno stato moderno, 1796–1814* (Milan: Fondazione Treccani, 1946)

Rodriguez-Pereyra, Gonzalo, 'Descartes's Substance Dualism and his Independence Conception of Substance', *Journal of the History of Philosophy*, 46 (2008), 69–89

Romanelli, Raffaele, 'Electoral Systems and Social Structures. A Comparative Perspective', in *How Did They Become Voters? The History of Franchise in Modern European Representation*, ed. by Raffaele Romanelli (The Hague and London: Kluwer Law International, 1998), pp. 1–36

— (ed.), *How Did They Become Voters? The History of Franchise in Modern European Representation* (The Hague and London: Kluwer Law International, 1998)

Romano, Andrea, *Famiglia, successioni e patrimonio familiare nell'Italia medievale e moderna* (Turin: Giappichelli, 1994)

Romano, Ruggiero, *Paese Italia: venti secoli di identità* (Rome: Donzelli, 1997)

Rossi-Doria, Anna, *Il primo femminismo: 1791–1834* (Milan: UNICOPLI, 1993)

— *Dare forma al silenzio. Scritti di storia politica delle donne* (Rome: Viella, 2007)

Ruggiero, Guido, *The Boundaries of Eros: Sex Crime and Sexuality in Renaissance Venice* (Oxford: Oxford University Press, 1989)

Russo, Carla (ed.), *Società, Chiesa e vita religiosa nell'Ancien Régime* (Naples: Guida, 1976)

Sabbatucci, Giovanni and Vittorio Vidotto (eds), *Storia d'Italia*, 6 vols (Rome and Bari: Laterza, 1994), I, *Le premesse dell'unità*

Salonen, Kirsi, *Papal Justice in the Late Middle Ages: The Sacra Romana Rota* (London: Routledge, 2016)

Sanson, Helena, *Women, Language and Grammar in Italy, 1500–1900* (Oxford: Oxford University Press for the British Academy, 2011)

— '"La Madre Educatrice" in the Family and Society in Post-Unification Italy: The Question of Language', in *Women and Gender in Post-Unification Italy: Between Private and Public Spheres*, ed. by Katherine Mitchell and Helena Sanson (Oxford: Peter Lang, 2013), pp. 39–63

— 'Widowhood and Conduct in Late Sixteenth-Century Italy: The Unusual Case of *La Vedova del Fusco* (1570)', *The Italianist*, 35 (2015), 1–26

— 'Conduct for the *Real* Widow: Giulio Cesare Cabei's *Ornamenti della gentildonna vedova* (1574)', in *Conduct Literature for and about Women in Italy, 1470–1900: Prescribing and Describing Life*, ed. by Helena Sanson and Francesco Lucioli (Paris: Classiques Garnier, 2016), pp. 41–62

— 'Introduction: Women and Conduct in the Italian Tradition, 1470–1900: An Overview', in *Conduct Literature for and about Women in Italy, 1470–1900: Prescribing and Describing Life*, ed. by Helena Sanson and Francesco Lucioli (Paris: Classiques Garnier, 2016), pp. 9–40

Sanson, Helena and Francesco Lucioli (eds), *Conduct Literature for and about Women in Italy, 1470–1900: Prescribing and Describing Life* (Paris: Classiques Garnier, 2016)

Santoncini, Gabriella, 'Appunti per una bibliografia critica sulla seconda Restaurazione pontificia', *Proposte e ricerche*, 32 (1994), 156–85

— *Sovranità e giustizia nella Restaurazione pontificia. La riforma della organizzazione della giustizia criminale nei lavori preparatori del Motu Proprio del 1816* (Turin: Giappichelli, 1996)

Santoro-Passarelli, Francesco, *Libertà e autorità nel diritto civile: altri saggi* (Padua: CEDAM, 1977)

Saraceno, Chiara, 'Le donne nella famiglia: una complessa costruzione giuridica.1750– 1942', in *Storia della famiglia italiana, 1750–1950*, ed. by Marzio Barbagli and David I. Kertzer (Bologna: Il Mulino, 1992), pp. 103–28

Satta, Maria Margherita, 'Struttura familiare e modelli di trasmissione dell'eredità', in *Donne e società in Sardegna: eredità e mutamento: materiali e strumenti di ricerca*, ed. by Anna Maria Cecaro and others (Sassari: Iniziative culturali, 1989), pp. 59–78

Scaraffia, Lucetta, 'Essere uomo, essere donna', in *La famiglia italiana dall'Ottocento a oggi*, ed. by Piero Melograni and Lucetta Scaraffia (Rome and Bari: Laterza, 1988), pp. 193–258

Schiaffino, Andrea, 'Quelques données sur le remariage dans un milieu urbain: Bologne aux dix-neuvième et vingtième siècles', in *Marriage and Remarriage in Populations of the Past*, ed. by Jacques Dupâquier and others (London: Academic Press, 1981), pp. 397–409

Schiebinger, Londa, *The Mind Has No Sex? Women in the Origins of Modern Science* (Cambridge, MA; London: Harvard University Press, 1991 [1989])

Schutte, Anne Jacobson, *By Force and Fear: Taking and Breaking Monastic Vows in Early Modern Europe* (Ithaca, NY: Cornell University Press, 2011)

— 'Genitori, figli e monacazione forzata: norme ecclesiastiche versus patria potestà (secc. XVII–XVIII)', in *Famiglia e religione in Europa nell'età moderna. Studi in onore di Silvana Seidel Menchi*, ed. by Giovanni Ciappelli, Serena Luzzi, Massimo Rospocher (Rome: Edizioni di Storia e Letteratura, 2011), pp. 147–59

Schwegman, Marjan, 'Horrific Heroines: Female Brigandage, Honour and Violence in Post-Unification Italy, 1860–1870', in *Women and Gender in Post-Unification Italy: Between Private and Public Spheres*, ed. by Katherine Mitchell and Helena Sanson (Oxford: Peter Lang, 2013), pp. 111–31

Scoca, Franco Gaetano, *Il brigantaggio postunitario nel dibattito parlamentare (1861–1865)* (Naples: Editoriale Scientifica, 2016)

Scott, Joan Wallach, *Gender and the Politics of History* (New York: Columbia University Press, 1988)

Segalen, Martine, 'Mentalité populaire et remariage en Europe occidentale', in *Marriage and Remarriage in Populations of the Past*, ed. by Jacques Dupâquier and others (London: Academic Press, 1981), pp. 67–76

Seidel Menchi, Silvana, 'I processi matrimoniali come fonte storica', in *Coniugi nemici. La separazione in Italia dal XII al XVIII secolo*, ed. by Silvana Seidel Menchi and Diego Quaglioni (Bologna: Il Mulino, 2000), pp. 15–94

— 'Percorsi variegati, percorsi obbligati: elogio del matrimonio pre-tridentino', in *Matrimoni in dubbio. Unioni controverse e nozze clandestine in Italia dal XIV al XVIII secolo*, ed. by Silvana Seidel Menchi and Diego Quaglioni (Bologna: Il Mulino, 2001), pp. 17–60

Seidel Menchi, Silvana and Diego Quaglioni (eds), *Coniugi nemici. La separazione in Italia dal XII al XVIII secolo* (Bologna: Il Mulino, 2000)

— (eds), *Matrimoni in dubbio. Unioni controverse e nozze clandestine in Italia dal XIV al XVIII secolo* (Bologna: Il Mulino, 2001)

— (eds), *Trasgressioni. Seduzione, concubinato, adulterio, bigamia (XIV–XVIII secolo)* (Bologna: Il Mulino, 2004)

— (eds), *I tribunali del matrimonio (secoli XV–XVIII)* (Bologna: Il Mulino, 2006)

Semeraro, Cosimo, *Restaurazione. Chiesa e società. La 'seconda ricupera' e la rinascita degli ordini religiosi nello Stato pontificio (Marche e Legazioni 1815–1823)* (Rome: LAS, 1982)

Serri, Mirella, 'La piccola grande tessitrice. Clara Maffei', in *Donne del Risorgimento*, ed. by Elena Doni and others (Bologna: Il Mulino, 2011), pp. 111–22

Shorter, Edward, 'Emancipazione femminile, controllo delle nascite e fecondità nella storia europea', in *Famiglia e mutamento sociale*, ed. by Marzio Barbagli (Bologna: Il Mulino, 1977), pp. 317–59

Shusterman, Noah C., *The French Revolution: Faith, Desire, and Politics* (London: Routledge, 2014)

Sledziewski, Elisabeth G., 'Rivoluzione e rapporti fra i sessi. La svolta francese', in *Storia delle donne. L'Ottocento*, ed. by Georges Duby and Michelle Perrot (Rome and Bari: Laterza, 1991), pp. 34–50

Smith, Charles Edward, *Papal Enforcement of Some Medieval Marriage Laws* (Port Washington, NY: Kennikat Press, 1972 [1940])

Sodini, Elena, *Le carte di Felicita Bevilacqua. Famiglia, nazione e patriottismo al femminile in un archivio privato (1822–1899)* (Verona: Cierre, 2010)

Soldani, Simonetta 'Introduzione', in *Fare gli italiani. Scuola e cultura nell'Italia contemporanea*, ed. by Simonetta Soldani and Gabriele Turi (Bologna: Il Mulino, 1993), pp. 9–34

— 'La fortunosa conquista di un'istruzione secondaria da parte delle giovani italiane', in *La donna in Italia: 1848–1914: unite per unire*, ed. by Emanuela Bruni and others (Cinisello Balsamo: Silvana, 2011), pp. 15–26

— (ed.), *L'educazione delle donne. Scuole e modelli di vita femminile nell'Italia dell'Ottocento* (Milan: FrancoAngeli, 1989)

Soldani, Simonetta and Gabriele Turi (eds), *Fare gli italiani. Scuola e cultura nell'Italia contemporanea* (Bologna: Il Mulino, 1993)

Solimano, Stefano, *Il letto di Procuste: diritto e politica nella formazione del Codice civile unitario. I progetti Cassinis (1860–1861)* (Milan: Giuffrè, 2003)

— 'L'edificazione del diritto privato italiano: dalla Restaurazione all'Unità', *forum historiae iuris* <http://www.forhistiur.de/2005-05-solimano/> [accessed 6 December 2020]

Soresina, Marco, *L'età della Restaurazione, 1815–1860. Gli Stati italiani dal Congresso di Vienna al crollo* (Milan: Mimesis, 2015)

Southon, Emma, *Marriage, Sex and Death: The Family and the Fall of the Roman West* (Amsterdam: Amsterdam University Press, 2017)

Sperling, Jutta Gisela, *Convents and the Body Politic in Late Renaissance Venice* (Chicago, IL: University of Chicago Press, 1999)

— 'Marriage at the Time of the Council of Trent (1560–70): Clandestine Marriages, Kinship Prohibitions, and Dowry Exchange in European Comparison', *Journal of Early Modern History*, 8 (2004), 67–108

Stolleis, Michael, 'Judicial Interpretation in Transition from the *Ancien Régime* to Constitutionalism', in *Interpretation of Law in the Age of Enlightenment: From the Rule of the King to the Rule of Law*, ed. by Yasutomo Morigiwa, Michael Stolleis and Jean Louis Halpérin (Dordrecht: Springer, 2011), pp. 3–17

Tenenti, Alberto, *L'Italia del Quattrocento. Economia e società* (Rome: Laterza, 1996)

Tieri, Natascia, *Il brigantaggio post unitario. Un'analisi di sociologia storica* (Rome: Aracne, 2013)

Tilche, Giovanna, *Maria Gaetana Agnesi* (Milan: Rizzoli, 1984)

Tonini Masella, Ginevra Diletta, *Donne sole, modelle, prostitute. Marginalità femminili a Roma fra Sette e Ottocento* (Rome: Edizioni di storia e letteratura, 2012)

— 'Il buon nome delle donne. Matrimonio, professione e reputazione nella Roma dell'Ottocento', *Storia delle donne*, 6/7 (2010/2011), 139–55

Trifone, Romualdo, *Il fedecommesso: storia dell'istituto in Italia* (Naples: Pierro, 1914)

Turchi, Laura, 'Adulterio, onere della prova e testimonianza. In margine a un processo correggese di età tridentina', in *Trasgressioni. Seduzione, concubinato, adulterio, bigamia (XIV–XVIII secolo)*, ed. by Silvana Seidel Menchi and Diego Quaglioni (Bologna: Il Mulino, 2004), pp. 305–50

Turnaturi, Gabriella, *Signori e signore d'Italia. Una storia delle buone maniere* (Milan: Feltrinelli, 2011)

Turner, David M., *Fashioning Adultery: Gender, Sex, and Civility in England, 1660–1740* (Cambridge: Cambridge University Press, 2002)

Turno, Michela, *Il malo esempio. Donne scostumate e prostituzione nella Firenze dell'Ottocento* (Florence: Giunti, 2003)

Ulivieri, Simonetta, *Educare al femminile* (Pisa: ETS, 1995)

— *Le bambine della storia dell'educazione* (Rome and Bari: Laterza, 2003)

Ungari, Paolo, *Il diritto di famiglia in Italia dalle costituzioni giacobine al Codice civile del* 1942 (Bologna: Il Mulino, 1970)

— *Storia del diritto di famiglia in Italia (1796–1942)* (Bologna: Il Mulino, 1974)

Valsecchi, Chiara, 'L'istituto della dote nella vita del diritto del tardo Cinquecento: i *Consilia* di Jacopo Menochio', *Rivista di storia del diritto italiano*, 52 (1994), 205–85

Varriale, Marcella, 'Marianna De Crescenzo', in *Dizionario biografico degli italiani*, 100 vols (Rome: Istituto della Enciclopedia Italiana, 1960–2020), xc (2017) <https://www.treccani.it/enciclopedia/sangiovannara_%28Dizionario-Biografico%29/> [accessed 1 June 2021]

— '"Perché anche noi siamo cive[s]": reti amicali e familiari nel Carteggio Ranieri', *Chronica Mundi*, 12 (2017), 73–98

Vecchio, Giorgio, *Profilo storico della famiglia. La famiglia italiana tra Ottocento e Novecento* (Cinisello Balsamo: San Paolo, 1999)

Ventrone, Alfonso, *L'amministrazione dello Stato pontificio dal 1814 al 1870* (Rome: Edizioni universitarie, 1942)

Verdile, Nadia, 'Tra leggi illuminate e lettere private: il 1789 di Maria Carolina d'Asburgo', *Archivio per la Storia delle Donne*, 5 (2008), 71–106

— (ed.), *L'utopia di Carolina. Il Codice delle leggi leuciane* (Naples: La stamperia digitale, 2007)

Vermiglioli, Pietro, *Elementi ossiano Istituzioni Civili di Giustiniano Imperatore* (Perugia: Baduel, 1830)

Vinciguerra, Sergio (ed.), *Diritto penale dell'Ottocento. I codici preunitari e il codice Zanardelli* (Padua: CEDAM, 1993)

— (ed.), *Codice penale universale austriaco (1803)* (Padua: Cedam, 2001)

— (ed.), *Codice dei delitti e delle pene pel Regno d'Italia (1811)* (Padua: Cedam, 2002)

Viora, Mario E., *Consolidazioni e codificazioni. Contributo alla storia della codificazione* (Turin: Giappichelli, 1967)

Visceglia, Maria Antonietta, 'Corpo e sepoltura nei testamenti della nobiltà napoletana', *Quaderni Storici*, 50 (1982), 583–614

— 'Linee per uno studio unitario dei testamenti e dei contratti matrimoniali dell'aristocrazia feudale napoletana tra fine Quattrocento e Settecento', *Mélanges de l'Ecole française de Rome. Moyen-Age, Temps modernes*, 95 (1983), 393–470

— 'Introduzione', in *Signori, patrizi, cavalieri in Italia centro-meridionale nell'età moderna*, ed. by Maria Antonietta Visceglia and Renata Ago (Rome: Laterza, 1992), pp. V–XXXIII

Vismara, Giulio, *L'unità della famiglia nella storia del diritto in Italia* (Rome: Apollinaris, 1956)

— 'Momenti di storia della famiglia sarda', in *Studi sassaresi* (1971), 181–203

— *Il diritto di famiglia in Italia dalle riforme ai codici. Appunti* (Milan: Giuffrè, 1978)

Vovelle, Michel, *Piété baroque et déchristianisation en Provence au XVIIIe siècle. Les attitudes devant la mort d'après les clauses des testaments* (Paris: Plon, 1973)

— 'La morte nella mentalità e nella pratica religiosa', in *Società, Chiesa e vita religiosa nell'Ancien Régime*, ed. by Carla Russo (Naples: Guida, 1976), pp. 231–82

Webley, Lisa, 'Stumbling Blocks in Empirical Legal Research: Case Study Research', *Law and Method* (October 2016), 1–21

Weinrib, Jacob, 'Kant on Citizenship and Universal Independence', *Australian Journal of Legal Philosophy*, 33 (2008), 1–25

Willson, Perry, 'Introduction: Gender and the Private Sphere in Liberal and Fascist Italy', in *Gender, Family and Sexuality: The Private Sphere in Italy, 1860–1945*, ed. by Perry Willson (Basingstoke: Palgrave Macmillan, 2004), pp. 1–19

— (ed.), *Gender, Family and Sexuality: The Private Sphere in Italy, 1860–1945* (Basingstoke: Palgrave Macmillan, 2004)

Wood, Sharon, 'Murder in the Harem: Cristina di Belgiojoso', in *Women and Gender in Post-Unification Italy: Between Private and Public Spheres*, ed. by Katherine Mitchell and Helena Sanson (Oxford: Peter Lang, 2013), pp. 135–52

Woolf, Stuart J., *Napoleon's Integration of Europe* (London: Routledge, 1991)

Yin, Robert K., *Case Study Research: Design and Methods* (Thousand Oaks, CA: Sage, 1994)

Zaffignani, Giovanni, *L'università e la ragazza. La verità sulla prima laurea in legge ottenuta in Europa da una donna Maria Pellegrina Amoretti, Pavia, 1777* (Acirerale: Bonanno, 2010)

Zamagni, Vera, *Industrializzazione e squilibri regionali in Italia. Bilancio dell'età giolittiana* (Bologna: Il Mulino, 1978)

Zanetti, Dante, *La demografia del patriziato milanese nei secoli XVII, XVIII, XIX* (Pavia: Università di Pavia, 1972)

Zarri, Gabriella, 'Monasteri femminili e città (secoli XV–XVIII)', in *Storia d'Italia. Annali 9. La Chiesa e il potere politico dal Medioevo all'età contemporanea*, ed. by Giorgio Chittolini and Giovanni Miccoli (Turin: Einaudi, 1986), pp. 357–429

— *Recinti. Donne, clausura e matrimonio nella prima età moderna* (Bologna: Il Mulino, 2000)

— 'Presentazione', in *Arcangela Tarabotti, Lettere familiari e di complimento*, ed. by Meredith Kennedy Ray and Lynn Lara Westwater (Turin: Rosenberg and Sellier, 2005), pp. 7–17

Zorzoli, Maria Carla, 'Della famiglia e del suo patrimonio: riflessioni sull'uso del fedecommesso in Lombardia tra Cinque e Seicento', *Archivio storico lombardo*, 115 (1989), 91–148

Index

a sa sardisca 105
ab intestato inheritance 111, 116, 121, 156, 166, 169, 180, 183, 221
Accademia dei Ricovrati 53
Acquotta, Gioanni 169
ad sustinenda onera 89, 198, 221
Agnesi, Gaetana 67
Aiassa, Giovanni 15
Ajrasca 176
Albano 108
Albericus of Rosciate 31, 33
Alberti, Giuseppe 15
Albertine Statute 117
Albertini, Maria Teresa 184
Allgemeines Bürgerliches Gesetzbuch 113
Alzate 192
amasia 201
Amoretti, Maria Pellegrina 67
Ancien Régime 44, 99–100, 105, 139, 180, 215
Annali di giurisprudenza 16, 155–58, 170, 206
Antaldi, Augusta 37
antifactum 90, 221
Arienti Lattanzi, Carolina 44
Aristotle 50
Austrian Empire 24, 25
Authority 2, 9, 10, 18, 32, 34–35, 44, 59, 78, 85, 101, 103, 122–23, 148–49, 154, 215, 221
Balbo, Cesare 64–65, 80
Ballaro, Lorenzo 192
Baracchini, Caterina 47
Barbarigo family 94
Bartolus of Saxoferrato 31, 194, 201
Bassi, Felice 169
Belgiojoso, Cristina 45
Bellomo, Giovanni 60
Besana Fé, Camilla 46
Bettanini, Camilla 131
bona extra dotalia 110, 221
Bonacci, Maria Alinda 119
Bonaccorsi Dolcini Tredozio, Anna 38
Bonino, Giuseppe 170
Bonizi Poggi, Serafina 108
Boschetti, Margherita 185
Bouvard, Giuseppa 144
Boves 170
Browne, Thomas 51–52
Busto Arsizio 150
Buttarini, Andrea 131, 216

Cabanis, Pierre Jean George 57, 64, 81
Cagliari, court of 139–40
Caimi, Giulio 15, 185
Califronia, Rosa 44
Calleri di Sala, Francesco Zeffirino 169
Calleri di Sala, Zeffirino 169

Camerino 93
Caminer Turra, Elisabetta 42
Campan, Jeanne Louise Henriette (Madame Campan) 62
Carbonari movement 46
Carcano, Giovanni 29, 75–76, 79
Carlo Alberto, King of Sardinia 112
Carlo Emmanuele III, King of Sardinia 172
Carlo Felice, King of Sardinia 112, 139
Carmignani, Giovanni 42, 74, 77
Carnevale, Giovanna 169
Carrara Spinelli Maffei, Clara 45
Casale 160, 181
  court of 16, 160, 162–64, 166–74, 181, 192–93, 197
Casanova, Giacomo 56
Casati Confalonieri, Teresa 45
Cassinis, Giovan Battista 120
Catholic Church 3–4, 68, 102, 120, 149, 152–53, 195
celibacy 27, 86, 100
Chambéry 148
  court of 143
Charles II, King of Naples 94
Chassay, Frédéric-Edouard 69
chastity 5
Civali, Amalia 151
Civieri, Giovanni Battista 132–34, 216
Civitavecchia 108
Code Civil des Français, see Codice Civile di Napoleone il Grande pel Regno d'Italia
Codice Civile di Napoleone il Grande pel Regno d'Italia 4, 34, 36, 44, 78, 98–102, 104, 111, 114, 121–22, 156, 162–63, 177, 189, 202, 204, 215
Codice civile del Regno d'Italia 121
Codice civile per gli Stati di S. M. il Re di Sardegna 196
Codice civile universale austriaco pel Regno Lombardo-Veneto 113, 182, 194, 196
Codice Estense 36, 97, 102–03, 109
Codice penale dei crimini, dei delitti e delle contravvenzioni 137
Codice penale dei delitti e delle gravi trasgressioni di polizia 138, 144
Codice per lo Regno delle Due Sicilie 102, 113
Codice per gli Stati di Parma, Piacenza e Guastalla 102, 113, 190
Commissione Provvisoria di Governo dello Stato Romano 116
commune 88, 90, 92–93, 221
commune civitatis, see commune
communes opiniones doctorum 97, 147
Concone, Francesco 33
Condorcet, Nicolas 42
conduct literature 6, 49, 136, 188, 196
Confalonieri, Federico 46
Congress of Vienna 23–24, 35, 101, 103, 111, 156
consilia 91
controdote, see antifactum
copula perfecta 200
Corpus Iuris Civilis 1, 87, 90–91, 135, 188–89
corredo 89
Cosci, Cristoforo 205
Costituzione della Repubblica Romana 117
Council of Trent 1, 128–31, 134, 149
Crema 182–83
  tribunal of 183

D'Oria, Paolo Mattia 52
De Crescenzo, Marianna 119
De Cristoforis, Giovan Battista 62
De Previde Massara, Lucia 169
decorum 5, 36, 106, 108, 117, 179
Decreto legislativo luogotenenziale 217
Decreto sull'ordinamento de' municipj 118
Decreto relativo alle successioni intestate 111
Delacoux, Alexis 66
Delbuono, Maria 169
Della Porta, Giambattista 51–52
Descartes, René 56
dispensatio natalium 142
Dondena, Pietro 169
dowry 15, 17, 19, 35, 37–39, 44, 86–95, 97–98, 105–11, 116, 123, 136–37, 155–64, 166, 168–89, 191–94, 198–200, 208, 210–13, 216–17, 221–22
droit intermédiaire 99, 163, 166

education 9, 26, 42, 52–57, 60–62, 64–74, 81–82, 109, 198
elemosina, *see* dowry
Ellena, Giovanni Pietro 15, 176–77
Enlightenment, the 7, 9, 12, 30, 38, 40, 44, 52, 55, 82, 97, 99, 104, 141–42, 215
exclusio propter dotem 88

faderfio 87, 89
Falcidian quarter 88
Falloppio, Gabriele 51
Fardello, see corredo
Ferdinand I, King of the Two Sicilies 24, 113
Ferdinand III, Grand Duke of Tuscany 24, 110
Ferdinand the Catholic, King of Naples 94
Ferriani, Lino 141
fertility 28
fideicommissum 86, 92, 98, 100, 103–04, 221
Filangieri, Gaetano 54
filiusfamilia/filiafamilia 87, 221–22
Foligno 94
Fonseca Pimentel, Eleonora 42
Fornasio, Giacomo Domenico 176
Forti, Francesco 76
Fracavalli, Paola 183
fragilitas 135
Franceschi Ferrucci, Caterina 72–73
Francesco III, Duke of Modena 36
Francesco IV, Duke of Modena and Reggio 24
French Revolution 7, 40, 42, 44, 82, 98–99, 104, 116
Fusi, Francesco 168

Galdi, Domenicantonio 75, 121
Galen 50
Gallea Bussolino, Maddalena 158
Gallone, Antonio Maria 162, 166–67
Gallone, Evasio 164
Gallone, Giacoma 164
Gambarana Frecavalli, Maria 46
Gambone, Giovanni Maria 198–99
Garello, Carlo 190
Garello, Giuseppa 190
Garello, Ignazio 190
Garello, Teresa 190

Genoa
  commune of 90
  court of 115
  Republic of 24
Ghione, Felice 176–77
Ghione, Michele 176
gifts *propter nuptias* 89
Gioberti, Vincenzo 79
Giornale di giurisprudenza pratica 17
Giurisprudenza del codice civile 16–17, 136
Giurisprudenza degli Stati Sardi 17, 176, 181
Giurisprudenza pratica secondo la legislazione austriaca 144, 146, 182–83
Giurisprudenza teorico-pratica secondo la legislazione austriaca 17, 182, 206
Gouges, Olympe de 42
Guarrini, Alessandro 183
Guarrini, Giacomo Antonio 182
Guarrini, Giovanni Battista 182
Gusberti, Maria 168

hereditament 183–84, 221
hotchpot 183–84, 221

imbecillitas 50, 74, 77, 200
impediments, canonical 102, 127, 130–31, 147, 150
industrialisation 23, 26, 28, 123
in facie ecclesiae 128–29, 192
infanticide 12, 123, 127, 141–46
infirmitas 50, 74
inter vivos donation 86, 222
ius commune 4, 8, 14, 90, 97, 222
ius proprium 4, 8, 88, 102, 130, 222

Jacini, Stefano 25
jus occidendi 200
Justinian 1, 32, 86–87, 90–91, 107, 122, 135, 172, 188–89, 193
justus dolor 204

Kant, Immanuel 41–42
Kuliscioff, Anna 217

Lambruschini, Raffaello 29, 60–61, 72
Lavater, Johann Kaspar 51
Law 6 Thermidor V (24 July 1797) 166
Legge sulle successioni intestate 110
Leggi civili del Regno di Sardegna 112
Leggi e costituzioni di S. M. il Re di Sardegna 97, 111
legitima portio 88, 105, 107–08, 110–13, 166, 169–71, 174, 183–85, 190–91, 221–22
legitime, *see legitima portio*
levitas 50, 74
Livi, Francesco 107–08
Livi, Umbellina 107–08
Lombardy-Venetia, Kingdom of 1–3, 14–18, 24–25, 75, 88, 113–16, 118, 121, 127, 131, 139, 142, 144, 149, 152, 155, 159, 180–82, 185, 196, 204–07, 217, 219
Lombroso, Cesare 52
Longhi, Giacomo 163
Longhi, Maria 160–64
Longhi, Pietro Paolo 163
lower classes 3, 39, 69, 86, 105, 131, 133, 145, 193
Lucca
  Duchy of 24, 111
lucrum dotis 163, 211–14, 222

Maggi, Lorenzo 15
Majorat 86, 92, 100, 103–04, 222

Mantegazza, Francesca 168
Mantegazza, Pietro Giorgio 168
Mantelli, Cristoforo 16
Marchisone, Anna Maria 174–79
Marchisone, Bartolomeo 174–79
Marchisone, Giuseppe 174–79
Marchisone, Margherita 174–79
Marchisone, Michela Maria 174–79
Marchisone, Vincenzo 174–79
Maria Beatrice, Duchess of Duchy of Massa and Carrara 24
Maria Luigia, Duchess of Parma and Piacenza 24
Maria Luisa, Duchess of Lucca 24, 111
marriage, *ratum sed non consummatum* 195
Massa, Carlo 170
Massa and Carrara
  Duchy of 24
Massone, Clelia 115
Mazzini, Giuseppe 81–82
meffio 89
Mellana, Filippo 163, 166–67
Mellana, Gioanni Francesco 162, 166–67
Merci, Giuseppe 15
Meta 89
Middle Ages 9, 11, 31, 87, 89, 92, 97, 106, 114, 128, 135, 189, 202
Miglietti, Vincenzo 120
Milan 14–15, 45, 59, 62, 67, 150, 159, 167, 182–85
  Archbishop's Curia of 14
  Duchy of 159
  Statutes of 160
Milesi, Bianca 46
Modena and Reggio, Duchy of 24, 36, 83, 97, 102, 104, 109, 219
Molino Colombini, Giulia 71–72
Montabone, Cattarina 190, 216
Monti delle Doti 95
Monti di Maritaggi, *see* Monti delle Doti 95
Monti Perticari, Costanza 188
Morardo, Bartolomeo Raffoni 184
Morardo, Gaspare 58
morbo gallico 206–08
Morelli, Salvatore 82, 217
morgengabe 89
Mozzoni, Anna Maria 217
Muratori, Ludovico Antonio 96, 104, 135–36

Naido, Palma 185
Napoleon, Emperor of France 23–24, 34–36, 101, 109, 202
Napoleonic Code, *see Codice Civile di Napoleone il Grande pel Regno d'Italia*
Nathan, Sara 47
Negri, Giovanni Maria 33
Negroni, Giuseppe Antonio 160
Negroni, Teresa 168
Novara 167
  tribunal di Prefettura of 192

odium quartae 90, 222
Old Regime, *see* Ancien Régime
Oldrati, Luigi 138
Omegna, Statute of 201
Orbassano 176–77
Ornati, Regina 169

Pagani, Giovanni Battista 132–33
Paladini, Luisa Amalia 73–74
Paoletti, Anna 198–99
Papa, Giuseppe 131
Papal States 3, 24, 37–38, 46–47, 77, 107–09, 114, 116, 150, 188, 190, 219
paraphernalia 89

Parma, Statute of 88, 93
Parma, Piacenza and Guastalla
Code, *see Codice per gli Stati di Parma, Piacenza e Guastalla*
Duchy of 24, 78, 190, 219
Partiti, Giovanni Antonio 15
Patente sovrana 12 aprile 1816 N. 45 118–19
paterfamilias 32–35, 88, 118, 165, 167–68, 170, 176, 188, 221–22
paterna paternis, materna maternis 34, 94, 189, 222
Patto di Capuana e Nido 94–95
Peano, Giacomo 170
peculium 87, 222
Pellegrini, Angelica 169–70
Pellegrini, Bartolomeo 169–70
Pellegrini, Maddalena 169–70
Pellegrini, Maria 169–70
Pellegrini, Michele 169–70
Pepoli Sampieri, Anna 70–71
Pesaro 37
Statute of 92
Piedmont 88, 119, 159, 164, 176, 181, 190, 192
Senato of 170, 171
Pinerolo 15
tribunal di 15, 177–78
Pisanelli Code, *see* Codice civile del Regno d'Italia
Pisanelli, Giuseppe 120, 122
Pius VII, Pope 24, 107
Pius IX, Pope 106, 117
Polatti, Giacomo 68
Potestas 32–33, 115, 121–22
Pouget, Firmin 63
pratiche disoneste 147
propter dotem 88, 105, 157, 222

quarta uxoria 189–90, 192–93, 216

Rabezzana, Bartolomeo 169–70
Rabezzana, Francesco 169–70
Rabezzana, Giuseppe 169–70
Rabezzana, Maria 169–70
Rabezzana, Teresa 169–70
Raffoni Morardo, Anna Maria 184
Raffoni Morardo, Bartolomeo 184
Raffoni Morardo, Elisabetta 184
Raffoni Morardo, Giuseppe 184
Rainoldi, Federico 168
Ravizza, Carlo 29–30, 36, 67–68
Rebizzo, Bianca 45
Regie Costituzioni 4, 111–12, 156–57, 162, 165–69, 172–73, 178, 189, 194
Regio Editto 103, 156
Regis, Domenico 158
Regis, Giacinta 158
Regolamento Legislativo e Giudiziario per gli affari civili 104, 107–08, 114
Renaissance, the 11, 93–96
Renazzi, Filippo Maria 79
Repubblica Partenopea 42
Restoration, the 1–2, 13, 25–26, 44, 101–02, 104, 107, 114, 121, 123, 202, 217
Ricasoli, Bettino 38
Risorgimento, the 5, 23–25, 40–49, 79, 82, 116
Riva, Maria 169
Romagna, the 38
Romagnosi, Gian Domenico 78
Roman law 3, 32, 34–36, 89–90, 102, 107–08, 111, 173–74, 178, 190, 200
Roman Republic, the 47, 116, 118
Roncalli, the 159–74, 179, 181
Roncalli, Giacoma 160–74
Roncalli, Gioanna 160–74
Roncalli, Giuseppa 160–74

Roncalli, Giuseppe 160–74
Roncalli, Rosa Anna 160–74
Roncalli, Teresa 160–74
Roncalli, Vincenza 160–74
Roncalli, Vincenzo 160–74
Rossi Gabardi Brocchi, Isabella 69
Rossi, Pellegrino 77
Rousseau, Jean-Jacques 55–56, 64
Roussel, Pierre 57, 80–81
Ruzzenenti, Luigia 132

Sacerdote, Speranza 181–82
Sacra Rota, the 108–09, 114, 137
saevitia 205–14
Salvatori, Filippo Maria 153
Sanchioli, Marianna 164
Sanchioli, Serafino 160
Santibusca, Antonio 15
Sardinia, Kingdom of 16, 18, 24, 34, 46, 83, 103, 105, 111–15, 119–20, 124, 127, 136, 139, 142–44, 147, 152, 155–56, 159, 167, 180, 189, 194, 204, 206, 211, 219
Sassi, Clara 160, 162
Scarpazza, Faustino 203
Scherpa, see corredo
Senigallia, Statute of 92
sibisufficientia 41
Sieyès, Emmanuel Joseph 41
socia criminis 135
Società delle Giardiniere 46
Sopranzi Agazzini, Teresa 46
Sperotti, Luigi 15
spinsterhood 27, 86, 100
sponsalia 129–30
Statuto fondamentale pel governo temporale degli Stati della Chiesa 117
Stella, Luigi 77, 117
Stramigioli, Tomaso 37
stuprum 135–37
substancia 31, 85, 92, 119
sui juris 32, 222
Susa 190
    Regio Tribunale di Prefettura of 190–91
syphilis 206–09, 211–13, 216

Tametsi decree 128
Tarabotti, Arcangela 96
Tassoni, Alessandro Maria 58–59
Tensini, Giovanni Battista 182
Tensini, Marianna 182
tertia 89–90, 222
Thermidorian Reaction, the 99
Tivoli, Statute of 201
Tommaseo, Niccolò 65–66
Turin 14–16, 46, 72, 170, 176, 197
    Bishop of 213
    Corte di Cassazione 16, 178–79
    court of final appeal 143
    Senato 191–92
    Statute of 211
    Tribunal 178, 198, 212
Turri, Francesco Gerardo 151
Tuscany
    Grand Duchy of 24, 110, 116, 118, 189, 219
    Regolamento comunale 118
Two Sicilies, Kingdom of the 24, 38, 113, 219

Ulpian 32–33
uso di Proceri e Magnati 94

Vacca, Giuseppe 120
Valbassora, Luigi 192
Valentino, Giovanni 192–93

Valentino, Pietro 192–93
Vandoni, Lorenzo 192–93
Vandoni, Maria 192–93, 216
Venice 14–15, 68, 94
  Republic of 24
  Tribunale di Appello Generale 16
  Tribunale Civile di Prima Istanza di Venezia 16
verba de futuro 129
verba de praesenti 129
Vercelli, Archbishop's Curia of 137
Verona 14–15, 131–33, 184–85
  Bishop's Curia of 14, 131–33, 152, 216
  San Zeno Maggiore 133
  Supremo Senato of 210
  Supremo Tribunale of 14, 16, 183
Vigevano 159, 168
  Statute of 88, 162, 166–68, 172–73
  Tribunal of 166–67
Villafranca 15, 176–77
Viscontini Dembowski, Metilde 46
Vita-Levi, Raffael 181
Vittorio Emanuele II, King of Italy 119
Volpi, Giovanni Antonio 54

White Mario, Jessie 47

Zallinger zum Thurn, Jacob Anton 129–30
Zecchini, Petronio Ignazio 56
Zini, Giovanni Francesco 16
zitella onesta 134, 136–37, 210
Zorzoli, Giovanni Battista 169

CPSIA information can be obtained
at www.ICGtesting.com
Printed in the USA
LVHW051644121121
703028LV00003B/10

9 780854 572786